THE
NATHANIEL
HAWTHORNE
JOURNAL
1974

Nathaniel Hawthorne—U.S. Signal Corps photograph No. B-6207 (Brady Collection) in the National Archives.

T:

THE
NATHANIEL
HAWTHORNE
JOURNAL
1974

C. E. Frazer Clark, Jr., Editor

 **Microcard Editions Books**
An Indian Head Company
A Division of Information Handling Services

Copyright© 1975 by Indian Head, Inc.
Library of Congress Catalog Card Number: 75-148262
ISBN: 0-910972-50-8

Published by Microcard Edition, Books,
5500 South Valentia Way, Englewood, Colorado 80110,
a division of Information Handling Services,
an Indian Head Company.

Printed in the United States of America.

Editor: C. E. Frazer Clark, Jr.
1700 Lone Pine
Bloomfield Hills, Michigan 48013

Design and Layout: Margaret Swanson Clark

Address all editorial correspondence to the editor.

Address orders and inquiries to: Microcard Editions Books
5500 South Valentia Way
Englewood, Colorado 80110
Telephone (303) 771-2600

For
Dorothy Potter
who is Essex.

CONTENTS

ILLUSTRATIONS

THE
NATHANIEL
HAWTHORNE
JOURNAL
1974

December 11th Monday.

Last night Mary O'Brien went to bed very late & waked me out of a sound sleep with the noise of doors. My dearest husband had come to bed without disturbing my repose as usual, though I had a consciousness of his advent. But Mary completely roused me, & I felt as if I should never sleep again. It was nearly eleven. ~~[several lines crossed out]~~ My lord told me of his early life in Raymond ~~[lines crossed out]~~ My husband ~~[crossed out]~~ got me some of Mr Bridge's ancient wine & a cracker at about twelve. These were of admirable effect & in ten minutes I was composed & almost asleep. Very soon I was quite — I know he saved me from being ill. I slept till six in the morning very well. The bath was particularly reviving this morning. The day was cloudy & I sewed instead of painting & finished a little pelt & made a wee apron. My lord wrote till four in the P.M. Then he went to the village & brought me thence letters from Mary & Mother. After tea he read the Two gentlemen of Verona partly. I do not like it much. What a queer mood Shakespeare must have been in to write it. He seems making fun.

Facsimile of entry for 11 December [1843] from Sophia Hawthorne's Journal (1843-1844). Henry W. and Albert A. Berg Collection, The New York Public Library, Astor, Lenox and Tilden Foundations. Reproduced with permission.

A Sophia Hawthorne Journal, 1843-1844

EDITED BY

JOHN J. McDONALD

Though voluminous, Nathaniel Hawthorne's journals rarely afford that sort of detailed attention to daily activity which allows reconstruction of those specific conditions which so much determine the mood of an individual life. Hawthorne used his journals largely as a place to set down details of "reality" and of "ideality" that might later be worked into a story or a romance. His wife's journals are different. They revel in detail, often becoming the kind of diaries which Hawthorne never kept. Perhaps it is their personal tone which caused someone so to mutilate those entries in Hawthorne's *American Notebooks* that were made by Sophia.[1] But the tone is personal, not *intime*. Rarely is Sophia anything less than decorous, nor do her surviving journals unduly concentrate on trivial gossip. They are simply a record of day-to-day events made in an attempt to capture the joy and pain of life as immediately as it was being lived. This immediate quality makes Sophia's journals most valuable to the biographer trying to recapture the way in which Hawthorne and his wife spent their days. In 1846 Hawthorne said: "It is the age itself that writes newspapers and almanacs, which, therefore, have a distinct purpose and meaning at the time, and a kind of intelligible truth for all times."[2] To newspapers and almanacs he might have added diaries, at least such diaries as Sophia kept.

The journal printed here was written between 1 December, 1843, and 5 January, 1844, on which day it was abandoned without evident ceremony. It consists of eleven sheets, each folded once and placed within one another to make a single folio-style gathering. The sheets lack any binding and are not numbered. I have added pagination, which is given within square brackets in the text. Between pages [2]

1

and [3] there is a lacuna in sense which indicates the loss of at least one, although probably not more than one, sheet of manuscript. I have not assigned page numbers to the missing sheet(s). The end of the journal would fall on the other leaf of the missing sheet, since pages [43] and [44] of the surviving manuscript are blank. Several other, shorter lacunae are described in the running text of the journal. Only short portions of the diary have previously been printed (in Rose Hawthorne Lathrop's *Memories of Hawthorne*, pp. 64-69), but these are treated as excerpts from letters written by Sophia to her mother. I have enclosed published sections between brackets: { }, but have made no attempt to indicate the many editorial changes in the Lathrop transcription.

The time period covered by this diary occurs nearly a year and a half after Sophia's marriage to Nathaniel and their removal to the old manse at Concord. Winter is fast approaching, and the isolation which the combination of winter and Concord roads habitually imposed is evident throughout. Hawthorne is writing magazine pieces at a furious rate, for him, which leaves Sophia much to herself.[3] The isolation is yet more intensified because Sophia is in her last trimester of pregnancy with Una, the Hawthornes' first-born (b. March 3, 1844). If Nathaniel sometimes appears overly concerned for Sophia's health, forbidding walks when it rains or snows slightly, this is to be understood in light of the fact that Sophia had miscarried in February, 1843. The coming *accouchement* may also contribute to Sophia's occasional nervousness, but she had been prone to nervous headaches for several years. Her troubles recounted in these pages are mild compared to descriptions of incidents prior to her marriage.

Since the journal was meant for entirely private uses, there are a few quizzical characteristics of the holograph. It is not always possible to distinguish a period from a comma or a dash, as in Emily Dickinson's holograph, so I have occasionally chosen the proper punctuation from context. There has been no attempt to reproduce the spacing in the manuscript, but original spelling has been preserved.

The Henry W. and Albert A. Berg Collection of The New York Public Library, Astor, Lenox, and Tilden Foundations, has generously granted its permission to publish the journal. I want to express my thanks both to the Berg Collection and to the descendents of Nathaniel and Sophia Hawthorne, who have also given me their kind permission to publish their great grandmother's diary.

[1]*December 1st 1843. Friday.*
This is the first day of winter & I am going to write from this date, if possible, a journal of household events principally. It is very convenient to have such archives & some-things quite interesting will inevitably insert themselves, though my plan is a dry one. I shall look back one

day, because it was Thanksgiving. It was a dim morning, but cleared off reluctantly by the middle of the forenoon, & shone all the rest of the day. I was uprisen by the dawn & before breakfast put together the manifold parts of my plum pudding, which was to be boiled seven hours. After breakfast my dear husband went to his study to write, & I did not paint upon Endymion,[4] because I felt rather nervous about it, & showed pale in the glass & was lazy. So I took "The Mysteries of Paris",[5] a horrible & interesting book & read. At half past two I went to make some superlative sweet sauce for the pudding, while Mary O'Brien[6] was roasting the turkey in the store-room. At quarter past three we dined, my husband & I alone, with the sunshine. The turkey was excellently cooked, & the dinner very good. After dinner I continued to read the Mysteries in the study while my Prince[2] read Rousseau & Mr Mann's July oration.[7] I did not feel like walking, & we sat reading our separate books till we went to bed. I was quite nervous, but found repose on my husband's heart & slept very well. We awoke to a grey morning. I could not paint, because there was no sun, & I wrote a long letter to Mother after breakfast[8] & at half past eleven went to the village in a gentle snow storm, for the first time carrying an umbrella in Concord. At the Post Office there was nothing for us, nor at the Stage House could I find the valise.[9] Soon after my return, my dear husband went to dine at Mr. Emerson's, with Messrs Bradford, Thoreau, Channing &c. I dined stupidly, solitaire, upon rice & squash & a bit of turkey & of pudding, but there was no beauty in it, because my lord was not opposite me. After dinner I read Cannilla[10] a few moments, & then mended my husband's summer gown & a shirt, & sewed upon my night robe till dark. I sent Mary to the village to get Horace Walpole's letters[11] for my husband & some yeast. So I sat still in my chair & at last I heard the [one word here is illegible because of an accidentally torn MS] *known entrance & ran out to meet* [3] [hiatus in MS][12] *true purpose of woman's much disapproved love of dress. Mere love of dress is the abuse of this legitimate tendency.* {*For the world's eye I care nothing.*} *Not at balls & routs should I care to walk in silk attire,* {*but in the profound shelter of this home, I would put on daily a velvet robe and pearls in my hair to gratify my husband's taste*} *& appear to him alone as beautiful as possible. Behold* {*a true wife's world!*} *It is her husband only. If each separate woman could but once know this fact, how happy would she be! There would be an end to personal vanity & aimless fashion.* {*Directly after dinner, my lord went to the Athaeneum*} *& Post Office, & took my india rubber[13] to the shoemaker's. But I do not often invite my Apollo to be a Mercury. During his absence I sewed. I have a great deal of sewing to do in preparation for my accouchment. Most sweet thoughts I have over my work. It is different from all other work. Except when I am using the needle for my*

*husband, it is to me the pleasantest sewing I ever did, for I do not like it
in itself as some persons do. For him I like* [At this point a piece of
MS has been torn away. It contained five lines of writing, with
only parts of words written near the inner margin remaining]. [4]
Imp's[14] *pump is very inferior in taste. At last {my husband returned.}
Oh it is always such a refreshment & awakening to hear him open the
front door! He brought no letters nor news, but himself is enough to
bring. Then {he sat reading Horrace Walpole till he went out to the
woodhouse to saw & split.} As soon as daylight was gone, I put on my
mantle, & walked up and down the gallery. The moon shone into every
eastern & southern window with bountiful glory. {Presently I saw
hastening up the avenue Mr George Bradford. He stayed to tea} & till
nine o'clk. We were very glad to see him as usual. {His beautiful
character makes him perennial in interest. As my} dear {husband says
we can see Nature through him straight without refraction.} He told us
much about the Community*[15] *& has not decided about coming to Concord. He wants to dwell near the sea.*

December 4th Monday.

I ent [At this point the same destruction which marred page [3]
causes the loss of six lines of writing. A few words written near
the inner margin survive, including "Sunday," which is the day
that what follows is describing.] [5] *I forgot to take a book to read in
the tub & so had to use my thoughts. {The water was deadly cold, instead of livingly cold as usual, & I knew it must have been taken from
the wash-tubs which The Imp filled.} So it proved. I begged Mary to
draw henceforth from the well. She said it was because the bucket had* [a
four-letter fragment, probably of "frost," is here crossed out] *ice in it
that she did not. Mary gave us another nice Indian cake for breakfast,
but I ate rice principally[.] After breakfast my lord came to his study, &
I wrote a short letter to Mother to send by Mr Thoreau, & a note to Mrs
Emerson,*[16] *& then read Montaigne's Essays. He is pretty wise, I think,
but I do not like his Individuality much. His style is strong & to the
point & he has wonderful sense. Mary came into the dining room as
usual on Sundays, to read & write. My purpose is to cultivate her particularly on Sundays, as the best use I can make of the day. But she does
not accomplish much, because it tries her to sit still & stupefies her to
be in a warm room long at a time. She wrote very well, & then began to
read, but asked to be excused after half a page because she had no mind
for it, & wanted to take the air. She went to the avenue, & as my
husband* [6] [The word "asked" is here crossed out.] *requested me to
go out before dinner, I followed her & walked three quarters of an hour
up & down beneath the leafless trees. Puss accompanied me backward &
forward till she was weary, & then she sat on her tail in the middle of*

the path. I took her up once for a muff, but she was too heavy to hold long. The day was very superb & the air full of keen life. We dined upon the finale of the turkey. After dinner we came to the dear study, & my husband wrote a letter to Count Louis,[17] & I went to sleep in my chair, & finally ended my nap on my lord's bosom, which was very sweet. He read Walpole while he held me. From this dulcet rest I was roused by Mary, who came for letters to carry to Mr Thoreau. So I made up a pacquet of mother's & Count Louis's & sent her away with them. As I was weary with reading, I then sewed till dark, while my husband read. Mary came back as I was promenading the gallery according to my husband's wish, just before tea. Mary was called for as we went down to tea by her friends Elizabeth & Ann & took [7] leave without waiting to eat anything. She is very indifferent always to her supper. {She brought with her from Mrs Emerson "The Mysteries of Paris" & I read it all the evening,} while my love read Walpole's letters. This morning 4th there was another golden dawn. I rose early & waked Mary for her washing. There was a mistake about calling me to the bath & so I lost half an hour—no, not lost it, for I read all the time I waited, but breakfast was delayed. I painted upon Endymion's right arm & hand. The arm Mr Bradford had criticised. Between twelve & one I went to the village—I met Mr Rice & spoke to him of our oil w'h seemed to burn dim. He convinced me that the fault was not in the oil. I called at Dean's & spoke for some pieces of zinc for a hearth & back to my stove.[18] Then I went to Mrs Emerson's, but could not see her. At the Post Office I found a Salem Gazette.[19] It was a beautiful day, with a mild south west wind. I came to see my dear husband before dinner. We dined upon roast-beef. The butcher left twelve pounds and half this morning to be cut up for various purposes. After dinner I was very lazy & sleepy & slept in my chair & then upon the couch [8] till almost sunset & my husband went out to exercise. Then I reluctantly uprose & dressed myself & finally sat down to write this till he should return. He will have to read the Mysteries of Paris this evening & I shall sew.

December 6th Wednesday.

I forgot my journal again last evening. Yesterday morning, (Tuesday 5th) I waked very early & the northern window was full of moonlight. I thought at first it was daylight—I tried to keep awake, for it stupefies me to sleep again after being once completely roused. But it was so still, I could not. I dozed unawares & was startled by a loud singing, & found it came from some men & boys near the house. It was still moonlight, but I then rose, & found it a little after five. My husband's study is always warm, & so I lighted a little lamp & sat down here to sew. The moon set at about quarter before six. It was beautiful, & very soon the orange dawn lightened the east. I got through my bath by half past *seven. After breakfast the day promised fair & the south west wind still prevailed. But when I began to paint the sun played hide & seek so provokingly, that the light was continually changing & I became so perplexed that after two hours' trial, I gave up & at eleven went to walk. I called at Mr Rice's & spoke for a barrel of flour, & then at Mr Dean's to [9] get a chafing dish for coals & told him to make one. There I found Mr Edmund Hosmer buying a cooking stove.[20] Mr Dean said the Zinc was ready for me. Then I proceeded to the P. O. & found a letter from Louisa, explaining the mystery of the long silence & the non arrival of the valise.[21] The family had all been ill with colds. I went on to Mrs Emerson's. Behold, the dining room was bouleversed & carpenters were there, & so Abby put me into the parlor. Madam Emerson[22] came in, looking very ill with a cold. I went up to see Mrs E. & found her for the first time up & dressed since a long time. I carried in my muff, my little darling's netted pelisse which Mary Shaw sent me, & they admired it & I thought Mrs. envied[?] me somewhat. She said Mr Emerson had gone to lecture at Providence, & one or two other places, to be absent till Saturday. From there {I went to see Ellen Channing.}[23] She was just out of the bath, & {looked very pretty} & I gave her much counsel about her diet which she intends to follow. She feels very badly all the time. Her pregnancy is not so happy as mine, but she says she is very happy in her mind. {She has a dog, named Romeo, w'h Mr S. Ward[24] gave Ellery.} The dog & cat peacefully lay upon the floor together. It was a very mild day, south west, & the sun shone lustrously all my way. {I borrowed a book about sainted women of Ellen.} I came in to see my dear husband before [10] dinner. After that ceremony I looked over the book for a good while, until I was summoned to see Mrs Prescott. She took home with her all the rest of baby's diapers, twenty five, to make them, benevolent as she is. She insisted upon it, & could not be denied. In the evening my lord read the Mysteries, & I sewed upon a tiny petticoat for my little fay. In the midst came a pacquet from Boston, quite rich. There was a sumptuous present from Rose Forbes of a french [?] embroidered robe, a flannel petticoat of exquisite texture & workmanship, four silk-flannel bands, soft as love, a pair of netted shoes & a netted bonnet. Mother sent the large blanket & flannel for night pettis—& Sally Gardner muslin for my night caps. Ellen Hooper a pair of knit shoes made by herself, & Mary Shaw four yards of beautiful thread lace edging.[25] Then there were many notes from Mary Mann to mother & E. for me to read, & a letter from Mother. the Democratic Review[26] & a bundle for Ellen Channing. {In the Democratic was my husband's "Fire Worship." I could not wait to read it. It is perfectly inimitable} & inimitably perfect {as usual. His wit is as subtle as fire,} his wisdom as searching. To read anything of his after all other reading is like lifting one's head out of the bogs & quagmires of earth into the [11] clear empyrean. He is the wonder & glory of my life & of his time also. He is constantly a new sun rising on midnoons. I went down & heard Mary read a good while before I went to bed. This morning (6th Wednesday) {I was up at moonlight again & sewed till Mary got my bath ready.} The house was full of moonlight, very bright. {The moon did not set till after dawn.} The room was so cold I could not sit down in my tub to day. After breakfast I painted till half past twelve & then walked till nearly two. I went to the Post Office, & found nothing, & then called at Miss Ward's—she was not at home.*[27] *I went to Rice's store also. The day was very still, colder, but superbly bright & cloudless. I painted af-ter dinner till 1/2 past three on drapery. Then I came to my beloved, & sewed on little petticoat till dusk, while he read. After he went to take the fresh, I called Mary into the study, & dressed. After tea, my husband read aloud the rest of Hamlet & I finished little pett:*

December 7th Thursday

I waked very early this morning & it looked quite light & yet the moon did not seem to shine. I arose & looked out & found a slight sprinkling of snow—& then saw it was five o'clk, & concluded not to go to [12] bed again. I came into the study & opened the stove & lighted a small lamp & sat down to mend my tunic—. After that was done, I felt a little sleepy & lay down upon the couch till it should be time to call Mary to get my bath. At half past six, it was still quite dusky, but I summoned her. In the tub I read a part of Count Louis's article upon Mr Brownson in the Demo:[28] *& my dear husband came in before I was out. After breakfast, as it was too dark to paint, I sewed. First I altered the collar of my lord's purple blouse & then made a little cambric robe. I in-vited Mary OBrien to sit with me & knit till it were time to get dinner. She has such a pretty way of talking & is so full of innocent fresh feelings & thoughts, that she is a very pleasant companion. After twelve, I wrapped up, & bustled about the chambers to get air & exer-cise, as it had been diligently snowing all the morning, & I could not walk out. My dear husband wrote till two, I believe. After dinner I came to the study with him & sewed on tiny garments while he read till after four, when he went out & soon {I began to promenade the gallery with muff & tippet & wadded dress,} even my [13] lord's purple blouse. Oh I forgot that directly after dinner, he went to the village, & brought me a letter from Mary Mann, dated 13th November! It had been mislaid all this while. {After tea, my love read Jones Very's criticism upon 'Hamlet',}*[29] *& then two acts of 'Taming of the Shrew' to me. After that I heard Mary read nearly an hour—It has snowed all day.*

December 8th Friday.

This morning I was again early awake, between four & five. It was

*bright moonlight. The snow storm had ceased & the wind was still. I
returned to bed after excursing a little & lay till dawn. The deep snow
had so blocked up the pathway to the well, that I did not intend Mary
should go for water for my bath, especially as she had a bad cold. But I
intended to wait till after breakfast, when my dear lord would bring it,
{heaps of snow being trifles to his might.} So I did not wake Mary, but
sat down to sew, & mended my husband's stockings & shirt. {The morning was very superb.} The earth was delicately white {& the gold
sunlight played on it like the glow of rubies upon pearl. My beloved
was truly satisfied with the beauty (of its kind) & he is so seldom
satisfied with any thing—weather, things or people that I am always
glad to find him pleased. [14] His demand is for perfection, & nothing
short can content him. How can seraphs be contented with less? After
breakfast, as I should not be able to walk out on account of the snow, I
concluded to housewife.} I swept chambers & entries & dusted all things
& it was fine exercise with windows open, letting in the magnificent
weather. {My husband shovelled paths & sawed & split wood &
brought me water. To such uses do seraphs come when they get astray
on earth.} After my housewifery was over, I bathed, & then {painted
till after one o'clk} on drapery. Then I came to see my dear husband till
dinner. I thought to paint in the afternoon, but did not feel like it &
sewed on tiny robe till dusk. My love went to the village after dinner &
then read till sunset. {It was a purple & gold sunset.} When he went
out, I lay down on the couch & called Mary O'Brien to sit with me till
he should return. In the evening he read the rest of the Taming of the
Shrew to me, & then I descended to hear Mary read, but she did not on
account of her cough. I staid an hour to let her have a chance to talk, as I
left my lord on the couch to take a nap. "My William" brought the flour
to day.*

[15] *December 9th*

*It was after six when I rose to day for a wonder. I had time to do
nothing till after breakfast, except to read more of Count Louis's article
as I sat in the tub. When I first looked out upon the world, the moon
shone, but by the time it was fully daylight, it snowed again, & the
morning & day were dark so that I could not paint. I sewed therefore for
dearest baby, & made a little long sleeved apron. Then as I could not
walk out, I housewifed for more than an hour. It was very mild weather,
& thawed a little. {After dinner my love went to the village & brought
back a Salem Gazette.} I sewed all the afternoon while he read Walpole
till sunset. There was no shine of sun, but the clouds broke in the west &
tried to look pleasant. {As usual my} sweet {husband went out to find
exercise till quite dark} & I called Mary. When he returned, he coun-
selled me to walk the gallery till tea-time, which I did. After that*

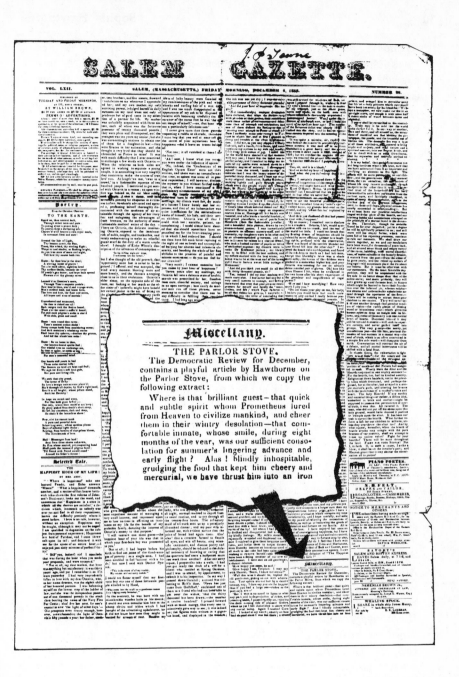

Miscellany.

THE PARLOR STOVE.

The Democratic Review for December, contains a playful article by Hawthorne on the Parlor Stove, from which we copy the following extract:

Where is that brilliant guest—that quick and subtle spirit whom Prometheus lured from Heaven to civilize mankind, and cheer them in their wintry desolation—that comfortable inmate, whose smile, during eight months of the year, was our sufficient consolation for summer's lingering advance and early flight? Alas! blindly inhospitable, grudging the food that kept him cheery and mercurial, we have thrust him into an iron

Salem Gazette 8 December 1843. Collection of C. E. Frazer Clark, Jr.

ceremony, {he read aloud part of the Tempest & I sewed} little pett: &
finally spent an hour with Mary down stairs. {Some one had the im-
pudence to speak of my husband as "gentle Nat Hawthorne" in the
Gazette. I cannot concieve who could be so bold & so familiar & so
unapt. 'Gentle' surely he is, but such an epithet does not comprehend
him & gives a false idea.}[30]

[16] *December 10th Sunday.*

I wake later now, for which I am very glad. This morning it was six
before I was fully aroused I believe. Mary slept long as usual on Sunday morning, & as I did not feel like the tub, I did not summon her. After breakfast I wrote many notes & a letter to Mother. They were to
Sally Gardner, Anna Shaw, Mary Shaw, Ellen Hooper, Count Louis
O'Sullivan & Rose Forbes.[31] It was a pleasant day with mild west wind,
& at twelve, I went out & walked half an hour from the front door to the
well along the path my dear lord shovelled. It was most reviving to be in
the air again. After dinner, I wrote more & then read Montaigne & the
rest of Count Louis's article. I wonder what Mr Brownson will say to
it. Mary was with me all day, but felt too stupid with a cold to read or
write till in the afternoon she tried a little. My beloved wrote all day
long till sunset. Then he called me & I was glad enough to be with him
again. But he soon had to go out for air & exercise & it was not till after
tea that I felt as if I had possession of him. He read the rest of the Tempest. Mary went to the village. The moon shone bright by nine of clock.

[17] *December 11th Monday.*

Last night Mary O'Brien went to bed very late & waked me out of a
sound sleep with the noise of doors. My dearest husband had come to
bed without disturbing my repose as usual, though I had a consciousness
of his advent. But Mary completely roused me, & I felt as if I should
never sleep again. It was nearly eleven. [Here two and a half lines of
the MS have been obliterated.] {My lord told me of his early life in
Raymond} [Three and one half lines destroyed] {My husband [Two
words obliterated] got me some of Mr Bridge's ancient wine}[32] & a
cracker at about twelve. These were of admirable effect & in ten minutes
I was composed & almost asleep. Very soon I was quite—I know he
saved me from being ill. I slept till six in the morning very well. The
bath was particularly reviving this morning. The day was cloudy & I
sewed instead of painting—& finished a little pett: & made a wee
apron. My lord wrote till four in the P.M. Then he went to the village
& brought me thence letters from Mary & Mother.[33] {After tea he read
the Two gentlemen of Verona partly. I do not like it much. What a queer
mood Shakspere must have been in to write it. He seems making fun.}
[18] I came down to see Mary after he stopped reading, but she felt too

sick with her cold to do any thing. It has been a very mild, thawing day with South west wind. I walked half an hour in my path before dinner.

December 20th Wednesday.

My journal is sadly behind hand. Just a week ago this morning, my Mary went to bed sick, & threatened with a fever, perhaps Typhus, which is very prevalent now in Concord & many places. It was the coldest day by far we had yet had, & clear & splendid. I had just taken up my brush to paint, when poor Mary opened the door, looking very ill, & said she must go to bed. I went to Mrs Prescott's to ask her advice, & she told me to get her into a perspiration, if possible, & to send for Dr Bartlett.[34] I put her on the little couch in my chamber & gave her some hot tea of lemon balm & put a jug of hot water to her feet, & made a fire in the air-tight stove. I will not enter into details of her illness. That day & the next continued bitterly cold, but bright. Mrs Prescott was an angel of aid to me & spent the first night with Mary—The next day I had Betsey come, who officiated in the kitchen & chambers & waited upon Mary a little. I became pretty tired going up & down stairs & feeling the great responsibility, but chiefly was wearied by the excessive anxiety of my beloved husband, who thought I should be injured [19] by so much extra exertion. Betsey could not stay, & I sent to Mother for Margaret, Mary's sister, who arrived Friday night. Mary was better then, & has been getting well ever since, & now is quite restored, though lacking appetite. She was very patient & considerate & behaved exceedingly well. It was her first sickness. I did nothing, not even any sewing till Saturday, my mind & hands were so occupied. Margaret brought me from mother some letters & perryan pens & Hill's bill. I prepared some work for the Antislavery ladies to do for me on Saturday. Sunday morning I wrote to Mother & Sarah Clarke & Mrs Sturgis.[35] Oh—on Saturday I recieved a bundle from Mother by Miss Adams, containing a pair of polish boots, flannel for baby, a budget of letters from Mary to mother & E. & a Stove almanack & a letter from Sarah.[36] I read a little of Montaigne on Sunday. Monday I prepared work all the morning. Mary came down stairs for the first time, & sat with me in the dining room. In the afternoon I sewed upon a little robe. In the evening my dearest husband read the Merry Wives of Windsor to me. Tuesday I rose at five & sewed two hours before my husband was up & finished the little robe. It was very pretty. We recieved from the Count an hundred dollars on Monday 18th. Yesterday (Tuesday) morning, we went to the village early to change the bill at the bank. The bank would not because it was New York money, but Mr Shattuck did.[37] I went to see [20] Mrs Emerson while my husband went to the Athenaeum. I wanted to send a pacquet to Boston by Miss Adams. But she was gone. Mr [Mrs?] Emerson, however, was to go this morning, & would take it.

It was a superb day. Every tree & twig was snowy white & the sun
shone lustrously. I never saw so beautiful a spectacle of its kind. The
earth & all that thereon was, was white, white, white. The tracery of the
trees against the blue sky was exquisite—I called at Dean's & scolded
him for not coming to fix my stove. I paid the baker fifteen cents for
bread, & we went to Mr Rice's & bought cheese & crackers. Coming
home, I called at Mr Prescott's & engaged George to carry my pacquet to
Mrs Emerson's in the afternoon. By this time the sun was overshadowed
& shone no more that day. Last evening my husband read aloud "What
you will". In the afternoon he had written, & I sat in the dining room
with Margaret & Mary, sewing on little pett. I continued to sew on it
all the evening. This morning I rose a few minutes before six & sewed
an hour before my husband came, still upon tiny pett. It was cloudy.
Just now the sun breaks forth & I must paint.

I painted from 10 till after one, or rather sat during that time before
Endymion, brush & palette & mahl stick in hand, [21] but was very
lazy & did not paint all the hours. After dinner I went to the village
with my dear husband & sat in the Athenaeum with him while he read.
I read a story in the Knicker-bocker called 'The Venus of Ille"—which
was quite original.38 We met Mr Emerson at the foot of the Athenaeum
stairs. He said Ellery was chopping wood eight hours a day—& had
been doing so for ten days. We were at home by four o'clk. I sewed upon
little pett then & all the evening. My beloved finished "Twelvth night".

December 21th Thursday.39

This morning I woke before five & soon after five rose after a few
moments waking with my sweet husband. I wrote to Michael O'Brien &
to Mother before light & then lay down on the couch.40 I could not tub
this morning. It was a most beautiful day—mild, still & shining. After
breakfast I meant to paint, but was so sleepy I lay down & slept all the
morning! After dinner I went to village with my lord, & proceeded to
Elizabeth Hoar's. She was gone to Boston to Dr Randall's funeral. I
went back to the Athenaeum & staid there till my husband was ready to
come home—. Soon after we arrived Mrs. Brown made me a visit.41 She
wanted to see tiny garments, & I showed her some. [22] She came up
into the study & greatly admired Loch Lomond illumined by the evening
sun, as it shone upon the wall where it hung.42 In the evening, my
dearest husband read the first part of "Much ado about Nothing-" & I
sewed Mamma-cap, & wrote to Louisa.43

December 22d Friday

A cloudy warm morning. I rose much later than usual & had time
only to bathe before breakfast. After breakfast {I wrote to Mrs Follen &
made up a budget to her of a paper from my husband for her "Child's

Friend".[44] It was the incident of Mr Raike's life with regard to his founding of Sunday-schools, most exquisitely told & set in a frame of precious jewels. Whatever he touches turns to gold in the intellectual & spiritual world.} I wish for his sake it might be so for a season in the material. It is exactly as if he had taken that fact & placed it among the constellations in stars. During my cessation of record here, on the 12th December, he finished quite a long sketch, "The Christmas Banquet" "One of the Unpublished Allegories of the Heart". He read it to me that day before he sent it to the Count. I thought it very extraordinary—perfectly original & very profound. I must have it in print & read it again before I can speak of it. After making up the pacquet for Boston, I sewed on mamma-cap & attended to Margaret & Mary who were to go to Boston in the Harvard Stage. When they had gone, my dearest husband came [23] down to see me, & I got the dinner with his assistance & it was quite a good one. We think {we will have the luxury of being alone during Mary's absence.} After dinner & dish washing, my husband went to the village, & did not want me to go with him for fear of rain. So I remained behind & {sewed on purple blouse till dusk.} He returned pretty soon. Before dark Mrs Prescott called for a few moments. In the evening my lord finished "Much ado about Nothing" & I sewed cap till he implored me leave off. The wind rose in the evening after a long sleep of two or three days, so that I supposed it would grow colder. It has been wonderfully warm for winter lately.

23d December Saturday.

This morning we woke alone in the house. {My Apollo} to day has helped me keep-house, for we enjoy so much being by ourselves for a while that we do not hire any one during Mary's absence. My lord {made the fires} in the kitchen & dining-room, & {I warmed some rice for me,} because I do not eat bread during pregnancy (as a habit) {& I had the happiness of toasting his bread} & of making him tea. He very rarely takes tea, & never except in the morning, but I wanted him to have some today. After breakfast I came up & arranged his study which I love to do, for whatever for him, & having put him in possession, I went down & washed my breakfast dishes & made order [24] below stairs. It was eleven when I finished & my dearest husband wanted me to sit with him while he wrote. This was enchanting—I was not to be separate from him all day. I sat here & sewed till about two. At one my love went to the village & thought I had better not accompany him, because it looked like rain. At two we made hot some potatoes & rice & dined soon after three on cold meat, those vegetables, & stewed apple—a very excellent dinner. I did not wash dishes after dinner, but put them nicely together to wash in the morning with the breakfast things, & then we were to be uninterrupted the rest of the time—for we did not intend

Pandora attired by the Graces

A tracing of a Flaxman drawing made by Sophia Hawthorne for the Concord Fair. *Collection of C. E. Frazer Clark, Jr.*

to have any supper. My husband brought me from the village a budget
of letters from Boston—from Mary & Mother.[45] I was very sorry to
hear that my brother Horace had injured his eye with a stick of wood.
So they are not in Boston yet perhaps. They have engaged three rooms at
the old Coolidge House in Bowdoin Square. Before dark came from
Salem the long expected valise from dear Louisa. It contained many articles for thee, my sweet baby. Material for night robes & two little
gowns already made by thy Aunt Luly.[46] silk flannel to make thy little
shirts [25] for cold weather & linen cambric to make them for warm.
Cambric edging to adorn thy dayrobes & the prettiest little brush &
comb for thy silken hair that were ever seen. Thou shalt see them when
thou art old enough. Above all were two linen cambric shirts wh thy
dear father wore when he was an infant! I am sure they will consecrate
with a new charm thy sweet, pure little form. There was also a letter
from Louisa, containing the sad news of her own & our Mother's
illness—which had caused the delay of the valise.[47] In the evening my
beloved {husband read to me "Love's Labor Lost"} & I sewed till half-
past eight. {He said that play had no foundation in Nature.

Sunday. December 24th

Another dim morning. Yesterday I could not paint; it was so dark.
{To day there have been bright gleams, but no steady sunshine. Apollo
boiled some potatoes for breakfast. Imagine him with that magnificent
head bent over a cooking stove & those star-eyes watching the pot! There
never were such good potatoes before in consequence.} I prepared the
study before breakfast a little—& finished afterwards. It did not take
me so long to housewife to day, & again my dear lord wanted me to sit
with him, and all day I did so. We [26] dined at quarter past three &
made an end of the boiled meat. {We did not succeed in warming the
potatoes effectually, but they were edible, & we had cheese & apple
besides.} In the evening was finished 'Love's Labor Lost'. I rose before
five this morning.

Monday December 25th.

{Christmas day—which I consider the most illustrious & sacred day
of the year. Before sunrise a great, dark blue cloud in the east made me
suppose it was to be a dark & dismal day: but I was quite mistaken. It
has been uncommonly beautiful}—a mild, still, shining day with a sun
of real heat. {Peace has seemed brooding with "turtle wing" over the
world. There has seemed no one stirring & as if all men obeyed the command of the elements which was "Be still as we are."}[48] I did not rise
quite as early as usual. At sunrise a rosy gleam turned the snow to
opaline hues & not a breath of wind broke the sacred calm. We break-
fasted upon baked potatoes, milk, bread & apple. {I intended to make a

*fine bowl of chocolate for my husband's dinner; but he proposed to
celebrate Christmas by having no cooking at all for dinner.}* [27] *I
should have painted as it was sunny; but my lord asked me to sit with
him Christmas day & I was only too glad to do so. I was through my
morning housekeeping by ten, I believe, & then I came to the study, &
made little silk-flannel shirts till one o'clk while he wrote. {At one we
went together to the village.} My furs & velvet bonnet were very op-
pressive in the warm noon sun. It was rather difficult walking on account of the thawing. I parted with Myself at the Court-House. {He
went to the} Post Office & {Athenaeum.} I called at Mr Rice's & then
at Mr Dean's to scold him for not coming to fix my fire board. He is a
very careless man, I think. {Then I went to Mrs Emerson's.} They had
just dined, & the table was not quite cleared off. Edith still sat at it in
her high chair, looking very happy, rosy & smiling.*[49] *Mrs Browne was
there {& Mr Thoreau to dine.} I carried the tiny comb & brush to show
& they were much admired. Mr Emerson was in Boston.* [Here almost
four lines of holograph have been scratched out in the same way
as page [17] was partially obliterated.] *Mrs Emerson was uncommonly well for her. She said Mr Alcott had dined with them, &
thought of coming to live in Concord again.*[50] *{At last I came* [28] *away
& saw soon in the distance the form of forms approaching.} I was glad
enough, for I feared I was so late that he had gone home. We came
slowly along. The wicked Dr Gallup rode behind in a sleigh without
bells. After coming home, we proceeded to arrange our Paradisiacal dinner. {It consisted of preserved quince, stewed apples, dates, cheese, bread
& butter & milk, quite elegant & very nice.} Towards dark my dear
husband went out to exercise—By quarter past five we were seated for
the evening—I made little shirts & my love read the first acts of the
Comedy of Error, & then Milton's beautiful Christmas Ode.*

Tuesday December 26th

*This morning was dark with no sign of a gleam. I rose at six, &
braided my hair & began a little shirt before my husband came. After
the bath I joined him downstairs. He was cooking me some rice. We had
it for breakfast. {What a miracle he is!} He gives me a greater sense of
universal power than any person I ever knew or heard of except
Shakspere. He resembles him more than any one else. {He has the
faculty of accommodating himself to* [29] *all sorts of circumstances
with a marvellous facility & grace of soul.} I have found new cause to
admire him during Mary's absence. He is the wholest person that ever
lived. I had the felicity of sitting with him again all day. Directly after
breakfast came the reprehensible Mr Dean & fixed my fire board. I
made little shirt in the morning. At one my lord went to the village &
would not let me go, because it snowed a little. Mrs Prescott came at*

twelve & brought some of baby's napkins which she had made for me—two dozen—most kind lady.[51] *While my husband was gone, I wrote a letter to Mary Pickman*[52] *& then sewed. We had some warm rice for dinner with preserved pear & quince, apple, cheese, bread & molasses & milk. In the afternoon I cut into napkins an old damask table cloth Louisa sent me & made one. A pedler came to sell honey & essences & I sent him away without buying. I never buy any thing of pedlars, especially to eat. In the evening my lord read the rest of the Comedy of Errors & I sewed on little night gown. {He brought from the post office for me a letter from } Mother & from {Ellen Hooper & some* [30] *verses from Ellen, inspired by his article upon "Fire Worship."*[53] *The motto is "Fight for your stoves" & the versification*[54] *is that of "Scots who hae." It is very good.} The letter was delightful. Soon after six {Mary O Brien arrived} from Boston, our familiar spirit ushering her in with all her luggage in his arms & sitting down in the dining room with us as if he meant to spend the evening. His presence prevented me from asking Mary any questions & after waiting a while for him to go of his own will, I called Mary out of the room & took the lamp. He still sat, till I said 'Come Ben'—I thanked him for his attention & bade him good night without ceremony.*[55]

Wednesday December 27th

{We awoke to a mighty snowstorm. The trees stood white-armed all round us.} It was also very mild weather. I did not paint but sat with my dearest husband. Mary washed. I made little nightgown. We concluded to continue our practice of but two meals a day & so dined after three. Mary thinks it a delightful plan. {In the PM. some one knocked at the front door. I was amazed, supposing no one could overcome the roads & thought it must be a government officer. As Mary opened I heard a voice "Where is the man?" It was Ellery Channing [31] *who said as he appeared at the study door that it was the very time to come. He liked the snow. He looked like a shaggy bear—but his face was quite shining as usual. He brought some novels & Reviews which Queen Margaret had sent Ellen to read.*[56] *We had to leave him to dine. He would not join us, & made his exit while we were down stairs.} Towards dusk my, beloved moved a bureau into our chamber, & I arranged in one of the drawers the few baby clothes I have ready. Then I walked the gallery a little while he was out of doors. In the evening he read to me the first acts of "As you like it"—while I sewed little nightgown & finished it. At eight I went down to see Mary & found her quite cheery & not inclined to read.*

Thursday 28th December.

No more snow falling, but a grey day & mild. I did not sleep so well as usual last night & felt lazy & stupid this morning. Yet I was resolved to paint, willing or unwilling. I mended my husband's socks before light & then lay down till the bath was ready. Then I mended my own stockings till Mary had prepared the breakfast room & left it—& I began to paint. But soon I was overwhelmed with drowsiness & stupidity & lay down [32] upon the carpet for forty minutes, nearly sleeping. I painted afterwards till half past twelve, much against my mood. Then I went up stairs & peeped in to see my husband, for I had been terribly homesick down stairs without him. He was extended on the couch, reading. I returned soon to painting & he went to the village. Then I came up & with the intention of putting a pocket in his blouse & mending his coat; but was obliged to lie down & go to sleep upon the couch. There I was when he returned. He brought a letter from Ellery, enclosing part of the money he owed us. five dollars. I did not feel[57] well, but feverish & lifeless & after dinner could not do much of any thing. At dusk, as I sat with my hand over my eyes, half asleep, my dear husband attempted to shut a drawer of his secretary, & tipped over the lovely Ceres, who came tumbling down, scattering her remains over me & the room with an astounding crash. I was amazed—but seemed very quiet at first. Then I began to feel nervous & shocked & as if I must have a thunder gust of tears to relieve myself. I found it would not do, however, for this immediately [33] [Here three-quarters of a line is obliterated] & I made a great effort to stop. But I could have done nothing without the tenderest & best husband in the world, who held me in his arms & soothed & calmed me with his divine caresses & seraph-tones. A tiny glass of Mr Bridge's antique wine seemed to do some good, & soon I got quite over it, except a little headach. I did not accomplish any thing in the evening, & my dear love did not read, aloud[58] because I thought I could not lend attention. I read the Foreign Review, & looked over "The Czarina" & ripped off thread lace for baby's robes—& paid a few minutes' visit to Mary.[59]

Friday 29th December

A grey morning. My dear husband advised me so strongly not to paint as I did not feel very bright, that I yeilded, not against my will, but much against my purpose. He wanted me to sit with him too & that was too tempting. I did not do much. I tried to sew & read a little of the "Nabob at Home" as I had done in the tub.[60] Soon after eleven he proposed going to the village & I went with him. Mr Flint overtook us in a few minutes & I made him take me into his sleigh upon the top of his meal-bags, & he rode me to Mrs Brown's. [34] There I made a call. She showed me some baby clothes & lent me a linen cambric embroidered robe for a pattern & a piece of little shirt. She also displayed her London doll, as large as a babe of four or five months.

From her I went to Mr Rice's—& bought a piece of narrow tape for baby's robes—Mr Hosmer came into the shop & pulled off his great mitten to shake hands. Thence I went to Wardwell's, but he had nothing I wanted, & to Hastings' to leave Mary's india-rubber. I then called at the Athaeneum for my husband & took again Mary's rubber & we came home[.] My love had found a letter from Mrs Sturgis in the Post O. for me & when we were home, he unfolded a letter from the Count.[61] *I was greatly benefitted by the oxygen I had inhaled. I cannot stay in the house over a day without detriment, I find. I need pure air more than ever now that I am two. When I returned I arranged the guest chamber somewhat & put away my scattered work—& then read Nabob a little before dinner. After dinner I sewed no night gown. The sun broke forth & filled the study, & my lord read aloud more of "As you like it", till dusk. After lamp light he read Foreign Reviews.*[62] *I paid Mary a visit between 8 & 9 o clk—& was not in bed till ten for a wonder.*

[35] *December 30th Saturday.*

A very windy night was last night, rather disturbing to slumber. The morning proved cold but not bitterly so, & very lustrous. I did not [Here two and a quarter lines of holograph have been neatly cut out of the leaf.] *After breakfast I painted upon drapery but with a most stupid mind. I am possessed with an obstinate fiend as soon as I sit down to this picture now. It is strange & most provoking.* {*As I painted the wind arose & howled & swept about & clouded the sun & wearied my spirits. I was obliged to put away my palette at 1/2 past twelve & then came up & looked at my husband. He was writing & I was conscience stricken for interrupting him.*} *I returned to the dining room, & found Mary had spread the door open & moved the chairs & was all ready for a great sweeping, supposing I had left till dinner. I felt desolate & nervous & as if I wanted to sit down & weep a river. I had to return to the study, it was so cold & comfortless below, & the wind all the while confusing my brain. My return spoiled my dear husband's vein for writing & that was very hard for me to bear & I was more nervous still. I concluded to go to the village, though the* [36] *weather was so unpropitious, because I knew if I stayed at home a thunder-gust would come.* {*So we went.*} *At the foot of the* [Here two and a quarter lines of holograph have been lost because of the cutting done on this leaf—see p. [35].] *his sleigh; but he slackened as he drew near, &* {*invited us to drive to town. I accepted, but my husband would not. The Imp sprang on as we passed his house, & then I found the kind old man was Mr Jarvis of the hill.*} *He deposited me at Shattuck's & thence I went to the Athenaeum to find my husband—first to* {*the Post Office however, where he was reading a letter.*} *There was one to me from Louisa & for him* {*from Mr Hillard.*}[63] *Louisa was worried about the valise because I had not written of its arrival. {We stayed in the Athenaeum till after two, & then braved the warring wind homewards.} I was better for the oxygen & exercise, but still a little nervous all the rest of the day. I sewed in the afternoon & evening, mending night cap & making little nightgown. {We had no reading for the wind was too noisy.} I went to see Mary a little—& Gaffer Flint came to apologize [37] for not calling as he promised in the day to get my message to Mrs Emerson.*

December 31st Sunday.

A sunny but windy day. We were much disturbed in the night by the wind. I dreamed of women in fits & many horrors. After breakfast I wrote to Mother & Mary & Mrs Sturgis & Louisa—& read Foreign Review. In the afternoon my husband read aloud to me "As you like it" till dusk. Then I walked half an hour in the gallery. I recieved this afternoon a budget from Mother—a note & a thermometer.⁶⁴ In the evening my dear love read more—Mary went to the village.

Monday January 1st 1844

{A quiet morning at last. The wind had howled itself dead as if it were the breath of the old year, by midnight.} The relief was very great. It was clear & sunny. I wrote more to mother after breakfast & made up a pacquet to Boston to send by Mr Emerson's opportunity—& put in also a letter to Mary Mann. Gaffer Flint was coming to get my messages to Mr Emerson, & I put up all the books we [38] had borrowed from him, & some tiny garments Mrs E. had lent me for patterns—& sent the rake also. I sent to Mr Rice's the Brown sugar Bucket & the White Havana & the Rice bucket. Then I took my painting, but did not accomplish any thing. We went to the village at half past one. I called at Rice's & explained the buckets that were to come, & went half way to E. Hoar's; but found I should be too tired & therefore returned to the Athenaeum to my husband. {Coming home Dr Bartlett met us & offered to take us both along—but took only me. On the way he spoke of} his wife & her retiringness & of {George Bradford's worshipping Mr Hawthorne.} There was such a huge drift of snow at the gate of the avenue that he could not drive me in. After dinner I sewed, & in the evening also & my dearest love finished "As You like it. Mary went to the village & so I did not go to see her. It was superb moonlight.

January 2d. Tuesday

A perfect day, very mild, still, & bright. I read Foreign Review in the tub, a quite interesting account of the Cossacks & Ukrainian poetry—& of Galy.⁶⁵ After breakfast I sewed till eleven & then painted till after three o'clk; for my love wished to write [39] till dinner time. {I had a

The Old Manse (early photo). *Collection of C. E. Frazer Clark, Jr.*

fine time painting. Every thing went right & I succeeded quite to my mind. I felt sure my husband above me must also be having a propitious morning} with his muse, or I could not feel so altogether content. {When he came to dinner, I asked him, & he said he did not know as he ever felt so much like writing on any one day. We seemed to respond to one another exactly, as if particularly united, & I think it was so. [One word scratched out, seemingly as an error.] Were we two persons? After dinner Miss Cath: Barrett called & {Mr Emerson.} I took the lady into the dining room & Mr Emerson went to the study. Miss B. wished to make some small garment for me, & took a flannel petticoat, which she desired to embroider. When she had gone, I went to the study & found no husband! I dressed myself as soon as possible, & proceeded to the village. I searched in the Athenaeum for my lord, but he was not there. The world seemed empty of all things because I did not know where Mr Emerson had carried him. I wanted very much to go to Elizabeth Hoar's & as I could not think of coming home & not finding him here, I went there, tho' it was rather late. I saw Mrs H. & E—E. had a bad cold approaching. I borrowed of her for my love the Antiquary & the Promessi Sposi. I saw there Miss Frances Jane Pritchard.[66] [40] *I was pretty tired before I got home. I had a sharp pain beneath my left shoulder & wanted to sit down on a snow bank to rest, but continued on till I came to Mrs Prescott's & went in there to rest a moment. When I came out, my dear husband was in the road, awaiting me. I was glad enough to see him again. In the evening he read to me "The Merchant of Venice" & I sewed edging on little robe. The moon was dim to night. Mary went to the village again.*

January 3d Wednesday.

A dark morning—& soon after sunrise it began to snow. I concluded to arrange my chamber as I could not paint, & had a fire put there. I stuffed the cracks of two windows with cotton & left the third to be opened for airing the room. I put up the white curtains & fixed the closet, & draped the couch, & it looked very pretty. My husband went to the village after dinner without me as then it rained hard. In the evening he finished the 'Merchant of Venice' & I put a ruffle on my nightgown & cut out tiny aprons. I was rather tired with my day's labors, & my dear love felt tired & sleepy.

January 4th Thursday.

The morning promised fair, but clouded soon. I gave George Prescott[67] [41] *La Fontaine's Fables for a New Year's present. The sun did not shine all the morning; but there was an even bright light so that I could have well painted; but before eleven, when I meant to begin, I found myself so very weary from yesterday's housewifery, so sleepy, that I sat in the great chair, leaning back, fit for nothing but a little sewing on a tiny apron. Mary was with me, writing a letter to Mike. She composes remarkably well. At one I was obliged to go to bed where I lay & slept till nearly three. In the morning the bath exhilarated me so much that I thought I was quite rested. I read Promessi Sposi in the tub. After dinner I felt still too tired to go out, though I wanted some air. The sun shone[68] at about four & set beneath cold, blue clouds. In the evening my dearest husband read "Troilus & Cresseida"—Mary went to the village & was gone till nine. The moonlight was magnificent. I sewed upon little apron.*

Friday. January 5th

A very cold morning. I rose at five, but my lamp soon went out, & I had to lie down upon the couch in the study—There I was too cold & so I sat by the stove till I thought it late enough to wake Mary, & then I got her lamp, & [42] sewed till the bath was ready. In the tub I read Promessi Sposi. The morning was clear & sunny—After breakfast I sewed till eleven, & then painted till three very successfully. There seems no difficulty now in the picture. I always go through the valley of Shadow of death in painting every picture, & the more worth the picture has, the more dismal is my journey. But at last I stand on the delectable mountains—& now I seem to be there with Endymion.[69] After dinner the wind blew so furiously & it was so very cold, I could not go to the village; but went with my dear husband as far as Mrs Prescott's to get a little oxygen. He had written to the Count.[70] I made call upon the Prescotts, & Abba escorted me down the slippery steps that I might not fall. Then I went into Miss Barrett's & found her working on very little petticoat. She is going to embroider it famously—I do not know whether I shall like it as well as my plainer & more elegant way—but perhaps it will look better than I think. When my husband returned from the village, I went out & came home under his guard angelic.

University of Notre Dame

---

[1]It has always been assumed, largely on Julian Hawthorne's authority (see Claude M. Simpson, ed., *The American Notebooks*, vol. VIII of *The Centenary Edition of the Works of Nathaniel Hawthorne* [Columbus: Ohio State U. P., 1972], 686-90, 703), that Sophia did all the physical "editing" of the Hawthorne notebooks, but that may not be entirely the case. The present journal by Sophia, though not intended for publication at any time, is mutilated in exactly the same manner as Nathaniel's notebooks. Why would Sophia go to the trouble of "editing" a journal which she had no intention of publishing? Particularly troubling is some crossing-out that is done in blue ink rather than the more

usual black used by both Nathaniel and Sophia.

[2][*The Works of Nathaniel Hawthorne: Riverside Edition*] (Boston: Houghton, Mifflin, 1882), II, 30-31.

[3]For a detailed account of Hawthorne's production during this time, which included "The Christmas Banquet," "A Good Man's Miracle," and "Earth's Holocaust," see my article, "The Old Manse Period Canon," *The Nathaniel Hawthorne Journal 1972*, ed. C. E. Frazer Clark, Jr. (Washington, D.C.: NCR Microcard Editions, 1973), p. 28.

[4]For a description of this painting, see Rose Hawthorne Lathrop, *Memories of Hawthorne* (Boston: Houghton, Mifflin, 1897), pp. 71-73. The MS of this passage from *Memories* is in the Berg Collection. In *The Peabody Sisters of Salem*, Louise Hall Tharp remarks that the bas relief from which Sophia copied "Endymion" was an especially attractive subject for her because she "had become enamored of sculpture and this picture combined both sculpture and painting in the problems it presented" (p. 161). The immediate source of Sophia's copy was a print(?) owned by Emerson. She began to paint it sometime after August 20 and described it as "about finished" in a letter to her mother dated December 8, 1843 (MS: Berg). The actual completion date, however, was January 26, 1844 (see her letter to Maria Louisa Hawthorne, February 4, 1844—MS: Berg). Rose Hawthorne Lathrop's comment on the painting (*Memories*, p. 72) indicates that it still existed in 1897, but present inquiries have failed to uncover it.

[5]Eugene Sue's novel of Parisian low life, *The Mysteries of Paris*, caused a small stir at the end of 1843. Written and published serially by Sue in 1842-43, it had been published in an American French Language edition and in at least two American translations by January, 1844. The earliest translation was done by Charles H. Town and was published by Harper & Brothers in late 1843. See *Knickerbocker*, 22 (Dec., 1843), 602.

[6]Mary O'Brien, whose name is variously spelled and who is often called "Molly," was the Hawthornes' maid from sometime in late August or early September, 1842, until late June, 1844. Mary was dismissed for undetermined reasons, although there are several vague allegations bruited about in Sophia's letters to and from Mrs. Peabody. She was replaced by Margaret Sullivan, who stayed a month or less, and the Hawthornes gained "the luxury of an *American* & a *Protestant* maid" only in early January, 1845 (SH to Mrs. Peabody, January 12, 1845—MS: Berg). This maid's name was Mary Pray.

[7]Horace Mann, "An Oration Delivered Before the Authorities of the City of Boston, July 4, 1842" (Boston: J. H. Eastburn, city printer, 1842). Horace Mann married Sophia's sister, Mary Peabody, on May 1, 1843.

[8]The incomplete, four-page MS of this letter is now in the Berg Collection. The letter was sent to Boston *via* Ralph Waldo Emerson (a usual way to save postage), so no doubt Hawthorne took it with him when he went to dinner at Emerson's on the evening of December 1.

[9]The valise was expected from Salem, specifically from Hawthorne's sister, Maria Louisa. It finally arrived on December 23, on which date Sophia writes a detailed description of its contents—see below.

[10]Almost certainly this is a mistake for Camilla. Most probable reference is, then, to Mme. Frances (Burney) d'Arblay, *Camilla: or, A Picture of Youth*, first published in London in 1796. First American edition is 1797.

[11]*The Letters of Horace Walpole, Earl of Orford*, 4 vols. (Philadelphia: Lea & Blanchard, 1842). According to the Library of Congress catalog, this American edition is a reprint of an English 1840 edition done by John Wright in 6 volumes. In his notebooks, Hawthorne recorded an extract from Walpole's

"Reminiscences," printed in the 1840 English edition, I, lxiv-lxv. Hence the date *a quo* for the passage in Hawthorne's notebooks is December 1, 1843. See Simpson, ed., *The American Notebooks*, pp. 241, 614.

[12]Caused by a sheet missing from the manuscript (see my introductory remarks). Since the date of the next entry in the journal is December 4, and since the December 4 entry also describes events of December 3, the missing sheet no doubt contains the date December 2, 1843—Saturday. It may also contain part of the January 5 entry, and/or a possible entry later than January 5, since the other leaf of this sheet would follow the point at which the journal now ends.

[13]The O.E.D. lists "india rubber" as a U.S. colloquialism for an overshoe made of india rubber. The first citation for this usage is dated 1840.

[14]The "Imp" is Ben Barrett (see SH to Maria Louisa Hawthorne, December 31, 1843), the son of a Mrs. Barrett who lived with her family about 600 yards south of the Old Manse, nearly into the center of Concord village. Sophia consistently called him "Imp" or "familiar spirit," probably because of his country manners and frequent visits (see below, entry for December 26). For locations of the Barrett and other homes in Concord, see the early 1850's map in Robert F. Stowell and William L. Howarth, *A Thoreau Gazetteer* (Princeton: Princeton Univ. Press, 1970), pp. 10-12.

[15]Brook Farm, at which George Bradford was a close friend and companion of Hawthorne's in 1841. Sophia's mention of Bradford's indecision about coming to Concord probably means that Hawthorne's invitation to Bradford (that he live with them at the Old Manse) was still open. See NH to Margaret Fuller, August 28, 1842 (MS: Huntington).

[16]Of these two letters and one note, only the letter to Thoreau is now extant. The manuscript is in the John Pierpont Morgan Library (M1918). In it, Sophia asks Thoreau to take a letter to O'Sullivan (see below, note 17) in New York and a letter to Mrs. Peabody—both dated December 3, no doubt.

[17]John Louis O'Sullivan, editor of *The United States Magazine and Democratic Review*. The MS of this letter is not extant.

[18]Mr. Rice was Reuben Nathaniel Rice (1814-1885), owner of the grocery store in Concord and the first Secretary-Treasurer of the Concord Athenaeum. Rice didn't prosper as owner of the "Green Store," so he became the railroad's first station agent in Concord (1844). Later he went to Michigan, where he helped build the Michigan Central Railroad. He finally retired to Concord as a most substantial citizen. For a biographical sketch and an engraved portrait, see D. Hamilton Hurd, *History of Middlesex County, Massachusetts* (Philadelphia: J. W. Lewis & Co., 1890), II, 610-12.

[19]Sent by Maria Louisa Hawthorne, according to her usual practice. Even when Louisa failed of writing letters (she was the nearly exclusive line of communication between the Salem Hawthornes and the Concord Hawthornes during these years), she seemed never to fail of the *Salem Gazette*. See SH to M. L. Hawthorne, November 26, 1843, for one of many references to Louisa's not writing but sending the neswpapers.

[20]Hosmer was the Concord farmer idealized as a kind of American yeoman by Emerson in "Agriculture in Massachusetts," *The Dial*, III (July, 1843), 123-26. Hawthorne had met him on August 14, 1842 (see Simpson, *The American Notebooks*, pp. 334-36).

[21]This letter is dated December 2, 1843. MS: Berg.

[22]Ruth Haskins Emerson, R. W. Emerson's mother, who lived with her son until her death in 1853.

[23]*Mary Shaw* (nee Mary L. Sturgis) is no doubt the wife of Robert G. Shaw and

sister to Ellen Hooper (see below, note 25). Robert G. Shaw was an older brother of *Anna Shaw* (mentioned later in this journal) and an uncle to Robert Gould Shaw, the Boston leader of black troops in the Civil War who is memorialized in a bronze relief by Saint-Gaudens that stands opposite the State House on Beacon Hill, Boston. *Ellen Channing* was Margaret Fuller's sister. She had married William Ellery Channing in 1841 or 1842.

[24]Samuel Gray Ward (b. 1817) was a Boston banker, friend to Emerson, Margaret Fuller, Elizabeth Peabody, and an occasional contributor to *The Dial*. See George Willis Cooke, *An Historical and Biographical Introduction to Accompany The Dial* (New York: Russell & Russell, 1961; first published in 1902 by the Rowfant Club), II, 36-39.

[25]*Mrs. Prescott* was the widow of Timothy Prescott and mother to George and Abba Prescott (the latter two are often mentioned in SH's letters and journals of the period). The Prescotts lived across the road from the Manse and about 150 yards towards Concord. *Rose Forbes* (nee Rose Green Smith) had married Robert Bennet Forbes in 1834. In 1843 "Ben" Forbes was well along the way towards making a fortune in the China trade. I have not been able to identify *Sally Gardner*. *Ellen Hooper* (nee Ellen Sturgis, daughter of William Sturgis of Boston) was a regular contributor to *The Dial*. She married Robert Hooper, a Boston physician. For a biographical sketch of her, see George Willis Cooke, *An Historical Introduction to The Dial*, II, 54-61.

[26]"E." is Elizabeth Palmer Peabody, the famous maiden sister of Sophia. The practice of circulating letters among the Peabody family (and among their friends as well) was of long standing. The most celebrated example is "The Cuba Journal," letters written by Sophia and Mary to Elizabeth and Mrs. Peabody while the two sisters were in Cuba in the early 1830's. Many years later these letters were still intact as a group, and were being circulated to new friends of the family. In this instance, Mrs. Peabody forwarded Mary Mann's letters on Sophia's request (see SH to Mary Mann, December 8, 1843—MS: Berg) because Mrs. Mann had not been able to write Sophia recently. Mary had returned from Europe with her husband in early November, and was busy settling a house and helping to organize her husband's report on European educational methods. The letter from Mrs. Peabody mentioned here does not seem extant in manuscript. The "Democratic Review" is the December issue of *The United States Magazine and Democratic Review*.

[27]Miss Prudence Ward, daughter of Mrs. Colonel Joseph Ward, came to Concord in the early 1830's with her widowed mother. According to F. B. Sanborn, she was "an inmate of the Thoreau household for years," probably after her mother died in 1844. Both Ward ladies were active in the Concord Women's Anti-Slavery Society, which is probably why Sophia was visiting her (The "Anti-Slavery Ladies" did sewing cheaply to raise money for their cause, and Sophia often patronized them—see below, p. [19]). See F. B. Sanborn, "A Concord Note-Book," *The Critic*, 48 (1906), 257, 350, 409. Concerning SH's intent to use the services of the Anti-Slavery Society, see her letter to her mother dated November 15, 1843 (MS: Berg).

[28]John Louis O'Sullivan, "Mr. Brownson's Recent Articles in The Democratic Review," *The United States Magazine and Democratic Review*, 13 (Dec., 1843), 653-60.

[29]The November 13, 1843 letter from Mary Mann is not extant in manuscript. "Jones Very's criticism upon Hamlet" is in his *Essays and Poems* (Boston: Charles C. Little and James Brown, 1839), pp. 83-104. His "Hamlet" is said to have been written or revised while he was an inmate of the McLean Asylum at Charlestown, Mass.

[30]The offending epithet occurs in *The Salem Gazette* for Friday, December 8, 1843 (volume 42, number 98), p. 2. *The Salem Gazette* reprints, on page 1 of this issue and under the prosaic title "The Parlor Stove," a section of "Fire Worship," which had appeared in the December number of *The Democratic Review*. The page 2 piece which mentions Hawthorne is an essay on winter which refers back to "The Parlor Stove:" "It is *possible* that one may enjoy one's self in a social domestic way before a close stove—but, with gentle Nat Hawthorne, we have our misgivings." It is difficult to understand Sophia's strenuous objection to the characterization unless she thought that Hawthorne deserved better at the hands of Caleb Foote, then editor of *The Salem Gazette*. Sophia was a long-time friend of Foote's wife, Mary Wilder Foote.

I am indebted to Mr. C. E. Frazer Clark, Jr., for generously responding to my request for aid in locating this *Salem Gazette* reference.

[31]None of the six notes and one letter here mentioned appears to survive in manuscript. All but the last letter to Mrs. Peabody and the note to O'Sullivan were no doubt thank-you notes for recently received baby presents. *Anna Blake Shaw* was Mary Shaw's sister-in-law. See above, note 23. She later married Colonel William Batchelder Greene. On this day (December 10), Sophia also finished a letter to Mary Mann which she had begun on December 8. MS: Berg.

[32]This wine was a gift from Hawthorne's old friend, Horatio Bridge, made in March, 1843, a month or so prior to Bridge's sailing for Africa on the trip that resulted in *The Journal of an African Cruiser*. See NH to Horatio Bridge, March 25, 1843 (MS: Bowdoin College Library), printed, although with several errors, under the date March 24 in Horatio Bridge, *Personal Recollections of Nathaniel Hawthorne* (New York: Harper & Brothers, 1893), pp. 88-91.

[33]Neither of these letters survives in manuscript.

[34]Dr. Josiah Bartlett, first president of the Concord Total Abstinence Society. See Townsend Scudder, *Concord: American Town* (Boston: Little, Brown, 1947), pp. 171-73.

[35]None of the letters mentioned on p. [19] survives in manuscript. *Sarah Clarke* (1808-1896) was the sister of James Freeman Clarke, the clergyman who officiated at Hawthorne's wedding to Sophia. For a brief biography of her, see George Willis Cooke, *An Historical Introduction to The Dial*, II, 67-8. Mrs. Sturgis is no doubt Mrs. William Sturgis, mother of Ellen Sturgis Hooper, Mary Sturgis Shaw, and Caroline Sturgis Tappan. Caroline Sturgis Tappan was the Hawthornes' "landlady" when they lived in Lenox during 1850-51.

[36]Miss Adams is Abby Larkin Adams, the adopted daughter of Abel Adams, a close friend of Emerson's. According to a letter written by Emerson on December 17, 1843, Abby Adams was "a guest for a few days" about this time. See *The Letters of Ralph Waldo Emerson*, ed. Ralph L. Rusk (New York: Scribner, 1939), III, 229. Miss Adams may also be the "Abby" mentioned on p. [9] of this journal. The words "& a letter from Sarah" are added in Sophia's hand above the normal line of the text, with a caret marking the point of proper insertion.

[37]This $100 was certainly in partial payment for articles which Hawthorne had contributed to O'Sullivan's *Democratic Review*. As of 18 December, he had given O'Sullivan seven pieces since January, 1843, and it is probable that he had been paid for only one of these. It further seems that O'Sullivan had to consider this $100 as payment in full for five articles. The Hawthornes had expected $5 per page (which would have amounted to somewhere between $130 and $155, depending on how the pages were counted). Instead, O'Sullivan could pay them only $20 per article—see SH to Mrs. Peabody, January 9, 1844 (MS: Berg). See also Rose Hawthorne Lathrop, *Memories of Hawthorne*, p. 70).

Mr. Shattuck is Daniel Shattuck, a banker and justice of the peace in Concord.

He was the brother of Lemuel Shattuck, an historian of Concord.

[38]John Hunter, transl., "The Venus of Ille. Rendered from the French of P. Merimee by the Translator of 'The Galley Slave'," *The Knickerbocker*, 22 (December, 1843), 537-58.

[39]The "1" of "21th" was originally written as a narrow "O" and then filled in (almost certainly by Sophia) to make the "1."

[40]Neither of these letters is now extant in manuscript. Michael O'Brien is Mary O'Brien's brother.

[41]*Elizabeth Hoar* was the woman who had been engaged to marry Emerson's brother Charles at the time of his death in 1836. She never married, living most of her life as a slightly mysterious but unfailingly benevolent citizen of Concord. It was Elizabeth who anonymously decked the Manse with flowers to greet the Hawthornes on their wedding day. *Mrs. Charles Brown* (nee Lucy Jackson) was Lydia Jackson's sister and, hence, Emerson's sister-in-law. She lived just across the road from the Emersons.

[42]"Loch Lomond" was a painting done by Sophia for her husband. It hung in Hawthorne's study at the Manse along with two pictures of Lake Como, also done by Sophia. (See SH to Mrs. Peabody, November 19, 1843—MS: Berg, printed in Rose Hawthorne Lathrop, *Memories of Hawthorne*, pp. 63-64.) The two pictures of Lake Como are still in the Hawthorne family, but "Loch Lomond" appears to be lost.

[43]MS not extant.

[44]The manuscript of Sophia's letter to Mrs. Eliza Follen is not now extant. Hawthorne's "paper" mentioned here is "A Good Man's Miracle," published in the February, 1844 issue of *The Child's Friend*.

[45]Neither MS is now extant.

[46]Almost certainly "Aunt Luly" is one of Hawthorne's sisters, Elizabeth Manning Hawthorne or Maria Louisa Hawthorne—probably the latter. It is most likely that Sophia had not yet seen either Elizabeth or Mrs. Hawthorne since her marriage to Nathaniel. The first meeting appears to have occurred on November 18-25, 1844, when Sophia went to Salem to introduce Una to her Hawthorne relatives. (There is a possible, although unlikely, meeting in Salem during the ten-day period October 21-31, 1842, but it seems that Sophia spent this time in Boston while Nathaniel was in Salem.) Sophia's relationship with her sister-in-law Elizabeth was at best too formal to square with her using a nickname such as "Aunt Luly" in late 1843. She did, however, have a much closer relationship with Maria Louisa Hawthorne, who had visited the Manse and with whom she carried on a regular and friendly correspondence.

[47]This letter is dated from Salem, December 21, 1843 (MS: Berg).

[48]"Turtle wing" is taken from line 50 of Milton's "On the Morning of Christ's Nativity." "Be still as we are" appears to be Sophia's phrasing of the theme with which Milton deals in lines 53-68.

[49]Edith Emerson, Ralph Waldo Emerson's child, had been born on November 22, 1841, just two months prior to the death of Emerson's son Waldo.

[50]Amos Bronson Alcott, together with his English friends Charles Lane and Henry Wright, had started their utopian community, Fruitlands, in June of 1843. Sophia's intelligence here is correct, as the community folded by mid-January, 1844. Alcott did not, however, return immediately to Concord, taking up, instead, a temporary residence in Still River, Massachusetts, near the site of Fruitlands. He returned to Concord in the Autumn of 1844.

[51]The words "some of" are added in SH's hand above the regular line of the text, with a caret to indicate point of interpolation.

[52]Mary Pickman was Sophia's first cousin. She was the daughter of Sophia

Palmer (Mrs. Thomas) Pickman, who was Sophia's mother's sister. The letter mentioned is not extant in manuscript.

[53]Neither of these letters survives in manuscript, nor are the verses inspired by "Fire Worship" now extant.

[54]The word "measure" is written in SH's hand between the regular text lines, above "versification," but neither word choice seems to have been preferred by SH.

[55]The "Ben" here mentioned is Ben Barrett. See above, note 14.

[56]The novels no doubt included *The Czarina* and *Nabob at Home*, both mentioned later in this journal. The "Reviews" were back issues of *The Foreign Quarterly Review*, also mentioned later in this journal. Queen Margaret is Margaret Fuller. Ellen is her sister, Ellen Fuller (Mrs. Ellery) Channing.

[57]The word "feel" is written, in Sophia's hand, above the normal text line, with a caret to indicate proper point of insertion.

[58]The word "aloud" is written, in Sophia's hand, above the normal text line, with a caret to indicate proper point of insertion. The comma before "aloud" is left standing despite its incorrect placement.

[59]*The Czarina: An Historical Romance of the Court of Russia* was written by Barbara (Wreaks) Hoole Hofland (1770-1844). It was published both in London and the United States in 1842. The London edition is a three-decker; the U.S. edition is a 152 page redaction (Harper & Brothers). Sophia could be "looking over" either edition.

[60]*The Nabob at Home; or, The Return to England* is an anonymous three-decker published in London, 1842. As with *The Czarina*, there is an American edition (Harper & Brothers) also in this year. See review in *The Ladies Companion*, 18 (January, 1843), 153.

[61]Neither the letter from Mrs. Sturgis nor the one to NH from John L. O'Sullivan is now extant in manuscript. *Mr. Flint* is probably "Gaffer" or "John" Flint, who is mentioned by Hawthorne in notebook entries for November 8, 1842 and April 8, 1843. In the latter entry, NH calls him "our next neighbor, in one direction" (see Simpson, *American Notebooks*, 363, 370, 644). The 1852 map in *A Thoreau Gazetter* (ed. William Howarth and Robert F. Stowell) shows a "J. Flint" residence north of the Manse, just across the Concord River. *Hastings'* is Jonas Hastings' shoe shop. Emerson said of him: "Let every one mind his own. Hastings makes a good shoe because he makes nothing else." See *The Journals and Miscellaneous Notebooks of Ralph Waldo Emerson*, IX, ed. Ralph H. Orth and Alfred R. Ferguson (Cambridge: Harvard U. P., 1971), 353.

[62]The word "light" in this sentence is added in Sophia's hand above the normal line of text. "Lamp" is partially crossed out.

[63]Neither the letter from George Hillard nor that from Maria Louisa Hawthorne now survives in manuscript. The letter from Louisa is also mentioned in Sophia's letter to her dated December 31, 1843.

[64]Only one of the letters noted on p. [37] survives in manuscript—the one to Maria Louisa Hawthorne. It is dated December 31, 1843, but has a postscript dated January 1, 1844 (MS: Berg). The letter to "Mary" is probably to Mary Mann, although it may be to Mary Caleb Foote. There *is* a letter to Mrs. Peabody printed under the date December 27, 1843, in Julian Hawthorne, *Nathaniel Hawthorne and His Wife*, I, 273-74. It is possible that Julian's date is in error, since Sophia mentions no such letter in her journal entry for December 27.

[65]"Art. II.—Piesni Ukrainski, wydam przez P. Maxymowicza, w Moskwie, 1834 [running title: "Songs of the Ukraine"], *The Foreign Quarterly Review*, 26 (January, 1841), 266-89.

[66]*Mrs. H.* is probably Mrs. Edmund Hosmer; *Mrs. E.* is certainly Mrs. Ralph Waldo Emerson. *The Antiquary* is no doubt Sir Walter Scott's novel of that title (the third Waverly Novel to be published [1816]). *Promessi Sposi* is Allessandro Manzoni, *I Promessi Sposi*. Walter Harding, *Emerson's Library* (Charlottesville: Univ. of Virginia U. P., 1967) shows that Emerson had copies of the Waverly Novels (an incomplete set as it now survives) and of the second Italian edition of *I Promessi Sposi*. English translations of Manzoni's popular (and lengthy) novel were available, however, since at least 1834. *Miss Frances Jane Prichard* was a daughter to Moses Prichard of Concord. The Prichards are mentioned often in Emerson's letters and occasionally in his journals.

[67]Mrs. Timothy Prescott's son (see above, note 25). For further identification, see Claude Simpson, *The American Notebooks*, pp. 636-37, note 316.6.

[68]At this point the word "after" is written and crossed out (by Sophia) with a single line.

[69]This passage, beginning with "I always go..." and ending with "...Endymion," is published in Louise Hall Tharp, *The Peabody Sisters of Salem* (Boston: Little, Brown, 1950), p. 181.

[70]This letter does not survive in manuscript.

New Light on Hawthorne and the *Southern Rose*

WAYNE ALLEN JONES

After comparing "The Lily's Quest" with the general fare of the *Southern Rose*, no one could be surprised that the editor of the *Rose* was pleased to print Hawthorne's short story. A puzzle about the first appearance of "The Lily's Quest" has, however, been presented to Hawthorne readers and bibliographers—why would Hawthorne give first refusal on any story to a small, bi-weekly magazine published in Charleston, South Carolina? By early 1839, when the story appeared in the *Rose*, Hawthorne had already published his work in the *New England Magazine*, the *American Monthly Magazine*, and the *Knickerbocker Magazine*, and in 1838, his pieces had appeared regularly in the *Democratic Review*.[1] Hawthorne could have found outlets for his work more prestigious than the *Southern Rose*—outlets that also promised, at least, to pay for published material. The *Southern Rose* had no money to offer.

The answer to this puzzle and to other questions about Hawthorne's response to his then new, public identity as "Author" have come to light as a result of the discovery at the Massachusetts Historical Society of a letter Hawthorne wrote to Mrs. Caroline Gilman, editor of the *Southern Rose*. The letter, dated 25 September 1837, has also led to the recovery of a previously unnoticed review of *Twice-Told Tales* and three reprintings of Hawthorne short stories.

Mrs. Gilman was born Caroline Howard in Boston, 8 October 1794.[2] When Caroline was three, her father died, and afterwards she moved often, always in New England, until her mother settled the family in Cambridge, Massachusetts. Throughout her childhood, poetry and religion developed complementary aspects of her personality. When she was sixteen, her first published poem appeared in a newspaper

31

Salem, September 25th. 1837.

Mr. N. Hawthorne has recently been favored with a number of the Southern Rose, containing a very favorable notice of his "Twice-told Tales." He feels far too much gratification in praise from such a source, not to maintain a sturdy faith in the correctness of the judgement there passed, although modesty might whisper him that the writer has been greatly more kind than critical. But the truth is, he has himself been so much delighted with certain productions from the pen, as he believes, of the Editor of the Rose, that he feels as if he might accept all the approbation that she can possibly bestow on him, and still leave her in his debt. He particularly remembers, in perusing the Recollections of a Housekeeper, a year or two since, how hopelessly he compared his own writings with the nature and

Nathaniel Hawthorne to the editor of The *Southern Rose* [Mrs. Caroline Gilman], 25 September 1837, reproduced by permission of the Massachusetts Historical Society.

without her knowledge. Seven years later, the *North American Review* published her poem, "Jairus's Daughter." Caroline moved to South Carolina following her December 1819 marriage to the Rev. Samuel Gilman, a minister appointed to the Second Independent Church of Charleston.

In the summer of 1832, Mrs. Gilman launched a four-page tabloid for young boys and girls. She titled her venture the *Rose Bud, or Youth's Gazette*. In the "Editor's Address" to the first issue (11 August 1832), she envisioned children opening the *Rose Bud* and exlaiming, "What . . . a real newspaper like father's!" According to the conventions of such addresses, she explained her motives, hopes, and limits:

> I have always loved to write for children, and hope I can do something, in· my present arrangement, for your pleasure and improvement.
>
> I propose to publish the Rose Bud every Saturday. It will contain original prose and poetry, notice of new books and toys, extracts from children's works that are not common, and many other interesting things which cannot be detailed here.
>
> . . . If any of you, my young readers, are disposed to write for me, you must not mention Political parties, or Religious controversy. Be patient, and wait until the Rose Bud is *fully blown*. I hope however that I shall always encourage your holy feelings, and assist you in being pious and humble.[3]

Besides the kinds of material mentioned in the address, Mrs. Gilman offered her readers long stories and travel narratives printed serially, humorous anecdotes, snippets of world history, special items for her "Younger Readers," bits of world news, conundrums, and even obituaries of children and infants.

In the prospectus for Vol. II, Mrs. Gilman announced a change of the paper's name to the *Southern Rose Bud*, and a change in the intended readership: "[the paper] will be adapted in many points to mature readers, though not relinquishing the juvenile department."[4] Further sophistication of content, including a change of format and of interval between appearances, was announced for the third volume:

> The Southern Rose Bud, Vol. III, will be issued on a *double sheet*, comprising more matter than has been formerly contained in two single ones. . . .
>
> It is proposed to adapt it to family reading, and though a department will still be left to Juvenile subscribers, the taste of young gentlemen and ladies of maturer years will be carefully studied.[5]

In the last several numbers of Vol. III, notice was given that the paper would again be "enlarged and improved," and that the title would also change to reflect the improvements. Though the format truth of that little work.

Mr. Hawthorne has delayed this acknowledgment, in the hope of being able to offer a tale or sketch for publication in the Rose; but anxieties of various kinds have kept his pen idle, and his fancy produces no flowers, nor hardly a weed that looks like one. In conclusion, he begs permission to express his high respect for the Editor, and for one* whom the inhabitants of Salem are proud to claim as a native townsman.

    Editor of the Southern Rose.

*Dr Gilman was born in Gloucester Cape Ann.

continued to evolve to a sixteen-page magazine bound in wrappers, the fourth through seventh volumes were titled the *Southern Rose.*

Mrs. Gilman's own work provided much of the paper's copy at all stages of its evolution. In addition to sundry poems, she printed several series of letters and essays that were later collected and published separately: *Recollections of a Housekeeper* (1834), *Recollections of a Southern Matron* (1836), *The Letters of Eliza Wilkinson during the Invasion of Charleston* (1839), and *Ruth Raymond* (1840). She also wrote most of the material for the incidental departments, particularly the "Literary Notices."

The bulk of her notices and reviews, over 200 in all, appear in volumes three through six, and they cover a wide spectrum of material for "family reading": from *Uncle Philip's Conversations with Young Persons on the Evidence of Christianity* (12 July 1834), and *A Compendious History of Italy* (15 Oct. 1836) to works by W. G. Simms, J. K. Paulding, and Mme. de Stahl and new editions of 18th century English novelists.

One further item will help define the environs in which Hawthorne's "The Lily's Quest" first appeared. The Rev. and Mrs. Gilman, transplanted in South Carolina, retained throughout their lives a strong devotion to New England. Tidbits of news about Harvard crop-up from time to time, and journals of travel through New England, or from Boston to Charleston appear with surprising frequency. The nature of their expatriot feelings, however, can be guessed while reading the poem written by the Rev. Gilman and printed in the 6 January 1838 issue of the *Rose.* The poem had been "sung at the nineteenth anniversary of the New-England Society of Charleston, Dec. 22d, 1837." It begins, "New England! receive the heart's tribute that comes/From thine own Pilgrim-sons far away...."[6] In their exile, the Gilman's had also kept in touch with people in Boston and Salem, as shown by the occasional Boston and Salem address on the lists of subscriptions received, e.g. the wrapper of Vol. 7, no. 6, lists a "Mrs. J. G. King, Salem, (Mass.)." The *Southern Rose* also had agents in Boston: Gilman Davis, 91 State St. (listed 3, 17 Sept. 1836), and William Crosby, 147 Washington St. (listed 17 Sept. 1836 and afterward passim).

Hawthorne's link with the *Southern Rose,* as C. E. Frazer Clark, Jr. has pointed out,[7] was first mentioned in print by Hawthorne's earliest bibliographer, John P. Anderson, who noted the appearance of "The Lily's Quest" in the *Southern Rose* for the bibliography in Moncure Conway's *Life of Nathaniel Hawthorne* (London: Walter Scott, 1890). Victor Hugo Paltsits, who helped organize the two 1904 Hawthorne exhibitions at the New York Public Library and the Grolier Club, was also fascinated by Hawthorne's tie with the Charleston publication. The manuscript of "The Lily's Quest," one of the few remaining of Hawthorne's short story manuscripts, was part of the Grolier exhibit,[8] and it must have sparked Paltsits' interest. He sought out and acquired a run of *Southern Rose* issues, hoping to find other Hawthorne work. Although he found nothing of Hawthorne's, he discovered an anonymous article titled, "A Day of Disappointment in Salem," which recounts the futile attempt by a Southern gentleman and admirer of Hawthorne to meet the elusive Salem author. In 1916, Paltsits reprinted the anonymous article as *A Pilgrimage to Salem in 1838*, with an introduction speculating about the identity of the author.[9] He argued that William Gilmore Simms was the most likely candidate, but he also included "Another View," an argument by John Robinson of the Peabody Museum of Salem that Hawthorne himself was the author of the anonymous sketch. Paltsits answered Robinson by concluding the pamphlet with a point-by-point rebuttal of the Hawthorne theory. Frazer Clark has finally resolved the debate by proving the author to be the Rev. Samuel Gilman, husband of the *Southern Rose* editor.

The identification, however, did not resolve the other mystery that Paltsits also was the first to articulate in print: "how did it come about that Hawthorne sent his manuscript of 'The Lily's Quest' to *The Southern Rose*, so far afield from his own stamping ground"?[10] Paltsits could only suggest that Hawthorne "had some source of southern admiration which elicited a contribution from him...."[11] Uncovering the Hawthorne-Gilman letter at the Massachusetts Historical Society and reviewing the contents of the *Southern Rose* have made possible the reconstruction of a sequence of events that explains the first appearance of "The Lily's Quest" in Charleston, South Carolina.

In late May or early June 1837, Mrs. Gilman obtained a copy of *Twice-Told Tales* (published in March of that year) from a Charleston bookseller.[12] Whether she found the book while browsing, or had it pointed out to her by one of the local booksellers, Burges or Babcock, Mrs. Gilman was so impressed by what she read that she reprinted two of Hawthorne's tales in successive issues: "The Minister's Black Veil" on 24 June 1837 and "David Swan" on 8 July 1837.[13] These reprintings have not been previously noted by Hawthorne bibliographers. The haste with which Mrs. Gilman rushed "The Minister's Black Veil" into print may be judged by the fact that Hawthorne's name appears misspelled in the by-line: "By NATHANIEL HAWTHORN."[14]

Another item appearing in the 8 July 1837 issue, immediately following "David Swan," has also escaped the notice of Hawthorne students. Mrs. Gilman followed up her reprinting of the two Hawthorne stories by publishing one of the earliest reviews of Hawthorne's *Twice-Told Tales*. Her review appeared in the department called, "The Turf-Seat Shade, or Notice of Books."

Twice Told Tales, by Nathaniel Hawthorne; published by the American

Stationers' Company, Boston, *and Samuel Colman,* New York.

There is a purity and freshness about this work perfectly fascinating. Most if not all the tales and sketches, have been previously published in Souvenirs or Journals, but the pearls are now strung together in an attractive looking volume. It may seem like heresy, but to us there is more animation in the style, with as much purity and good sense, as in the writings of Irving. No one can read it without a glow of youth stealing over his feelings. The Minister's Black Veil, selected for the last number of The Rose, is one of the most original, rather than the best story in the collection. Among the most exquisite are, *A Sunday at Home,* and *David Swan.* The edition has had a rapid sale in this city.[15]

Mrs. Gilman's notice was preceded by ones in the *Salem Gazette* (14 March 1837), the *Knickerbocker Magazine* (April 1837), and the *North American Review* (July 1837). Hawthorne learned of this last review before its July publication date, as shown in his 19 June 1837 letter to Longfellow, the author of the *North American* piece.[16]

Although Mrs. Gilman's short review offers little insight into Hawthorne's work, the comparison of Hawthorne and Irving recalls the earlier and more reserved remarks of Park Benjamin in the *New England Magazine* and the *American Monthly Magazine.*[17] Yet, regardless of how positive her review was, it could not have greatly influenced either Hawthorne's literary reputation or the national sales of the book. What seems striking about Hawthorne's response to the review is the absence of any substantive distinction between that response and the one to Longfellow's review. Hawthorne was greatly pleased by both, even though Longfellow's was immensely more important. Hawthorne's reaction to Mrs. Gilman had nothing blase or contemptuous about it. On the contrary, Hawthorne was extraordinarily grateful for her favorable notice.

During the years before the appearance of his first collection of tales, Hawthorne had enjoyed the safety of anonymous publication. As long as his work was printed with no by-line or with a number of limited ascriptions such as "By the Author of Sights from a Steeple," Hawthorne had no public literary reputation to risk, no large arena in which his work and his pride could be trampled. Samuel G. Goodrich, editor of the *Token* and the Peter Parley series, and Park Benjamin, editor of the *New England Magazine* and the *American Monthly,* had both disguised their dependence on Hawthorne as a source of good material; they omitted by-lines and manipulated anonymous credits so that no more than two pieces in the same monthly or annual issue were ascribed to the same "Author of. . . ."[18] Although Goodrich and Benjamin exploited Hawthorne's inclination toward anonymity and kept him unknown to the public longer than seems reasonable, Hawthorne himself must take some of the responsibility for the belated appearance of his work under his own name. Anonymity became a comfortable habit, and at times

Hawthorne actively sought to remain unknown. On 27 January 1832, Hawthorne wrote to the Philadelphia publishers Carey and Lea offering his authorial services to their annual, the *Atlantic Souvenir*, and after he mentioned four stories he had written for the 1832 *Token*, he enjoined them, "I should not wish to be known as the author of those, sketches."[19]

When Hawthorne decided, however, to abandon his safety and lay public claim to his work, he must have done so with some uneasiness attending his new visibility—he was allowing himself to become more vulnerable to attack by literary critics. Much to Hawthorne's relief, all the reviews spoke favorably of *Twice-Told Tales*. One measure of that relief can be inferred from the careful attention he paid to the review from so remote a place as Charleston, South Carolina, and so obscure a forum as the *Southern Rose*. Hawthorne responded to Mrs. Gilman's kind review with a letter dated 25 September 1837. The facsimile of his letter (which precedes this article) appears with the permission of the Massachusetts Historical Society; a transcription of the letter follows here:

Salem, September 25th, 1837.

Mr. N. Hawthorne has recently been favored with a number of the Southern Rose, containing a very favorable notice of his 'Twice-told Tales.' He feels far too much gratification in praise from such a source, not to maintain a sturdy faith in the correctness of the judgment there passed, although modesty might whisper him that the writer has been greatly more kind than critical. But the truth is, he has himself been so much delighted with certain productions from the pen, as he believes, of the Editor of the Rose, that he feels as if he might accept all the approbation that she can possibly bestow on him, and still leave her in his debt. He particularly remembers, in perusing the Recollections of a Housekeeper, a year or two since, how hopelessly he compared his own writings with the nature and [p. 2] truth of that little work.

Mr. Hawthorne has delayed this acknowledgement, in the hope of being able to offer a tale or sketch for publication in the Rose; but, anxieties of various kinds have kept his pen idle, and his fancy produces no flowers, nor hardly a weed that looks like one. In conclusion, he begs permission to express his high respect for the Editor, and for one whom the inhabitants of Salem are proud to claim as a native townsman.

Editor of the Southern Rose.

[Pencil note not in Hawthorne's hand] Dr. Gilman was born in Glouchester Cape Ann.

Hawthorne's diffidence here about his own work, and his flattery of Mrs. Gilman at his own expense are characteristic of the man and the masks he donned to protect himself from a public display of pride. The mock-despair called forth by comparing the fancifulness of his writing

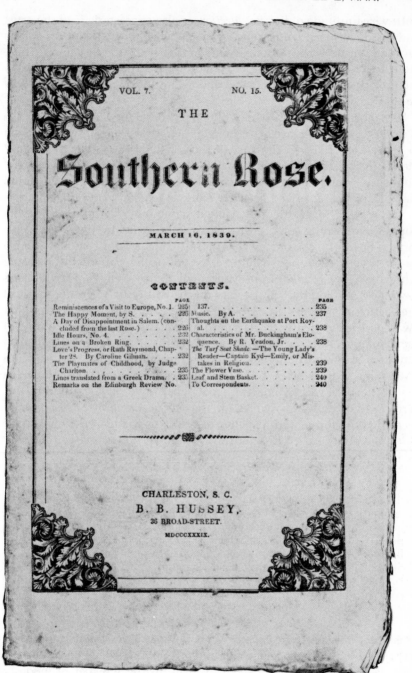

VOL. 7.   NO. 15.

THE

Southern Rose.

MARCH 16, 1839.

CONTENTS.

CHARLESTON, S. C.

B. B. HUSSEY,

36 BROAD-STREET.

MDCCCXXXIX.

Collection of C. E. Frazer Clark, Jr.

with verisimilitude of her *Recollections* is also characteristic of the artist and his doubts that truth could persuade as well when clothed by the imagination as when left naked in more "realistic" discourse. These same doubts recur frequently in Hawthorne's writings, most notably in the prefaces to the four romances and to the 1851 edition of *Twice-Told Tales*.

Hawthorne's letter to Mrs. Gilman echoes four statements in his previous correspondence with Longfellow about Longfellow's reaction to *Twice-Told Tales*. In the first of those letters, the one written on 7 March 1837, Hawthorne told Longfellow that the American Stationers' Company would be sending a complimentary copy of the *Tales*, and Hawthorne characterized his early work as "a good many idle attempts in the way of Magazine and Annual scribbling."[20] And touching the hopes for returning some of the pleasure provided by the work of his former Bowdoin classmate, Hawthorne concluded, "I should like to flatter myself that they would repay you some part of the pleasure which I have derived from your own Outre Mer."[21] Hawthorne's awareness of the effect praise had on his ability to judge the merit of the criticism appears in two later letters to Longfellow, and that awareness is coupled with Hawthorne's equally clear understanding of the demands of the situation felt by his critic. In the long letter dated 4 June 1837, Hawthorne wrote, "I am glad to find that you had read and liked some of the stories. To be sure, you could not well help flattering me a little; but I value your praise too highly not to have faith in its sincerity."[22] Longfellow's review for the *North American Review* greatly pleased Hawthorne, and his letter of response written on 19 June 1837 is infused at once with his gratification and an honest view of his own motives and reactions:

> I have to-day received, and read with huge delight, your review of 'Hawthorne's Twice-told Tales.' I frankly own that I was not without hopes that you would do this kind office for the book; though I could not have anticipated how very kindly it would be done. Whether or no the public will agree to the praise which you bestow on me, there are at least five persons who think you the most sagacious critic on earth—viz. my mother and two sisters, my old maiden aunt, and finally the sturdiest believer of the whole five, my own self. If I doubt the sincerity and correctness of any of my critics, it shall be those who censure me. Hard would be the lot of a poor scribbler, if he may not have this privilege.[23]

This letter reveals the ease and good humor with which Hawthorne responded to the early reviews of his first acknowledged book, and his relief is also reflected, in a subdued form, in the whisper of modesty mentioned in his letter to Mrs. Gilman.

Mrs. Gilman's response to Hawthorne's letter appears in the section, "To Correspondents," of the 14 October 1837 issue of the *Southern Rose*:

"The new Salem correspondent of The Rose, is earnestly requested to fulfill his generous intention. Will he accept of a series of the current numbers by mail?"[24] The earnestness of Mrs. Gilman's may have sprung from her seeing how desirable snaring Hawthorne as a regular contributor would be. But her adjective "generous" also bespeaks her knowledge that Hawthorne might be more interested in publishing his stories elsewhere for money, and that any story he sent to Charleston meant a loss of income for him.

Nevertheless, Hawthorne finally made good his promise of sending "a tale or sketch for publication in the Rose," but only after considerable delay. On 27 December 1838, Hawthorne wrote another letter to Mrs. Gilman, in which he enclosed the manuscript of "The Lily's Quest" and regretted the year long delay. The following text of that letter is transcribed from a facsimile in the Anderson Auction Company catalogue for 14-15 January 1926, item #367:

Salem Dec. 27th, 1838

Mr. Hawthorne regrets that he has not been able to send an earlier contribution to the Rose, and that at last, he can repay the editor's kind attention with nothing better than the above. If this little tale may claim the praise of some degree of fancy and prettiness, it is all he can expect for it. Such as it is, he commends it to Mrs Gilman's kind consideration, and will be proud to see it among her own beautiful productions, in the Southern Rose.

Some of the later numbers of the Rose have not reached him. He is grateful to the Editor for her long patience, and cannot wonder that it should have failed at last.[25]

The Anderson catalogue misidentified this letter, saying it referred to "The Wedding Knell," but Clark has convincingly demonstrated the catelogue's error.[26] "The Lily's Quest" appeared in the *Southern Rose* on 19 January 1839, and Mrs. Gilman placed the apologue on the first page, giving it prominence as the lead article.

In the 12 May 1838 issue of the *Rose*, Mrs. Gilman reprinted another of Hawthorne's *Twice-Told Tales*, "Foot-Prints on the Sea-Shore."[27] The last Hawthorne-related item to appear in the *Southern Rose* was the two part publication, on 2 and 16 March 1839, of "A Day of Disappointment in Salem." When the Rev. Gilman reprinted this piece in his collected works,[28] he referred to it as a *"jeu-d'esprit"* he wrote in 1838. Rev. Gilman's word *jeu-d'esprit* may suggest that the whole story could have been a fantasy given life by his intimate knowledge of Salem. Hawthorne's 25 September 1837 letter attests at least to Rev. Gilman's public reputation in Salem (whatever the mix-up about his true birthplace), but fixing the relationship between the sketch and any actually incident awaits the discovery of some record of the Reverend's travels through New England.

In 1839, "The Lily's Quest" was also reprinted in two places of interest. On 12 March 1839, the story appeared on page one of the *Salem Gazette* with the note, "[From the Southern Rose.]," and that same year Otis, Broaders of Boston printed the story in a book for the first time. The book was *The Picturesque Pocket Companion, and Visitor's Guide, through Mount Auburn.*[29] Both of these reprintings help make one final point about the spread of Hawthorne's literary reputation, his failure to make a living wage by writing for periodicals, and the nature of the literary industry in nineteenth century America. The editorial community in the U.S. was close-knit, and as a result of their common desire to survive, a high degree of cooperation prevailed among editors and publishers—more often, of course, among those not competing for the same readership. The *Salem Gazette* seems to have had a direct link with the *Southern Rose* (whether or not Hawthorne provided the link can only be guessed), and Otis, Broaders had a link with one or the other, probably the *Gazette*. Broaders had another indirect link with Hawthorne: they published *Youth's Keepsake*, an annual edited by Park Benjamin, which in 1835 contained Hawthorne's story "Little Annie's Ramble."[30]

The interlocking network of author-editor-publisher relationships can be further illustrated to show how people associated with Hawthorne's literary career worked together and provided each other with material. Benjamin had given special notice, in his several reviews of The *Token*, to Hawthorne's anonymous work. As editor of the *New England Magazine*, he printed fourteen Hawthorne pieces, and later, for the *American Monthly Magazine*, he selected five others.[31] Benjamin himself contributed frequently to The *Token* before he began attacking Goodrich as a poet and editor in 1835.[32] Benjamin also wrote for the *Boys' and Girls' Magazine*. Among the contributors to the June 1843 issue of the magazine, Benjamin appeared under his title, "Editor of Youth's Keepsake."[33] Hawthorne's story "Little Daffydowndilly" appeared that same year in the August issue of *Boys' and Girls'*.[34] This children's magazine was edited by Mrs. S. Colman, and her husband, Samuel, was a partner in the firm that published the magazine.[35] Samuel Colman's name also appears with that of J. Munro and Co. in a *Southern Rose* advertisement as a reference for Wm. W. Hooper, a New York wood engraver.[36] For some as yet unknown reason, Mrs. Gilman, in her review of Hawthorne's book, listed Samuel Colman as the publisher of an 1837, New York edition of *Twice-Told Tales.*[37] And J. Munro and Co. published the 1842 expanded edition of *Twice-Told Tales*, in which "The Lily's Quest" was collected for the first time.

Much bibliographic work remains to be done to trace the routes by which editors and publishers passed along Hawthorne's work, but it will show how Hawthorne's literary reputation grew while his pockets stayed empty, and editors and publishers filled their columns, pages, and purses.

University of Illinois at Chicago Circle

A Checklist of Hawthorne Items
in the Southern Rose

"The Minister's Black Veil"	24 June 1837	*SR*, 5, no. 22, 173-175.
'David Swan"	8 July 1837	*SR*, 5, no. 23, 181-183.
Notice of *Twice-Told Tales*	8 July 1837	*SR*, 5, no. 23, 183.
"To Correspondents"	14 October 1837	*SR*, 6, no. 4, 64.
"Foot-Prints on the Sea-Shore"	12 May 1838	*SR*, 6, no. 19, 298-302.
"Children's Books for the Season" [Notice of Parley's *Universal History*][38]	24 November 1838	*SR*, 7, no. 7, 106.
"The Lily's Quest"	19 January 1839	*SR*, 7, no. 11, [161]-164.
"A Day of Disappointment in Salem" Pt. I Pt. II	2 March 1839 16 March 1839	*SR*, 7, no. 14, [209]-211. *SR*, 7, no. 15, 226-232.

A Checklist of Other Items Linking Hawthorne
and the Southern Rose

NH to editor of the *Southern Rose* [Mrs. Caroline Gilman]	25 September 1837	Mass. Hist. Soc.
NH to [Mrs. Caroline] Gilman	27 December 1838	MS in NN-Berg; facsimile in *NH Journal-1971*, p. 208.

"The Lily's Quest," reprint[39]	16 February 1839	*New Yorker*, 6, 341-342.
"The Lily's Quest," reprint	12 March 1839	*Salem Gazette*, p. 1.
"The Lily's Quest," reprint	1839	*The Picturesque Pocket Companion, and Visitor's Guide, through Mount Auburn*, Boston: Otis, Broaders, pp. [230]-239.
"The Lily's Quest," collected	1842 edition, 2v.	*Twice-Told Tales*, Boston: Munro, 1842.
"A Day of Disappointment in Salem," reprint	1856	*Contributions to Literature Descriptive, Critical, Humurous, Biographical, Philosophical, and Poetical*, Boston: Crosby, Nichols, by Samuel Gilman, pp. 474ff.
"A Day of Disappointment in Salem," reprint	1916	*A Pilgrimage to Salem in 1838*, Salem: Newcomb & Gauss, 1916.

---

[1]*Checklist of Nathaniel Hawthorne*, C. E. Frazer Clark, Jr., compiler, (Columbus, Ohio: Merrill, 1970), pp. 3-14, passim.

[2]Information about Mrs. Gilman's life was obtained from the *Dictionary of American Biography*.

[3]*Rose Bud*, 1, no. 1 (11 Aug. 1832), 1.

[4]*Rose Bud*, 1, no. 51 (17 Aug. 1833), 204.

[5]*Southern Rose Bud*, 2, no. 48 (26 July 1834), 191.

[6]*Southern Rose* (hereafter *SR*), 6, no. 10 (6 Jan. 1838), 158.

[7]C. E. Frazer Clark, Jr., "In Quest of A Southern Admirer of Nathaniel Hawthorne," *Nathaniel Hawthorne Journal 1971*, (Washington, D.C.: NCR Microcard Editions, 1971), pp. 208-226.

[8]*First Editions of the Works of Nathaniel Hawthorne*, (New York: Grolier Club, 1904), p. 61.

[9]Victor Hugo Paltsits, ed., *A Pilgrimage to Salem in 1838, by a Southern Admirer of Nathaniel Hawthorne*, (Salem, Mass.: Newcomb & Gauss, 1916).

[10]Paltsits, p. 3.

[11]Paltsits, p. 5.

[12]Cf. the last sentence in Mrs. Gilman's review of the *Tales* [*SR*, 5, no. 23 (8 July 1837), 183]: "The edition has had a rapid sale in this city."

[13]MBV, *SR*, 5, no. 22 (24 June 1837), 173-175; and DS, *SR*, 5, no. 23 (8 July 1837), 181-183.

[14]*SR*, 5, no. 22 (24 June 1837), 173.

[15]*SR*, 5, no. 23 (8 July 1837), 183.

[16]NH to HWL, 19 June 1837, at Houghton Library, Harvard. See p. 000 for quotation. For Elizabeth Peabody's March 1838 review in the *New Yorker* see, in this volume Arlin Turner's article "Elizabeth Peabody Reviews *Twice-Told Tales*," p. 000-000.

[17]*NEM*, 9 (Oct. 1835), 294-298; *AMM*, 2 n.s., (Oct. 1836), 405-407.

[18]A more detailed discussion of this matter can be found in Chapter III of my unpublished dissertation. *The Divided Worlds: Studies of Hawthorne's Separation Between the Material and Spiritual Realms,* (Harvard), and in a forthcoming article on the Hawthorne-Goodrich relationship.

[19]Moncure D. Conway, *Life of Nathaniel Hawthorne,* (London: Walter Scott, 1890), p. 44.

[20]NH to HWL, 7 Mar 1837. This letter and those of 4 June 1837 and 19 June 1837 are quoted by permission of the trustees of the Longfellow Estate.

[21]NH to HWL, 7 Mar 1837.

[22]NH to HWL, 4 June 1837.

[23]NH to HWL, 19 June 1837.

[24]*SR*, 6, no. 4 (14 Oct. 1837), 64.

[25]Reproduced as part of Clark, "A Quest," *NHJ-1971*, p. 208.

[26]Clark, "A Quest," p. 208-226.

[27]*SR*, 6, no. 19 (12 May 1838), 298-302.

[28]Samuel Gilman, *Contributions to Literature, Descriptive, Critical, Humorous, Biographical, Philosophical, and Poetical,* (Boston: Crosby, Nichols, 1856), p. 474.

[29]Noted in Nina Browne, *A Bibliography of Nathaniel Hawthorne,* (Boston: Houghton, Mifflin, 1904), p. 88; and in Jacob Blanck, *BAL,* v. 5, 5. For pointing out the *Picturesque Pocket Companion,* and for his kindness and helpful suggestions, I would like to thank C. E. Frazer Clark, Jr.

[30]"Little Annie's Ramble," by the Author of "The Gentle Boy," *Youth's Keepsake,* (Boston: E. R. Broaders, 1835), pp. 147-159. The table of contents of the annual mistakenly lists p. 146 as the first page of the story.

[31]*Checklist of NH,* pp. 3-14, passim, for Hawthorne's work in *NEM* and *AmMM.* Benjamin's reviews appeared in *NEM*, 3(Nov. 1832), 425-426; 5(Oct. 1834), [331]-333; 9(Oct. 1935), [295]-298; and *AmMM*, n.s. 2 (Oct. 1836), 405-407.

[32]Benjamin even reviewed his own work that had appeared in *The Token.* In one review of the annual he wrote, "The little poems, by Park Benjamin, display a rich use of language, and are quite acceptable" (*NEM*, 5[Nov. 1833], 437). Benjamin began his attack on Goodrich in the review of *The Token* for 1836 (*NEM*, 9[Oct. 1835], 295-298).

[33]*Boys' and Girls' Magazine,* (Boston: T. Harrington Carter), 2, no. 2 (June, 1843).

[34]*Checklist of NH,* p. 8.

[35]*Boys' and Girls' Magazine,* 1, no, 1 (Jan. 1843), inside the front wrapper: "T. Harrington Carter & Co. 118 1/2 Washington Street, Boston Publishers and Booksellers T. Harrington. Samuel Colman."

[36]*SR*, 5, no. 26 (19 Aug. 1837), inside front wrapper.

[37]No such book is known to exist, and no reference, besides Mrs. Gilman's has ever been found to suggest that a New York edition existed. Colman may have been the New York distributor for the American Stationers and hence the

source from which the Charleston booksellers received their supply of Hawthorne's book, but this conjecture has as yet no biographical or bibliographical support.

[38]A note on this item will be forthcoming.

[39]See Arlin Turner, "Park Benjamin on the Author and the Illustrator of 'The Gentle Boy,' " in this volume p. 85.

Francis Bennoch. From *Hawthorne and His Circle* (NY. Harper's, 1903), p.154.

Bennoch and Hawthorne

RAYMONA E. HULL

As Henry Bright was the Englishman in Liverpool most closely associated with the Hawthorne family, so Francis Bennoch was the most intimate London friend. Like Bright, Bennoch was a commoner, not a member of the landed gentry, and he had no university education.

The two men were also strong contrasts in age and appearance: Bright, who was only twenty-two when he met Hawthorne in Concord, is described as a tall, thin young man with brown hair, light eyes, and a prominent nose; Bennoch, who was forty-one when he met Hawthorne in Liverpool, is pictured as short, fat, and jolly, with handsome features, black eyes, and black wavy hair. Part of this description may be slightly inaccurate in view of the fact that it comes from childhood impressions recalled long afterwards by Hawthorne's daughter Rose,[1] but early portraits attest to the dark eyes and hair and the handsome features.

In later years Sophia Hawthorne paid tribute to both of these men when she pointed out that though their relationships with her husband had been very different, they were the only two people in England that Nathaniel deeply regretted leaving behind when he returned to the States.[2] Because she felt that Bennoch had not received sufficient recognition, she dedicated *Passages from the English Notebooks* to him with this statement:

To Francis Bennoch, Esq.

The dear and valued friend who, by his generous and genial hospitality, and unfailing sympathy, contributed so much to

48

render Mr. Hawthorne's residence in England agreeable and homelike these English notes are dedicated with sincere respect and regard by

The Editor [no name given in
this edition by Strahan, 1870]

If, aside from parts of these *English Notebooks*, not much is known of Bennoch's life in London, even less material is available about his Scotch background. He was born in Drumcrool, in the parish of Durisdeer, county of Dumfries, on June 25, 1812, the son of Robert and Jean Kennedy Bennoch and the sixth one of nine children. Apparently at that time his father was a tenant farmer on the Drumlanrig estate of the Duke of Buccleuch and Queensberry. Nearly one hundred years earlier Daniel Defoe had written a most vivid description of this part of the Nith valley, praising the Duke's castle much more than its surroundings. He was, in fact, depressed by the barrenness of the valley:

> ...the Vale on either Side of the River [the Nith] is pleasant, and tolerably good: But when these rapid Rivers overflow their Banks, they do not, like *Nile*, or even like the *Thames*, and other Southern streams, fatten and enrich the Soil; on the contrary, they lodge so much Sand and Splinters of Stone upon the Surface of the Earth, and among the Roots of the Grass, that spoils and beggars the Soil; and the Water is hurried on with such Force, also, as that in a good light Soil it washes the best Part of the Earth away with it, leaving the Sand and Stones behind it.... But that which was more surprising than all the rest, was to see a Palace so glorious, Gardens so fine, and every Thing so truly magnificent, and all in a wild, mountainous Country, the like we had not seen before...[3]

After a description of the castle itself, Defoe observed finally that he had been sent there by the Duke to see what the opportunities might be for improvements, and that he had discovered evidence of lead-mines such as those in Derbyshire and Somersetshire, which "are said never to fail." The poetry that Bennoch wrote in his early days says nothing of such commercial matters as lead-mines. Poems like "The Storm" picture the rural scene and the life of a sheep-herder, which he had known during his boyhood on his father's farm.

Bennoch's mother's family had also been tenant farmers for the Duke, but we know little about them. *Bennoch*, however, is a well-known family name in Nithsdale, an area of S.W. Scotland not far from what was then one of the major ports of the Lowlands, the town of Dumfries. According to tradition, the Bennochs had been active Covenanters in Dumfriesshire, but long before that time the family gained fame through the romantic tale of William *Bunnoch* (as he spelled it), an ancestor who helped Robert Bruce in 1313 by a ruse to seize the castle at Linlithgow, one of the last two strongholds retained by the English army of Edward I.[5] Nathaniel Hawthorne mentions the fact that Bennoch had once spoken of such an ancestor's exploits.[6] Circumstantial evidence connects the ancestor with this legend.

No records have been discovered to explain why Bennoch at the age of sixteen left his home in Scotland for a business career in London. The poems alone reflect his background as a farm boy. In a memoir of Bennoch, William Jerdan, editor of the *Literary Gazette,* referred to the Scottish scenes in the poems as refreshing to one's "jaded senses." "Thus we find young Bennoch, amid the clatter of the great city, turning to the quiet of his native valley to sing the charms of the Nith."[7]

The reader of these now forgotten poems can easily understand why Bennoch looked back on his native land with fondness, and though for the rest of his life he worked in London and lived in its suburbs, he did return to Scotland for visits. In moving to London in 1828 Bennoch passed up the woolen mills of Dumfries for a job as a merchant's clerk in the City. After about nine years of such apprenticeship he became senior partner in his own company, Bennoch, Twentyman, and Rigg, wholesalers in silks and ribbons, 77 Wood Street, City. Thus Bennoch as a young man became a self-made business executive whose abilities quickly led him to prominence in business and civic affairs.

Here there exists a hiatus in the formal records. At this time he must have married Margaret Raine, also of Scotch background. They chose to live in the suburbs, first in Greenwich, then in Blackheath. By the time the company was fifteen years old, Bennoch had made a name for himself in London. In 1852 he was elected to membership in the Royal Society of Arts, an organization devoted to sponsoring both industry and the arts. Speeches that he subsequently delivered to the Society reveal his knowledge of technical processes: "Thread or Fibre Gilding" (1856); "Metropolitan Improvements and Thames Embankment" (1857); and "Silk and Velvet Manufactures," a report on the London International Exhibition of 1873.[8] The layman reading these addresses may be baffled by some of the technical details, but he realizes that Bennoch's information derived immediately from his personal experience.

Business activities evidently had not absorbed all of Bennoch's energies after his arrival in London. His first volume of poems, printed privately in 1837, had received favorable notice. As a result of this, Bennoch sent a copy to Wordsworth, who in his reply quoted Sir Walter Scott that "poetry as a staff was a pleasant companion to walk with, but perilous as a crutch to lean upon."[9] Bennoch took the advice and kept his writing of poetry as an avocation, but some poems continued to be published in anthologies of Scotch poetry. Among these poems we find such titles as "Auld Peter Macgowan," "The Flower of Keir," "My Bonnie Wee Wifie," "Hey My Bonnie Wee Lass," and "The Nith." They were chosen no doubt as representative of the Scotch background to which Bennoch belonged.[10]

When in 1877 he finally gathered together the verses from his early volume and those written afterwards, Bennoch commented to his readers:

> Their appearance now will, I dare say, surprise many of my associates, who have hitherto only looked upon me as a merchant, or as a hard-headed financier, to whom the beauties of nature or the grace of poetry could have little fascination....[11]

In this collected volume the poems range widely in subject and style—from love songs to "occasional verse" to Scotch ballads, from formal English to Scotch dialect. During the years of Hawthorne's stay in England, Bennoch was averaging about six poems a year. This total does not account, however, for many undated poems. One such poem, obviously written after Hawthorne's arrival in England, was entitled, "I Will Try." The footnote following the poem reads: " 'I will try' is one of the truest principles, and expresses all that one man has any right to expect from another. I think I shall adopt it as a motto. —Nathaniel Hawthorne."[12]

Of particular interest also to American readers are two poems composed on board the Cunarder *Niagara*, when Bennoch was en route to the States for the first time in 1848. One, entitled "Our Ship," was set to music by Mr. Hatton, a fellow passenger, and sung by him in his "professional tour in the U.S."[13] The other poem describes the westward movement of the ship. Curiously enough, this was the same vessel that five years later carried the Hawthorne family to Liverpool.

Meanwhile Bennoch had concerned himself also with civic affairs, proposing a plan for a bridge across the Thames;[14] trying unsuccessfully to persuade companies like the Goldsmiths to open their art collections to the public;[15] and eventually serving as common councilman for the city of London and as deputy of a ward.[16] Some of these activities appear to have taken place after the Hawthornes reached England in 1853, for at that time Bennoch was giving much of his effort to the success of his company, then a flourishing business. Suddenly on November 9, 1857, Bennoch, Twentyman, and Rigg declared bankruptcy. Bennoch blamed himself for not keeping track more carefully of his junior partners' desires for expansion, but newspaper accounts list other factors as causes: deterioration of large quantities of silk in stock, and suspension of two affiliated companies in other parts of the country.[17] Mrs. Bennoch helped to liquidate the debts by contributing sixty shares of her own stock in the Gas Consumers' Company. In spite of great difficulties the company was re-established, and it flourished once more with Bennoch as head man until his retirement in 1874.

By his own account Bennoch had, early in his life, through his poetry become friends with some of the leading writers of his day: Allan Cunningham, his countryman; Samuel Rogers, Miss Mitford, Southey, DeQuincey, and Walter Savage Landor.[18] He had also on his first visit to American met Bryant, Longfellow, Bayard Taylor, Grace Greenwood, and "that most genial of men, James T. Fields."[19] It was through Fields, junior partner of Ticknor and Fields publishers, that Bennoch became acquainted with Hawthorne. Years later Bennoch wrote of this friendship:

> During the whole period of his residence in England we were as brothers. My house was as his own home, and to me more than to any living man, was disclosed the inner workings of his marvellous genius. . . . Those who read his English Notes will discover how intimate we were, and will judge how sacred I have held the privilege of such a friendship.[20]

This passage, written nearly thirteen years after Hawthorne's death, reveals the hospitable nature of the man who first met Hawthorne in 1853, not long after the Consul arrived in Liverpool. Bennoch and William Jerdan traveled from London to Liverpool and crossed the Mersey by ferry to visit the Hawthorne family in their Rock Park home.[21] Hawthorne did not return the visit for a year and a half because he did not wish to take time out from his work at the Consulate. Then, for the sake of her health, Sophia, together with her daughters, Una and Rose, accepted an invitation to spend the winter of 1855-56 with Ambassador O'Sullivan's family in Lisbon. Nathaniel, depressed by a lonely Christmas and the gloom of a Liverpool winter, planned a vacation by himself in London. He decided to leave his son Julian behind in Liverpool in the care of the Brights and the family of W.H. Channing, Unitarian minister from Boston, then serving as pastor of the Renshaw Street Chapel.

It was late March before Hawthorne could get away from the work load at the Consulate. He had previously arranged by letter to stay at #32 St. James' Place with Mr. Bowman, "a very agreeable companion." (EN, 282) In London he called on Bennoch for the first time at the company office in Wood Street, and they planned an expedition to Greenwich Fair for Easter Monday. In the evening after the fair, Hawthorne and Bowman were entertained at dinner at Bennoch's house in Blackheath, not far from Greenwich. The house had already become the scene of numerous dinner parties and entertainments, for Bennoch gravitated to other literary people in his leisure hours. Descriptions of the Bennochs as charming host and hostess are to be found not only in the English Notebooks, but also in the memoirs of some of their guests.

Captain E. M. Shaw
from the Author —
March 8 — 1860 —

TRANSFORMATION:

OR, THE

ROMANCE OF MONTE BENI.

BY

NATHANIEL HAWTHORNE,

AUTHOR OF "THE SCARLET LETTER," ETC. ETC.

IN THREE VOLUMES.

VOL. I.

LONDON:
SMITH, ELDER AND CO., 65, CORNHILL.

M.DCCC.LX.

Collection of C. E. Frazer Clark, Jr.

Following this first informal dinner at the Blackheath house Hawthorne recorded his early impressions of Bennoch (EN, 391-2):

> Bennoch is an admirable host, and warms his guests like a household fire by the influence of his broad, ruddy, kindly face, and glowing eyes, and by such hospitable demeanor as best suits this aspect. After the cloth was removed came in Mr. Newton Crosland, a young man who once called on me in Liverpool; the husband of a literary lady, formerly Camilla Toulmin. The lady herself, it appeared, was coming to spend the evening. The husband (and, I presume, the wife) is a decided believer in spiritual manifestations, and spoke of the subject with a quiet, self-satisfied consequence that was amusing to see .... [22]

Another guest on that evening was Philip Bailey, author of the popular poem, "Festus."[23] On this particular occasion Hawthorne had little to say of him; his comments were limited to those concerning Bennoch and Mrs. Crosland, who was evidently an admirer of *The Scarlet Letter.*

After a few days of sightseeing in London and meeting Bowman for dinner at their lodgings, Hawthorne apparently decided to return to Liverpool. At this this point Bennoch said that he took Hawthorne in hand in an attempt to see to it that he really enjoyed himself. Accounts by the two writers show vast differences. Hawthorne in his guidebook fashion recorded a series of incidents (EN, 294-310): a visit at Aldershot Camp, where they were received by Lieutenant Shaw of the North Cork Rifles; a railroad trip to Albury, where they were greeted by Martin Tupper, the popular writer, taken to his home for dinner, and called upon later in the day by Mr. Evelyn, descendant of the famous diarist; a Sunday at Tunbridge Wells; a visit to Battle Abbey; and then a drive to Hastings, where they lunched with Theodore Martin, author of Bon Gaultier's ballads, and his actress wife, Helena Faucit.[24] The one exception to Hawthorne's rather factual reporting is an unflattering picture of Martin Tupper, a picture about which Tupper in his autobiography expressed reesentment for its "unkindly remarks."[25]

The reader familiar with Hawthorne's account in the *English Notebooks* may be astonished by Bennoch's version of the same trip, giving quite a different slant on the story. The time lapse, of course, makes it subject to probable inaccuracies, but it does raise a question in the reader's mind: how much romanticizing is present in these reminiscences? According to Bennoch, the entire trip after their visit to Aldershot was a surprise to Hawthorne. He accepted Bennoch's decisions on when to leave the train without knowing where he was going. Neither, according to Bennoch, did Hawthorne know until afterwards the name of his luncheon host at Hastings. Bennoch said that he had kept the identity of Martin and his wife a secret because Hawthorne, in a conversation earlier on that very day, had rather severely criticized Martin as a poet. Afterwards, Bennoch reported,

Hawthorne admitted to being much chagrined by his comments made before he had met the poet.[26]

Bennoch's great enthusiasms implied in his account of the trip were no doubt due to the mighty effort he had put forth to cheer up his lonesome friend, for as he said concerning their first meeting in London, "I never saw a man more miserable. London was detestable. It had only one merit; it was not so bad as Liverpool."[27] Some of his friend's effervescence seems to have begun to work on Hawthorne, since at the end of the account Bennoch's comment was: "I found Hawthorne utterly prostrated by depression. I hoped to lift him out of himself, and I think I succeeded."[28] The degree of his depression is something Hawthorne himself never directly admitted except in letters to his wife. Undoubtedly variation in accounts by the two men is due not only to differences in personality, but also to differences in the times of recording the events—almost thirty years.

From this point on Hawthorne seems to have settled down to the kind of busy social life that would have frightened him in earlier days. The notebook entries show that for two weeks after the first of April, 1856, his London social calendar was incredibly full. First, he dined with Bennoch at the Milton Club, where the other guests included mostly writers and editors (EN, 310-313): Martin Tupper; S.C. Hall, editor of the *Art Union Journal*;[29] Charles Mackay, editor of the *London Illustrated News*; Herbert Ingram, proprietor of the same paper and new member of Commons for Boston; and William Howitt, previously editor of *People's Journal* and then of *Howitt's Journal*. At the end of the dinner Bennoch made a speech introducing his "honored guest" and Hawthorne was pleased, though he could not recall afterwards what either of them had said. Later they went to supper at the home of Eneas Dallas, editorial writer for the *Times*, along with John C. MacDonald, another *Times* writer.

Two days later in the same week Hawthorne went to the Reform Club as a guest of Charles Mackay (EN, 314-16). Here he met Douglas Jerrold, whom he offended at first during their discussion of Thoreau. Again, accounts of the event differ. Hawthorne's was matter-of-fact; Mackay's was very critical of Hawthorne's clumsiness in the conversation.[30] After the misunderstanding with Jerrold was somewhat cleared, they all went together to the Haymarket Theater for a performance of a Spanish ballet.

The next affair was supper party, again at Dallas's house (EN, 136-7). Guests included Thomas Faed, a painter of Scotch ancestry; John Elliotson, former physician at London University, then practising mesmerism; and Charles Reade, popular novelist. Hawthorne said little about these men, though elsewhere he praised Reade's works.[31] Most of his remarks concerned his hostess, Dallas's wife, Isabella, a successful actress known professionally as Miss Glyn. She had just returned from the theater, and Hawthorne was astonished to discover "how exhausting stage exertions are." (EN, 317)

On Sunday, April 6, Bennoch, Mackay, and Hawthorne traveled by train to Woking, where they were met by S.C. Hall's carriage and driven to Addleston for dinner at Firfield, the Halls' home (EN, 317-9). Most of Hawthorne's comments on this occasion praised the merits of his hostess, whom he found to be "a genuine and good woman, unspoiled by a literary career." Later references to her reveal that Hawthorne continued to appreciate Mrs. Hall more than he did her husband. In view of Hawthorne's usual scorn for "scribbling females" this was real tribute.

Of all the events during this London vacation the most famous is the Lord Mayor's dinner on Monday, April 7 (EN, 319-323). Bennoch had of course managed to obtain this invitation and from his office in the City accompanied Hawthorne to the Mansion House, where David Salomons, Lord Mayor, was entertaining a great crowd of people.[32] At the dinner the guest of most interest to Hawthorne was the Lord Mayor's sister-in-law; in fact, Hawthorne was so fascinated by her appearance that he devoted two pages of his notes to a description. Readers have always assumed that she furnished the model for Miriam in *The Marble Faun*, and although Hawthorne never exactly admitted this, she probably did. The surprising part, which Hawthorne did not survive long enough to discover, is that the "miraculous Jewess," later married this same Lord Mayor after her first husband died.[33]

The following day included visits to Downing Street and the House of Commons. Together Bennoch and Hawthorne visited the speaker's gallery, saw Lord John Russell and Disraeli, and dined with Mr. Ingram, member for Boston (EN, 324-6). After dinner in "the refectory of the house," they went to Albert Smith's lecture on Mont Blanc. This writer for *Punch*, nicknamed "Albert the Great," had ascended the mountain in 1851, and thereafter until 1858 he presented a type of illustrated lecture each summer.[34] Smith then took Hawthorne and Bennoch to Evans's supper-rooms, where Hawthorne said he enjoyed watching the crowd until 1 or 2 a.m. (EN, 326). The supper-rooms were evidently favorites with others besides the *Punch* staff. Newton Crosland referred to the place as "one where women were excluded, capital suppers were to be had, and the assembled company were entertained with singing, which was really excellent, but the songs were most highly improper, and spiced with *double entendres* in every sense." Crosland also suggested that it could be compared with Judge and Jury and the Coal Hole.[35] Any one who has read about the performances of Judge and Jury may safely assume that Bennoch probably laughed hilariously, Hawthorne might have been mystified at the English jokes

4 Pond Road, Blackheath. The residence loaned to the Hawthornes by Francis Bennoch. *Photograph by Raymona E. Hull.*

but would have been amused in his usual quiet way, and Sophia—had she been allowed to attend—would have been genuinely shocked!

"Nothing of moment happened the next day," says Hawthorne (EN, 326), until evening, when J.B. Davies, former secretary of the American legation, took Hawthorne to dine at "Vermont House" in Camden, the home of Henry Stevens, antiquarian and hunter of rare books for libraries. Naturally Hawthorne was interested in Stevens' collection of books, but he was also attracted by the brilliant conversation of Tom Taylor, a witty writer for *Punch*.[36] The other guests, except for Mackay, Hall, and the Howitts, were less known figures in London society, and Hawthorne had little to say about any of them. Bennoch apparently was not there.

This was the last of the social events for a time, since late in the afternoon of the next day Hawthorne said goodbye to Bowman, having planned their trip to Scotland for the beginning of May, and departed for Liverpool. "And so ended my London Excursion, which has certainly been rich in incident and character, though my account of it be but meagre." (EN, 328) Other people's references to Hawthorne at these various social events are scattered among the memoirs of the literary people whom he met chiefly through Bennoch's efforts. Significantly, there is little mention by his British guests of the man who played host to his more famous American guest of honor. Praise of Bennoch was a matter left chiefly to his contemporaries among American writers.

The trip to Scotland with Bowman lasted for about one week. From that time in the middle of May until Sophia returned from Lisbon in mid-June Hawthorne was hard at work at the Consulate, except for an overnight stay with Bennoch in Manchester, where Bennoch seems to have had business connections (EN, 350-2). At the dinner party at the Albion Hotel given by him on May 22, the guests besides Hawthorne were Charles Swain, engraver and poet;[37] Alexander Ireland, editor of the Manchester *Examiner*, the man who had formerly entertained Emerson during his lecture tour of England;[38] and Mr. Watson, a merchant of Manchester. According to Hawthorne's account, all three men were pleasant company. Swain was a quiet man whose poetry Hawthorne could not seem to recall. Ireland he admired as a sensible man with unusual knowledge of American authors. Watson, Hawthorne said, was also a "sensible man" because he was frank enough to admit that the English *did* "cherish doubt, jealousy, suspicion, in short, an unfriendly feeling towards the Americans." (EN, 351)

After the other guests had retired, Bennoch and Hawthorne sat talking until late. It was at this time that Bennoch first proposed his invitation to the Hawthornes to occupy his Blackheath house during the coming summer months while he and his wife were to be in Germany.

Hawthorne said that the matter depended upon ratification by the two wives (EN, 352).

When Sophia arrived from Lisbon in June 1856, the Hawthornes did accept Bennoch's offer for July and August. Since the fogs of the Mersey River were so inimical to Sophia's bronchial condition, the family were delighted with the prospect of two months in a suburb easily accessible to London. After a short stay at Clifton Villa near Southampton and a trip to Stonehenge, they arrived in Blackheath early in July while the Bennochs were still there, and they stayed until early September when they moved to Southport. During the two months Nathaniel occasionally commuted to the Consulate in Liverpool. The rest of the time the whole family relaxed in the quiet atmosphere of Blackheath Park and made frequent excursions by train to London for sightseeing. Of their stay in Bennoch's house Hawthorne wrote, "I, for my part, have spent some of the happiest hours that I have known since we left our American home." (EN, 424)

When the Hawthornes arrived, however, they found that the Blackheath house, which Hawthorne described as "not so big as his [Bennoch's] heart," was too small for two families. In fact, it gives the impression today of being barely large enough for the Bennochs themselves and their two servants. Of course there has been extensive remodeling resulting in fewer and larger rooms, and the grounds have probably been reduced in size through sale of some of the property. A small garage has been added on the left side in front. The two-story stucco house standing on the corner lot at #4 Pond Road is now marked by a plaque, above the pillared entrance, that reads:

L.C.C.
[London County Council, but it was Kent then]
Nathaniel Hawthorne
1804-1864
Stayed here in 1856

In the rear a large garden is enclosed by a red brick wall that is not high enough to shut out the view of an apartment building on the lot behind #4.[39] In Bennoch's day that garden was the scene of numerous outdoor parties, one of which William Ticknor, Hawthorne's publisher and close American friend, described when he was there in 1853.[40]

To relieve the crowded condition of the house the Hawthornes arranged for Una, Rose, and the nurse to rent rooms and prepare their own meals in a house near enough so that they could visit the "old folks" daily (EN, 372).

Before the Bennochs departed for Germany, there was further social life, like the "conversazione" which took place at the home of the Croslands, also in Blackheath (EN, 373-5). Then there was an evening at the S.C. Halls' London house, where the guests were literary people such as Catherine Sinclair, the Scotch author;[41] Samuel Lover, the Irish song-writer;[42] and Geraldine Jewsbury, author of both fiction and children's books, who had moved from Manchester to London two years before this date.[43] The guest of honor was the famous singer, Jenny Lind, then known as Madam Goldschmidt, but Hawthorne was "not greatly interested in her" (EN, 376).

The next night, while Bennoch was dining again with the Lord Mayor, Hawthorne went to the London house of Mrs. Heywood, Henry Bright's aunt, whom he had known since his first days in Liverpool (EN, 376). Here, after dinner, he met a number of people including the sprightly Tom Taylor, who greeted him again cordially. Hawthorne was much impressed by Mrs. Monckton Milnes for her lack of snobbishness and her interesting comments on Tennyson.[44]

The result of their talk was an invitation to breakfast two days later at the Milnes' London home, where Hawthorne met Elizabeth Barrett Browning and the mother of Florence Nightingale, in addition to George Ticknor, the historian of Spanish literature, the Marquess of Lansdowne, Robert Browning, and several other guests (EN, 379-84).

Meanwhile the Bennochs left for Germany, and the Hawthornes continued their round of sightseeing in London and rambles in Greenwich Park. Nathaniel made a trip now and then to Liverpool, and in August one to Southport, a seaside resort north of Liverpool, to see whether it would be a suitable place for his family to live. Late in August Bennoch returned by himself, leaving his wife for a time to further improve her health on the Continent.

Two important events mark the early fall. One occurred when Nathaniel and Sophia, Bennoch, S.C. Hall, and Joseph Durham, a well-known sculptor, were all guests of Richard Spiers, an ex-mayor of Oxford, for about a week in Oxford (EN, 399-423). Hawthorne's account of this trip is chiefly one of sightseeing. Bennoch evidently left no comments.

The second occasion was a dinner arranged by Hawthorne, to be held at the Adelphi Hotel in Liverpool, in return for all the kindnesses he had received from Bennoch.[45] The correspondence reveals that Bennoch went to Southport for the entire week-end. To his American publisher and friend, William Ticknor, Hawthorne described the dinner party on Saturday, October 4. He included the menu, the cost, and the guest list. The only other literary guests present besides Bennoch were Henry Bright and Charles Swain. The majority were Liverpool business men with residences in the suburbs, all of whom Hawthorne

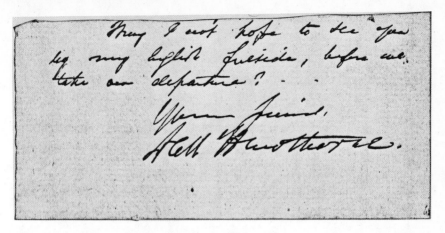

Collection of C. E. Frazer Clark, Jr.

had met in his position as consul, and most of whom had already entertained him in their homes. They included: Benjamin Franklin Babcock, merchant, of Hayman's Green, West Derby (the same town in which Bright lived); Richard Ely, merchant and agent to the New Orleans Canal and Banking Company, of 9 Bedford Street South; Charles Holland, merchant, who had entertained the Hawthornes at his home in Liscard Vale; George Melly, merchant, of 5 Bedford Place (later the brother-in-law of Henry Bright); Albert Mott, merchant, of Orchard Hey, Rice Lane, Walton; and Joseph Pollock, Judge of County Court, Wollasey Road, Poulton.[46] The dinner, as reported by Hawthorne, included turtle, "haunch of venison, etc.," ice creams and cakes, grapes, tea and coffee, all kinds of liquors from sherry to port and brandy, and cigars. All told the cost was over twenty-two pounds, or more than one hundred dollars. This was the only occasion on which Hawthorne entertained lavishly.

In only two ways were Bennoch and Hawthorne together directly involved with literary production. One was the famous Delia Bacon affair of 1856, when Bennoch took over the task of seeing that her book on Shakespeare was published. This action was at the request of Hawthorne, who so angered Miss Bacon by admitting her right to be heard, but by refusing to agree with her conclusions that she broke off relations with him after he had written the preface to her controversial book. She never knew that Hawthorne had financed the printing of the book, for the two men managed to keep from her all knowledge of the cost. Neither did she know that Bennoch contributed his work as literary agent without payment.[47]

philosophy, wherein they join close. namely, that same
"Primum quaeries". For divinity saith: "Seek first the
Kingdom of God, and all other things shall be added to
you; and Philosophy saith "Primum quaerite bona
animi caetera aut aderunt, aut non oberunt."

And who will now undertake to say, that it is
indeed written in the Book of God, in the Book of the
Providential design and creative Law, or that it is
writ in the Revelation of a divine good will to
men that those who cultivate and cure the soul,
who by a divine appointment to the office of its cure,
shall thereby be qualified to ignore its laws, or that
they shall find this in the scientific investigation of
its actual history, or in this new, so new, this so wonderful
and beautiful science, which is here laid out in all its
parts and points on the basis of a universal science of
practice, "no ministery and suppeditation" to new end.
Who shall say that the Regimen of the mind, that
that its Education and healthful Culture as well as its
Cure, shall be able to accept of no instrumentalities
from the advancement of learning? Who shall say,
that this department of the human life — this alone
is going to be held back to the past, with bonds and
cramps of iron while all else is advancing, that this
is going to be held forever as a place where the
the old Aristotelian logic, that we have driven out of every
field can keep its unchallenged state, as a place for
the metaphysics of the school-men

Manuscript page from Delia Bacon's The Philosophy of The
Plays of Shakespeare Unfolded. *Collection of C. E. Frazer
Clark, Jr.*

The other matter was a favor that Hawthorne did for Bennoch's friend, Miss Powers, who was then editing an annual, the equivalent of our coffee table books. Although while he was consul Hawthorne persisted in refusing all opportunities to write and publish—on the grounds that he could not spare the time and energy from his work—he did on this occasion take notes from his manuscript of what was later to become the *English Notebooks*. From these he worked out the sketch entitled, "Uttoxeter." Written just before Sophia's return from Lisbon in June 1856, it was not published until the end of that year in the 1857 issue of *The Keepsake*. Hawthorne would never have taken the time to produce an article if Bennoch had not asked it as a favor.[48]

Bennoch's action in helping Miss Powers was typical of his many endeavors to assist artists of all kinds.[49] Among those he helped was Mary Russell Mitford—first in getting her collected plays and also a volume of short stories published, and later in establishing a memorial to her.[50] Most notable, perhaps, was the case of the painter, Benjamin Haydon, to whom Bennoch's company is listed as having made generous contributions.[51]

The years of 1857 and 1858 were, as indicated by the bankruptcy previously described, rather unhappy ones for Bennoch and his wife. When Hawthorne resigned as U.S. Consul and with his family traveled around England while waiting for his records to be completed and his successor to arrive, Hawthorne and Bennoch saw little of each other. In fact, Hawthorne learned of the bankruptcy not from Bennoch, but from another friend who had read the announcement in the London *Gazette* (EN, 590-1). When Hawthorne called on Bennoch in London, he found the latter a saddened man, not yet certain what his future might be. Then the Hawthornes departed for eighteen months in Italy, the *English Notebooks* ceased, and our knowledge of the friendship thereafter depends chiefly upon a few letters, plus scattered entries in unpublished diaries of Nathaniel and Sophia.

By the time the Hawthornes returned to London in June 1859, Bennoch was once more his cheerful self. He found a boarding house for the Hawthornes in London and urged his friend to remain in England for another year. Nathaniel was persuaded to stay abroad in order to write the final draft of *The Marble Faun* and to obtain an English copyright before going home to Concord. Since London was not a congenial place for writing, the Hawthornes moved to Yorkshire, first for a week in the resort town of Whitby, where they could find no inexpensive housing, and then to Redcar, a quiet town also on the coast, farther north than Whitby.[52]

The Hawthornes had no visitors at the seaside house in Redcar while Nathaniel was busy writing, but after they moved to Leamington in

THE

KEEPSAKE

EDITED BY

MISS POWER

FOR 1857.

LONDON:
DAVID BOGUE, 86 FLEET STREET;
BANGS, BROTHER, AND CO., NEW YORK; H. MANDEVILLE, 15 RUE DAUPHINE, PARIS.

Hawthorne's sketch "Uttoxeter" first appears in *The Keepsake, 1857. Collection of C. E. Frazer Clark, Jr.*

October for the winter months, the book was completed except for the printing, and they saw more of Bennoch and other friends. Bennoch visited them in October, and since he could not go back there for Christmas, he sent the family a barrel of oysters. In February he invited Nathaniel, Sophia, and Una to meet him in Conventry for dinner with Mr. Bill, another ribbon manufacturer. Then in March of 1860 he produced, at Hawthorne's request, a birthday poem for Una. It was a six-stanza ode entitled, "To Nathaniel Hawthorne on the Anniversary of His Daughter Una's Birthday." The first part concerns the beauties of spring, particularly the month of March. The last stanza alone makes a personal reference:

> Oh! sacred season, ever blest,
> When saints their offerings bring,
> Thou to thy heart an offering prest
> More fair than flowers of Spring.
> A miracle!—long ere the yoke
> Of winter passed away,
> Thy Hawthorne into blossom broke,
> Anticipating May![53]

The footnote at the end of the poem when it was later published reads:

The foregoing verses were composed at the urgent request of the late Nathaniel Hawthorne, my intimate and very dear friend, on the anniversary of the birthday of his daughter Una. Hence the allusion in the last verse, which, without this explanation, would not be understood. The verses were written several years ago. Mr. Hawthorne was then staying at Leamington, in Warwickshire, busy with the last sheets of his Italian romance "Transformation." In the words of a relative, "The verses bring up many pleasant recollections, dimmed by the remembrance that he, who could rouse with a skill unequalled the tenderest emotions, and depict with infinite power the deepest passions of the human heart, is mouldering in the tomb. Those who knew Mr. Hawthorne best loved him most: and all who were acquainted with the plans he had hoped to carry out, regret that death should have stilled the heart and stayed the hand before his greatest work was accomplished."

The last two months of that spring of 1860 passed slowly for the Hawthornes. Though apprehensive about their return to the States, they were all beginning to be homesick, but transatlantic travel was not advisable for Sophia until the more pleasant weather of summer. The family left Leamington for a brief stay in Bath. Hawthorne went up to London to see his publisher about the copyright on *The Transformation*, as Smith and Elder insisted on calling the novel that became *The Marble Faun* in its American edition. Bennoch visited the family once in Bath.[54]

Footstone of grave of Sophia Hawthorne, Kensal Green
Cemetery, London. Wording is as described in Rose
Hawthorne Lathrop's *Memories of Hawthorne* (Boston and
New York: Houghton, Mifflin, 1897). *Photograph by
Raymona E. Hull, with David Young.*

Then at the end of May, Henry Bright invited Hawthorne to Cambridge for commencement week-end at Trinity College, where he was
receiving his M.A.[55] From there Hawthorne went to Canterbury with
Bennoch—their last excursion together—back to London, and on to his
family in Bath. This London stopover was the last that Hawthorne and
Bennoch saw of each other. When the Hawthornes sailed from Liverpool in mid-June, Bright probably saw them off, though there seems to
be no record of this. From that time until early in 1864, a few months
before his death, Hawthorne continued the correspondence with both
Bright and Bennoch, though the letters became fewer and fewer in
number. Neither man forgot his friendship with Hawthorne, for in
later years they made every effort to help the Hawthorne family.

Meanwhile, although Bennoch had moved from 4 Pond Road to The
Knoll, Eliot Hill, he was still a resident of Blackheath. He became a
prominent member of the Blackheath Golf Club, and in spite of win-

ning no medals, in 1860 he was made captain for the year. The portrait of him painted at that time shows the same handsome, sparkling personality seen in his earlier pictures.[56]

When, after her husband's death, Sophia sold The Wayside and took the rest of her family to Dresden, she continued her letters to both Bright and Bennoch. By this time she had quarreled with James Fields over the income from her husband's writing. Whether Bennoch was the one responsible for making arrangements for her with an English publisher is not certain. He did give her all kinds of advice, and when she returned to England for a visit from Dresden, she stayed at the Bennochs' home, The Knoll.[57] She also consulted with Bennoch about renting a house in Kensington in 1870. Julian had gone back to the States to work in New York, and Sophia and the two girls decided to settle in England, for war had driven them from the Continent, and they no longer felt at home in Concord.

Although she visited Fanny Wrigley, the former family nurse, Sophia had no desire to live in Liverpool. This factor probably accounts for her dependence upon Bennoch rather than on Bright, whose home was still in a Liverpool suburb. Furthermore, letters show that Bright had troubles of his own.[58] His father died, and he and his wife (whom he had married in 1861 and whom the Hawthornes never met) lost an infant daughter. Una Hawthorne evidently visited Bright's sister in Malvern, and Bright himself came to London once to see them all. But Sophia continued to depend upon Bennoch for advice to the end of her life.

During the last week of Sophia's final illness Mrs. Bennoch and her servant, Ellen Deacon, were the only persons in the Kensington house to help Una, Rose, and their servant.[59] On March 4, 1871, the day of the funeral, Francis Bennoch was one of the pall-bearers, along with Browning, Channing, and Russell Sturgis, all friends of the family from earlier days.[60]

At the time of his mother's death Julian, then married, was living in America, but when he and his family came to England several years later, Bennoch once more helped the Hawthornes. As a beginning novelist, Julian was not making enough to support his growing family. Bennoch gave both financial assistance and advice. His letters to Bright indicate that while Bennoch spent evenings advising Julian on ways out of his dilemma, Bright wrote to Lord Houghton and succeeded in persuading him to obtain one hundred pounds from the Literary Fund to save Julian from bankruptcy. This did not completely solve Julian's financial problems, but Bennoch continued to do all he could to help, and Julian never ceased to be grateful to his father's friend.[61]

In the late 1870's, probably after Bennoch had retired from the company in Wood Street, he moved his home from Blackheath to

Tavistock Square, London. This does not mean that he ceased to take an interest in business matters, for he was one of the most active members of the Council of Foreign Bondholders. In this capacity he paid another visit to the U.S. about 1880. Following his return, the London Councilhouse published *A Report by Mr. Francis Bennoch on Virginia*, in which the author analyzed, for the benefit of his fellow-bondholders, the post-war financial status of Virginia. In his years of retirement Bennoch also had some connections with a number of other commercial enterprises: the Debenture Guarantee and Investment Trust, the Federal Fire Insurance Company, the City of Potsdam Waterworks, the Stanley Fire-proof Lathing Company, and the Venezuela Telephone and Electric Appliances Company.[62] Exactly what these connections were is not explained. He may have served as director in one or more of the companies; that he held stocks is suggested by the fact that at his death he left a substantial sum of money to his wife, who, three years later, left an almost equal sum to numerous nieces and nephews.[63]

One of Bennoch's last acts in memory of Nathaniel Hawthorne concerned settling the question of the three photographs made of Hawthorne in London in May, 1860. Bennoch's extensive correspondence with George Holden, of Providence, reveals the story of how the photograph owned by Bennoch differed from the other two, all of which were made on the same day by photographer Mayall, and how from Bennoch's photograph Alexander Johnston painted a portrait in oils. Bennoch saw to it that this painting was shipped to Bowdoin College, Hawthorne's alma mater. It does not seem that Bennoch paid for the entire work; it is more likely that he headed a subscription list, but for his efforts he was made an honorary member of the Historical Society of Maine, which, he quipped, was an honor "seldom conferred."[64]

In the last few years of his life Bennoch continued his business trips, but he also made sojourns to various watering places, presumably for the health of both himself and his wife. The word *gout* is mentioned only once in his letters, but references to "attacks" seem to imply that this was his chief physical difficulty.

When Julian Hawthorne saw Bennoch for the last time in the summer of 1889, the latter was visiting in Paris. He invited Julian to dinner on a week-end, but warned that he might be called away on business at any time. Julian's description of Bennoch, taken together with the photograph made of him in late years, records the change from the black-haired young man to a white-bearded gentleman resembling one of our "household poets" of the nineteenth century.[65] Julian wrote of him on that occasion:

We dined together at one of the cafe's. [sic] His beard and hair were snow white; his ruddy, handsome, hearty face gave him the aspect of the ideal Santa Claus, beloved of chidren. He was over seventy-five years of age, but his voice was still full and vigorous, his sturdy figure unbent, his friendly eyes sparkled as of yore, and the grasp of his hand was firm and pithy. His wonderful vitality, and the well of human love in his heart, had kept him young. Nevertheless, when I bade him farewell, we both felt that it was for the last time. Neither spoke of it; but I saw tears in his eyes. Then came once more the genial smile, the hearty handshake, the cheery goodbye. . . .[66]

It was on another trip to the Continent, about one year later, that death came to Bennoch. He and his wife were traveling in Germany, en route from Kempen to Berlin, late in June. It was July before the news reached Julian. By this time all of Bennoch's oldest friends were gone—Bright had died in 1884—but Julian, now a middle-aged man living in Sag Harbor, Long Island, discussed for the public his 37-year friendship with Bennoch. Excerpts from his long letter to the editors of *The Critic* suggest how it happened that Nathaniel Hawthorne, the shy reserved writer, and Francis Bennoch, the cordial, effervescent poet-business man, developed a strong friendship:

His [Bennoch's] laugh was as rich and contagious a chuckle as ever issued from a man's lungs, and his whole genial visage, at such times, was the incarnation of jollity. He had an inexhaustible fund of story and anecdote, told with a spirit and energy, and a sense of humor, that were a delight apart from the stories themselves. To see and hear Francis Bennoch, at his generous table, was to experience the perfection of British hospitality. . . . His many-sided mind met and harmonized with men of the most diverse characters, drawing out the best in them and giving the best in return.[67]

Descriptions by James Fields and other American contemporaries express the same admiration for Bennoch as a person. The feeling for delicate poetry and the energetic spirit of a successful business man, plus a keen sense of humor, pervade all of Bennoch's unpublished letters. They reveal him as a man deserving more recognition than that of being Hawthorne's closest London friend. He was in his own rights a charming man—as the Scotch would say, "a darling of a man."[68]

Indiana University of Pennsylvania

---

[1]Rose Hawthorne Lathrop, *Memories of Hawthorne* (Boston: Houghton Mifflin, 1897), p. 224-5 on Bright; p. 308 on Bennoch.

[2]Sophia Hawthorne, Letter to Henry Bright, November 23, 1870. The original

is among the Bright papers now deposited in Trinity College Library, Cambridge.

[3]Daniel Defoe, *A Tour Thro' the Whole Island of Great Britain...*(Clifton, New Jersey, rpt. 1968), p. 726-7. I have translated the long *s*'s of this edition into modern type for easier reading.

[4]Ibid., p. 729.

[5]Moray McLaren, *If Freedom Fails: Bannockburn, Flodden, and the Union* (London: Secker and Warburg, 1964), p. 105.

[6]*English Notebooks*, edited by Randall Stewart, Entry for July 8, 1857 (New York: Modern Language Association, 1941; reissued, New York: Russell & Russell, 1962), p. 582. Hereafter references to this edition will be included within the text and labeled *EN*.

[7]William Jerdan, "Francis Bennoch," introductory section in *The Modern Scottish Minstrel* (Edinburgh: Adam and Charles Black, 1857), V, 2. Jerdan reported that Bennoch's poems were first published in the Dumfries *Courier;* so far I have been unable to verify this statement. However, the Dumfries County Council Library supplies the information that one poem, untitled, beginning " 'Tis Christmas morn—the merry bells..." appeared in the Dumfries *Courier* on January 11, 1837. The poem is dated London, December 26, 1836. No doubt a complete search of the newspaper files would prove Mr. Jerdan's assertion.

[8]*Journal for the Society of Arts*, I, 1; IV, 373, 424; V, 345, 387; and Obituary, XXXVIII, 786.

[9]Francis Bennoch, Preface to *Poems, Lyrics, Songs, and Sonnets* (London: Hardwicke and Bogue, 1877, p. vii.

[10]*The Scottish Minstrel: the Songs and Song Writers of Scotland Subsequent to Burns* (Edinburgh: William F. Nimmo, n.d.), second edition. Although no copyright date is included, prefatory remarks on Bennoch indicate that publication of this anthology preceded that of Bennoch's collected poems.

[11]Bennoch, *Poems...*,p. xiii-xiv.

[12]Ibid., p. 327n.

[13]Ibid., p. 87n.

[14]Francis Bennoch, *The Bridges of London: Are More Bridges Needed? Answered Affirmatively* (London: Effingham Wilson, 1853). See also *Journal for the Society of Arts*, IV, 373, 424.

[15]Francis Bennoch, Letters under the heading, "The Fine Arts," *Illustrated London News*, 21, August 21, 1852, p. 130, col. 2 and 3.

[16]Frederick Boase, ed. *Modern English Biography* (New York: Barnes and Noble, rpt. 1965), Supplement IV, 364-5.

[17]A description of all the action taken at the creditors' meeting is given in "Bennoch, Twentyman, and Rigg," London *Times*, November 28, 1857, p. 7, col. b.

[18]Bennoch, *Poems,...*,p. ix.

[19]Ibid., p. x.

[20]Ibid., p. x-xi.

[21]Rose Hawthorne Lathrop, *Memories of Hawthorne*, quoting part of Sophia Hawthorne's letter to her father. The original of this letter, dated December 6, 1853, is in the Berg Collection of the New York Public Library.

[22]Newton Crosland (1819-1899) was a wine merchant, born in Philadelphia of English parents. In 1848 he married Camilla Toulmin (1812-1895), who was already well-known as a writer. Her *Landmarks of a Literary Life* (New York: Scribner's, 1893) records her impressions of Hawthorne, especially upon this occasion, on p. 210-213.

[23]Philip James Bailey (1816-1902), though educated in the classics and later

admitted to the bar, achieved a temporary, but brilliant fame by the publication of "Festus." The poem went through eleven editions in England and thirty in the U.S. Though he wrote other poems, this is the one that maintained his lifetime reputation. See A. H. Miles, ed., *Poets and Poetry of the Century* (London: Trubner, 1859), IV, 467.

[24]Theodore Martin's popularity is indicated by the sixteenth edition of *The Book of Ballads*, ed. by Bon Gaultier (Edinburgh: Blackwood, 1903). In *A Biography of Helena Faucit (Lady Martin)* published by her husband (Edinburgh: Blackwood, 1900), Martin described their pleasure in meeting Hawthorne and their surprise in finding him cordial and frank, instead of "reserved and distant," as they had expected (p. 259).

[25]Martin Farquhar Tupper (1810-1889) was the author of *Proverbial Philosophy*, which sold 5,000 copies in England alone. None of his other works was as popular. *My Life as an Author* (London: Sampson, Low et al, 1886), which gives impressions of literary contemporaries, refers to Hawthorne's and Bennoch's visit on p. 246-7.

[26]A 25-page description of this trip, written to Sir Theodore Martin, was enclosed in a letter to George Holden, dated November 15, 1884. The originals of the Bennoch-Holden correspondence are in the Francis Bennoch Collection of the Clifton Waller Barrett Library, University of Virginia Library.

[27]Ibid., p. 2 of the manuscript letter.

[28]Ibid., p. 25.

[29]Samuel Carter Hall (1800-1889), editor of many periodicals and books, gave his impressions of Hawthorne in his *Book of Memories* (London: Virtue & Co., 1871), p. 184, where he described Hawthorne as "a handsome man of good 'presence,' reserved—nay, painfully 'shy,' and apparently unconscious of his status in society."

[30]Mackay's *Forty Years' Recollections of Life, Literature, and Public Affairs* (London: Chapman and Hall, 1877) contains an entire chapter on Jerrold and Hawthorne at the Reform Club (p. 271-293). However, Mackay did not remain angry at Hawthorne, for in September of the following year he wrote to Hawthorne asking for letters of introduction to take with him on his coming voyage to the U.S. The original of this letter is the University of London Library.

[31]Charles Reade (1814-1884), though a barrister, was better known for a long list of plays and novels. Hawthorne mentioned *Christie Johnstone*, a Scotch story which Bennoch may also have enjoyed. Hawthorne had read *It Is Never Too Late to Mend* shortly after its publication, and Sophia probably read *Love Me Little, Love Me Long* while she was in Redcar in 1859.

[32]It is worth noting that Sir David Salomons (1797-1873), a London banker and a county sheriff, became the first Jewish magistrate for Kent, Middlesex, and Sussex. By special act of Parliament he then became the first Jewish Lord Mayor. When he left office he received the "unique distinction of congratulations" from leading merchants and bankers. He was created a baronet in 1869. (DNB, XVII, 100)

[33]David Salomons was married twice: first to Jeannette, daughter of Solomon Cohen; then in 1872 to Cecilia, widow of P.J. Salomons. Undoubtedly this was "the miraculous Jewess," wife of Philip Salomons when Hawthorne saw her.

[34]As a staff member for *Punch*, Smith was reputed to be the butt of practical jokes, particularly by Douglas Jerrold, who once remarked that when he first saw Albert Smith's initials, he believed they were "only two-thirds of the truth..." M. H. Spielman, who recounts various incidents in his *History of*

Punch (London: Cassell, 1895), says that Smith remained to the end "the best abused humorist of his day." (p. 304)

[35]*Rambles Round My Life* (London: E. W. Allen, 1898), p. 201.

[36]Tom Taylor (1817-1880), newspaper man, professor of English Literature and Language at London University, and barrister, was also for many years an art critic for the *Times* and the *Graphic*. He wrote over 70 plays, including the famous *Our American Cousin*, produced in New York in 1858, edited the *Life of Benjamin Haydon*, and was best known at the end of his life as editor of *Punch* (1874-1880). See Boase, III, 902-3, and the above-mentioned *History of Punch* by Spielman.

[37]Charles Swain (1801-1874), a Manchester native, was a well-established poet by this time; he had acquired a wide reputation "as a graceful and elegant, though not a powerful writer." Some of his songs were set to music, and he became honorary professor of poetry at Manchester Royal Institution. His collected poems were published a year later in Boston. (DNB, XIX, 189-190)

[38]Alexander Ireland (1810-1894) is of interest to us for his account of Hawthorne's shyness and refusal to be introduced to Tennyson at the Art Exhibition in Manchester in 1857. Ireland had previously invited Hawthorne to meet Swain at a dinner honoring the poet. Hawthorne was unable to accept. His letter of November 28, 1853, copied in Ireland's handwriting, is included in a letter dated April 6, 1890. The originals are in the Nathaniel Hawthorne Collection of the Clifton Waller Barrett Library, University of Virginia Library.

[39]#4 Pond Road is privately occupied. The owner kindly received this writer, permitted photographs, and suggested sources of information about the house. An early history is contained in the unpublished notebooks of Leslie J. Baker and was obtained by courtesy of the London Borough of Lewisham Library Service.

[40]William D. Ticknor, of Ticknor and Fields, had been entertained at the Bennochs' home in 1853, when he accompanied the Hawthornes to Liverpool and then traveled in other parts of England. His impressions are recorded by his daughter Carolyn in *Hawthorne and His Publisher* (Boston: Houghton Mifflin, 1913), p. 54 and 62-3.

[41]Catherine Sinclair (1800-1864), daughter of a Scotch baronet, first introduced "cooking depots" and drinking fountains for the lower classes in Edinburgh. Besides her charity work she was a popular author of both fiction and non-fiction. It is said that *Beatrice* sold over 100,000 copies in a few weeks. Her obituary in *Gentleman's Magazine*, November 1864, p. 659-60, contains an excellent account of her work.

[42]Samuel Lover (1797-1868) was first a portrait painter, especially of miniatures, in Dublin. Later he became popular for Irish songs and entertainments in London.

[43]Geraldine Endsor Jewsbury (1812-1880) is known also for the extensive correspondence which she carried on with Jane Carlyle before she moved from Manchester to Chelsea in 1854. She was admired by some and satirized by others, including her friend Jane Carlyle, who called her "Miss Gooseberry of Manchester."

[44]R. M. Milnes had not yet been created a baronet, but with his wealth and social position he was already famous in Parliament and as host to leading literary figures.

[45]Nathaniel Hawthorne, Letter to Ticknor, Southport, October 10, 1856. The original of this letter is in the Berg Collection of the New York Public Library.

[46]Hawthorne gave only the last names. Additional information comes chiefly from *Gore's Liverpool Directory for 1857*.

[47]The story is revealed in a long series of letters, some of which are the property of the Bacon family. Others are in the Francis Bennoch Collection in the Clifton Waller Barrett Library, University of Virginia Library. I am indebted to Norman Holmes Pearson, of Yale University, for the opportunity of a first reading of all such letters from his forthcoming edition of the letters of Nathaniel Hawthorne.

[48]Nathaniel Hawthorne, Letter to Francis Bennoch, June 9, 1856. See note #47.

[49]Bennoch had already contributed a poem to the 1856 issue of *The Keepsake.*

[50]See Jerdan's memoir of Bennoch in *The Modern Scottish Minstrel,* p. 6.

[51]Benjamin Haydon, *Autobiography and Memoirs* ((London: Peter Davies, 1929), II, 820.

[52]Life at Redcar is covered in the unpublished diaries of both Nathaniel and Sophia Hawthorne; the originals for the year 1859 are in the Berg Collection of New York Public Library.

[53]Published in Bennoch's collected *Poems, Lyrics, Songs, and Sonnets,* p. 265-7.

[54]Information on the Leamington and Bath periods of 1859-1860 comes from unpublished letters of Hawthorne in several different libraries. Copies of all of these are in the collection of Hawthorne's letters in the possession of Norman Holmes Pearson.

[55]Hawthorne never recorded the story of his visit to Cambridge. Letters in the Bright papers at Trinity College Library, Cambridge, give some details. Other information comes from the records of Cambridge University and from the local town newspapers of that week. Bright's M. A., like his B.A. of 1857, was delayed because as a Non-conformist he was not eligible for a university degree until rulings were changed in 1856. He and his cousin, James Heywood, were the first Non-conformists to receive B.A. degrees at Trinity after the new rule went into effect.

[56]W. E. Hughes, ed. *Chronicle of Blackheath Golfers* (London: Chapman and Hall, 1897) has a print, opposite p. 173, of Bennoch playing golf, with a Greenwich pensioner as caddy in the background. This print was made from an oil painting. A water color copy hangs on the wall of Lewisham Public Library.

[57]Various letters from Sophia Hawthorne to Henry Bright in the years from 1868 to 1870 give us this information and other details. The originals are among the Bright papers in Trinity College Library, Cambridge.

[58]Sophia Hawthorne, Letters to Henry Bright, dated February 13, 1870 and July 3, 1870; the originals are in Trinity College Library, Cambridge.

[59]Julian Hawthorne, *Hawthorne and His Wife* (Boston: James R. Osgood, 1885; rpt. Scholarly Press, 1968), quoting Una's account of her mother's illness and death, II, 353-371.

[60]Recorded by Moncure Conway, who described his attendance at the funeral at the end of the chapter on the Hawthornes in *Emerson at Home and Abroad* (London: Trubner, 1883), p. 225.

[61]The Bright correspondence at Trinity College Library, Cambridge, contains letters from Bennoch and Julian Hawthorne.

[62]Obituary, *Athenaeum,* #3271, July 5, 1890, p. 37; also London *Times,* July 2, 1890, p. 5, col. f.

[63]The Bennoch wills are recorded in the Probate Court of London, 1890 and 1893. They had no children.

[64]Bennoch correspondence with George Holden from 1884 to 1888 is in the Francis Bennoch Collection in the Clifton Waller Barrett Library, University of Virginia Library.

[65]The portrait of Bennoch in Julian Hawthorne's *Hawthorne and His Circle* (New York: Harper's, 1903), opposite p. 154, is labeled "Francis Bannoch," which may have been either the original spelling of the name or an error in printing. Since no information is given on the artist, it is impossible to tell.

[66]Julian Hawthorne, "The Late Francis Bennoch of London," Letter to *The Critic*, July 19, 1890, p. 36, col. 1.

[67]Ibid.

[68]Ibid.

[Permission from the various libraries has been given for references to and quotations from the unpublished materials included in this article.]

Elizabeth Peabody
Reviews *Twice-Told Tales*

ARLIN TURNER

In April, 1838, Sophia Peabody received at Salem a parcel of New York magazines from her cousin George Palmer Putnam. In one of them, she wrote her sister Elizabeth on April 17, "is your review of Mr. Hawthorne."[1] Her reference was to an unsigned review of *Twice-Told Tales*, some 3,500 words in length, published in the *New-Yorker* for March 24 (V, 1-2). This review, which seems to have escaped notice, is printed below.

Elizabeth Peabody was spending the spring and summer with her brother Nathaniel and his family at West Newton. During her absence, packets of letters were exchanged between her and the Peabody household, with letters between her and Hawthorne sometimes included. Sophia commented further on Elizabeth's review: "It is beautiful. I like it all but the expression, 'sweet story-teller, with the flowery name, whose caged melodies' &c. It sounds too much like 'the rose baptized in dew.'" Elizabeth would recognize, she assumed, the phrase quoted from the beginning of a review of *Twice-Told Tales* in the *American Monthly Magazine* for March (n.s. V, 281-283), presumably by Charles Fenno Hoffman: "A rose bathed and baptized in dew—a star in its first gentle emergence above the horizon—all types of the soul of Nathaniel Hawthorne; every vein of which (if we may so speak) is filled and instinct with beauty."

In the year between the publication of *Twice-Told Tales*, March 6, 1837, and the appearance of Hoffman's review, no review of consequence had been published except that by Henry Wadsworth Longfellow in the *North American Review* for July (XLV, 59-73). The *Salem Gazette* of March 14 had published a note to introduce a reprinting of one of the tales, "Fancy's Show Box," and the *Knickerbocker Magazine* for April (IX, 422-425) had included slight comment, along with several quotations. The reviews by Hoffman and Elizabeth Peabody were both published in the same month, March, 1838, and both in magazines edited by Park Benjamin, who thus continued the effort he had exerted over several years to win recognition for Hawthorne's work.[2]

Elizabeth Peabody's review, published a year later than the book and in its length and its nature suggesting less a review than an evaluative essay, testifies that both the reviewer and the editor valued the work highly and wanted to give it greater acclaim than it had received. The review was but one of many efforts Miss Peabody made to encourage and assist Hawthorne to the high literary achievement she had become certain was possible for him. Before *Twice-Told Tales* was published, she had learned that he was the author of stories she admired in magazines and annuals, but only in November, 1837, did she meet him. By early 1838 she and her sisters Mary and Sophia were unabashedly devoted to the handsome, retiring young author. Within a few months Elizabeth Peabody was busy tring to secure for Hawthorne employment that would support him and leave time for his writing, and to find publishers for what he would write. His appointment as inspector in the Boston custom house in January, 1839, was in part in response to her efforts, and she herself published in 1841 three children's books from his pen.[3]

This review of *Twice-Told Tales* reveals Miss Peabody's judgment of Hawthorne's writings at the beginning of their acquaintance. (It is in fact the only criticism of his works she published until after his death.) She obviously had the contents of the volume well in mind. Inaccuracies in some of the short quotations from the tales suggest that she knew them so well as to risk quoting from memory.All of the contents but three receive comment, and all are praised, though not equally. She demands work of the highest order. "The Gray Champion" and other stories of American history please her greatly, but on second thought, "we cannot spare him from the higher paths, to confine him to this patriotic one." "The Prophetic Pictures" is "a masterpiece in its way," but "First-rate genius should leave the odd and peculiar, and especially the fantastic and horrible, to the inferior talent." Such tales would be to "Sunday at Home," "Sights from a Steeple," and "Little Annie's Ramble" as the effects of Byron are to Wordsworth's poetry.

In stating that to her mind "Sunday at Home" is worth a thousand sermons and that "The Gentle Boy" is "worth a thousand homilies on fanaticism in all its forms, contrasted with the divinity of the natural sentiments, and the institutions growing therefrom," Elizabeth Peabody might have been thinking of Emerson as a reader of Hawthorne's tales. Less than three months after her review appeared, she took Emerson the sketch "Footprints on the Sea-Shore" to read and had him reply "that there was no inside to it. Alcott and he together would make a man."[4] When she visited Emerson at Concord a year later, she brought him a volume of *Twice-Told Tales* to replace her own copy, which she had left with him earlier and now found he had not read. "He is in a good mood to do so," she wrote on June 23, 1839, "and I intend to bring him to his knees in a day or two, so that he will read the book, and all that Hawthorne has written."[5] Her review may be read as a Transcendentalist evaluation of this book and Transcendentalist guidance for works to be written. She quotes from Emerson's poem "The Rhodora." Emersonian phrases and turns of thought abound: "know thyself"; "the eye of Reason"; "the faculty of fancy is below the imagination"; "every man's mind is the centre of the whole universe—the *primum mobile*—itself at rest, which wheels all phenomena, in lesser or greater circles, around it"; "the poetic story-teller...will draw his materials from the wells of nature and involve the sanctities of religion in all his works"; "the ideal beauty may be seen clearest and felt most profoundly in the common incidents of actual life"; "the true story-teller...sits at the fountain-head of national character, and he must never stoop below the highest aim, but for ever seek the primal secret—for ever strive to speak the word which is answered by nothing less than a creation"; "the track of his footsteps will be hallowed, and every thing become sacred which he has touched.—Then, and not till then, we shall have a country; for then, and not till then, there will be a national character."

A long letter Elizabeth Peabody wrote Hawthorne's sister Elizabeth at about the time she was writing her review for the *New-Yorker* reflects no less certainty as to Hawthorne's genius and no less firmness in outlining the course he must follow: "...there is good reason for believing that he is one of Nature's ordained priests, who is consecrated to her higher biddings....I feel sure that this brother of yours has been gifted and kept so choice in her secret places by Nature thus far, that he may do a great thing for his country." The men of affairs to whom Hawthorne may turn for patronage "live in too gross a region of selfishness to appreciate the ambrosial moral *aura* which floats around our ARIEL,—the breath that he *respires*. I, too, would have him help govern this great people; but I would have him go to the *fountains* of greatness and power,—the unsoiled souls,—and weave for them his 'golden web,'...—it may be the *web of destiny* for this country. In every country *some one man* has done what has saved it. It was one Homer that made Greece, one Numa that made Rome, and one Wordsworth that has created the Poetry of Reflection."[6]

In her review in the *New-Yorker* Elizabeth Peabody found Hawthorne to be Wordsworthian, and said so with emphasis; without naming Emerson, she proved him Emersonian, as if she were demon-

strating that he measured up to the criteria of the essays "Nature" and
"The American Scholar"; she had published a review of these two
works a month earlier.[7] With the *Twice-Told Tales* as evidence, she had
a prediction to make of its author: Genius "wells up at the top of the
hill; and in this instance descends in many streams—...may it
preserve the sweetness and purity of its fountains, far up in the
solitudes of nature! We can wish nothing better for Mr. Hawthorne or
for ourselves. He will then take his place amongst his contemporaries,
as the greatest artist of his line; for not one of our writers indicates so
great a variety of the elements of genius."

REVIEW

TWICE-TOLD TALES; By Nathaniel Hawthorne. Boston; American
Stationers' Co.—John B. Russell. 1837.[8]

The Story without an End, of which all true stories are but episodes, is
told by Nature herself. She speaks now from the depths of the un-
measured heavens, by stars of light, who sing in a distance that the understanding cannot measure, but which the spirit realises; now from
clouds, that, dropping sweetness, or catching light—to soften it to weak
eyes—bend with revelations of less general truth over particular regions
of earth's surface; and now from the infinitely varied forms, and hues,
with which vegetable life has clothed the nakedness of the dark
unknown of this rock-ribbed earth, (whose secrets who may tell?) And
not only does she speak to the eye and ear, but to the heart of man; for
taking human voice and form, she tells of love, and desire, and hate; of
grief, and joy, and remorse; and even of human wilfulness and human
caprice, when, as sometimes, these break the iron chains of custom, and
scatter, with the breath of their mouths, the cobwebs of conventionalism.
  Therefore must every true story-teller, like the child of the German
tale, go out of his narrow hut into Nature's universal air, and follow
whatsoever guides may woo him: her humble-bee, her butterfly, her
dragon-fly, each in their turn; lying down in her caverns, and with heart
couchant on her verdant breast, ever listening for her mighty voice. If,
like one class of modern novelists, he prefers to listen to his own narrow
individuality, to generalise his own petty experience, to show us the
universe through the smoky panes of a Cockney window, he shall not
give us any of that immortal story; its sphere-music will be drowned in
that discord. Or if, like another class, he is mainly intent on some theory
of political economy—some new experiment in social science—the
dogmas of some philosophical or theological sect, he shall not make a
work of art—he shall not open or clear up the eye of Reason, but rather
thicken that crowd of phenomena that overwhelms it with fatigue. The
confessions of egotism, and the demonstrations of modern science, have
their place, but not where the true story-teller—who is the ballad-singer
of the time—has *his*. He sits at the fountain-head of national character,
and he must never stoop below the highest aim, but for ever seek the
primal secret—for ever strive to speak the word which is answered by
nothing less than a creation.

In this country, the state of things is so peculiarly unfavorable to that quiet brooding of the spirit over the dark waters, which must precede the utterance of a word of power;—our young men are so generally forced into the arena of business or politics before they have ever discriminated the spirit that they are, from the formless abyss in which they are, that it argues a genius of a high order to soar over the roaring gulf of transition in which the elements of society are boiling, into the still heaven of beauty. Such genius, however, there is amongst us. The harmonies of Nature, like the musical sounds in the ancient rites of Cybele, so fill the souls of her chosen priests, that they are insensible to all meaner sounds;[9] and one of these true priests is the sweet story-teller, with the flowery name, whose little book of caged melodies we are now to review.

We have heard that the author of these tales has lived the life of a recluse; that the inhabitants of his native town have never been able to catch a glimpse of his person; that he is not seen at any time in the walks of men. And, indeed, his knowledge of the world is evidently not the superficial one acquired by that perpetual presence in good society—so called—which is absence from all that is profound in human feeling and thought; but, on the contrary, it is the wisdom which comes from knowing some few hearts well—from having communed with the earnest spirits of the past, and mainly studied in the light of that Pythian temple "not built with hands—eternal in the spirit," whose initiation is—"know thyself."[10] There is throughout the volume a kindliness and even heartiness of human sympathy—a healthy equilibrium of spirits, and above all, a humor, so exquisitely combined of airy wit and the "sad, sweet music of humanity,"[11] that it contradicts the notion of misanthropical or whimsical seclusion. We will venture our reputation for sagacity on the assertion that he is frank and communicative in his character, winning thereby the experience of whatsoever hearts come in his path, to subject it to his Wordsworthian philosophy.

Wordsworthian philosophy we say, and with consideration; not that we would imply that he has taken it from Wordsworth. We mean to speak of the kind of philosophy, which cannot be learnt except in the same school of Nature where Wordsworth studied, and by the same pure light. We mean that he illustrates the principle defended by Wordsworth in his prose writings, as well as manifested by him in his metrical compositions, viz: that the ideal beauty may be seen clearest and felt most profoundly in the common incidents of actual life, if we will but "purge our visual ray with euphrasie and rue."[12] Mr. Hawthorne seems to have been born to this faith. His stories, generally speaking, have no dramatic pretension. Their single incident is the window through which he looks

"into the mind of man—
His haunt, and the main region of *his* song."[13]

In none of the little pieces before us has he succeeded more completely in suggesting the most general ideas, than in the "Sunday at Home," the "Sights from a Steeple," and "Little Annie's Ramble." These pieces also exhibit in perfection the objective power of his mind. With what a quiet love and familiar power he paints that sunrise stealing down the steeple opposite his chamber window! We turn to this passage, as we do to a painting upon canvass, for the pleasure it affords to the eye. The motion and sentiment so mingled with the forms and hues do not obscure the clear outlines—the sharp light and shade. What a living as well as tangible being does that meeting-house become, even during its week-day silence! The author does not go to church, he says; but no one would think he stayed at home for a vulgar reason. What worship there is in his stay at home! How livingly he teaches others to go, if they do go! What a hallowed feeling he sheds around the venerable institution of public worship! How gentle and yet effective are the touches by which he rebukes all that is inconsistent with its beautiful idea! His "Sunday at Home" came from a heart alive through all its depths with a benignant Christian faith. *"Would that the Sabbath came twice as often, for the sake of that sorrowful old soul!"* This is worth a thousand sermons on the duty of going to church. It quickens the reader's love of religion; it shows the adaptation of Christianity to our nature, by adding to the common phenomena of the sacred day the pathos and grace which are to be drawn up from the wells of sympathy, and reproduces the voice that said "the Sabbath is made for man,"[14] in its very tones of infinite love, even to our senses. And "Little Annie's Ramble," though still lighter in execution, is no less replete with heart-touching thought. We feel as if to dwell upon it in our prosaic manner would be to do some injury to its airy structure. The more times we have read it, the more fully we have realised the force of its last paragraph:

> "Sweet has been the charm of childhood on my spirit throughout my ramble with little Annie! Say not that it has been a waste of precious moments, an idle matter, a babble of childish talk, and a reverie of childish imaginations, about topics unworthy of a grown man's notice. Has it been merely this? Not so—not so. They are not truly wise who would affirm it. As the pure breath of children revives the life of aged men, so is our moral nature revived by their free and simple thoughts, their native feeling, their airy mirth for little cause or none, their grief soon roused and soon allayed. Their influence on us is at least reciprocal with our on them. When our infancy is almost forgotten, and our boyhoods long departed, though it seems but as yesterday;—when life settles darkly down upon us, and we doubt whether to call ourselves young any more, then it is good to steal away from the society of bearded men, and even of gentle woman, and spend an hour or two with children. After drinking from these fountains of still fresh existence, we shall return into the crowd, as I do now, to struggle onward, and do our part in life, perhaps as fervently as ever, but, for a time, with a kinder and purer heart, and a spirit more lightly wise. All this by thy sweet magic, dear little Annie!"

Not so grave is the effect of the "Vision of the Fountain." But who would ask for more than meets the eye and touches the heart in that exquisite little fancy?

> "Sure, if our eyes were made for seeing,
> Then Beauty is its own excuse for being."[15]

But nothing about our author delights us so much as the quietness—the apparent leisure, with which he lingers around the smallest point of fact, and unfolds therefrom a world of thought, just as if nothing else existed in the outward universe but that of which he is speaking. The hurried manner that seems to have become the American habit—the spirit of the steam-engine and railroad, has never entered into him. He seems to believe and act upon what is seldom ever apprehended, that every man's mind is the centre of the whole universe—the *primum mobile*—itself at rest, which wheels all phenomena, in lesser or greater circles, around it. Thus, "David Swan" goes down from his father's house in the New Hampshire hills, to seek his fortune in his uncle's grocery in Boston; and being tired with his walk, lies down by a fountain near the way-side for an hour's repose. Our philosophic, or, more accurately, our poetical story-teller, marks him for his own, and sitting down by his side, notes the several trains of phenomena which pass by and involve the unconscious sleeper; and comparing these with that train in which he is a conscious actor, reads the great lesson of superintending Providence, with the relation thereto of the human foresight. Again, his eye is struck with an odd action related in a newspaper, and his attentive mind is awakened, and may not rest until he has harmonised it with the more generally obeyed laws of human nature. Thus we have "Wakefield," and the terror-striking observation with which it closes:

> "Amid the seeming confusion of our mysterious world, individuals are so nicely adjusted to a system, and systems to one another, and to a whole, that *by stepping aside for a moment*, a man exposes himself to a fearful risk of losing his place for ever. Like Wakefield, he may become, as it were, the outcast of the universe."

"The Rill from the Town Pump" has been praised so much—not too much, however—that we have hardly anything left to say. It shows that genius may redeem to its original beauty the most hackneyed subject. We have here what would make the best temperance tract;[16] and it is a work of the fine arts too—something we could hardly have believed possible beforehand.

"The Gray Champion," "The Maypole of Merry Mount," and "The Great Carbuncle," form another class of stories, for which it has often been said that this country gives no material. When we first read them, we wanted to say to the author, "This is your work:—with the spirit of the past, chrystallized thus, to gem the hills and plains of your native land; especially let every scene of that great adventure which settled and finally made free our country, become a symbol of the spirit which is too fast fading—the spirit that in Hugh Peters and Sir Henry Vane laid down mortal life, to take up the life which is infinitely communicable of itself." But, on second thought, we feel that we cannot spare him from the higher path, to confine him to this patriotic one; although we would recommend him frequently to walk in it. Why will he not himself give us the philosophical romance of Mt. Wallaston, of which he speaks? We can see but one objection; and that is, that into his little tale of "The Maypole," he has already distilled all the beauty with which he might have garnished the volume. "The Great Carbuncle" combines the wild imagination of Germany, and its allegoric spirit, with the common sense that the English claim as their characteristic; and these diverse elements are harmonized by the reliance on natural sentiment which we love to believe will prove in the end to be the true American character. The story awakens first that feeling and thought which is too fine in its essence for words to describe. A practical philosophy of life, that gives its due place and time to imagination and science, but rests on the heart as a solid foundation, is the light that flashes from the "Great Carbuncle" upon the true soul; which absorbing it, leaves the outward rock only "opaque stone, with particles of mica glittering on its surface."

The momentous questions with which "Fancy's Show Box" commences, and the "sad and awful truths" interwoven with its light framework, and the expressed hope with which the author relieves these at the end, where he suggests "that all the dreadful consequences of sin may not be incurred unless the act have set its seal upon the thought," would make the story interesting, even if it were not half so well done. Yet it does not denote a character of genius so high as the others that we have mentioned. It is as much inferior to the "Great Carbuncle" as the faculty of fancy is below the imagination. In quite an opposite vein is Mr. Higginbotham's catastrophe; but the variety of power proves the soundness of the author's mind. Where there is not the sense and power of the ludicrous, we always may fear weakness.

"The Gentle Boy" we have not neglected so long because we like it least. It is more of a story than any of the rest; and we, perhaps, are the most fond of it, because it was the first of the author's productions we saw. We took it up in the Token, where it was first told, not expecting much, and found ourselves charmed by a spell of power. That sad, sweet, spiritual Ibrahim, with "eyes melting into the moonlight," seeking a home on the cold tomb of his murdered father, while his deluded mother is wandering over the earth to awaken, with the concentrated force of all human passions that she has baptized into the name of the Holy Ghost, the spiritually dead to spiritual life, is worth a thousand homilies on fanaticism in all its forms, contrasted with the divinity of the natural sentiments, and the institutions growing therefrom. In this angelic child, we see human nature in its perfect holiness, its infinite tenderness, its martyr power, pleading, with all the eloquence of silent suffering, against the time-hallowed sins and ever renewed errors of men. On the judgment seat sits Time; and he shows himself, as usual, a very Pilate, delivering up the innocent victim to the furies of the present. They crucify him, and bury him in its stony bosom. Bury him, did we say? No—we saw his feet "pressing on the soil of Paradise," and again his soothing spirit coming "down from heaven, to teach his parent a true religion."

We have now spoken, as we could, of our chief favorites in this volume. A few more stories are left, which are indeed treated with great skill and power, and with as severe a taste as their subjects admit—especially the "Prophetic Pictures," a masterpiece in its way. As specimens of another vein of the author's art, we would not give them up. But we cannot avoid saying that these subjects are dangerous for his genius. There is a meretricious glare in them, which is but too apt to lead astray. And for him to indulge himself in them, will be likely to lower the sphere of his power. First-rate genius should leave the odd and peculiar, and especially the fantastic and horrible, to the inferior talent which is obliged to make up its own deficiency by the striking nature of the subject matter. Doubtless, we are requiring of genius some self-denial. These very tales are probably the most effective of the volume, at least with readers of Tokens and Magazines. They are the first read and oftenest spoken of, perhaps, by all persons; and yet, we would venture to say, they are the least often recurred to. They never can leave the reader in so high a mood of mind as the "Sunday at Home," or "Little Annie's Ramble." The interest they excite, in comparison with the latter, is somewhat analogous to the difference between the effect of Byron and Wordsworth's poetry.

But it is with diffidence we offer counsel to Mr. Hawthorne. We prefer to express gratitude. Can we do it more strongly, than to say, "We would hear more and more and forever"? Nor do we doubt that we shall hear more. Talent may tire in its toils, for it is ascending a weary hill. But genius wells up at the top of the hill; and in this instance descends in many streams—and the main stream is augmented and widened and deepened at every conflux. As it approaches the dwelling places of men, and spreads out to bear the merchandise of nations on its bosom, may it preserve the sweetness and purity of its fountains, far up in the solitudes of nature! We can wish nothing better for Mr. Hawthorne or for ourselves. He will then take his place amongst his contemporaries, as the greatest artist of his line; for not one of our writers indicates so great a variety of the elements of genius.

And this is a high quarry at which to aim. The greatest artist will be the greatest benefactor of our country. Art is the highest interest of our state, for it is the only principle of conservatism our constitution allows—a beauty which at once delights the eye, touches the heart, and projects the spirit into the world to come, will be something too precious to be weighed against the gains of a break-neck commerce, or the possible advantages held out by empirical politicians. While all the other excitements of the time tend to change and revolution, this will be a centre of unity. Let the poetic story-teller hasten, then, to bind with the zone of Beauty whatever should be permanent amongst us. In order to discharge his high office worthily, he will draw his materials from the wells of nature, and involve the sanctities of religion in all his works. Being, thinking, loving, seeing, uttering himself, without misgiving, without wearisomeness, and, like the spirit which hangs the heavens and clothes the earth with beauty, for ever assiduous; he yet need do nothing with special foresight. We would not yoke Pegasus to the dray-cart of utility; for the track of his footsteps will be hallowed, and every thing become sacred which he has touched.—Then, and not till then, we shall have a country; for then, and not till then, there will be a national character, defending us alike from the revolutionist within, and the invader without our borders.

Duke University

---

[1] This letter is in the Berg Collection, New York Public Library. It has been made available to me, along with other letters in the Berg Collection mentioned below, by the curator, Mrs. Lola L. Szladits.

[2] For a survey of the tales and sketches by Hawthorne that Benjamin published initially, the others that he reprinted, and his criticism of Hawthorne's writings, see my article "Park Benjamin on the Author and the Illustrator of 'The Gentle Boy,'" pp. 85-91 of this volume.

[3]Letters exchanged among Elizabeth, Mary, and Sophia Peabody, Nathaniel, Elizabeth, and Mary Hawthorne are in the Berg Collection. Selections appear in Julian Hawthorne, *Nathaniel Hawthorne and His Wife* (Boston: J. R. Osgood, 1885), and in Rose Hawthorne Lathrop, *Memories of Hawthorne* (Boston: Houghton, Mifflin, 1897). See three important articles by Norman Holmes Pearson: "Elizabeth Peabody on Hawthorne," *Essex Institute Historical Collections*, XCIV (July, 1958), 256-276; "A Good Thing for Hawthorne," *Essex Institute Historical Collections*, C (Oct., 1964), 300-305; and *Hawthorne's Two Engagements* (Northampton, Mass., 1963). See also Louise Hall Tharp, *The Peabody Sisters of Salem* (Boston: Little, Brown, 1950), pp. 113-132.

[4]Ralph Waldo Emerson, *The Journals and Miscellaneous Notebooks, VII, 1838-1842*, ed. A. W. Plumstead and Harrison Hayford (Cambridge, Mass.: Belknap Press of Harvard University Press, 1969), p. 21, June 6, 1838).

[5]Rose Hawthorne Lathrop, *Memories of Hawthorne*, p. 29.

[6]Julian Hawthorne, *Nathaniel Hawthorne and His Wife*, I, 165-167.

[7]In the *Democratic Review*, I (Feb., 1838), 319-329. A letter of Hawthorne's to Louis O'Sullivan, editor of the *Democratic Review*, April 19, 1838, calls this review unworthy of Miss Peabody, "particularly poor," but recommends another essay of hers, which appeared in the *Democratic Review*, III (Nov., 1838), 253-268, under the title "Claims of the Beautiful Arts." (Professor Norman Holmes Pearson has kindly made available to me this letter and others, in the texts he has prepared for the edition of Hawthorne letters.) William Ellery Channing wrote Elizabeth Peabody a similar judgment, saying that this review "would be a bad model for a book which seeks general circulation." See her *Reminiscences of Rev. Wm. Ellery Channing, D. D.* (Boston: Roberts Brothers, 1877), p. 393.

[8]*New-Yorker*, V (March 24, 1838), 1-2.

[9]Cybele, in Greek religion the Great Mother, identified with Rhea, mother of the gods. The rhythm of music was invented among her followers, and her rites included frenzied dancing.

[10]The Delphic oracle was situated in the temple of Apollo, on which were the inscriptions "Know thyself" and "Nothing too much." The priestess Pythia transmitted messages from the oracle through priests to the seekers of information.

[11]William Wordsworth, "Lines Composed a Few Miles above Tintern Abbey," 1. 91 ("still, sad music of humanity").

[12]John Milton, *Paradise Lost*, XI, 11. 414-415, Michael clearing Adam's eyes after the expulsion from Paradise, before showing him from a hilltop the history of mankind down to the flood ("...Then purged with euphrasy and rue / The visual nerve, for he had much to see").

[13]William Wordsworth, "The Excursion," Preface, 11. 40-41 ("The Mind of Man— / My haunt, and the main region of my song:).

[14]Mark, II, 27: "The Sabbath was made for man, and not man for the Sabbath."

[15]Ralph Waldo Emerson, "The Rhodora," 11. 11-12. ("Sure, if our" replaces "Tell them, dear, if.")

[16]This story was in fact published as a temperance tract in 1841 and 1857. See Jacob Blanck, *Bibliography of American Literature* (New Haven: Yale University Press, 1955-), IV (1963), 24, 25.

Park Benjamin on
the Author and the Illustrator
of "The Gentle Boy"

ARLIN TURNER

In the *New-Yorker* for January 26, 1839, Park Benjamin reviewed *The Gentle Boy, a Thrice-Told Tale,* Hawthorne's story in a separate publication, which included a preface by the author and a drawing by Sophia Peabody. This review, printed below, was the longest comment Benjamin published on Hawthorne, apparently, but in the preceding five years he had presented Hawthorne prominently and favorably in the journals he edited. Benjamin had published initially a dozen and a half tales and sketches by Hawthorne, had reprinted others, and had published also several brief statements of his own, all highly laudatory of Hawthorne's works.

Benjamin had been associate editor of the *New-England Magazine* in 1834 when it received, through Samuel Griswold Goodrich, a collection of tales and sketches which Hawthorne had enclosed in a narrative frame tracing the career of an itinerant story-teller, and hoped to publish in two volumes entitled "The Story-Teller."[1] Since a publisher had not been found, Goodrich apparently picked some of the stories for future numbers of his annual, *The Token,* and left the remainder of the manuscript with the *New-England Magazine,* which began publishing from it in November and December with "Passages from a Relinquished Work" (VII, 352-358, 449-459). Very likely "Little Annie's Ramble" was in the manuscript and was selected by Benjamin for the 1835 *Youth's Keepsake* (pp. 146-159), printed late in 1834, which had Benjamin as editor and the same publisher as the *New-England Magazine.* With Benjamin editor from March of 1835 onward, the *New-England Magazine* had something from Hawthorne in every month of that year except September and October. These selections probably were all from "The Story-Teller" manuscript, and when the *New-England Magazine* merged with the *American Monthly Magazine* at the end of 1835 and Benjamin moved to New York as editor, he took the remainder of Hawthorne's manuscript with him and published from it the sketch "Old Ticonderoga" in February, 1836 (n.s. I, 138-142). He and Hawthorne apparently became estranged in the succeeding months, likely because of the editor's laxness in paying for contributions; for on February 1, 1837, Horatio Bridge wrote Hawthorne that he was glad they were reconciled.[2] Another selection from "The Story-Teller," "Fragments from the Journal of a Solitary Man," was published in the *American Monthly Magazine* in July, 1837 (n.s., IV, 45-46). In January of the next year Hawthorne's sketch of Thomas Green Fessenden appeared (n.s. V, 30-41), and in March "The Threefold Destiny" (n.s. V, 228-235) and a review of *Twice-Told Tales*, presumably from the pen of Charles Fenno Hoffman (pp. 281-283).

In addition to publishing a score of pieces by Hawthorne, Benjamin had raised a persistent voice praising his works. In the *New-England Magazine* for October, 1834 (VII, 331), his phrasing ran, "writer of some of the most delicate and beautiful prose ever published this side of the Atlantic"; in April, 1835 (VIII, 316), "originality and graphic freshness of coloring"; in October, 1835 (IX, 298), "the most pleasing writer of fanciful prose, except Irving, in the country." In the *American Monthly Magazine* a year later (October, 1836, n.s. II, 405-407) Benjamin identified the author—the first time in print. He continued, "If Mr. Hawthorne would but collect his various tales and essays into one volume, we can assure him that their success would be brilliant—certainly in England, perhaps in this country." He was writing about *The Token* for 1837, in which Goodrich had included eight pieces by Hawthorne. Since his contributions to *The Token* appeared anonymously, Goodrich once wrote the author, May 31, 1831,[3] he could run several in one number. Benjamin was engaged in a vituperative literary war with Goodrich at the time and probably thought his identifying Hawthorne as author of so many pieces in one issue of *The Token* would embarrass Goodrich. He advised the editor to have Hawthorne write the next number entire.

At the beginning of 1838 Park Benjamin became literary editor of the *New-Yorker* (after being named an associate editor earlier)[4] and at once brought his support of Hawthorne to yet another magazine. Horace Greeley had founded the *New-Yorker* in 1834; he continued it and remained editor until he established the New York *Tribune* in 1841. Early in 1838 Greeley became editor also of the *Jeffersonian*, a weekly published at Albany to support Whig candidates in the state. He appointed Benjamin literary editor of the *New-Yorker* and began in midwinter preparing the first number of the *Jeffersonian* for release on March 3.[5]

Before Benjamin became literary editor, the *New-Yorker* had reprinted three pieces by Hawthorne, presumably chosen by Horace Greeley:

July 9, 1836 (I, 247), "The Science of Noses," from the *American Magazine of Useful and Entertaining Knowledge,* II (March, 1836), 268.
March 18, 1837 (II, 405), "A Bell's Biography," from the *Knickerbocker,* IX (March, 1837), 219-223.
November 25, 1837 (IV, 563-564), "Night Sketches Beneath an Umbrella" ("By S. G. G.," Samuel Griswold Goodrich), from *The Token* for 1838, pp. 81-89.

Benjamin began at once giving Hawthorne greater prominence in the *New-Yorker*; he reprinted four selections in the first three months:

January 6, 1838 (IV, 660-662), "Thomas Green Fessenden," from the *American Monthly Magazine,* n.s. V (January, 1838), 30-41.
January 27, 1838 (IV, 709-710), "Footprints on the Sea-Shore," from the *Democratic Review,* I (January, 1838), 190-197.
February 17 (IV, 759-760), "Snow-Flakes," from the *Democratic Review,* I (February, 1838), 355-359.
March 3 (IV, 787-788), "The Three-Fold Destiny: A Faery Legend," by Ashley Allen Royce, from the *American Monthly Magazine,* n.s. V (March, 1838), 228-235.

The *New-Yorker* for March 24 contained a long review-essay on the *Twice-Told Tales* written by Elizabeth Peabody, in which she said of Hawthorne, "He will then take his place amongst his contemporaries, as the greatest artist of his line; for not one of our writers indicates so great a variety of the elements of genius."[6]

Benjamin left the *New-Yorker* in April, 1838; Greeley had discovered that editing the *Jeffersonian* left him time to edit both the literary and the political sections of the *New-Yorker.* But the *American Monthly Magazine* ceased publication with the October number, and Benjamin returned to the *New-Yorker* as literary editor.[7] He indicated soon that his interest in Hawthorne had not lessened. On January 13, 1839 (VI, 259), he reprinted "The Sister Years" (omitting the final two sentences), with the following introductory note: "One of the best—nay, the very best thing of the season, is the Carrier's Address of the Salem Gazette, with this title. It is manifestly from the pen of Nathaniel Hawthorne, author of 'Twice-Told Tales,'—original, striking, yet full of quiet beauty. By the way, why have not the publishers sent us 'The Gentle Boy'? In this felicitous strain commences the Address."

This appeal to the publishers produced a copy of *The Gentle Boy*, and Benjamin published his review on January 26. He was eager to praise both the story and the drawing by Sophia Peabody, whom he had known since the early 1830's in Boston.

The Gentle Boy, a Thrice-told Tale: by Nathaniel Hawthorne.—[8] We have at length received from the publishers, Weeks, Jordan & Co. of Boston, a copy of this affecting and beautiful story. It originally appeared in 'the Token,' and the reason for its publication at the present time and in its present shape, is to offer the public an original illustration from the pencil of Miss Sophia A. Peabody. Even if we had not learned from the author's preface that this performance had received "the warm recommendation of the first painter in America," (he might have written "in the world,"—ALLSTON, of course,)[9] we should have pronounced it a display of the most exquisite genius. Though softly and delicately drawn, it has all the effect of one of Retsch's—though it does not remind us so much of his manner as of Flaxman's.[10] The expressions of both faces in the etching are angelic—the attitudes of the figures natural and therefore graceful. The conception is highly poetic. The mind that prompted and the hand that drew this illustration, must be obedient to the sweetest and happiest influences of Imagination.

Mr. Hawthorne tells us in his preface that the story was at first little noticed. His observation suggested to us the following statement, which will be regarded as a curious instance of the effect of prejudice. We were five years ago engaged in editing the New-England Magazine, and, having just completed a University education,[11] were doubtlessly looked upon as a novice in literature, who assumed too much in undertaking the conduct of a journal of criticism. Of course no good thing could emanate from such a Nazareth. Yet, during the first months of our direction, that Magazine contained many remarkable articles, wholly unnoticed at the time, which, subsequently published under other forms, have attracted the noisiest approbation. Among them were the best sketches and stories in the volume—lauded to the skies by the North American Review[12] and other sapient journals—issued under the title of "Twice-told Tales, by Nathaniel Hawthorne." This same Mr. Hawthorne, who is now ranked by some enthusiastic admirers with Lamb and Irving, did not elicit more than common inquiry when writing paper after paper of the most beautiful description in the New-England Magazine, and in 'the Token.' We were so much impressed with 'The Gentle Boy,' on its first publication, as to consider that it must be the production of one of our most celebrated authors.

We have in reserve other anecdotes of the same kind, illustrative of that low-minded prejudice, which cannot discover merit. till it is trumpeted through the country. People here will understand Mr. Hawthorne's position, when we say that he is *wondered at* in Boston as much as Mr. Stephens is in New-York. Perhaps the most popular book of the day is the latter gentleman's 'Incidents of Travel in Egypt, Arabia Petraea and the Holy Land'—and yet very copious extracts from this work, long before its publication, could appear in the American Monthly Magazine without eliciting observation.[13] 'The Gentle Boy' in its present shape will probably be called everything that is remarkable, while, issued modestly in the Token, nobody but an Editor or two ever dreamed that it was superior to the trash by which it was surrounded.

Three weeks after publishing this review, the *New-Yorker* reprinted "The Lily's Quest," February 16 (VI, 341-342), from the *Southern Rose* of January 19, 1839 (VII, 161-164). The *New York Review*, founded in 1837 with Benjamin as business manager, printed a note on *The Gentle Boy, a Thrice-Told Tale* in the number for April, 1839 (IV, 493), which parallels this review in the *New-Yorker* closely enough (in the phrasing and in the reference to Retzsch) to identify Benjamin as its author.[14] In October, 1839, Benjamin left the *New-Yorker* to found his own weekly, the *New World*. He brought the author and the illustrator of "The Gentle Boy" into this new journal, among marriage announcements on July 16, 1842 (V, 50): "July 9, at Boston, by Rev. James F. Clarke, Nathaniel Hawthorne, (author of 'Twice-Told Tales,' etc.) and Sophia Amelia[,] daughter of Dr. Nathaniel Peabody."

The *New World* had reprinted "The Three-Fold Destiny" on December 25, 1841 (III, 401-402), and on the next February 26 (IV, 145) had published the following note on the new edition of *Twice-Told Tales*, issued in two volumes by James Monroe and Company:

> There exists a certain class or *clique* of readers, who entirely overestimate the writings of Mr. Hawthorne. On the other hand, we are inclined to think that the great body of the reading public do not sufficiently regard them. These twice-told tales are of very unequal merit. Some of them are excellent; "The Gray Champion," "The Gentle Boy," "A Rill from the Town Pump," "Little Annie's Ramble," and a few others, have a great and peculiar merit, displaying considerable originality in thought and expression, and being related in a style of charming simplicity. Others, again, of a more ambitious character, are, comparatively, failures. On the whole, however, these tales form two entertaining volumes, and are a valuable addition to our stock of native literature.

In the ensuing months Hawthorne's name appeared again and again in the *New World*, chiefly among the editor's notes on current magazines. On December 10, 1842 (V, 383), he was named among contributors to *Sargent's New Monthly Magazine*, which had "The Old Apple Dealer" in its January number; on January 21, 1843 (VI, 90), the editor praised the first issue of the *Pioneer*, naming one contribution in particular, but added, "It should have been attended, however, by one of Hawthorne's quiet, quaint, and most appropriate papers." The editor noted on February 4 (VI, 156-157) that Hawthorne opened the second number of the *Pioneer* "with an article, full of genuine sentiment and showing a finely regulated imagination." The article he meant was

"The Hall of Fantasy," which he reprinted elsewhere in the same number (pp. 146-149). He listed Hawthorne as a contributor to *Sargent's New Monthly Magazine* for February, in which "The Antique Ring" appeared; and he designated "The New Adam and Eve" in the February *Democratic Review* as "a delightful story." Readers of the *New World* for March 11, 1843 (VI, 302-303), learned that Hawthorne was in the *Democratic Review* for March with the story "Egotism." On June 10 (VI, 696) they learned that he had contributed to the June number "Buds and Bird-Voices," "a very pleasing and graceful essay on spring."

Duke University

[1]See Nelson F. Adkins, "The Early Projected Works of Nathaniel Hawthorne," *Bulletin, Bibliographical Society of America*, XXXIX (First Quarter, 1945), 119-155.

[2]Julian Hawthorne, *Nathaniel Hawthorne and His Wife* (Boston:James R. Osgood, 1885), I, 149. See Merle M. Hoover, *Park Benjamin, Poet and Editor* (New York: Columbia University Press, 1948), 62-64, 71-74.

[3]Julian Hawthorne, *Nathaniel Hawthorne and His Wife*, I, 132.

[4]See F. L. Mott, *A History of American Magazines* (Cambridge, Mass.: Harvard University Press, 1930), I, 358.

[5]For information on the *Jeffersonian* and on Benjamin's connections with the *New-Yorker*, see James Parton, *The Life of Horace Greeley* (Boston: Houghton, Mifflin, 1897), pp. 117-119, 139-140; Merle M. Hoover, *Park Benjamin*, pp. 82-94.

[6]This review is reprinted in my article "Elizabeth Peabody Reviews *Twice-Told Tales*," pp. 257-267 of this volume.

[7]See editorial announcements in the *New-Yorker* for April 7, October 13, and November 3, 1838 (V, 45; VI, 49, 109).

[8]*New-Yorker*, VI (Jan. 26, 1839), 301.

[9]In an essay entitled "Claims of the Beautiful Arts" published in the *Democratic Review*, III (Nov., 1838), 253-268, Elizabeth Peabody had spoken of Allston as the greatest artist in America and possibly in the world.

[10]Frederick August Moritz Retzsch (1779-1857) was a German painter known for his illustrations of Goethe, Schiller, and Shakespeare. John Flaxman (1755-1826) was an English artist whose outline drawings illustrating Homer were among Sophia Peabody's favorites.

[11]After attending Harvard College two years, Benjamin graduated at Washington College, Hartford, 1829, and later studied law at Harvard and Yale. He contributed to the *New-England Magazine* as early as its second number, August, 1831, and had an editorial connection before he became owner and editor with the March number, 1835. See Merle M. Hoover, *Park Benjamin*, pp. 16-53; also Lillian B. Gilkes, "Hawthorne, Park Benjamin, and S. G. Goodrich: A Three-Cornered Imbroglio," *Nathaniel Hawthorne Journal 1971*, pp. 83-112.

[12]Henry Wadsworth Longfellow reviewed *Twice-Told Tales* in the *North American Review*, XLV (July, 1837), 59-73.

[13]John Lloyd Stephens (1805-1852) sent back from the Eastern Mediterranean a series of travel letters that were published in the *American Monthly Magazine*, supposedly without his authorization but probably by arrangement with

Charles Fenno Hoffman: I (Oct., Nov., Dec., 1835), 89-99, 174-183, 262-268; II (Nov., 1836), 480-489. The full work was published in two volumes in 1837 under the title *Incidents of Travel in Egypt, Arabia Petraea, and the Holy Land*, and went through six editions within a year. See Victor Wolfgang von Hager's introduction to an edition of the work published by the University of Oklahoma Press in 1970.

[14]This note in the *New York Review* was reprinted in the *Salem Gazette* on April 12, 1839.

Wayside, April 18th '63

Dear Fields,

I received the cheque, and pocketed it with great satisfaction. I shall begin to write the last article (which will come first in the volume) in a day or two. I don't think the public will bear any more of this sort of thing.

I had a letter from Bennoch the other day. He has had a fit of the gout, but seems to be comfortable enough now. He sends me the enclosed verses, and, I think, would like to have them published in the Atlantic. Do it if you like. I pretend to no judgment in poetry, and shall therefore refrain from recommending or dissuading.

Hawthorne to James T. Fields 18 April 1863. *From the Collection of Rare Books and Manuscripts, Memorial Library, University of Wisconsin, Madison. Reproduced by permission.*

The Hawthorne-Fields Letterbook: a Census and Description

JEROME KLINKOWITZ

In June of 1867 James T. Fields assigned a unique task to the copyists of his firm, Ticknor, Reed & Fields. They were to transcribe all remaining letters written to Fields by his close friend and most important author, Nathaniel Hawthorne. Fields then bound these copies into a volume and added the preface, "These letters were written by N. H. to me during the years between 1850 and 1864 (the year of his death). Many other letters from him have been either given away or mislaid."

These letters were to be the basis for the chapter on Hawthorne in Fields' *Yesterdays With Authors* (Boston: J. R. Osgood, 1873). Parts of nearly every letter were included, and the copies bear Fields' pencilled excisions. In most cases only a line or two referring to a celebrity was quoted, although in a few instances entire letters were reproduced. The originals are now widely scattered: some among Fields' papers in the New York Public Library, others in the collection of Professor Norman Holmes Pearson at Yale University, and at least one in a place indicative of the fate of so many Nineteenth Century manuscript items: in a special edition of *Yesterdays with Authors* prepared by Mrs. Annie Fields as a wedding gift for Lucia Fairchild, October 25, 1893. Mrs. Field tipped in letters to her husband from such illuminaries as Emerson, Whittier, Dickens, Longfellow, Stowe, and one from Hawthorne dated April 18, 1863 (copied in the Letterbook).The Fairchild gift is presently in the collections of the Rare Book Room of the University of Wisconsin Memorial Library, Madison, and was brought to my attention by the curator, Mr. Felix Pollak.

The Hawthorne-Fields Letterbook remained a family heirloom for several generations, and was given to Harvard University on May 3,

Bennoch also sent his Epi-
thalamiũ by Mrs. Crosland; and
I doubt not that the good lady will
be pleased to see it copied
into one of our newspapers with
a few landatory remarks. Can't
you do it in the Transcript (let
Michael Angelo write the remarks, if you have not the time)
and send her a copy? You cannot imagine how a little praise
follifies us poor authors to the
marrow of our bones. Consider,
if you had not been a publisher
you would certainly have been
one of our scribbled tribe, and
therefore ought to have a fellow-
feeling for us.

        Your friend,
        Nath'l Hawthorne

1940, by Mr. Boylston A. Beal. It consists of a leather-bound volume its spine stamped in gold, "Hawthorne's Letters to James T. Fields." Sixty-eight letters are copied, dated from January 15, 1850, to April 9, 1864, on ruled pages numbered from 1 through 182, with three additional pages interpolated between pp. 37-38, and sixteen additional pages between pp. 69-70. In the following census, "Y" denotes quotation from the letter in *Yesterdays With Authors.* The Letterbook is housed in the Houghton Library of Harvard University; this census is published with the kind permission of Mr. Rodney G. Dennis, Curator of Manuscripts.

The Hawthorne-Fields Letterbook

1. Salem, January 15, 1850.
    Encloses all but last three chapters of *The Scarlet Letter.* Fears for delicacy of the subject matter. "The Custom-House" as a necessary introduction, which has purged Hawthorne's ill feelings. Uncertain of title for the volume, perhaps "Old-Time Legends; together with sketches, experimental and ideal."

2. Salem, January 20, 1850. (Y)
    Disinclined to let *The Scarlet Letter* stand alone without adding other tales, since it is too uniformly gloomy. Suggests printing title in red.

3. Lenox, October 1, 1850. (Y)
    Will prepare a new preface for *Twice-Told Tales.* Will begin a new romance after the first frost in November. Scene will be an old projecting-story house in Salem. Considering titles.

4. Lenox, November 3, 1850. (Y)
    Considering titles for new romance, which is harder to write than *The Scarlet Letter.* Special problems of writing a romance.

5. Lenox, December 9, 1850. (Y)
    Bogged down in new romance.

6. Lenox, January 12, 1851. (Y)
    Encloses new preface for *Twice-Told Tales.* Finishing *The House of the Seven Gables,* must submit first to his wife's

reading. Uncertain of title. Mrs. Hawthorne sends her thanks for the copy of *Evangeline,* Hawthorne comments on the poem. Cautions against enquiry about *Fanshawe.*

7. Lenox, January 27, 1851. (Y)

   Has finished *The House of the Seven Gables,* Mrs. Hawthorne prefers it to *The Scarlet Letter.* Suggests that Fields publish the Bible in a twelve-volume edition.

8. Lenox, February 22, 1851. (Y)

   List of presentation copies of *The House of the Seven Gables,* including Pierce, Bridge, Emerson, Longfellow, Sumner, Holmes, and Lowell. Fears *The House of the Seven Gables* will not be as successful as *The Scarlet Letter,* which profited by its introduction.

9. Lenox, March 6, 1851. (Y)

   His portrait for *The House of the Seven Gables.*

10. Lenox, May 23, 1851. (Y)

    Whipple's reviews have been enlightening. Hawthorne believes *The House of the Seven Gables* to be a better book than *The Scarlet Letter,* and hence may be less popular. The existence of an actual Pyncheon family. Plans a book of classical myths—*A Wonder Book.*

11. Lenox, June 5, 1851. (Y)

    Another original Pyncheon. To send first part of *A Wonder Book* in two weeks.

12. Lenox, July 15, 1851. (Y)

    Encloses the rest of *A Wonder Book.* Comments on the reception of his romances in London.

13. Lenox, August 18, 1851. (Y)

    Sends drawing of his porch at Tanglewood for *Tanglewood Tales.* Acquires a set of DeQuincey. Writes a Pyncheon disclaimer.

14. Lenox, September 13, 1851. (Y)

    Is tired of the Berkshires.

15. Concord, June 17, 1851. (Y)

    Written to Fields in London. Describes his new estate

at The Wayside. Calls Ticknor a bookseller compared
to Fields' superior talents and friendship. Requests
British editions of his romances. Will write a campaign
biography of Franklin Pierce. Encloses a letter to Barry
Cornwall.

16. Concord, December 17, 1852. (Y)
    Complains about women authors. Interest in Portugal.

17. Liverpool, August 19, 1853. (Y)
    Good feeling in England.

18. Liverpool, September 16, 1853. (Y)
    Sending Ticknor home, settling in Rock Park. Seeks
    information on his ancestor William Hawthorne, who
    left England in 1634, hopes to find a family gravestone.

19. Liverpool, October 14, 1853.
    Obtaining copies of *Tanglewood Tales.*

20. Liverpool, January 20, 1854. (Y)
    His delight in autobiographies.

21. Liverpool, April 13, 1854. (Y)
    Writing a new preface for the *Mosses*, remarks on his
    change since first writing. Restores preface to "Rap-
    paccini's Daughter" from the *Democratic Review.* Ad-
    mires DeQuincey.

22. London, September 13, 1855. (Y)
    Enjoying London. Comments on the English character.

23. Liverpool, March 27, 1857. (Y)
    Delia Bacon angry with him. Visit with Leigh Hunt,
    writes a sketch on him. Literary life otherwise dull.
    His house robbed.

24. Leamington, September 9, 1857. (Y)
    Enjoying the English countryside, planning a visit to
    Paris. Writing an English journal which he will let be
    published in one hundred years.

25. Near Florence, September 3, 1858. (Y)
    Enjoys his present isolation. Describes house and

tower, plans for setting of a new romance. Needs atmosphere of England and Massachusetts to finish other works. Has many ideas. Is growing old faster in Italy, greying fast.

26. Rome, February 3, 1859. (Y)
    Dismal time in Rome, Una sick with fever. Detests Rome and its history. Working hard on new romance, but its development is often interrupted. Not expected to be happy once he returns to America, England is more liveable. Plans to enlarge his home or build another.

27. Redcar, August 6, 1859. (Y)
    Book bogged down, is revising heavily.

28. Leamington, October 10, 1859. (Y)
    Romance is almost finished, Mrs. Hawthorne likes it but Hawthorne is mercurial. Speculates on titles with names of characters or place.

29. Leamington, November 28, 1859. [out of sequence]
    English publication of the new romance deferred.

30. Leamington, November 17, 1859. (Y)
    Comments on Italian and British climates. British publisher requests a title other than "Romance of Monti Bene," Hawthorne sends twelve. Thinks it his best romance. English notebooks unpublishable.

31. Leamington, December 30, 1859. (Y)
    New romance being printed. British insist on *The Transformation* as title, Hawthorne prefers *The Marble Faun.*

32. Leamington, February 11, 1860. (Y)
    Regards himself as not a popular author. His own taste is for writing quite unlike his own, especially Trollope's. *The Marble Faun* will be American title.

33. Bath, April 26, 1860. (Y)
    The Marble Faun daringly imposes absurdities by style and narrative. Whipple analyzes his unpopularity. Wants to purge the devil from his pen and write more genial books.

James T. Fields, Hawthorne's friend and publisher.
Photograph from the collection of C. E. Frazer Clark, Jr.

34. Bath, May 3, 1860.
    Travel arrangements for return to America.

35. Concord, September 21, 1860. (Y)
    Una still ill with Roman fever.

36. Concord, September 23, 1860. (Y)
    Adds note to "Dr. Heidegger's Experiment" con-
    cerning an imitation by Dumas.

37. Concord, February 27, 1861. (Y)
    Gratitude to Fields for his success. Julian to visit
    Fields, is warned of his behavior.

38. Concord, July 14, 1861.
    Concerning Longfellow's misfortune.

39. Concord, October 6, 1851. (Y)
    Plans for a new story.

40. Concord, November 6, 1851. (Y)
    Can serialize new story, but thinks it too monotonous.

41. Washington, April 2, 1862. (Y)
    Portrait by Leutze, kept cheered during sitting. Com-
    ments on the sinking of the Cumberland, describes its
    wreck for Holmes. Prospect of war not hopeful from
    near at hand. His hair lightened by Washington sun.

42. Concord, May 23, 1862. (Y)
    Omit section on Lincoln from his essay.

43. Concord, October 5, 1862. (Y)
    Sends an article from his English journal. Suggests that
    for life of Scott Fields is publishing, clarifying details
    be added.

44. Concord, October 9, 1862.
    Cannot find title for his English article.

45. Concord, October 12, 1862.
    Seeks a method to send letters postage free to England.

46. Concord, December 6, 1862. (Y)

Another essay on England. Glad to be rid of Julian.

47. Concord, January 4, 1863.
    Sends another article.

48. Concord, January 8, 1863.
    Will write on London and suburbs to finish volume.

49. Concord, January 30, 1863. (Y)
    Appreciates Fields' encouragements regarding the
    English essays. Louisa Alcott home from Washington
    with typhus.

50. Concord, February 14, 1863. (Y)
    Declines invitation to Boston.

51. Concord, February 22, 1863. (Y)
    Sends an essay on Leigh Hunt.

52. Concord, April 18, 1863. (Y)
    Finished last essay for book, comments on Bennoch's
    verse.

53. Concord, April 30, 1863. (Y)
    Sends his last article and suggests the title, *Our Old
    Home.*

54. Concord, May 3, 1863. (Y)
    Plans dedication for Pierce, Bennoch, or none at all.

55. Concord, May 28, 1863. (Y)
    Correcting proof for *Our Old Home.*

56. Concord, July 1, 1863.
    Prefatory matter to *Our Old Home.* Will dedicate to
    Pierce.

57. Concord, July 14, 1863. (Y)
    Requests changes in preface to *Our Old Home.*

58. Concord, July 18, 1863. (Y)
    Insists on retaining dedication to Pierce, despite his
    unpopularity and chances it might harm the book. Will
    make one small modification.

James T. Fields, Hawthorne, William D. Ticknor (1. to r.).
From a photograph, collection of C. E. Frazer Clark, Jr.

59. Concord, September 16, 1863. (Y)
    Presentation copies for *Our Old Home.*

60. Concord, October 18, 1863. (Y).
    Cautions against lending money to Julian. Reflects on his criticisms of the English. Is reluctant to begin a new romance.

61. Concord, October 24, 1863. (Y)
    Declines invitation to organ recital. To begin romance with a preface about how Thoreau told him a similar legend about his own house. Uncertain of title. Needs money.

62. Concord, November 8, 1863. (Y)
    Beginning his romance. The importance of prefaces. Comments on his criticisms of the English.

63. Concord, November 14, 1863. (Y)
    Encloses a photograph.

64. Concord, December 9, 1863. (Y)
    Proceeding with *The Dolliver Romance.* More problems with pens and paper.

65. Concord, December 15, 1863. (Y)
    Happy with new paper. Terrible reluctance to proceed with his new work. In ill health.

66. Concord, January 17, 1864. (Y)
    Ill disposed to write.

67. Concord, February 25, 1864. (Y)
    Whimsical announcement to public of his failed powers.

68. Philadelphia, April 9, 1864.
    Ticknor very ill on their journey.

University of Northern Iowa

FANSHAWE,

A TALE.

"Wilt thou go on with me?"—SOUTHEY.

BOSTON:

MARSH & CAPEN, 362 WASHINGTON STREET.

PRESS OF PUTNAM AND HUNT.

1828.

Hawthorne's Gothic Discards: Fanshawe and "Alice Doane"

NINA BAYM

As Elizabeth Hawthorne remembered it, her brother decided to become a professional author while he was in college.[1] *Fanshawe* and "Alice Doane's Appeal" (insofar as we can discern the early version of this tale through the existing revision) were both written either while Hawthorne was still at Bowdoin or within a year after his graduation in 1825.[2] Virtually the earliest surviving writings, they are also the first fruits, so to speak, of his professional commitment. Since he never acknowledged writing either of them, evidently he later judged them as failures. Possibly they never satisfied his aims even from the beginning, but perhaps the actualities of authorship made the early aims themselves seem superficial or inadequate.

The idea of the literary work implicit in these neophyte productions, whether the works themselves are good or bad, gives us a means of better understanding of the shape of Hawthorne's career by showing us how he thought about writing when he began. I would agree with Roy Harvey Pearce's statement that Fanshawe represents Hawthorne's "calculated attempt" to write for a popular audience, "a role he later came so heartily to damn,"[3] while disagreeing strongly with the implication that there was a certain insincerity in this calculation. A fresh literary commitment would not be likely to contain such an admixture of cynicism. On the contrary, all the evidence suggests that Hawthorne sincerely and wholeheartedly wanted to be a popular writer when he began, and that his idea of the literary work as well as his idea of authorship was controlled by the example of popular authors.

In the United States in 1825 there was no literary tradition, but in England where the tradition was august, the conditions of authorship themselves were changing dramatically. Briefly, the modern profession

of authorship which had been slowly developing during the eighteenth
century became an emphatic and dramatic reality with the successes of
Byron and Scott. The careers of these men essentially established the
model for authors who followed them, and both of them were
thoroughly in the "business" of supplying literature to an enormous
reading audience: were genuine popular authors. The same can be said
for the first successful American professional authors as well, Cooper
and Irving.[4] Indeed a successful professional author in the modern
sense is by definition popular since his success is measured exactly in
terms of how widely his works are read. If, by 1855 when Hawthorne
referred in exasperation to the "damn'd mob of scribbling women," the
idea of the professional author had become overlaid with ironies and
bitterness, these were unsuspected developments twenty-five years
earlier.

The idea of the author came from the example of a handful of men
and so did the idea of the literary work. There is again no need to
imagine any skepticism in young Hawthorne's attitudes. His early letters testify to the fact that his favorite books were written by these men
and their forerunners, and it seems natural that he would try to write
the kind of book he loved to read. In practise, then, the literary work
would have to be in the tradition of Scott and Byron and the gothic
genre from which their works derived.[5] The "romance" of which
Hawthorne became in later years so staunch a defender would have
been the natural model for one determined to succeed as an author. The
"novel" which began to flower in the late eighteen-thirties was still in
the bud in 1825 when writers embodied the novelistic urge to
reproduce daily life in the sketch. A versatile author demonstrated his
range, as Irving did in *The Sketchbook* (on which Hawthorne modelled
Twice-Told Tales) by writing gracefully and effectively in both modes.
But the sketch lacked plot, and therefore to tell a story meant to write
in the gothic mode.[6]

The model of professional authorship which attracted
Hawthorne—a man of letters writing popular fiction—would no doubt
have been enhanced by the rhetoric of literary nationalism. But the
discussions of a national literature inaugurated by the founding of the
North American Review in 1815 had not yet attained the scope or
precision which they were to have in the thirties or forties. At this time
the literary debate would probably have done little more than assure
Hawthorne that authorship was a worthwhile, even admirable
profession, and make him believe that whatever he wrote would
necessarily be a contribution to the building of the nation and its
reputation. It would, that is , justify his purpose without providing him
with specific directions.

The sense of division and alienation in Hawthorne's later works seems to have developed gradually as a result of inner and outer changes. Within, the growth of a set of serious concerns whose expression became increasingly the purpose of his writing; without, the jarring realities of the publishing business and the expansion and solidification of a reading public whose taste did not support the kind of book he wanted to write. It may partly be that because Hawthorne began to write with so complete, one might almost say so naive, a belief in the community of author and audience, that he was later embittered. And of course, to the extent that he thought of writing as an escape from the business orientation of most of his contemporaries, the commercial aspect of book-writing and selling must have been difficult for him to accept.

Hawthorne's career, then, it can be hypothesized, began with a remarkably clear impulse: a young man enthralled by certain books and inspired by the success of their authors, determined to become a writer. With both "Alice Doane's Appeal" and *Fanshawe* Hawthorne attempted to reproduce or recreate in his own imagination, the forms of the familiar. "Alice Doane's Appeal" is a fairly simple imitation of conventional gothic fiction. *Fanshawe* tries more subtly to domesticate the genre by modifying some of the conventions. The first pages of *Fanshawe*, insisting as they do on the New England setting, establish the story as an American fiction.[7] But the conventionality of the opening and its traditional rhetoric assimilate the book into the international tradition and imply that the book will be an American version of the well-known rather than a new departure. And in fact none of the national references have organic purpose in *Fanshawe*. The occasional set pieces of landscape description with their hills and dales, villages and fields, crags and waterfalls, do not seem particularly American. Fields are bounded by hedgerows, forests traversed on horseback within fifteen minutes. These are not the Maine woods in 1750, the time of the narrative. Dr. Melmoth, head of Harley College, is a type of country squire; the students range from "rusticity" to "models of fashion," and include "a few young descendents of the aborigines" (p. 336). The anachronisms of the description are obvious and laughable. The author cannot be said to be "using" American materials with purpose or consistency.

If, however, nothing in the externals creates an American tale, Hawthorne's "treatment" does show his intent to Americanize the gothic in *Fanshawe*. The many clear allusions to gothic types and situations are combined with a decided toning down of the extremes and excesses of the genre. The gothic, of course, is associated with intense states of feeling, extremes of good and evil, and events are extraordinary, mysterious, and terrible. As William Charvat points out, the earliest versions of American Gothic, which were novels of female misery, tended to have European villains because "even in the late eighteenth century, the 'more smiling' aspects of American life were beginning to be considered the more characteristic."[8] Throughout *Fanshawe* we can see Hawthorne carefully managing a sort of "smiling gothic," which avoids excess and tries to make events decorous and mild enough to appear probable in the calm American setting. This interesting approach to the problem of American Gothic, however, does not have a successful outcome because the quick of the gothic is in its very excess, its unremitting assertion of awfulness.

A combination of allusion and avoidance, then, marks *Fanshawe's* tone. Though we recognize the essential gothic in the heroine, the hero, the villain, and the various events—a forged letter, an abduction, a chase, a violent death—which comprise the action, we also realize that these essences have been greatly diluted.[9] Consider, for example, the heroine of *Fanshawe*. How does she compare with the "heroine of delicate sensibility and purest innocence" whose persecution by "a superior but evil male protagonist" is usually the locus of suffering in a Gothic plot?[10] Of course Ellen Langden is innocent, but she "differed from the multitude only as being purer and better" (p. 444). This sentence asserts her superiority, but stresses her ordinariness. "It must therefore be left to the imagination of the reader to conceive of something not more than mortal...but charming men the more, because they felt, that, lovely as she was, she was of like nature to themselves" (p. 341). She has "much of the gaiety and simple happiness, because the innocence, of a child" *(Ibid)*. She has "an affectionate disposition," and makes "herself useful where it is possible, and agreeable on all occasions," so that everyone loves her (p. 342). Her speciality is domestic art; at her guardian's, Dr. Melmoth's, "the nicer departments of cookery...were committed to her care; and the doctor's table was now covered with delicacies, simple indeed, but as tempting on account of their intrinsic excellence as of the small white hands that made them" *(Ibid)*. Our heroine, then, is an innocent and agreeable homebody with no special emotional or imaginative gifts.

Although Ellen prefers to read an old romance to the doctor rather than be instructed by him in the learned languages, this fact is not adduced to demonstrate a romantic imagination in her so much as a conventional "feminine" distaste of heavy intellectual engagement. She is not at all the conventional sort of gothic heroine, as Hawthorne makes clear. She is induced to put herself in the villain's power because he gives her a letter purporting to be from her father, which commands her to do so, and she is convinced that the letter is genuine. "The letter spoke vaguely of losses and misfortunes, and of a necessity for concealment on her father's part, and secrecy on hers; and to the credit of Ellen's not very romantic understanding, it must be acknowledged, that the mystery of the plot had nearly prevented its success" (p. 427). This comment reminds us that we are in a gothic romance while making clear how unusually quotidian this particular example of the romance is. The heroine's American pragmatic streak leads her to endure the appearance of loss of virtue with unconventional equanimity. Because her first attempt to run away with the villain has been discovered, a "stain had fallen upon her reputation—she was no longer the same pure being, in the opinion of those whose approbation she most valued." Consequently, "it was easier, now, to proceed" (p. 430). Her combination of practicality and fluff faintly heralds the "American girl" and makes Ellen an unlikely gothic figure.

The forged letter implies a gothic plot. In the calm precincts of Harley College where Ellen lives quietly with her guardian, loved by all the undergraduates, a mysterious villain appears whose plan is to abduct the girl and force her into marriage so as to control her fortune. The letter gives the girl over to him, and when she understands his dark designs he prepares to rape her in order to keep control of her. Fanshawe makes a timely appearance and in climbing a steep cliff toward him the villain falls and is killed. Where the gothic romance often repeats its plot pattern a number of times, *Fanshawe* offers but this one sequence of events, and the single device of the letter. Butler, the villian, is no decadent European aristocrat but a wandering sailor returned to his birthplace. He gets no more than a few miles out of town with Ellen; she is never imprisoned and the attack on her is prevented. Butler dies violently but he is not murdered. We have, in effect, a series of "almost" events, which recall the usual course of a gothic plot without actually following it.

The toning-down is most evident in the treatment of the hero. The gothic hero, according to William Axton's admirable summary already cited, is in reality a "hero-villain," a "two-sided personage, a figure of great power, latent virtue, and personal magnetism tragically stained by criminality. He is deliberately made larger than life, and his contradictory qualities are exaggerated."[11] The duality, the highly developed qualities of both good and evil is basic to this character type. The clash of impulses within him is a source of reader interest and makes it difficult to judge him. But Hawthorne has split the hero-villain into Fanshawe the hero and Butler the villain, thereby undoing the crucial tensions of the generic figure.

The gothic villain with no mixture of high human qualities becomes a melodramatic puppet. Butler, whose seaman's sunburn is the native substitute for the swarthy complexion of continental badmen, suffers not merely by being deprived of even vestigial good impulses but also by having his wickedness sharply circumscribed. Dialogue with the local innkeeper hints at a vicious life but the reader gets no details beyond neglect of his mother and designs on Ellen. Like Ellen he is a small-scale character, with an emotional range only from "wild and fierce" (p. 361) to "cold and hard" (p. 378) and on to "dark and fiend-like" (p. 422).[12]

The villain's scope is restricted by Hawthorne's desire to make him a believable figure in the pleasant American landscape and also by the young author's high-minded reluctance to believe that evil can coexist with virtue or breeding. Butler is low class while Fanshawe is a scholar. The characterization of Butler suffers by being denied the admixture of nobility, intellectuality, and elegance that complicates the gothic villain. Conversely, the characterization of Fanshawe suffers from the removal of coarseness, sensuality, aggressiveness. His are the mildest of heroic dissipations, though he is clearly meant to be cast in the heroic mold. He has a "nobleness on his high forehead" and features "formed with a strength and boldness, of which the paleness, produced by study and confinement, could not deprive them." His expression is "proud and high—perhaps triumphant—like one who was a ruler in a world of his own, and independent of the beings that surrounded him." Literally studying himself to death, "a blight, of which his thin, pale cheek and the brightness of his eyes were alike proofs, seemed to have come over him ere his maturity" (p. 346). Butler is animal nature, Fanshawe spiritual.

Fanshawe's character is further attenuated by Hawthorne's refusal or inability to give him an active part in the fiction. To be sure, he is Ellen's rescuer. The first time he performs this function he does so simply by staring the villain down.

> Fanshawe turned, calmly, and fixed his eye on the stranger. "Retire, sir," was all he said...The stranger endeavored in vain, borne down by the influence of a superior mind, to maintain the boldness of look and bearing, that seemed natural to him...but, quailing at length beneath the young man's bright and steady eye, he turned and slowly withdrew. (p. 363)

And the second time he simply stands at the top of a cliff while Butler, trying to reach him, in effect kills himself. Muting the gothic in this way, Hawthorne makes Fanshawe all good but makes his goodness entirely interior—a matter of thought, feeling, and sensibility. The glitter in his eye and the pallor on his cheek have no cause beyond excessive study. Refusing Ellen's grateful offer of marriage because he knows she does not love him, and because he feels himself to be set apart from common humanity, he dies a few years later unactualized. Perhaps this passive story is an adolescent fantasy of self-pity. Perhaps Hawthorne was unable to imagine any action without some component of selfish or evil motivation, and therefore could think of nothing for so purely

good a hero to do. But the result of this handling of Fanshawe's character is to avoid the real challenge of the gothic: its sense of moral complexity, the decadent heroism by which it defines the limits of the
human spirit. The book suggests that nothing very terrible can happen
in America, that evil is the province of the occasional outsider, and that
intense dreams and ambitions are bound to go unrealized. How far
such premises are from those we associate with the gothic as well as
with Hawthorne's best work! It is almost as though in his maturity
Hawthorne grew into the gothic rather than beyond it.

Hawthorne's attempt to blend a genre of the extreme and over-
wrought with an ideology of the plain and everyday produced an artistic failure. Pruning the excesses of the gothic in order to make it
likely, decorous, and fit for the middle road of American life, he
created a story that was neither gothic nor probable. The experiment of
Fanshawe clearly urged the author on toward much greater boldness of
conception and expression. "Alice Doane"[13] represents an attempt to
execute a gothic fiction in all its extravagances. But to be extravagant is
not necessarily to be bold, for though "Alice Doane" is comprised
purely of one gothic excess after another, all of them are perfectly
standard and none of them effectively given depth or purpose. A recent
generalization about early American fiction seems particularly apt for
this narrative: "plots at first strike one as inventive, even wildly so; but
it soon becomes evident that they merely achieve new combinations of
old and familiar elements."[14]

After *Fanshawe* Hawthorne concentrated for a number of years on
short fiction, and within this form he achieved technical mastery very
soon. Like Poe, he found the boundary condition of brevity useful for
focus and concentration. But "Alice Doane," though brief, does not observe the formal restraints of short fiction (this is not true, however, of
the revision, "Alice Doane's Appeal") for it reads like the condensation
of a long work, striving for its effect by the simple expedient of
squeezing the maximum number of gothic motifs and crises into the
shortest possible space. This work approaches the gothic in a manner
opposite to *Fanshawe,* but is not any more successful. The revision,
however, whose date we do not know (a reference in an 1830 letter
may imply either version[15]), is a mature, effective, artistic whole.
Given the evidence of such early stories as "Young Goodman Brown"
and "My Kinsman, Major Molineux," we can suppose that a change
had occurred in Hawthorne's artistry sometime between 1828 and 1830,
a change which would account for his refusing to acknowledge either
Fanshawe or "Alice Doane's Appeal" which, even in its revision,
revealed so much about the early work.

The story presents an author-narrator who, with two young lady
companions, strolls to the top of the Gallows Hill in Salem and there

reads to them from a manuscript which he identifies as "Alice Doane" (p. 282).[16] He does not reproduce the entire early manuscript for us but summarizes large portions, presumably to balance the length of the manuscript with its new context.[17] More than a frame, this context points up and rejects the literary premises on which "Alice Doane" had been based.

"Alice Doane" was a series of theoretically hair-raising incidents centered on Leonard and Alice Doane, "a young man and his sister; the former characterized by a diseased imagination and morbid feelings; the latter, beautiful and virtuous, and instilling something of her own excellence into the wild heart of her brother, but not enough to cure the deep taint of his nature" (p. 284). Here are pure examples of the gothic hero-villain and the innocent persecuted maiden. By making them brother and sister, Hawthorne introduces the standard incest motif of gothic fiction.[18] The other two characters are a fiendishly evil wizard to whose superhuman machinations all the crimes of the story are finally attributed (thus is the supernatural brought into the tale) and wicked Walter Brome whom the wizard manipulates into tempting Alice to shame and provoking Leonard to murder him. The climax of this farrago is a ghoulish graveyard scene where all the dead are cavorting; there it is revealed that Walter was really the unknown brother of Alice and Leonard—two more motifs, the hidden identity and the lost sibling, are thus worked in. The incest theme is compounded, for Alice is now the incestuous attraction for two brothers. And, making Leonard recall the murder of his father in an Indian raid, Hawthorne introduces a massacre and hints obscurely at parricide.

Crews' description of the tone of this tale as one of turbulent agitation (see note 18) is apt. Leonard's speeches, which are the chief passages read, are pure rant, and the narration appears to have proceeded in the same mode. There is no sign of the measured, reserved, balancing, and ironic speaker who is now reading his early effort to us, and the contrast in prose styles within the revised version is instructive. In summary, the plot of "Alice Doane" is the complications of foul crime, its purpose to display the horrible and the supernatural in high-keyed rhetoric. Its sole American reference is locating the corpse of Walter Brome about three miles from Boston. Like *Fanshawe* it does nothing with American materials; in contrast, it solves the problem of creating an American Gothic by producing an extreme and extremely conventional example of the wildest of the species. This is in a sense no solution at all, no more than is *Fanshawe*. And, because it is so conventional, it is no less flat than *Fanshawe*.

The flatness of the original narrative is brought out strongly in the new setting of "Alice Doane's Appeal." After reading this wild story, the narrator discovers to his chagrin that his auditors are unmoved by

it. (Let us remember that to engage the reader's emotions was the
preeminent goal of this type of literature—in Axton's phrase, "inciting
an energetic intuitive response."[19]) The ladies remain composed, their
cheeks do not blanch and after a moment of polite silence they begin to
laugh. The manuscript has clearly failed. Thereupon the narrator turns
to the scene around him for inspiration and makes "a trial whether
truth were more powerful than fiction" (p. 292). He improvises a
crowd-scene which is structurally parallel to the graveyard assembly of
"Alice Doane" but which draws its content from American history. He
describes the people of Salem gathering at the height of the witchcraft
persecutions. Instead of the unreal innocent maiden of convention, we
have an unexpected grouping of ordinary people: "a woman in her
dotage, knowing neither the crime imputed her, not its punishment,"
another "distracted by the universal madness, till feverish dreams were
remembered as realities, and she almost believed her guilt," a proud
man so broken "that he seemed to hasten his steps, eager to hide
himself in the grave" (p. 293).

The gothic hero-villain is Cotton Mather, "darkly conspicuous" and
"sternly triumphant." Instead of supernatural motives, the moving
forces are "vices of spirit and errors of opinion that sufficed to madden
the whole surrounding multitude" (p. 294). Hawthorne has found real
and particular events of an extremity, evil, and awe-inspiring quality
which correspond exactly to the requirements of the gothic but with
infinitely more urgency and meaning to his audience.[20] And this
literature, *this* American Gothic, succeeds: "But here my companions
seized an arm on each side; their nerves were trembling; and, sweeter
victory still, I had reached the seldom trodden places of their hearts,
and found the well-spring of their tears" (p. 294).

The priorities implicit in this remark of the narrator may not please
those who like to think of Hawthorne's art as designed primarily for a
moral purpose. It suggests that he turned to the American past as well
as to themes of moral significance because these, rather than the
standard overworked repertoire of gothic devices, produced a moving
literature. At the outset of his career, indeed, Hawthorne was
motivated less by the desire to express a moral vision than the drive to
write successful fiction. He had to learn that the American past was a
repository of moving events; and that significance could be more
effective than triviality. Even more importantly he discovered how to
be original while still gothic. Thereupon, with a minimal personal
commitment except to effectiveness, he wrote moral stories set in the
American past. His sense of a good story remained bounded by his basic
imaginative engagement with the gothic.

Over the many years that he wrote he did come to have important
concerns that he wanted to embody in his fiction; he learned, quite

probably from the years he spent in Concord with the Transcendentalists, that literature ought to be sincere and self-expressive and he became a more complex person himself. But he never abandoned the mode which had shaped him. In *The Marble Faun*, his last complete work, and one which is profoundly resonant with his private artistic dilemma,[21] there is an extraordinary compilation of traditional gothic elements. By setting his story in Rome, Hawthorne puts it in the Country of the Gothic romances, and he uses the catacombs and towers, the persecuting priests and decadent Italian aristocratic families even as they had been used a century before. He has a protagonist who is a hero and a murderer, one heroine who is abused, persecuted, maligned, but innocent and another who is spirited away to a nunnery. A little more consideration will remind us of an occasionally stated but frequently ignored truth: that every tale and romance Hawthorne wrote was gothic in its conception. If, then, *Fanshawe* and "Alice Doane" are failures, they are failures of direction within a mold that from first to last contained Hawthorne's literary imagination.

University of Illinois at Urbana-Champaign

---

[1]Julian Hawthorne, *Nathaniel Hawthorne and his Wife* (Boston: Haughton, Mifflin, & Co., 1884), I, 123-24.

[2]Roy Harvey Pearce, Introduction to the Centenary Edition of *Fanshawe* (Columbus: Ohio State Univeristy Press, 1964), p. 302. *Fanshawe* was published anonymously in 1828, and the revised "Alice Doane's Appeal," also anonymous, appeared in the *Token* for 1835.

[3]Pearce, p. 316.

[4]William Charvat, *The Profession of Authorship in America, 1800-1870* (Columbus: Ohio State University Press, 1968), p. 20. This book, along with *The Early American Novel* (Columbus: Ohio State University Press, 1971) by Henri Petter, and pp. 3-70 of Neal Frank Doubleday's *Hawthorne's Early Tales, A Critical Study* (Durham: Duke University Press, 1972), provide excellent background for understanding the context of Hawthorne's beginning writings.

[5]Much of the existing commentary on *Fanshawe* stresses its debt to the *Waverly* tradition. See Doubleday, p. 42 and G. Harrison Orians, "Scott and Hawthorne's *Fanshawe*," *NEQ*, 11 (1938), 388-94.

[6]Hawthorne read all the popular romances by Radcliff, Walpole, Maturin, Godwin, etc. One article, Jesse Sidney Goldstein's "The Literary Source of Hawthorne's *Fanshawe*," *MLN*, 60 (1945), 1-8, argues that *Melmoth the Wanderer* is the major source for Hawthorne's novel. I know of no direct evidence for Hawthorne's reading Byron at this early stage but given the Byronic vogue it seems impossible that he could have missed him. The character of Fanshawe clearly represents a kind of attenuated Byrnoic hero.

[7]Parenthetical page references are to Volume III of the Ohio State University Press's Centenary Edition of Hawthorne's works (Columbus, 1964).

[8]Charvat, pp. 22-23

[9]This dilution is not attributable to the vigorously active Waverly series; nor is the pale Fanshawe a typical Scott hero.

[10]William F. Axton, Introduction to *Melmoth the Wanderer* by Charles Maturin (Lincoln: University of Nebraska Press, 1961) p. viii.

[11]Axton, p. x.

[12]I would disagree here with Leo B. Levy who, in *"Fanshawe:* Hawthorne's World of Images," *SNNTS,* 2 (1970), 440-48, argues for the psychological complexity of the portrait of Butler; and more generally with Carl Bode, "Hawthorne's *Fanshawe:* The Promise of Greatness," *NEQ,* 23 (1950), 235-42, who rests his case for Hawthorne on the superior handling of character in this novel.

[13]To distinguish between them I will call the early story "Alice Doane" and the published revision "Alice Doane's Appeal."

[14]Peter, p. 397.

[15]*Nathaniel Hawthorne and His Wife,* I, 131-32.

[16]Parenthetical page references are to the text of "Alice Doane's Appeal" printed in V. XII of *The Works of Nathaniel Hawthorne* (Boston: Houghton, Miffling, & Co., 1883).

[17]I would take issue with Seymour L. Gross who, in "Hawthorne's 'Alice Doane's Appeal,' " *NCF,* 10 (1955), 232-36, argues that the purpose of summarizing is to cut out the strong incest motif in the story. Among my reasons is the fact that the motif is not cut out.

[18]Every study of the Gothic that I have consulted mentions this motif as a matter of course. Petter's *Early American Fiction* devotes a full section (pp. 242-56) to examples. It is unfortunate, therefore, that Frederick C. Crews in *The Sins of the Fathers* (New York: Oxford Press, 1965) extensively analyses "Alice Doane's Appeal" as evidence that at the outset of his career "Hawthorne felt impelled to treat the most shameful of subjects, and to so in a spirit of turbulent agitation" (p. 52). What Gothic story, one might rhetorically ask, is *not* done in a spirit of turbulent agitation.

[19]Axton, p. viii.

[20]Thus the two parts of "Alice Doane's Appeal" form a contrast, and cannot be considered as parts of a cumulative effect, as in argued by such critics as Robert H. Fossum, "The Summons of the Past: Hawthorne's 'Alice Doane's Appeal,' " *NCF,* 23 (1965), 294-303, or Roy Harvey Pearce, "Hawthorne and the Sense of the Past," *Historicism Once More* (Princeton: Princeton University Press, 1969), pp. 150-52.

[21]See my *"The Marble Faun:* Hawthorne's Elegy for Art," *NEQ* 44 (1971), 355-76.

Hawthorne and the Function of History: A Reading of "Alice Doane's Appeal"

STANLEY BRODWIN

"Alice Doane's Appeal" (1835) is one of the few stories of Hawthorne's that has not fared well with the critics. Both the composition of the tale—it was saved from the fire into which Hawthorne doomed his early *Seven Tales of My Native Land*[1]—and its "sensational" psychological matter dealing with incest, murder and persecution, have been the main concerns of critical scrutiny. Seymour L. Gross, in trying to protect Hawthorne from the charge of artistic ineptitude, has pointed out that "Alice Doane's Appeal" is the "...only story [of Hawthorne's] which is *told about* rather than *told*."[2] He argues that Hawthorne, in revising the story for publication, removed "the incestuous and sexual portions of the original version...whereas those portions of either pure description or of nonsexual psychological dimensions were allowed to remain dramatic."[3] Gross' theory is that, in doing this, Hawthorne was forced to create a clumsy "frame" device of a narrator telling a now toned-down and confused story to two young ladies. And Frederick C. Crews, who has given the story its fullest psychoanalytic reading, says that the tale has "contradictions" and "false starts."[4] Arlin Turner, however, sees the story in literary terms as a "...bridge between Hawthorne's earliest attempts and the remainder of his work."[5] He adds that "Unwilling to publish the story as it was first written, Hawthorne converted it by means of a superimposed framework into a study of the effects such a tale of sorcery and guilt would have on those hearing it read."[6] While this is a true statement of Hawthorne's intentions, Turner does not touch upon the larger implications of the tale. Finally, Hyatt H. Waggoner calls the story "fragmentary and chaotic," inviting "psychological rather than structural criticism."[7]

Given the weight of this "consensus," the burden lies heavy on the critic who would argue for the story's thematic unity and depth of meaning. Yet it can be demonstrated that the story, despite some flaws, possesses both. My argument is that the framework device gives structural meaning to the "Oedipal" triangle between Leonard Doane, his sister, Alice, and Leonard's twin-brother, Walter Brome, as well as the horror visions of the guilt surrounding the Salem witch trials, and serves to dramatize Hawthorne's concept of the function of history. In this story, Hawthorne concentrates on the value and force of history in converting the human heart from one state of being to another. Change is accomplished only by making people aware that they are *witnesses*—emotional martyrs, so to speak—to the truth of events they have ignored, forgotten or psychologically repressed. Hawthorne recognizes the problem that history, conventionally understood or studied as a body of "facts" about the past, lacks existential meaning or authenticity. This authenticity is best conveyed, ironically, through romantic art or the shaping force of the creative imagination. Art, whose function it is to explore human motives while recreating the historical landscape, confronts guilt and actualizes it. But guilt, to be a true homeopathic element in the tension between human motive and historical event, must liberate the deadened esthetic and moral center of the heart, and give it the capacity to see things feelingly, to paraphrase Gloucester in *King Lear*. History, art and guilt, always inter-related as they are in Hawthorne's view, lack meaning and purpose unless they effect such an existential conversion whose ultimate consequence is to bind individuals into genuine community.[8] Hawthorne's purpose in "Alice Doane's Appeal" is to dramatize the process by which the past, guilt, and art achieve their liberating and humanizing effects. The structure of the story is the structure of this process, and is by no means chaotic or incoherent. At the same time, the story preserves and considerably deepens its original nationalistic context, by being, possibly, a rebuke to those spokesmen like Rufus Choate, who, in 1833 at Salem (where Hawthorne was then living), called for American writers to use Puritan history in their romances, but to record "the useful truth...only,"[9] i.e., to ignore unpleasant episodes like the witch trials. "Alice Doane's Appeal" is clearly both about Americans and their inauthentic or non-relationship to American history, and a vision of the uses of history.

Turning to the story itself, we can see that the first section—the frame—establishes the major themes and structural form. The narrator accompanies two young ladies, possibly fictional "portraits" of his sisters, Louisa and Elizabeth, to Gallows Hill, now overgrown with a "vile and eradicable"[10] weed. This weed, the wood-wax, functions as a characteristic symbol of evil growing out of the soil of unexpiated crimes. The narrator knows that it signifies a "physical curse" (127) on the site where the martyred victims of the witch trials are buried. Hawthorne comments that "history blushed to record" (127) the event, but no blushes appear on the girls as they tread on ground made sacred, ironically, by moral pollution. Yet the narrator suggests that the girls only behave as most Americans do, "because we are not a people of legend or tradition" (127). And again: "But we are a people of the present, and have no heartfelt interest in the olden time" (127). Over against "the people of the present" stand the narrator himself who "often courted the historic influence of the spot" (127), and an historian (Bancroft? Joseph B. Felt?) who has performed the task of "converting the hill of their disgrace into an honorable monument of his own antiquarian lore, and of that better wisdom, which draws the moral while it tells the tale" (127).[11] Through ancient "lore" and a moral vision of the past, the historian and romancer may redeem the innocent, judge the guilty, and remind the forgetful.[12] Still, weeds cover the past and human motives. Until the artist or historian penetrates and reveals them, the contemporary observer will remain separated from his "roots" and spiritually alienated from those who relate authentically to the past. The narrator's goal is clearly to resolve this problem by bringing the girls into an authentic confrontation with the tragic meanings symbolically and literally buried beneath the weeds. Therefore the form of "Alice Doane's Appeal" becomes that of a strategy of conversion.

In beginning his strategy, the narrator first quickly assesses the difficulties he will find in his subjects. He recognizes their ability to catch and feel the "melancholy associations" of the place, but "feminine susceptibility" makes their emotions come and go with "quick vicissitude" (127). All this, combined with their being "people of the present," may be seen as a brief but pointed representation of American, or at least Hawthorne's "Token" readers. But Hawthorne is not content with this description alone. He reinforces it by indicating that his audience comes from a culture and society untouched by the dark shadows of life. Adjusting himself to his companions' changing moods, the narrator leads them to a spot where they can view the surrounding countryside. What they see from their "unhappy spot" of Gallows Hill is that "No blight had fallen on old Essex; all was prosperity and riches, healthily distributed" (128). Gallows Hill and old Essex: the two Americas, the dark and light yet again. The sun descending brings a "tender gloom" to the scene, and it then becomes an easy matter to throw, "in imagination, a veil of deep forest over the land," and to picture "...this old town itself a village, as when the prince of hell bore sway" (128). The little group is now able to imagine, fairly accurately, the town as it looked in 1692. Nevertheless,

Hawthorne cannot begin the story without voicing doubts and fears about his work, without giving us an *apologia* for what is to follow. We get the account of how the story was saved from the flames and knowledge of Hawthorne's "dread of renewing...acquaintance with fantasies that had lost their charm in the ceaseless flux of mind..." (129). Why does Hawthorne give the reader all this information rather than plunging into the story itself? Perhaps one reason is that he wished to endow the tale with a romantic cast which, in itself, would heighten the chances of its success. The story of how a scarlet letter was found by Mr. Surveyor Pue is, after all, only Hawthorne's most famous use of this device. By contrast, the story of saving "Alice Doane's Appeal" was at least *true* as well as "romantic." And possibly Hawthorne's admission that he wrote the original version under a "more passionate impulse within" than he was "fated to feel again" (129), is an appeal to his reading audience to recognize the emotional validity of what might seem merely "sensational." Yet he must return to those original, "passionate" sources of the tale despite the fact that his mind is now taken up with new fantasies. In revealing this about himself, Hawthorne may well be pointing to the problem of pulling away far less imaginative minds than his from *their* "ceaseless flux," and taking them into the forbidding past laden with repressed sexual and moral guilt. If the artist dreads to go over old common ground, what must his audience feel? Hawthorne seems to be implying that, in order to succeed, artist and audience have to agree to make the descent into the past together. Thus the tale can only begin when the three of them sit by a tree they *choose* to believe was the "death tree' (129). The artist justifiably hesitates a moment as he adjusts himself to renewing his "acquaintance" with these fantasies. Then the tale begins, "darkly, with the discovery of a murder" (129).

It is at this point that Hawthorne throws the full weight of his strategy on the esthetic and moral interplay between Leonard's dark confession and its effect on the two ladies. Hawthorne's concern is to develop only those portions of the confession that are psychologically disturbing to both the reader and the girls without going beyond the bounds of an assumed moral propriety. The structure must function to create the illusion that all the necessary "facts" of the confession are given to them, while at the same time intriguing, but not alienating, the actual reader. That is why the more "revelatory" aspects (Leonard's repressed incestuous feelings) are glossed over, but the details about the murder and Leonard's agonies are not. The discovery of Walter Brome's body is therefore made very vivid. The corpse is found by a traveller only because it is partly buried by a December snowfall "as if nature were shocked at the deed, and strove to hide it with her frozen tears..." (129-30). Here we have a double image in which the snow cover reinforces the image of the wood-wax cover on Gallows Hill. Nature hides both victims and victimizers. At the end of the story, we shall see that Hawthorne pleads for a monument to be placed on Gallows Hill, thus countering the anonymity the weeds partially symbolize, and at the same time succeeds in releasing the "well-spring" (139) of the girls' tears, in contrast to the townspeople's "frozen hearts" (134). Thus Hawthorne establishes image patterns which provide some thematic continuity in the story as a whole. The narrator can now "read on" (130), sketching in the main outlines of an obviously melodramatic and gothic plot.

We hear Leonard, who is "characterized by a diseased imagination and morbid feelings," giving his confession to a wizard "with fiendish ingenuity in devising evil." Listening, too, is Leonard's sister, Alice, "beautiful and virtuous," whose qualities have only partially refined "the wild heart of her brother" (130). The rather stereotyped story he tells is one that is not nearly so psychologically ambiguous as some critics suggest.[13] In good gothic tradition, he and his sister have a "consecrated" relationship because they alone were saved when an Indian raid killed "their race." Walter Brome, in reality Leonard's twin-brother and his "very counterpart" (131) spiritually and physically, attempts to seduce Alice. We later learn that this is at the instigation of the wizard. It is made quite clear that Walter fails, but he does arouse Alice's interest in him sufficiently to create a demonic jealousy in Leonard which was all he wished to do anyway. Leonard, recognizing "the hateful sympathy" (131) between himself and Walter, cannot allow him to have "more than the love which had been gathered to me from the many graves of our household—and I be desolate!" (131). But true villain that he is, Walter, helped by the ingenuity of the wizard, easily makes Leonard believe that Alice was seduced. Duped by self-hate and his own unhealthy desires toward Alice, Leonard's capacity to murder is unleashed. He kills Walter and confesses that "my spirit bounded as if a chain had fallen from it and left me free" (132). As might be expected in Hawthorne's work, such a release is followed by a return to a state pervaded by near-paralyzing guilt and the need for a judging, expiating authority. Gazing at the corpse, Leonard remembers the Indian raid and sees his dead father's image reflected in Walter's face. His euphoria gone, Leonard fully comprehends his own evil and loss of innocence. Not knowing that Walter is his twin-brother, he cannot grasp the "delusion" of the family resemblance and its meaning to him. He frantically *half*-buries the body, confused as to whom, psychologically, he has killed. Indeed, Leonard's vulnerability to deception was foreshadowed earlier when he began his confession to the wizard. There he is shown as being unable to distinguish between a gust of wind and the wizard's laugh which mocks the "indubitable proofs" (132) of Alice's guilt, proofs which the wizard knows are unreal. "I was deceived," (132) Leonard thinks to himself, as laugh and wind become indistinguishable. True to his gothic technique, however, Hawthorne does not reveal the full nature of the wizard's plot until later in the story when the spectral Walter responds to Alice's appeal and absolves her. Nevertheless, the deception theme is sufficiently developed so as to suggest that the entire tragedy—murder and witch trials—is the product of psychological instability and moral blindness.The wizard, though inadequately drawn as a personality, stands as a symbol of Deception, magnetically pulling to himself all those who live by delusions and betrayal. The human heart's greatest infirmity is defined by its inability to distinguish between appearance and reality and to follow its healthiest instincts.

Yet the structural problem remains. The appeal scene with its revelation of Alice's innocence and the wizard's deception comes short-ly after the narrator has created a powerful spectral vision of the puritan graveyard of the damned. A shift of interest and even meaning seems to have taken place. One explanation for this shift may be that Hawthorne probably felt that the revelation scene would have greater psychological and historical significance when seen against the background of a more general and dramatic metaphor of human evil. Also, Hawthorne needed to place Leonard's confused mental state into a situation most likely to create sympathy and fear among the listeners and reader, something the confrontation between Alice, Leonard, Walter and the wizard's damned minions theoretically would achieve. But as we shall see, Hawthorne fails to give the expiation scene the in-tellectual and dramatic substance it needs to fully succeed. The shift or placement itself is neither illogical nor chaotic, just inadequately fleshed out. Still, the narrator does manage to "carry over" the reader from the drama of Leonard's outpourings to the dark and icy world of Salem through which Alice and Leonard rush to meet the dead and the damned. And it is done rather simply by linking images of ice and cold (with the implied contrast of the fires of passion) drawn from Leonard's experience to that of the town, its inhabitants and graveyard.

First, Leonard's confession ends with a vivid account of how he failed to bury Walter successfully in an "icy sepulchre" (133). This image reinforces the association of snow and death already made earlier in the description of the snow cover with its "frozen tears." Then follows a short summary passage of Leonard's woes: he cannot make up his mind about Alice's guilt; he feels remorse for Walter's death, yet considers killing Alice; and, finally, he is filled by a sense "of some unutterable crime," probably an awareness that he has murdered his own flesh and blood in order to possess, sexually or otherwise, his sister. In despair, the tormented couple seek answers, ironically, from the master deluder, the wizard, who "had no power to withhold his aid in unravelling the mystery (133). The unravelling of the "mystery" becomes the subject of the following sections and allows the narrator to expand artistically the background and atmospere for the coming revelations. These will encompass Leonard's and Walter's relationship, Alice's innocence, and the knowledge that individuals are part of a larger community of self-deceived sinners. To prepare the proper mood and tone for these revelations, the narrator abruptly shifts from Leonard's passionate last words to the wizard, to a wholly new mood and scene. It is a typical Hawthorne scene, replete with bright moon, northern lights and strange transformations. Ice covers the trees and nearly everything else in the town with a "frigid glory" (133). The people themselves glitter in "icy garments" and have "frozen hearts" (134). Above all, the atmosphere is "ghostly" cold, and the living world seems the "creation of wizard power, with so much resemblance to known objects that a man might shudder at the ghostly shape of his beloved dwelling, and the shadow of a ghostly tree before his door" (133-4). The narrator has now created the "ghostly" mood of "moon-beams on the ice" (136) through which he intends his listeners and reader to experience the unravellment. It is his purpose to "throw a ghostly glimmer round the reader, so that his imagination might view the town through a medium that should take off its every-day aspect, and make it a proper theatre for so wild a scene as the final one" (134). Alice and Leonard are going to the graveyard where Walter has recent-tly been buried. They have an appointment with the dead in order to confront the reality of guilt, resolve tormenting suspicions and seek ab-solution. The narrator has brought his fantasy into the emotional and physical world of his listening audience. For the girls are sitting by the "death tree" where " so many had been brought to death by wilder tales than this..." (134). The irony is trenchant and sure; he has been telling a tale of guilt and woe in an extreme gothic setting which might well be rejected by the most credulous reader or listener. But we are suddenly reminded that the stories which condemned the innocent on Gallows Hill were indeed wilder and were *believed.* This perception is in keeping with one of the basic tensions in the story, the narrator's struggly to determine "whether truth were more powerful than fic-tion" (137). This contest constitutes a critical theme and structural prin-ciple in the story. In a convincing way, Hawthorne has brought his reader and two auditors to the point where fiction and truth—the "Ac-tual and Imaginary"—meet the graveyard of the puritan martyrs and the graveyard of Walter Brome in a community of the past. The auditors are now in a state of fear themselves. Their "bright eyes" are "fixed" on the narrator, their "lips apart" (134). Through his imagination, the narrator now brings the two girls to the brink of

Walter's grave. But "suddenly there was a multitude of people among the graves" (134). A new illusion or delusion is created by the wizard who has accompanied Alice and Leonard to the graveyard. Here the wizard functions as the artist-narrator's *alter ego*, a figure who gothically extends the imaginary boundaries the artist has established as "real" in the beginning. The artist creates the historical and psychological contexts of his fiction; then, through the fictional illusion of the story and its self-contained world, allows the wizard to create his own world of "accursed" souls and "fiends counterfeiting the likeness of departed saints" (135). Past and present generations of parents, children and clergy pass in review, revealing their sins and hellish torments. In the context of the story, this unholy rising is meant to be taken as "unreal" (136). It is there as a metaphor of universal deception embodied in a community coming to gloat over and to claim their own—Leonard and Alice. The dead are all "shadows" and have no "objective" existence. Then, after giving a brief and even casual account of Alice's successful appeal to Walter to absolve her, Hawthorne dissolves the whole scene. Alice's innocence routs the evil specters, but not before Leonard discovers that the wizard had used Walter to contrive the whole tragedy of temptation and murder. In short, we get a speedy denouement of an incredible gothic tale.

There is no doubt that this quick summary and conclusion deflates much of the moral and esthetic effect Hawthorne had built up to this point. And yet the flaw, as I have already indicated, does not lie so much in summarily concluding that part of the plot, as it does in Hawthorne's failure to give the moment its dramatic force. Given Hawthorne's strategy of conversion throughout the story, the absolution of Alice does not seem important because it does not deepen the auditors' emotional involvement with human suffering and the past; besides, her innocence is predictable as she is the stereotype of the falsely accused. The wizard's role in listening to confessions and symbolically showing how man is fated to tragedy by delusion and passion, was also suggested to the reader before the graveyard scene. And, finally, the description of the damned is powerful enough by itself to make it quite believable that the two ladies are in a state of fear and amazement. What happens, in effect, is that the contrived gothic ending of Alice's appeal really becomes emotionally and morally irrelevant to the final conversion of heart that is projected for the end of the story. I suspect Hawthorne recognized this weakness, but tried to make it appear that he could not develop the scene for fear of offending his audience. Thus, he introduces the summary with "I dare not give the remainder of the scene," and tells us that the devils and condemned souls had come to revel in a crime as "foul a one as was imagined in their dreadful abode" (136). The failure to flesh out sufficiently his "brief epitome" (136) breaks the tension which is meant to flow from the wizard's vision of the damned to the narrator's vision of the past with its "true" picture of the innocent being led to the slaughter. Fortunately, the story regathers strength when all its themes are finally merged in the narrator's last, powerful vision. Hawthorne must assure his triumph over the frozen minds of the "people of the present."

The story of Alice and Leonard now over, the narrator tries to assess what effect it has had on the listeners. The girls seem more entranced than profoundly moved; there is only silence as the narrator's voice mingles into a summer wind while night falls. He makes yet another effort to link the past and present by telling them that they are sitting next to the wizard's grave from which the wood-wax had originally sprung. "The ladies started; perhaps their cheeks might have grown pale had not the crimson west been blushing on them; but after a moment they began to laugh..." (137). The narrator now must face what seems to be either a failure of his art or of the "wild" gothic tale itself. He is "piqued" that his narrative should "be considered too grotesque and extravagant for timid maids to tremble at" (137). He realizes now that they have not fully comprehended the relationship between his tale of the forces of evil and the meaning of Gallows Hill. Yet, as a result of the story, and despite their defensive reaction to its horror, the listeners are still in the proper frame of mind to be authentically moved and illuminated. Through his imagination, he is able to conjure up before them a tragic procession of the "virtuous" being led to death, and to "communicate the deep, unutterable loathing and horror, the indignation, the affrighted wonder, that wrinkled on every brow, and filled the universal heart" (137). A whole society, trapped in "universal madness," carries the victims of its self-delusion to the gallows. So pervasive and intense is this delusion, that one of the victims, "a woman in her dotage, knowing neither the crime imputed to her, nor its punishment;...distracted by the universal madness, till feverish dreams were remembered as realities...almost believed her guilt" (138). Here Hawthorne has carefully drawn the historical and psychological parallels to the Leonard Doane confession.[14] But the tragedy is that there is no parallel appeal in the historical event for the absolution Alice Doane received. The innocent go to their death. Following behind them are the puritans, who, like the wizard, conspired in the event. "Villains" and "lunatics," their corporate evil is embodied by Cotton Mather whom the hearers mistake "for the visible presence of the fiend himself..." (138). Hawthorne has so mingled his historical and symbolical modes that they appear as one. And, as in the Leonard Doane story, the climax occurs when there is a confrontation with either the symbols of death, or death itself. Death becomes the great undeceiver. That is why the girls break down just as the narrator is about to describe the hangings. The artist's vision has brought them to the gallows, but cannot protect them from the terror of its reality. Unlike the fiction of the gothic tale, the hangings actually took place. The girls' defenses break down and a true consciousness of suffering and historical reality invades them. The narrator is triumphant: "I had reached the seldom trodden places of their hearts, and found the wellspring of their tears. And now the past had done all it could" (139).

Having accomplished his task, the artist can now savor his "victory" (139). For while there may be no absolution for the puritans who executed the innocent, history, as seen through an artist's vision, can provide an appeal for those who need absolution because they felt no "sympathy" with the afflicted communities of the past. History can be redemptive. That, indeed, is its greatest function, Hawthorne is saying, "while the human heart has one infirmity that may result in crime" (139). Clearly, the entire story is more a vehicle for Hawthorne's appeal to his countrymen's hearts than it is Alice's. And certainly, one important aspect of the narrator's success within the story is that the girls can now see why a monument should be placed on Gallows Hill. It will assist "the imagination in appealing to the heart" (139). The relationship between the imagination and heart, is, of course, a constant theme and concern of Hawthorne's. "Alice Doane's Appeal" is one of his most explicit treatments of this relationship. But the story also informs us that he was well aware that the "Imaginary" has its limitations without the presence of the "Actual."[15] The Leonard Doane story demonstrates that gothic passion and fantasy by themselves cannot easily touch the "seldom trodden places" of the human heart, despite being rooted in questions of human guilt. But link the fantasy to a base which is historically and humanly "real," however romanticized, and the artist will stand a better chance to humanize his reader, and, by extension, the community of which he is a part. The loneliness and isolation which describe Alice's and Leonard's final destinies, must be replaced by a more positive vision:

> We slowly descended, watching the lights as they twinkled gradually through the town, and listening to the distant mirth of boys at play, and to the voice of a young girl warbling somewhere in the dusk, a pleasant sound to wanderers from old witch times (139).

They return home, having grasped the moral meaning of their relationship to the past and the world they live in.

Hofstra University

¹See G. P. Lathrop, *A Study of Hawthorne* (Boston, 1876), p. 135, for an account of this event. Also, H. H. Waggoner, "Hawthorne's Beginning: 'Alice Doane's Appeal,' " *University of Kansas City Review*, 16 (Summer, 1950), 254-5. Elizabeth, Hawthorne's sister, in all likelihood was the one who saved the manuscript which was then revised, perhaps twice, before publication.

²"Hawthorne's 'Alice Doane's Appeal,'" *Nineteenth-Century Fiction*, 9 (December, 1955), 232.

³*Ibid.*, 236.

⁴*The Sins of the Fathers: Hawthorne's Psychological Themes* (New York: Oxford Univ. Press, 1966), p. 48

⁵*Nathaniel Hawthorne: An Introduction and Interpretation* (New York: Barnes & Noble, 1961), p. 16

⁶*Ibid.*

⁷In the "Appendix," in *Nathaniel Hawthorne: Selected Tales and Sketches*, Introduction by Hyatt H. Waggoner, 3rd ed. (San Francisco: Rinehart Press, 1970), p. 616. Also see Waggoner's *Hawthorne: A Critical Study* (Cambridge, Mass.: Harvard Univ. Press, 1955), pp. 40-45. Waggoner is one of the few critics to treat the story as an important attempt by Hawthorne to use the past as a way of appealing to the "heart." However, my analysis, though in general agreement with this point, is an attempt to reveal the inner structure of the tale and to explore certain thematic tensions (e.g., Art vs. History) and patterns not touched upon by Waggoner or other critics. But also see Robert H. Fossum's *Hawthorne's Inviolable Circle: The Problem of Time* (De Land, Fla., Everett/Edwards, Inc., 1972), pp. 13-22, who does give a structural analysis of the story in some points close to mine, but with some very basic differences in critical emphasis.

⁸Jean Normand perceives this in his study, *Nathaniel Hawthorne: An Approach to an Analysis of Artistic Creation*, trans. from the French by Derek Coltman (Cleveland: Case Western Reserve Univ. Press, 1970), p. 191: "Nor could the stories of Ilbrahim, Alice Doane, Hester Prynne, and the Pyncheons ever wipe out the abominable deaths of Giles Corey and Martha Hunt. They simply effect an esthetic and emotional conversion capable of touching the hearts of those now alive." This is beautifully said, but unfortunately it is not Normand's purpose to give extended structural criticism of these stories to show just how it is accomplished. And F. O. Matthiessen in his *American Renaissance* (New York: Oxford Univ. Press, 1941), p. 345, also points to Hawthorne's profound concern with emotional life. He quotes Hawthorne: "We are not endowed with real life...till the heart is touched. That touch creates us—then we begin to be." Matthiessen then cites "The Maypole of Merrymount" (1829) as a story exemplifying this belief. But the examples can be multiplied.

⁹From Choate's "The Importance of Illustrating New-England History by a Series of Romances like the Waverly Novels. Delivered at Salem, 1833," quoted in *Hawthorne: Tales of His Native Land*, ed. N. F. Doubleday (Boston: D. C. Heath, 1962), p. 134. We do not know if Hawthorne actually heard the address, but if he had, he certainly would have disagreed on this point at least.

¹⁰"Alice Doane's Appeal" in *Nathaniel Hawthorne: Selected Tales and Sketches*, Introduction by Hyatt H. Waggoner 3rd ed. (San Francisco: Rinehart Press, 1970). Unless otherwise noted, all references to the story will be from this edition and included in the body of my text.

¹¹It is possible that George Bancroft, whose first volume of his *The History of the United States from the Discovery of the Continent* was published in 1834, is the historian referred to. Bancroft was one of the earliest of major American historians to treat the witch trials as an outright moral scandal and tragedy. He particularly points to Cotton Mather as the "villain" in the piece, constantly

referring to his vanity and selfishness, e.g., "He [Mather] is an example of how far selfishness, under the form of vanity and ambition, can blind the higher faculties, stupefy the judgment, and dupe consciousness itself." From Bancroft's *History of the United States*, Vol. III (Boston: Little, Brown, 1864), p. 13. But since Hawthorne did not withdraw Bancroft's first volume from the Salem Atheneum until 1837, according to Marion L. Kesselring's *Hawthorne's Reading, 1828-1850* (New York: N.Y.P.L., 1949), p.44, we do not have proof that he was alluding to this work. Yet Hawthorne *may* have read the volume when it first appeared, or at least been aware of its point of view. Hawthorne also took out Felt's *Annals of Salem* in 1837 but probably read it before then so that he may be the historian referred to. Concerning the witch trials Felt wrote: "Hapless is the land which refuses to learn wisdom from such direful calamities." It is a statement Hawthorne himself might have written. In Joseph B. Felt's *Annals of Salem*, Vol. II (Boston, 1849), p. 484. In any case, whether or not Hawthorne was referring to any one of these men is finally less important than his own personal identification with the function of the historian.

[12]Hawthorne's artistic and philosophical concern with history is so amply documented that extended citation here is not necessary. But indispensable is Roy Harvey Pearce's "Hawthorne and the Sense of the Past, or, The Immortality of Major Molineux," *ELH*, XXI (1954), 327-349. Though Pearce regards "Alice Doane's Appeal" as unsuccessful, he writes that we can "interpret it as an experiment in the direct communication of a sense of the past" (338). For a good analysis of the historical problems and implications in "Alice Doane's Appeal," see Michael Davitt Bell's *Hawthorne and the Historical Romance of New England* (Princeton, N.J.: Princeton Univ. Press, 1971), pp. 68-76. Bell also feels that "Alice Doane's Appeal" is not a "coherent narrative" (p. 68), but goes beyond psychoanalytical criticism in order to show that Hawthorne's purpose was "to understand psychologically how the Puritans came to be 'Puritanical,' how the noble intolerance of the fathers became the superstitious intolerance of the sons" (p. 75). He likewise sees that Leonard's state of mind is emblematic of those who condemned the "witches." Though recognizing the importance of history in the story, however, he does not touch on the problem of conversion and the function of history in effecting it. Other helpful studies on Hawthorne and history are John E. Becker, *Hawthorne's Historical Allegory* (New York: Kennikat Press, 1971), especially pp. 155-78; David Levin, "Hawthorne's Romance: the Value of Puritan History," in his *In Defense of Historical Literature* (New York: Hill and Wang, 1967), pp. 98-117; Roy Harvey Pearce, "Romance and the Study of History," in Roy Harvey Pearce, ed., *Hawthorne Centenary Essays* (Columbus: Ohio State Univ. Press, 1964), pp. 221-44; Larzer Ziff, "The Artist and Puritanism," *ibid.*, pp. 245-69; and Leo B. Levy, "'Time's Portraiture': Hawthorne's Theory of History," in *The Nathaniel Hawthorne Journal 1971* (Washington, D.C.: Microcard Editions, 1971), pp. 192-200.

[13]See, for example, *The Sins of the Fathers: Hawthorne's Psychological Themes*, pp. 46-60. Crews gives us a thorough and fascinating analysis of the story. He argues that "the chief technical feature of 'Alice Doane's Appeal,' [is] its displacement of attention from its implicit center of interest," i.e., there is "factual obfuscation as to whether Alice really committed incest," and in the "narrator's efforts to make the story palatable to his empty-headed lady friends..." (p. 53). Now Hawthorne may have tried to do this by removing from the story certain sexual portions, as Seymour L. Gross has argued (see note 2 above), provided, of course, that such sexual passages existed. But the "displacement" seems more apparent than real. For one thing, Leonard's character is immediately presented to us as "diseased" and "morbid." His

"nobility" in avenging his sister's honor is at once blatantly compromised by descriptions of his "wild" nature, even to his "empty-headed" ladies and "casual" reader (p. 54), as Crews puts it. Any reader of Hawthorne's time who was used to such gothic stories, would be able to see the rather obvious ambivalence in Leonard's motivations. In fact, the listeners do not seem affected by the sensationalism of the plot precisely *because* the situation Hawthorne presents is not dramatically or psychologically original, though it does explore dangerous ground. Indeed, that is the problem Hawthorne sets up for himself, i.e., just how to make such a story affecting. Clearly, he does it by linking it with historical guilt. But the larger problem and contest, for Hawthorne, is between "truth" and "fiction." One more point: when Leonard hears the "indubitable proofs" (132) of Alice's guilt from Walter, it is in a situation where Leonard is being deceived by the wind and the wizard's laugh (132). It becomes rather obvious even then, that Alice is innocent. That is what makes the "revelation" scene of her appeal so weak.

[14]Crews likewise sees that "Leonard Doane's murder of a man who shares his own motives is a psychological counterpart to what the New England Magistrates did in 1692" (p. 59). For Crews, Hawthorne is so filled with guilt that he has the narrator back away "in disgust" from his own story, an illustration of Hawthorne sabotaging "his efforts at moral objectivity" (p. 60). That Hawthorne was filled with guilt few would deny. But that he was deflected from moral objectivity is open to discussion. Surely he had little doubt that the witch trials were evil; and certainly, he was not alone in his moral *judgment* of the event. What Hawthorne wishes to do is make his guilt work, through art, to humanize his readers. The narrator's problems derive from his struggle to do just that, and not, I think, because his own guilt disgusts him.

[15]The distinction between the "Actual" and "Imaginary," is, of course, in "The Custom-House" sketch prefacing *The Scarlet Letter.* But for good studies on Hawthorne's esthetics and concepts of these terms, see Millicent Bell, *Hawthorne's View of the Artist* (New York: SUNY, 1962); and Marjorie J. Elder, *Nathaniel Hawthorne, Transcendental Symbolist* (Ohio Univ. Paperback, 1969), pp. 89f.

Alice Doane's Story:
An Essay on
Hawthorne and Spenser

JOHN SHROEDER

I

About Alice Doane's story, we know several interesting things: That it represents either the earliest or else one of the two earliest of Hawthorne's extant short stories. That "represents" is the appropriate word because the story which we have is a truncation—Hawthorne's abstract of an earlier story now lost. That it is unusually strong, even after abstraction, in its evidences of authorial incest fantasy and parricidal impulse.

And a fourth thing, not nearly so well known and far from so interesting as the precedent three: That the Alice Doane story is the first of Hawthorne's many Spenserian paraphrases.

To readers unfamiliar with this subject, perhaps the most helpful introductory observation I can make is that Hawthorne's Spenserian paraphrases are just like Hawthorne's paraphrase of Bunyan in "The Celestial Railroad" save that where the latter is purposefully obtruded the former are by contrivance and cunning hidden. (I shall say something later about Hawthorne's probable motives for concealing his source whenever it was Spenser.) But once they have been found and laid out, Hawthorne's Spenserian paraphrases are always exquisitely obvious. Such is the case with the Alice Doane-Leonard Doane-Walter Brome plot, which plot is an elaboration of the Archimago episode in *The Faerie Queene* (I. i. 29—I. ii. 11) with some addition from the episode immediately after, the first Duessa episode (I. ii. 12-30).

Red Crosse and Una, their adventure in the Wandering Wood prosperously concluded, were entertained by the wizard Archimago, disguised, of course, as a pious recluse. Archimago, when his weary

guests had retired to sleep, inaugerated nigromantic treacheries. He
summoned up two sprites and a False Dream; the Dream he sent to Red
Crosse, to vex the good knight's sleep with unexpected though not
absolutely unwelcome images of an Una suddenly lascivious:

> And made him dreame of loues and lustfull play,
> That nigh his manly hart did melt away,
> Bathed in wanton blis and wicked ioy...(I. i. 47)

And that Dream Archimago capped by sending a simulacrum of
Una—one of the sprites transmogrified—to Red Crosse's bed. Red
Crosse came awake out of his dream "of loues and lustfull play" only to
find what seemed to be the table already set for him:

> Lo there before his face his Lady is...(I. i. 49)

And the knight, "cleane dismayd" and "halfe enraged," "thought haue
slaine her in his fierce despight" (I. i. 50); but mastering himself, he instead diverted the False Una with courtesies and sent her away, himself to fall then back into a troubled sleep, dreaming still of "bowres,
and beds, and Ladies deare delight" (I. i. 55).

So Archimago, his first plot failed though not exactly wasted, set a
second. He called the still confused Red Crosse, again out of slumber, to
witness the False Una merrily entangled with the other sprite, to
whom Archimago had given the form of a lusty young squire,

> In wanton lust and lewd embracement:
> Which when he saw, he burnt with gealous fire,
> The eye of reason was with rage yblent,
> And would haue slaine them in his furious ire,
> But hardly was restreined of that aged sire. (I. ii. 5)

Back to bed one more time went Red Crosse, "in torment great,/And
bitter anguish of his guiltie sight." No more sleep that night: he "did his
stout heart eat,/And wast his inward gall with deepe despight,/
Yrkesome of life" (I. ii. 6). And at the first dawn, Red Crosse rode off,
deserting Una:

> Still flying from his thoughts and gealous feare;
> Will was his guide, and griefe led him astray. (I. ii. 12)

And flying so, he encountered precisely the right object—which is to
say, another knight, Sans Foy, riding along with a beautiful woman (I.
ii. 12-13). At once the two men charged at each other ("As when two
rams...Do meete"). Red Crosse slew the stranger, so purging that murderous prompting which Archimago had repressed, and the Lady he
made his own, so anticipating the eventual satisfaction of that other

urging, unacknowledged but fierce, which the Dream, and the False Una, and the phantom squire abed with the False Una, among them had raised.

My summary has been necessarily prolonged and I hope the reader has attended to it carefully, for otherwise the finer similarities between it and the Alice Doane plot will likely be missed. In the Alice Doane plot, despite the truncation, we see a clear paraphrase of the Spenserian episode. We are given (and here I put in normal order the events which Hawthorne develops from the middle outward)—we are given, I say, a brother and a sister, Leonard and Alice Doane. There are two characters additionally, one a wizard, the other Walter Brome, mysteriously Leonard's counterpart and likeness and finally revealed as Leonard's lost twin. By the wizard's design, the two young men and Alice were implicated in a web of illusion, dark passion, and death. Leonard was first made suspicious of a "secret sympathy" obtaining between Walter and Alice, which suspicion maddened him with a "distempered jealousy." "Insane hatred" kindled Leonard's heart into "a volume of hellish fire." And "it appeared, indeed, that his jealousy had grounds..." At last, Walter and Leonard met on a lonely road; and there Walter taunted Leonard with "indisputable proofs of the shame of Alice," whereupon Leonard killed him. At a trial before a great crowd of damned souls, Alice was absolved: "all the incidents were results of the machinations of the wizard, who had cunningly devised that Walter Brome should tempt his unknown sister to guilt and shame, and himself perish by the hand of his twin-brother."

So the fable is precisely Spenser's, and either plot may be expressed by the one formula: A young man is caused to disbelieve in the purity of a spotlessly pure maiden, the disbelief issuing from the machinations of a scheming wizard; the consequence is in the young man jealous rage and murderous hatred, which rage and hatred eventuate in murder done. The characters match exactly, for Una, Alice; for Red Crosse, Leonard; for Archimago, the wizard; for the sprite in the form of the lusty squire, Walter Brome. Even Spenser's device of the deceptive simulacrum is preserved, though its sex is shifted and its origin rationalized, Spenser's False Una being paralleled by Walter Brome, Leonard Doane's twin and "very counterpart."

II

The relationship which I have just demonstrated, while not to my knowledge ever shown in its full development before now, is not here indicated for the very first time. Randall Stewart foresaw its announcement with two unconnected sentences in his edition of the *Notebooks*, forty years ago. Stewart at one place derived Hawthorne's wizard from

Spenser's and at another place paired the wizard's plot against Alice with Archimago's plot against Una (Introduction, pp. 1, 1i). The correspondencies, as my parallel summations ought to show, are more numerous, more precise, more coherent, much more striking than Stewart knew: but given no more than Stewart's hint, anybody could have puzzled the whole thing out long before this.

Perhaps it was not worth puzzling out. If, anyhow, that wasn't so in earlier decades, it likely is so in this one. Articles showing the derivation from Spenserian originals of this Hawthorne short story or that Hawthorne novel, have become so numerous as to rob of all present novelty additional announcements of A Hitherto Unnoticed Spenserian Source for Hawthorne's _____. To this date, "Lady Eleanore's Mantle, "Egotism; or, The Bosom Serpent," "The Man of Adamant," "Young Goodman Brown," "Rappaccini's Daughter," the Pyncheon mansion, the forest in The Scarlet Letter, the secret chamber in Dr. Grimshawe's Secret, and a very considerable part of The Blithedale Romance, have all been tracked back to Spenserian sources. So might be "My Kinsman, Major Molineux," too; though I don't recall seeing it done yet. That of all the literary influences on Hawthorne's fiction, the Spenserian was, quantitatively, anyhow, predominant, we need no more evidence.

Concerning the meanings and significances of this circumstance, on the other hand, we could perhaps stand a little speculation, for all the source studies thus far have been unusually neglectful of that. It seems to me to be in good order, therefore, to make some comments, quietly speculative and absolutely inferential, about the importance of the Spenserian influence to Nathaniel Hawthorne, and with some special reference to that short fiction in which the influence particularly appears.

So firstly: One of the major attractions which Spenser had for Hawthorne was, I infer, the striking character of what Hawthorne would have called Spenser's Psychological Romance. For the dedicated burrower in the depths of our human nature, the Spenser of, for instance, the Red Crosse—Una—Archimago episode could not but have held an extraordinary attraction. The episode is full of the most beautiful lights on Red Crosse's human, un-allegorical nature imaginable. We can readily believe of Red Crosse that he "waking euermore did weene" Una "To be the chastest flowre, that ay did spring/On earthly braunch" (I. i. 48). It is exactly what such a high-minded, earnest, sober young fellow fresh from the country should and would consciously imagine about the modest, beautiful young maiden-in-distress whose champion the Faerie Queene herself has named him. We can believe just as readily that the lad's unconsciousness would be treacherous and unsteady and liable to incursions by unbidden images of "loues and lustfull play"; his fantasies sometimes disturbing ("Lo there before his face his Lady is"); and his reaction to what dream and fantasy together suggest to him about himself, hostile and murderous. And then there comes, additionally, the shock of what he takes for ocular evidence that—never he!—the *Maiden - is* depraved,

Which when he saw, he burnt with gealous fire.

Not, mark you, moral indignation: just raw erotic envy, the immediate result of which envy is almost a double murder. And balked of the bloody revenge he thinks he wants to take, off he runs, "still flying from his thoughts and gealous feare," only to stumble on to a virtual duplicate of that scene which torments him: another man, another beautiful lady, riding along and making love as they ride ("With faire disport and courting dalliaunce"—I. ii. 14). Our young hero has, happily, the best conscious reason in the world for fighting and killing the stranger knight—the man is a paynim, a Sans Foy. And the best conscious reason, too, for taking the stranger's lady under his own wing after—she is a Helpless Damsel. It is not much longer before the two have dismounted in a nice shady spot and begun to play the prologue to a repetition of that scene which the night before so stimulated Red Crosse's "guilty sight."

That is marvelous psychological romance and, needless to say, not anything like what Hawthorne's age ordinarily say in *The Fairie Queene.* I don't think it would be extreme if I were to suppose that in Hawthorne's age only Hawthorne saw this particular side of Spenser's art. I have never been shown, in any event, a reason to believe that Hawthorne had a fellow in this.

That Hawthorne did find in Spenser the sort of thing I am talking about is, we all understand, inference. But it is a licit inference because it was exactly to the end of writing psychological romance that Hawthorne turned Spenser's Archimago episode. Spenser's episode, as a psychological romance, is a psychological romance about such burrows of our common nature as erotic fantasizing, sexual jealousy, repression, transference, ambivalence, homocidal hatred, compulsive violence. It is for the study of exactly those same that Hawthorne in Alice Doane's story adaps Spenser's materials, his only variants being reflections of his well-known personal biases. The erotic fantasy becomes incest and the homocide becomes parricide. Simple local coloring.

And—now Secondly—the conclusion I draw from all this is that Hawthorne, *so far as the evidence shows,* learned how to write psychological romance from copying the model of Spenser. The interior narrative of "Alice Doane's Appeal" is the earliest Hawthornean psychological romance we have. It is also his first known Spenserian paraphrase. The inference, "Ergo..." is, I hope, again at once permissible, modest, and unexceptionable as an inference.

And anyhow, there is more to it than an imperfect syllogism. In the growth of Hawthorne's art of psychological romancing, Alice Doane's story is preliminary as well as primal. The Alice Doane story is the earliest extant version of a plot which in its later versions—versions not, I think, usually associated by commentators with it in the gentic line I shall propose—becomes psychological romance in its full, mature Hawthornesque form.

These two are also short-story versions—that of "My Kinsman, Major Molineux" and that of "Young Goodman Brown." These, together with the Alice Doane plot, form a group of brief psychological romances having a common intent (the dramatization of perilous unconscious states, among which figure importantly sexual guilt and parricide), a common structure (the plot of each is controlled by the terms Question, Quest, Revelation), and common devices and stage properties (journeys, illusions, visions, devils, crowds of fiends, public illuminations). These too are close Spenserian paraphrases, and these paraphrase, likewise, the Archimago-Duessa episodes.

I have been discussing a significant line of Hawthorne's development. My inference has been that the particular variety of psychological romance represented by the three plots named—which is not the only variety of his psychological romance but which is a major one—Hawthorne evolved out of Spenser to begin with and thereafter regularly drew his models for from the same, one original storehouse.

That is much to infer about the Spenserian influence and, probably, more than any writer has found cause to suggest before. It raises one other problem, this an old one, which I shall address by way of an ending.

Put the question thus: Why Spenser in particular? Why, at the end of his career, even, was Hawthorne making notes to himself about more Spenserian paraphrases ("Compare it with Spenser's Cave of Despair. Put instruments of suicide there.")? Why should Spenser bulk so in the quantitative record of Hawthorne's literary indebtednesses?

Perhaps because he was so easily hidden, so safely paraphrased. The one thing you don't want your armature to do—to put the case by way of a metaphor—is poke out through the clay figure you build around it. If Hawthorne calculated that you can hide Spenserian armatures in a tale or novel, repeatedly, with no one ever the wiser because no one ever actually reads Spenser, then Hawthorne was certainly correct all during his own lifetime and nearly so over the long pull, too.

Brown University

Hawthorne and the
English Working Class

PATRICK BRANCACCIO

In the midst of the Civil War, Nathaniel Hawthorne reworked materials from his English notebooks into a series of essays published in *The Atlantic Monthly* and collected in book form as *Our Old Home*. The essays, which in their titles and general design suggested the Irvingesque sketch, must have struck many of Hawthorne's contemporaries as strangely escapist. The controversy over Hawthorne's dedication to his old friend and political patron, Franklin Pierce, suggested, even to his friends, a lack of touch with contemporary realities.

Yet the essays have proved to be much more tough minded than they at first appeared. Hawthorne's observations and judgments of English character and society have an incisive quality that is belied by the surface tone of genteel irony. The point of view of the observer in these pieces is that of a democratic gentleman conscious of his Puritan refinement and almost mockingly insistent about the clean, sunny prosperity of his native land which, as he writes, is being torn apart by bloody civil warfare.

In the next to the last essay in *Our Old Home* this point of view begins to break down. "Outside Glimpses of English Poverty" is interesting not only for the deep sympathy Hawthorne expresses for the English poor, but also for the self-questioning the discussion reveals.

The essay is structured around a visit to an almshouse in Liverpool. The main body consists of a tour through the wards of the West Derby Workhouse. This tour is introduced by a description of the physical and moral "dirt" of life in the poor areas of Liverpool and closes with the description of a mass wedding (which Hawthorne actually observed in Manchester) of poor couples who could not afford the minister's fee for a private wedding ceremony. More than the casual assemblage of travel notes suggested by the "Outside Glimpses" of the title, the essay emerges as a meditation on poverty that ranks with Hawthorne's critically probing best. The disturbing encounter with the depths of English poverty causes Hawthorne to shift between a moral and political perspective as he searches for categories to deal with his observations.

As an American he is somewhat smugly critical of the class system that makes such rigid distinctions. Though he is attracted to the good life made possible by the privileges enjoyed by the upper classes, he is painfully aware of the price paid for it by the lower ranks. At the beginning Hawthorne conceives of these differences in the broad terms of moral allegory. The air of Liverpool, polluted with "black snow-flakes of bituminous coal," seems first not a condition of the industrial system, but a judgment of God which falls equally and inescapably on *Wealth* and *Poverty*. Hawthorne tries to dispose of it with a conventional bit of "fancy" by describing the dirt as "the foul encrustation which began to settle over and bedim all earthly things as soon as Eve had bitten the apple."[1] He is especially disturbed at the surrender of the poor to their condition: "they starve patiently, sicken patiently, die patiently, not through resignation, but a diseased flaccidity of hope."[2] He cannot believe in a rebellion of the lower classes, although he certainly suggests that the conditions merit it: "If ever they should do mischief to those above them, it will probably be by the communication of some destructive pestilence."[3] Hawthorne is driven almost to despair because he is "uninventive of remedies for the evils that force themselves upon my perception."[4] In his frustration he snatches at another allegory by asserting "the speedy necessity of a new deluge."[5] Yet he cannot conceive of the deluge as a political uprising by the lower classes who, even in the poorhouse, are haunted by fantasies of identification with aristocratic superiority.

Nevertheless, a sense of responsibility continues to nag at Hawthorne. Though there is often a condescending tone to his expressions of sympathy, and a fear of being made to appear foolish by a begging trickster, he stresses the theme of brotherhood between high and low: "the whole question of eternity is staked there. If a single one of those little ones be lost, the world is lost."[6]

Allegory proves inadequate to the insistent demands of the real sufferings he encounters. Hawthorne begins to apply to himself the very crust image he had used to describe the universal "dirt." In discussing his resistance to beggars, for example, he wonders whether "(I am) doing myself a moral mischief by exuding a strong encrustation over whatever natural sensibility I might possess."[7] And later, the crust image appears again: "There is a decorum which restrains you (unless you happen to be a police constable) from breaking through a crust of plausible respectability, even when you ascertain that there is a knave beneath it."[8] Finally, Hawthorne puts aside the moralizing and speculates on the economic reasons which help to explain the suffering in the poorhouse:

> There may come a time, even in this world, when we shall all understand that our tendency to the individual appropriation of gold and broad acres, fine houses, and such good and beautiful things that are equally enjoyable by a multitude, is but a trait of imperfectly developed intelligence, like the simpleton's cupidity of a penny.[9]

The tour of the almshouse had led through the women's ward, the children's, the laundry, the basement schoolroom, and finally through the graveyard where the poor are buried in plain wooden boxes in mass graves. The essay closes with another grim and very moving scene as Hawthorne describes a mass wedding which is held during the Easter holidays when the clergymen charged no fee for their service. Everyone thought the scene was something of a joke. The minister smiled condescendingly, and even some of the brides giggled. But Hawthorne saw nothing funny, and later describes the sumptuous wedding of an aristocratic couple who can look forward to life on a large estate. The contract prompts him to this warning:

> Is, or is not, the system wrong that gives one married pair so immense a superfluity of luxurious home, and shuts out a million others from any home whatever? One day or another, safe as they deem themselves, and safe as the hereditary temper of the people really tends to make them, the gentlemen of England will be compelled to face this question.[10]

Though the essay stresses the patient resignation of the lower classes, the potentially explosive situation of mass suffering is made clearly apparent. Hawthorne had more direct knowledge of social unrest than the details of "Outside Glimpses" make manifest.To begin with there is the incident with the ballad singer in the Liverpool streets in November of 1853, a few months after Hawthorne's arrival in England. In "Outside Glimpses" he describes the incident in general terms:

> I noticed a ballad singer going through the street hoarsely chanting some discordant strain in a provincial dialect, of which I could only make out that it addressed the sensibilities on the score of starvation.[11]

The notebook entry on which this incident is based is more precise:

> The other day, I saw a man who was reading, in a loud voice, what seemed to be an account of the late riots and loss of life in Wigan.[12]

In both cases Hawthorne notes that there was a policeman accompanying the man to prevent a disturbance. The riots in Wigan, slightly to the northeast of Liverpool, were the result of an intense labor struggle underway in Lancashire in the autumn of 1853. The weavers in nearby Preston had been locked out of their mills after asking for a pay raise, and since September 23 the coal miners had been locked out of many of the mines in the Wigan area.[13] Violence broke out on Friday evening, October 28, 1853 when a crowd of colliers and weavers, awaiting the outcome of a meeting of the mine operators to decide whether to grant a raise, learned that the raise had again been denied. After a squabble in the streets, the crowd took to smashing windows in the hotels and in some public buildings. It then surged toward the homes of some of the factory owners and smashed the windows of some half dozen "cotten spinners," two provision dealers, and a pawnbroker. The crowd dispersed when the military were brought in from a nearby town.[14]

Two companies of soldiers maintained an uneasy order over the week-end, but trouble broke out again on Monday when the mine owners attempted to use Welsh workers, brought in secretly, to work down in the pits. As anticipated, a mass of workers, accompanied by fife and drum "had without the least ceremony commenced an attack on the Sawmills, a place where engines, etc. are made for the collieries, and where the Welshmen were housed."[15] The police fired into the crowd, and about eight or nine workers were shot. The men were again dispersed by the military who arrived a half-hour later from Wigan. On Tuesday morning it was clear that the strike was over:

> It is stated that the whole of the colliers (about 150) in the employment of Messers. J. Blundell and Son, Pemberton Colliery, returned to work on Tuesday morning, at the old prices, on an understanding that they are to receive an advance of wages within a month.[16]

Such events, which Hawthorne was obviously aware of through the full and continuing accounts in the Liverpool newspapers, suggests that the suffering was not always as patient as Hawthorne suggests in his essay.

A year and a half later, the situation of the poor was brought even closer to home as riots broke out in the streets of Liverpool itself. In February of 1855, during the Crimean War, there was large scale unemployment in Liverpool. Inflation produced high prices for bread and on Monday, February 19, riots broke out in the city as crowds began to storm the shops for bread and flour. The attacks spread throughout the city, and that very evening Hawthorne attended one of the sumptuous banquets "where I ate turtle soup, salmon, woodcock, oyster, and I know not what else, and might have eaten twenty other things."[17]

Later on his way to the Newsroom, he met crowds in the streets:

> (I) found the exchange pavement and its avenues densely thronged with
> people of all manner of dirt and rags. They were waiting, I believe, for
> soup tickets, and waiting very patiently too, without outcry or distur-
> bance, or even sour looks, only patience and meekness. Well, I don't
> Know that they have a right to be impatient of starvation; but still there
> seem to be an insolence of riches and prosperity, which one day or
> another will have a downfall.[18]

Meanwhile, the newspapers claimed that the crowds attacking the
breadshops were not the industrious poor who merited public sympathy, but idlers, the lowest elements of the unemployed. *The Liverpool
Courier* blamed the trouble on the Irish immigrants, "the lower orders
of Roman Catholics in this town....the mob was not made up of
Englishmen or Protestants, as the list of prisoners in Bridewell will
show."[19] Two days later, *The Liverpool Mercury* also attempted to deny
that the riots were expression of discontent among the working classes:

> we should scarcely consider it necessary to repeat that the working
> classes of this town took no part in the disgraceful outrages which occurred
> on the eve of our last publication....Our industrious poor are suf-
> fering severely, and their patience and endurance are severely taxed, and
> though their position at present is one of great trial, their resistance as a
> class, to vicious suggestions, has been conspicuous; and as one of them is
> reported to have said, they would rather die on the pavement than
> sacrifice their honesty by associating themselves in plundering move-
> ments of an idle and dissolute crowd.[20]

Clearly, Hawthorne read these accounts and interpretations of the
riots. A couple of days after the incident following the civic banquet,
people asking for food came to his home in Rock Park, a private community in the suburbs of Liverpool. Hawthorne's description of the incident reflects his familiarity with the newspaper interpretations:

> There have been disturbances within a day or two, In liverpool, and
> shops have been broken open and robbed of bread and money; but this is
> said to have been done by idle vagabonds, not by the really hungry
> people. These last submit to starvation meekly and patiently, as if it were
> an everyday matter with them, or, at least, nothing but what lay fairly
> within their horoscope. I suppose, in fact, their stomachs have the
> physical habit that makes hunger not intolerable, because customary. If
> they had been used to a full flesh diet, their hunger would be fierce, like
> that of ravenous beasts; but now, like the eels, they are used to it.[21]

The apparent insensitivity of these last remarks may in fact be
Hawthorne's reaction against the lack of rebelliousness on the part of
the starving poor. From today's perspective, Hawthorne seems to ac-

cept the glib assurance of the newspapers that the rioters did not express the antagonism of the working classes. Moreover, like Harriet Beecher Stowe, he seems at times to feel that the poor must merit their sympathy and charity by good behavior, although he is troubled by the sense of ignoble acceptance of oppression that "good behavior" reflects.

Two years later, Hawthorne was to get an even closer look at the effects of poverty and the social system in England when his home was robbed while he was living with his family in Southport, on the coast north of Liverpool. The clouds of industrial pollution that infected the atmosphere over Liverpool proved dangerous to Sophia Hawthorne's health so that Hawthorne sent her to Portugal with Una and Rose to stay with John O'Sullivan, the former editor of *The Democratic Review* who was now U. S. Minister to Lisbon. Mrs. Hawthorne was gone from October, 1855 to June, 1856. At the end of August, 1856 Hawthorne traveled to the resort town of Southport to look for a place so that Mrs. Hawthorne could profit from the sea air.

Hawthorne rented an apartment in a lodging house kept by Miss Bramwell, at 15 Brunswick Terrace, Promenade. The Hawthornes remained in Southport, which Hawthorne never liked, from September 18, 1856 until July 20, 1857.[22] It was here that Hawthorne was visited by Melville and where they had their famous talk on the sands. *The Southport Visiter* which listed guests staying in town in its weekly columns did not record the visit of Melville since he stayed for only three nights with the Hawthornes in their apartment, but it did list the O'Sullivans who stayed in an adjoining apartment in March of 1857.[23]

The Hawthornes did figure prominently in the local news when their apartment was burglarized on the night of February 19, 1857. Hawthorne gives an account of the incident in the notebook entry dated March 1, 1857. He tended to make light of the incident, claiming that he was thankful for the excitement in the dull life at Southport. The burglars were caught, and when Hawthorne saw them in court, he was very sympathetic toward them:

> The thieves were two young men, seemingly not over twenty (James and John MacDonald, brothers, I think) terribly shabby, jail-bird like, yet intelligent of aspect, and one of them handsome. The police knew them already; and they seemed not much abashed by their position. . . . So they were committed for trial at Liverpool assizes, to be holden some time in the present month. I rather wish them to escape.[24]

Julian Hawthorne concludes his account of the affair in this light way:

> They were young fellows; and although their appearance was that of thorough rascality, they steadfastly maintained a demeanour of more than infantile innocence; and one of them was something of a wag into the bargain, so that altogether, the affair appeared vastly entertaining to

EVEN NUMBERS.

Wellington Terrace.
Let Furnished.
11 .... *Mrs Price.*
John Aughton, Esq.
Mrs John Aughton and family
18 .... *The Misses Spencer.*
Mr and Mrs Foster, Bolton
Miss Foster, do.
Miss Hollins, Manchester
28 .... *Mrs Price.*
Mr and Mrs Pateson and family, Bow...

Union Terrace.
40 .... *Mrs J. Smith.*
48 .... *Mrs. Thornton.*
(Let Furnished.)
Mr Hindson and family, Liverpool
52 .... *Miss Thornton.*
Mr Burgess, Burton, Manchester
Miss Collier, Pendleton
54 .... *Mrs. Nixon.*
58 .... *Mrs. Mee.*
Mr. Lowe, Manchester
Mr. Barlow, Salford
62 .... *Mrs. Kross.*
64 .... *Mrs. Wilkinson.*
Mrs Smalley and family, Manchester
Mrs Comber, do.
Master Comber, do.

Union Hotel.
68 .... *Mr. Sharples.*
W. Huger, London
L. H. Jones, Esq. do.
W. R. Robinson, Esq. Ashton-le-Willows
Mr Cooper, Manchester
Mrs and Miss Cooper, do.
T. Smalle...we, Esq. Blackburn
J. Whittler, Esq. do.
Mr Walmsley, Creston

Union Place.
70 .... *Mrs. Hutt...worth.*

Gore's Terrace.
76 .... *Miss Warne.*

---

7 .... *Miss Jones.*
(Let Furnished.)
T. F. Beaver, Esq. and family, Liverpool
8 .... *Miss Jones.*
(Let Furnished.)
Charles Smithies, Esq. Liverpool
Mrs Smithies and family, do.

Rutley Place.
9 .... *Mrs. Berry.*
10 .... *Mrs. H. Johnson.*

Brunswick Terrace.
13 .... *Miss Bramwell.*
(Let Furnished.)
The Hon. Nathaniel Hawthorne, Consul, Liverpool
Mrs Hawthorne and family, do.
His Excellency the Hon. J. L. O'Sullivan,
U. S. Minister at the Court of Lisbon
16 .... *The Misses Brookes.*

Abergeldie Villas.
10 .... *Mrs. Newton.*
(Let Furnished.)
Captain Mawdsley
Mrs Mawdsley and family
20 .... *Mrs. Murray.*
Mrs Goodier, Preston
Miss Goodier, do.
Thomas Goodier, Esq. do.

Minshull Cottage.
21 .... *Mrs. Lunt.*
T. Wilson, Esq. Stanley, near Liverpool
Mrs Wilson, do.
Miss Wilson, do.
Miss J. Wilson, do.
Mrs and Miss Watson, Liverpool
Mrs and Master Cross, do.

Marine Cottage.
22 .... *Mrs. Smalley.*

Montague Cottage.
23 .... *Mrs. Edge.*
Thos. Guest, Esq. Cheetham Hill, Manchr
Mrs Guest, do.

---

6 .... *Mrs. H. Baker.*
7 .... *Mrs. Jump.*
8 .... *Mrs. E. Jump.*
9 .... *Mrs. Wm. Howard.*
10 .... *Mrs. Watson.*
11 .... *Mrs. Jeans.*
(Let Furnished.)
12 .... *Mrs. Riggs.*
13 .... *Mrs. Bowden.*
14 .... *Miss Tillotson.*
Miss Sergent, Green Hill, Edgeley
Miss M. I. Sladdon, do.

Crown Inn.
15 .... *Mrs. Roper.*
16 .... *Mrs. Kershaw.*

KING STREET.
Beech House.
1 .... *Mrs. Kay.*

Sandhill Cottages.
3 .... *Mrs. Mahr.*

Portico Cottage.
5 .... *Mrs. Duxfield.*

Cannon Cottages.
7 .... *Mrs. Howard.*
9 .... *Mrs. John Wood.*

NEVILL-STREET.
ODD NUMBERS.

Trafalgar House.
3 .... *Mr. W. Mercer.*

Samuel's Place.
7 .... *Mrs. Mecksom.*

Hampson's Terrace.
13 .... *Mrs. Fisher.*
17 .... *Mrs. Dixon.*
Mr Anderson, Manchester
Mr Middlewood, do.
Mr and Mrs Carter, Liverpool
Mr and Mrs Astonall, Blackburn
Mrs Hartley, do.
Mr Ramsden, Bolton

Burscough Villa.
28 .... *Mrs. Mchagan.*
29 .... *Mrs. Isherwood.*
30 .... *Mrs. Spencer.*
Mr and Mrs Widdows and family, Rock Ferry

Yew Tree Villa.
32.
Mr and Mrs Wright and family, Old Trafford, Manchester

UNION-STREET.
ODD NUMBERS.
3 .... *Mrs. Mckagan.*
9 .... *Mrs. Jones.*
11 .... *Mrs. Randle.*

Beech Hill.
15 .... *Mrs. Jones.*

EVEN NUMBERS.
2 .... *Mrs. Leadbeater.*
4 .... *Mrs. Blewin.*
Mr T. Cooper, Huddersfield
10 .... *Mrs. N. Wetherby.*
12 .... *Mrs. T. Ball.*
14 .... *Mrs. A. Ball.*
20 .... *Mrs. M. Ball.*

Union Cottages.
24 .... *Mrs. Sharples.*
26 .... *Mrs. Sturgess.*
Mrs Schofield, Mossley
Master Schofield, do.

Fleetwood Terrace.
28 .... *Mrs. Darbyshire.*
32 .... *Mrs. Edge.*
34 .... *The Misses Nixon.*

CASTLE STREET.
Ivy Grove.
1 .... *Mrs. Blake.*
2 .... *Mrs. Brown.*
3 .... *Mrs. Corlett.*

Apsley Terrace.

the younger members of the Consul's family. But the thieves got five and ten years respectively, which was probably no joke to them.[25]

It was even less of a joke than Julian suspected for his memory of the sentence for the MacDonald brothers was not accurate. *The Southport Visiter* reported that while the younger brother, James MacDonald received a one year sentence, his brother John was sentenced to prison for life.

It is clear from the above evidence that Hawthorne had accumulated enough experience of the English working classes to get a pretty fair view of their condition. His sympathy was a mixture of democratic indignation at the sight of such glaring class differences, impatience with the apparent resignation of the poor, counteracted by a genteel restraint in his concern for the "great unwashed." He continually seemed to raise the question, will the working classes revolt? And at times he seemed disappointed that the answer was such a clear "no." But he saw the system crumbling from within. The poor performance of the British in the Crimean War convinced him that aristocratic institutions would not survive and that the day of English dominance in the world had passed.

Colby College

Appendix — Burglary at Hawthorne's Home in Southport

The Southport Visiter, Thursday Afternoon, February 19, 1857, p. 5, Column 2, Local and District News

Burglary—Last night, a desperate burglary was committed at Miss Bramwell's, Brunswick Terrace, Promenade. The house is at present let furnished to the Hon. Nathaniel Hawthorne. The burglars entered at a back window which they had broken, and ransacked the lower part of the house evidently in search of the plate. Some small silver articles were missed, and a papeterie box; but the thieves fortunately missed a large box of silver which was in one of the rooms. The police are on the scent.

The Southport Visiter, Thursday Afternoon, February 26, 1857, p. 5, Column 4, "Burglary on the Promenade."

Last week, we gave a short account of a burglary which had been committed on the premises Brunswick-terrace, 15, Promenade, at present oc-

cupied by the Hon. Nathaniel Hawthorne, the American Counsul at
Liverpool. Intelligence of the facts, with a description of the principal articles missing, was forwarded to Liverpool and other places, and on
Saturday two stout young fellows, said to be notorious thieves, were apprehended under very suspicious circumstances, which will be found
detailed in the evidence subjoined. The prisoners, who are brothers, and
are named James and John Macdonald, were brought before the Liverpool magistrates on Monday, and in due course were handed over for
examination before the county magistrates for this district. On Tuesday,
they were brought up at the Town Hall. The magistrates present
were—Samuel Lees, Esq., J. H. Wrigley, Esq., James Glover, Esq., the Rev.
Jonathan Jackson, and Thomas Ridgway Bridson, Esq. The court room
was crowded throughout the whole of the proceedings, a case of veritable
burglary being happily a rare event in Southport.

The prisoners were placed in the dock, and informed that they were
charged with having burglariously entered the premises mentioned
above, and stolen therein a quantity of articles, the property of the Hon.
Nathaniel Hawthorne and others. The first witness called was—

Emily Hearn, a servant in the family, who stated that on the morning
of the 19th of February, when she got up, she found the side window
open, and the centre bottom square of the top sash broken. She went into
the kitchen, the door of which was open, and found all the drawers out,
and the cupboard door open, the whole having evidently been ransacked. The house maid came downstairs immediately after, and ran to
the window and got the master's hat, which was lying outside on the cill
(sic). Both of them then went towards the dining room. They found the
hall door open, and witness had heard the housemaid lock the door on
the previous night, after ten o'clock. She then missed her master's coat
from the tree in the hall. In the dining-room she found Mrs. Hawthorne's
box ransacked, and the mistress's workbox was moved on to the chair
near the door. She then missed two silver cups, one marked "Una," and
the other with no mark upon it, an electro-plate fork, marked "N.H.," a
silver salt spoon, a silver toast rack, a pair of Wellington
boots, a wooly jacket belonging to her mistress, a small brown jacket
worn by a baby, a shepherd's scarf, a quantity of buttons, a pair of
goloshes, and a piece of mutton, the whole of which belonged to her
master. There were also missing a papeterie box belonging to Miss
Brown, the governess, and a plated toast rack belonging to Miss Bramwell. She knew the coat produced to be her master's property, as also the
boots. About two or three hours before she got up in the morning, she
heard a noise: but thinking that it was the house maid getting up to light
the baby's fire she took no further notice of it—Cross-examined by the
prisoner James: She knew the boots from their general appearance, and
from having cleaned them herself many times. She had seen the thimble
and pencil case many times; her mistress had made them a present to the
housemaid.

Mary Sumner, the housemaid, remembered the night of the 18th of
February. She generally locked the front hall door and the side door. She
got up at twenty minutes to seven on the following morning. Two or
three hours before that she heard a sort of rummaging noise in the lower
part of the house; she went to the top of the stairs, but hearing nothing
more, she went to bed again. The rosewood box produced she identified
as belonging to Miss Bramwell, and the papeterie box also produced as

...ENCE.

ELLESMERE

...ave to announce
...d distinguished
...re paroxysms of
...ploms indicated
...ated by disease.
...arl left Worsley
...e the benefit of
...nowledge, skill,
...y sunk, and ex-
...welve o'clock at
...water House,
...ted a few years
...lery of pictures,
...gerton, was the
...ion dating from
...ount Bruckle..
...Duke of Suther
...eth, Countess of
...Lord Ellesmere
...ndon, in 180.
...year, He ma
...ter of Charl
...d daughter ma
...ortland, Lord
...land, Oxford
...lassics, in 182
...of Egerton, i
...on-Gower. O
...nly last year, the
...of the count
...be remember
...ng her visit t
...(with her roy
...and Countess o
...he peerages of
...st acquired by
...descendant re
...er. The estate
...nis nephew, the
...revival of these
...ministry in 1846.
...succeeded in his
...orge Granville
...y, He was born
...d, in 1810, the

that he was little better than a *gobe mouche.* Mr. Disraeli is a good enough Christian to "hold animosity" and he will certainly watch for the opportunity of annoying the man who has so little fear of him as Palmerston has shown. The "*judicium Paridis spretaeque injuria formæ*" were mere trifles compared with the indignity that Derby's Chancellor of the Exchequer has suffered at the hands of Palmerston.

WESLEYAN CHORAL MEETING.

The annual tea meeting in connection with the choir of the Wesleyan Chapel, Hoghton-street, was held on Monday evening last in the school-room adjoining that place of worship. There was a good attendance, and of the provision made it is almost superfluous to say that it was abundant and excellent, the tea, as was facetiously remarked, being decidedly "stronger of the caddy than of the kettle." After tea, the party adjourned to the chapel, where the efficient choir, who we sing several well chosen anthems, had the assistance of the splendid organ.

The hymn, commencing with the words,

"Come let us join our cheerful songs,"

having been sung, the Rev. J. D. BROCKLEHURST read the 149th and 150th Psalm, and the Rev. NEVISON LORAINE, of Waterloo, engaged in prayer.

The Rev. J. D. BROCKLEHURST then said that it afforded him great pleasure to inform the meeting that Dr. Wood had most promptly and cordially accepted an invitation to take the chair on this occasion. It would promote, he was sure, the harmony of this choral meeting to see him in his right position, and he would at once request him to take it.—(Cheers.)

Dr. WOOD—There are, my Christian friends, several circumstances which combine together to render these annual festivals full of interest and delight. One is, the power of tea—and its magic wonders none can tell. (Laughter.) I don't know whether the Chinese themselves drink much tea; but if they do they ought to be more civil and good tempered; for we find them to be the very churlish race.—(Hear.) Another is, the power of music, which delights our ears, calms the mind, expands the sympathies, and moves our hearts. Another is, the eloquence which is manifested by our various friends who come to help us—given us in every effect, and variety to gratify our taste, expand our intellect, and ennoble our hearts. Another is, the power of hope—and, perhaps, this is the secret, the soul and spring of our joy and delight in meeting together; because we know that these meetings on earth are but anticipatory of that grand, and final, and eternal meeting which we hope to have in our Father's house above, the palace of angels and of God. We meet on earth, and all may God grant, for his dear Son's sake, that we may all meet—in the mansions of the redeemed—in heaven. We sing on earth the songs of Zion, in the hope that we may sing in heaven the song of Moses and the Lamb.

Oh may we some humble part
In that immortal song?
Wonder and joy shall tune our heart,

Local and District News.

The following commissions have been signed by the lord-lieutenant:—3rd Regiment of the Duke of Lancaster's Own Militia—J. R. Pedder, Esq., to be captain, vice De Trafford, resigned; Ensign R. Blackmore, jun., to be lieutenant, vice Pedder, promoted.

A RARE EGG.—An enormous goose egg has been forwarded to our office, bearing the following inscription:—"This egg was laid by Old Granny Goose, aged 30 years, at Mawdsley Hall, on the 4th of February, 1857."

...OF THE SOUTHPORT VISITER by Mrs. Fye.

BURGLARY.—Last night, a desperate burglary was committed at Miss Branwell's, Brunswick Terrace, Promenade. The house is at present let furnished to the Hon. Nathaniel Hawthorne. The burglars entered at a back window which they had broken, and ransacked the lower part of the house evidently in search of the plate. Some small silver articles were missed, and a papeterie box; but the thieves fortunately missed a large box of silver which was in one of the rooms. The police are on the scent.

talented family surprised and delighted a Southport audience by their matchless performances; thus enabling us to endorse the high opinion expressed of them in other places which they have visited. The Town Hall was well filled by a fashionable audience. We are glad to find that they intend to repeat their visit on Saturday next, when two more concerts with many additional attractions are to be given. We are told that the playing of Mdlle. Bertha on the violin gains on you on a second or third hearing, there is some thing so sterling about it; and her face and ex-

Who had not felt this when listening to the soft tone of mellifluous voices blended with the sweet sounds of the finely-toned organ or harp, and observed the power to thrill with rapture the listening multitude, or to soothe into delicious sentimentalism, or pleasing melancholy, friends associated together in interchange of sentiment and feeling! The worthiest use to be made of melodious human voices and musical instruments was when they were appropriated to the celebration of Christian sentiment.—(Applause.) Worthy was the Divine Being, equally on account of the transcendant glories and perfections of his nature and the unfailing benevolence which he exemplifies to the children of men,—worthy was the Divine Being to whatever homage and thanksgiving they could bring before the throne. It was beautifully illustrative of the Divine condescension that, while all heaven was reverberating with mighty hallelujahs from numbers without number of "blest voices uttering joy," it was delightful to remember that God did not despise the meanest song chanted to Him from human voices; and, for their encouragement to engage in exercise of this description, He said to every one of them, whenever they approached Him, "Let me hear thy voice; for it is pleasant unto me." "Whoso offereth praise glorifieth God." They ought to be constantly prepared in the disposition of their minds for this delightful occupation. Mere melody of sound was not acceptable to the Divine Being; and they should discipline themselves into a capability of singing with the spirit and with the understanding also. In all their devotional exercises, sound should be subordinated to sentiment; and he maintained that church music did not answer its designed end, except it was employed to render more interesting and attractive, and to supply a more impressive and emphatic conveyance to religious sentiment. It might be extreme in the opinions he entertained; but he confessed that it seemed to him little less than profanation, when the distinct enunciation of the sentiment was lost in the commingling sounds, however scientific. At the same time fervour of devotion did not require that there should be what was slovenly and careless in their vocal performances. He did not think that the worship of Almighty God was acceptable in proportion to the voicelessness of sound. The worship of the sanctuary should not be after a fashion as if they meant to frighten away a certain, wil being...—(Laughter.) As to the incentive to appropriate and fervid utterance of adoration, the Divine goodness was so exuberantly, variously, and unfailingly exemplified towards them that they must feel that there was no hyperbole in the sentiment of the poet, when

...dious strains on ea
in the dust? Th
gentlemen) more
ciate. I would
spiritual world—t
stantly in that reg
that we are more
which are unseen
been expressed, if
of rhyme:—

But who are the
Falls like a sunt
O! they are hus
Who once beneat
But now escaped
Tread the brigh
Yet have to ling
Where first they
On wings of fait

O! they are the
With zeal forth
Whose glistenin
Jerusalem! thy
Thy sacred gate
I'll heard thy j...
Then cleave the...

With cheru
Seraphic ch
Celestial joy

A cloud of witn
A diadem'd titl

And urge us t
To lead th' trop
To spill the foe,
And with th...
(Loud applause.)

The Rev. N. Lo meeting. After a position," in which after the genial an Father Phillips, th had rolled forth ornamented the a the scientific and and learned disco that the man who "Speeches on all made to order,"— way in not beco were called upon sorts of platform Persons who thou him in quest of belonging to the governess. She had seen the coat the night before in the front hall. The pencil case and thimble belonged to her. She had used the thimble and had seen the pencil case the night before—Cross examined: Knew both the thimble and the pencil case well, and could swear to their being her's.

Prisoner James said he had bought a dozen thimbles at 2-1/2d. a-piece, and the pencil-case he had bought for 4s.

Jane Bramwell, the original tenant of the house, said she had let the house furnished to the Hon. Nathaniel Hawthorne. She left in the house a rosewood box, in which there was a pair of gold earrings old and much worn, a pair of gold earrings with drops, and a gold wedding ring rather thin, a feather fan of various colours, a bone fan painted, a bone needle case, a twopenny piece in copper, a guard fastener in the form of a hand, a large-sized common pin, and a number of letters from one correspondent. Hearing of the robbery on Thursday, she went to the house, and found the box missing. The two fans produced were her property.

A plaid scarf was also produced. It had been cut in two, but it was also identified as the property of Mr. Hawthorne. Emily Hearn said she knew it from having seen it many times.

Prisoner James—Oh yes; you may swear to a lamp-post by seeing it many times, if you swear only by appearances.

James Howe, a general dealer, residing at a No. 8, Fontenoy-street; Liverpool—I received information of this robbery on Friday morning last. On Saturday night, about eight o'clock, a person came to my shop. I had known him for three or four years; he was a tailor by trade. He offered for sale an overcoat, for which he asked 20s. I asked him where he got it, and he told me that it belonged to a young man who was outside, who had asked him to sell it for him. He called in the prisoner James Macdonald, and when he came in I asked him, was it his coat? He said it was. I asked him, was it his own wear? He told me no; he had exchanged jewelry for it the other side of London (sic)—I do not know the name of the town he mentioned. I then sent for P. C. Steadman, and gave the prisoner into custody.

William Laycock, detective-officer of the borough of Liverpool—About 8 o'clock on Saturday evening last, James Macdonald was brought to the central police office by P. C. Richard Steadman. I asked the prisoner where he got the coat from, and he stated that he had got them from a young man named John Macdonald. On further enquiry, he said that this John Macdonald lived in Stockdale-street. I went to the house in company with P. C. Steadman and James Macdonald. James there pointed out John as the man from whom he had bought the coat. I then asked John how he accounted for the coat that he had sold to the prisoner James. He replied, "I never did sell him a coat; we were both together; we met a man in the street in the Park, and we bought the coat off him for 16s; but I don't know who the man is." I then searched John Macdonald. In his coat pocket I found some papers—they were several small maps. He said that they were in the coat pocket when he bought it. I took from his neck a portion of a scarf shawl (which had been produced and identified), which he said he had bought, but did not state where. I then searched a box in the same room, which the prisoners said belonged to both of them, and there I found a bundle. The prisoners said that it contained goods that they hawked. In it I found two fans, a paper knife, a pencil-case, thimble, an electro-plate fork marked "N.H." (All these ar-

esenti-
ts.

TER.

a
ench of
curring
weight,
and had
n being
in fully
ntended
"lumps"
right for
have is
d." As
profit or
maker or
public of
uty sug-
in "the
aming."
nation of
mit-elf,

DID.

r.

6, 1857
d. We
tuation,
ity and
ers and
umbel-

amendment, which appears to have enlisted a good deal of favour on its side.

We have again been startled by one of those horrible catastrophes in connection with coal mines that every now and then occur. This one took place at what is called the Lund Hill Colliery, on the South Yorkshire Railway, and there is reason to fear that 170 lives have been lost. The violence of the explosion shook the earth for two or three miles round, and the flames at one time ascended to the height of 50 or 60 feet above the chimney. After the accident everything seems to have been done that vigour or science could suggest, but there is not the slightest hope of any one being left alive to think that as many as nineteen were rescued from the very jaws of death; but, as I say, there is no hope of any more being saved.

LESSONS FOR SUNDAY, MARCH 1.
FIRST SUNDAY IN LENT

MORNING—1st Lesson—Gen. 19; 2nd Lesson—Luke 12
EVENING—1st Lesson—Gen. 22; 2nd Lesson—Eph. 6

Local and District News.

A WIFE HUNTER.—A clever trap has been set by some of the "lads of the village," for an advertiser in search of a wife. The disinterested lover arrived in town this (Thursday) morning, and has afforded much amusement to a host of tormentors, who have supplied the place of his expected inammorata. We have no time for detail, which are very amusing, this week.

CROSSENS CHURCH.—While it is a christian duty to take every care of the temporal and spiritual welfare of all mankind, we should take care that our charity is not always telescopic. An appeal is to be made to the inhabitants of Southport next Sunday, to heat, paint, and repair the neighbouring church of Crossens. "Whose hath this world's goods, and seeth his brother have need," &c.

DRILLING.—Those who have observed the ready transformation which good drilling can make from the raw country clown to the smart-stepping soldier, must acknowledge the advantages in gait and carriage to be gained from a good system of physical training. Drilling now forms a part of the education of our public schools; and we draw attention to an advertisement in another column...

BURGLARY ON THE PROMENADE.

Last week, we gave a short account of a burglary which had been committed on the premises Brunswick-terrace, 15, Promenade, at present occupied by the Hon. Nathaniel Hawthorne, the American consul at Liverpool. Intelligence of the facts, with a description of the principal articles missing, was forwarded to Liverpool and other places, and on Saturday two stout young fellows, said to be notorious thieves, were apprehended under very suspicious circumstances, which will be found detailed in the evidence subjoined. The prisoners, who are brothers, and are named James and John Macdonald, were brought before the Liverpool magistrates on Monday, and in due course were handed over for examination before the county magistrates acting for this district. On Tuesday, they were brought up at the Town Hall. The magistrates present were—Samuel Lees, Esq., J. H. Wrigley, Esq., James Glover, Esq., the Rev. Jonathan Jackson, and Thomas Ridgway Bridson, Esq. The court room was crowded throughout the whole of the proceedings, a case of veritable burglary being happily a rare event in Southport.

The prisoners were placed in the dock, and informed that they were charged with having burglariously entered the premises mentioned above, and stolen therein a quantity of articles, the property of the Hon. Nathaniel Hawthorne and others. The first witness called was—

Emily Hearn, a servant in the family, who stated that on the morning of the 19th of February, when she got up, she found the side window open, and the centre bottom square of the top sash broken. She went into the kitchen, the door of which was open, and found all the drawers pulled out, and the cupboard door open, the whole having evidently been ransacked. The housemaid came down stairs immediately after, and ran to the window and got the master's h t, which was lying outside on the cill. Both of them then went towards the dining room. They found the hall door open, and witness had heard the housemaid lock the door on the previous night, about ten o'clock. She then missed her master's coat from the tree in the hall. In the dining-room, she found

[All these articles, with the exception of the paper-knife, had been identified.] I also found two steels in the bundle. The mark on the plate of the lock on the papeterie box, appears as if it had been forced open by such an instrument. Prisoner James said that he bought the steels at Mr. Stewards, of Paradise-street, at half-past eight on Friday night, and he hoped the gentleman—he did not know what they called his business (meaning the detective)—would call there, and find out if it was not true.—Laycock : I intend doing so.— Prisoner: Thank you, sir.—Prisoner was proceeding to argue that steels bought only on Friday could not have been used by them in a robbery committed on Wednesday, but he was informed that an opportunity would be afforded for making a statement.

P.C. Steadman confirmed the evidence of the previous witness, and added that at the Main Bridewell he took from James Macdonald a portion of a scarf shawl, which corresponded with another portion found by Laycock on the other prisoner. He also found on James Macdonald's feet a pair of Wellington boots, which he said he had bought in London.

P.C. Joseph Wood stated that on Sunday, the 22nd of February, he was on duty in Southport. From what a gentleman said to him he went along the shore in the direction of Liverpool. About a mile and a quarter from Southport he searched in the sandhills and found there a rosewood box and a small papeterie box, both of which were broken. [These boxes had been identified.] The papeterie box seemed to have been broken open with some blunt instrument. There were also several papers and letters lying about, which he gathered up and brought with him.

Richard Pickering, jun., assistant at the Birkdale station of the Lancashire and Yorkshire Railway, stated that on the afternoon of Wednesday, the 18th of February, just after the half-past three train from Liverpool had left the station, he saw two persons whom he now recognised as the prisoners. One of them was looking at a notice board, and the other asked of witness the road to Southport. He had never seen them since until this morning, when he picked them out from three others.—Prisoners tried to intimidate this ticles with the exception of the paper-knife, had been identified.) I also found two steels in the bundle. The mark on the plate of the lock on the papeterie box, appears as if it had been forced open by such an instrument—Prisoner James said that he bought the steels at Mr. Stewards, of Paradise-street, a half-past eight on Friday night, and he hoped the genteleman—he did not know what they called his business (meaning the detective)—would call there and find out if it was not true—Laycock: I intend doing so. Prisoner: Thank you, sir—Prisoner was proceeding to argue that steels bought only on Friday could not have been used by them in a robbery committed on Wednesday, but he was informed that an opportunity would be offered for making a statement.

P. C. Steadman confirmed the evidence of the previous witness, and added that at the Main Bridewell, he took from James Macdonald a portion of a scarf shawl which corresponded with another portion found by Laycock on the other prisoner. He also found on James Macdonald's feet a pair of Wellington boots, which he said he had bought in London.

P. C. Joseph Wood stated that on Sunday, the 22nd of February, he was on duty in Southport, From what a gentleman said to him he went along the shore in the direction of Liverpool. About a mile and a quarter from Southport he searched in the sandhills and found there a rosewood box and a small papeterie box, both of which were broken. (These boxes had been identified). The papeterie box seemed to have been broken open with some blunt instrument. There were also several papers and letters lying about, which he gathered up and brought with him.

Richard Perking, jun., assistant at the Birkdale stations of the Lancashire and Yorkshire Railway, stated that on the afternoon of Wednesday, the 18th of February, just after the half-past three train from Liverpool had left the station, he saw two person whom he now recognized as the prisoners. One of them was looking at a notice board, and the other asked of witness the road to Southport. He had never seen them since until this morning, when he picked them out from three others—Prisoners tried to intimidate this witness by accusing him of fake swearing, by asking him if "he knew the contents of an oath," &c., but he adhered to his positive identification and supported it by a statement that he had observed a tear on the back of James's coat, and that one of them carried a bundle.

Peter Pickup, a greengrocer, living at No. 47, Upper King-street, Southport, stated that he kept a stall in the pedler's market. Between three and four o'clock on Wednesday afternoon, the 18th instant, he saw the two prisoners. They came to his stall in the market. The one with the black head (both had dark hair, but John, whom the witness meant, was considerably the darker) asked him who took in lodgers. Witness asked them what they were? The same man said that they were jewellers, and that they had come here to stop for a month or six weeks. He asked them where their boxes were, and they said that they had left them in a back street. He then directed them where they might find his own house.

James—Did ye hear me speak?

Witness—Yes, and your speech now betrays you.

James—Ye ought to be a philosopher, to tell a man by his spache. (Laughter.)

The prisoner here whiningly said it was a shame to make a laughing stock of innocent men, and to make them stand in a degraded position for what they had honestly bought.

After having been cautioned, James told a long tale about where he had bought the various articles found upon him. The boots had been bought for him in London by his sister who was housekeeper to the Earl of Shrewsbury, before she went on the continent six months ago. They could get a respectable gentleman "in the Protestant line" to prove that they were in bed when this robbery was said to have been committed.

John contended that they could not have been "prised" the box with an instrument which had not been bought until after the robbery. They were brought into a room today with three other men, to see if they could be discerned by those who had stated that they had seen them in the town before. A woman came first, and she picked out a strange man whom he did not know. Since Saturday night until now they had never been in a bed. They had only had food once since they came here, and both of them being seemingly drowsy and wearied, the boy readily picked them out from among the rest. It had also been mentioned by the same boy, that they were seen here at half-past three o'clock in the day. How could they go up and down the town, and nobody see them all day? Where did they stay all that time? He desired to know whether any person saw them knocking about. It was not a very large town seemingly—that was, so far as he had read. Had any of the policemen seen them?

Mr. Welsby (sic)—It is evident that they have not, or they would have been called.

Mr. Lees then informed the prisoners that they were committed to the assizes on the charge of burglary. His worship added that the bench highly appreciated the conduct of the witness Howe, and commended the promptitude he had shown in furthering the ends of justice. If all dealers did the same, robberies would be more easily detected, and much less frequent.

The Southport Visiter, April 2, 1857, p. 8.
"The Late Robbery on the Promenade"

John M'Donald and James M'Donald, convicted of burglary at the resident of Nathaniel Hawthorne, Esq., American Consul, were sentenced, on Tuesday last, the former to penal servitude for life, and the latter to 12 months imprisonment, with hard labour. Before sentence was passed, John M'Donald pleaded earnestly for mercy, remarking that his crimes were the result of parental neglect. When 16 years of age, he was sentenced to transportation for 10 years; he conducted himself so well that he obtained a partial remission of the sentence, but when he returned home, he could not secure employment, as the prejudices against him, on account of his previous life, were so strong.

[1]Nathaniel Hawthorne. *Our Old Home: A Series of English Sketches,* ed. by Claude M. Simpson and Roy Harvey Pearce. Columbus, Ohio: Ohio State University Press, 1970, p. 277. All subsequent references will be to this edition.
[2]*Our Old Home,* p. 289.
[3]*Ibid.*
[4]*Our Old Home,* p. 304.
[5]*Ibid.*
[6]*Our Old Home,* p. 282.
[7]*Our Old Home,* p. 292.

[8]*Our Old Home*, p. 306.

[9]*Our Old Home*, p. 309. Of course, thoughts of cupidity were especially in Hawthorne's mind, perhaps, as he looked back on his English experiences and remembered the intensity of his efforts to accumulate funds to live on in the future. In one of his letters to W.D. Ticknor, to whom he regularly sent sums of 300 pounds of consular fees to invest at home, he wrote: "Invest—invest—invest! I am in a hurry to be rich enought to get away from this dismal and forlorn hole. If I can once see $20,000 in a pile, I shan't care much for being turned out of office; and yet I ought to be a little richer than that. It won't be quite so easy for me to live on a thousand dollars, or less, as it used to be. I am getting spoilt you see." (March 3, 1854). *Letters of Hawthorne to William D. Ticknor, 1851-1864.* Newark, New Jersey, 1910. Reprinted by Microcard Editions, Washington, D.C., 1972, pp. 31-32.

[10]*Our Old Home*, p. 309.

[11]*Our Hold Home*, pp. 288-289.

[12]Nathaniel Hawthorne. *The English Notebooks*, ed. by Randal Stewart. New York: Modern Language Association of America, 1941, p. 38.

[13]*The Wigan Times*, September 23, 1853, 5.

[14]*Liverpool Mercury*, November 1, 1853, 3.

[15]*Liverpool Mercury*, November 1, 1853, second edition, 5.

[16]*Liverpool Mercury*, November 4, 1853, 15.

[17]Hawthorne, *The English Notebooks*, p. 103.

[18]Hawthorne, *The English Notebooks*, p. 103.

[19]*The Liverpool Courier*, February 21, 1855, 71.

[20]*The Liverpool Mercury & Supplement*, February 23, 1855, 10.

[21]Hawthorne. *The English Notebooks*, p. 104.

[22]A detailed account of Hawthorne's stay in Southport is given by F. H. Cheetham. *Nathaniel Hawthorne and Southport*, Southport, 1903. Reprinted from *The Southport Visiter*, January 6, 8, 10, 1903.

[23]*The Southport Visiter*, March 12, 1857, 4.

[24]Hawthorne, *The English Notebooks*, p. 444.

[25]Julian Hawthorne. *Nathaniel Hawthorne and His Wife*. Boston, 1888, II, 137.

English Fruits, Yankee Turnips: Another Look at Hawthorne and England

DONALD KAY

Redclyffe: "O home, my home, my forefathers' home! I have come back to thee! The wanderer has come back!"

Hawthorne: "The truth is, there is a spirit lacking in England, which *we* do not lack...."

A polydipsic interest in the American experience in Europe, particularly on the part of nineteenth-century authors, has in recent years been augmented with the appearance of such publications as Philip Rahv's *Discovery of Europe* and Nathalia Wright's *American Novelists in Italy* (Philadelphia: University of Pennsylvania Press, 1965). The principal value of various descriptions of Old World scenes by New World authors, observes Mr. Rahv, "is the attitude of the given author, his subjective response, the turns and twists of his imagination when forced to cope with the challenge of the great European world...and to the challenge it offered Americans have reacted with sharp differences among themselves...."[1] Readers of Hawthorne have long been conscious of his especial attraction to England, but they have more often than not been perplexed by the ambiguity and intricacy of the "twists and turns of his imagination when forced to cope with the challenge" on the spot.

Most Hawthorne scholars, however, have been content to make their comments as sidelights to general biographical studies of Hawthorne's years in England in 1853-57. A notable exception is Randall Stewart who, as early as 1935, published an article in *The New England Quarterly* treating Hawthorne's patriotic motives in *The English Notebooks*; and who wrote in 1941 a masterly essay (published in his edition of *The*

150

English Notebooks) entitled "Hawthorne in England," which essayed to clarify the complex subject of Hawthorne's reactions to England. His biography of Hawthorne, published in 1948, also carefully analyzes much more than Hawthorne's mere comings-and-goings in the British Isles. It is with the particular inspiration of Professor Stewart's scholarship that this study, undertaking to comment upon (once more) what attracted Hawthorne to England and what caused his often openly-critical attitude during his years there, is written.

First of all, we need to recall that Hawthorne was never satisfied with his New England ancestors and his ancestral ties with them; their hands were red with the blood of Quakers and witches, and the tradition which they passed on to their off-spring was clouded with a sense of guilt. Hawthorne longed, then, to establish a pleasant link with his ancestral past, and to do so he was ultimately carried to the Old England his ancestors had left in 1635.[2] Hawthorne's discontent, his yearning for hereditary connections, and his longing for a wealth of "good" in his past is accurately summarized in these words spoken by Redclyffe (as Hawthorne's voice) in *Doctor Grimshawe's Secret:*

> "If you know anything of me, you know how . . . I was alone; how I grew up without a root, yet continually longing for one,—longing to be connected with somebody, and never finding myself so. Yet there was ever a looking forward to this time at which I now find myself [in England]. If my next step were death, yet while the path seemed to lead toward a certainty of establishing me in connection with my race, I would take it. I have tried to keep down this yearning, to stifle it, annihilate it, by making a position for myself, by being my own fact; but I cannot overcome the natural horror of being a creature floating in the air, attached to nothing; ever this feeling that there is no reality in the life and fortunes, good or bad, of a being so unconnected."[3]

The feeling of jubilation felt by Redclyffe upon arriving in England surely parallels Hawthorne's emotions: "Oh home, my home, my forefathers' home! I have come back to thee! The wanderer has come back!"[4]

When Hawthorne retraced the footsteps of his ancestors it was not with any sense of going to a foreign land or a strange country. England to him was Mother England, "Our Old Home." In *Our Old Home* he expresses his idea that America is but an extension of roots under the sea from the old tree of England:

> When our forefathers left the old home, they pulled up many of their roots, but trailed along with them others, which were never snapt asunder by the tug of such a lengthening distance, nor have been torn out of the original soil by the violence of subsequent struggles, nor severed by the edge of the sword.[5]

Indeed Edward Mather suggests that one of Hawthorne's motives for going to Europe was to find evidences of new life in these roots,[6] but, if this is true, Hawthorne looked in strange places—graveyards, old cathedrals, and ancient estates. It is most likely, or at least the evidence seems to indicate, that Edward H. Davidson's conclusion that "he was interested only in a country which might give him a vivid sense of the past and England was able to perform this service for him" is closer to the truth.[7] However, Mr. Davidson's statement fails to say that Hawthorne was interested not just in "the past," but in *his* past, his ancestral home, which was necessarily an English past. Hawthorne was primarily attracted to England, then, from a personal sense of past history; he was first of all concerned with the past not for the past's sake alone but because of the connection it had with his being. (For the most past, to be sure, this same feeling was presumably prevalent in the majority of New Englanders, since English settlements were plentiful there from 1620 on.) Arriving in England, Redclyffe in *Doctor Grimshawe's Secret* reveals the identical close association which Hawthorne himself felt with England:

> ...he began to feel the deep yearning which a sensitive American—his mind full of English thoughts, his imagination of English poetry, his heart of English character and sentiment—cannot fail to be influenced by,—the yearning of the blood within his veins for that from which it has been estranged; the half-fanciful regret that he should ever have been separated from...these habits of life and thought which...he still perceives to have remained in some mysterious way latent in the depths of his character, and soon to be reassumed...like habits native to him....[8]

The innate—shall we say instinctive?—sensation deep within Hawthorne's breast which made England seem like "our old home" to him is constantly supported and reinforced by things he saw there which seemed familiar. While visiting the abbeys and the ancient cathedrals and observing the English countryside, Hawthorne frequently had the feeling that he had been there before. "The ivy-grown English churches," says Hawthorne in *Our Old Home*, "...were quite as familiar to me, when fresh from home, as the old wooden meeting-house in Salem, which used, on wintry Sabbaths, to be the frozen purgatory of my childhood."[9] And in *Doctor Grimshawe's Secret* Redclyffe, in like manner, exclaims: "'How familiar these rustic sounds!...Surely I was born here!' "[10] As Newton Arvin notes, "England itself, England the island, so to say, England the garden, drew him to itself gently, magnetically, irresistibly. The sense of being on his own ground...was with him from the beginning and never left him."[11] The visualization, then, of England as "our old home"—the trunk of the tree from which American limbs had sprung—was perhaps the strongest attraction that the mother country had for Hawthorne. It was the same kind of attraction which will cause an orphan to seek his real mother. There is the feeling and the recognition that Hawthorne expresses in *The Ancestral Footstep:* "His [Middleton's] rights here were just as powerful and well founded as those of his ancestor had been, nearly three centuries ago."[12] Additionally, in *The English Notebooks,* he writes; "An American has a right to be proud of Westminster Abbey; for most of the men, who sleep in it, are our great men, as well as theirs."[13]

Another reason for Hawthorne's attraction to Europe, according to Austin Warren, was that "America had no past to speak of—no romance can be written about such a country."[14] Such literary purposes lying behind his trip to England are stated in a letter Hawthorne wrote to Longfellow in May 1855:

> It is good for the moral nature of an American to live in England, among a more simple and natural people than ourselves. Ale is an excellent moral nutriment; so is English mutton; and perhaps the effect of both will be visible in my next Romance.[15]

Edward Davidson also points out in *Hawthorne's Last Phase* that part of the pull of England for Hawthorne was its affording an opportunity for him to gather "material and impressions for novels he would write when he returned to the Wayside";[16] and the literary magnetism which England has for Hawthorne is pointed up time after time in *The English Notebooks.* As he toured the countryside, such places as Shakespeare's birthplace and Burns' grave were spots of great reflection; and in Westminster Abbey he was confronted with so much talent, so to speak, that he was awed:

> ...you can see the busts of poets looking down upon you from the wall. Great poets, too; for Ben Jonson is right behind the door; and Spenser's tablet is next; and Butler on the same wall of the transept; and Milton...with a profile medallion of Gray beneath it. It is a very delightful feeling, to find yourself at once among them.[17]

Again, however, the attraction was limited to the past, because Hawthorne formed not one close friendship with a literary figure of any significance while in England. What Hawthorne was seeking was inspiration from the "consciousness...of kind and friendly presences, who are anything but strangers...though heretofore you have never personally encountered them."[18] Hawthorne had discovered, just as Redclyffe had, that "the active tendencies of American life had interfered with him."[19] During his stay in England, therefore, one sees Hawthorne avidly putting new experiences into his notebooks to be used later in "my next Romance." The "limit of culture" in America[20] had become a limit to Hawthorne's literary aspirations; therefore he turned toward England.

Still another feature of England which Hawthorne admired and which naturally attracted him to England was a "singular tenderness" for her institutions.[21] This "singular tenderness" is shown primarily in *Our Old Home* and *The English Notebooks* as he explains his numerous visits to the old cathedrals, to the old historical points and homes of interest, and to the ruins of religious, political, or social institutions. Almost from the day of his arrival, Hawthorne showed this fondness. The English institutions, for Redclyffe, had a "charm, and besides it another intangible, evanescent, perplexing charm, full of an airy enjoyment," which along with the oldness and unchanging qualities, always impresses him as "the freshness of Paradise."[22] George P. Lathrop in *A Study of Hawthorne* has skillfully stated the importance of this fresh view of the old things Hawthorne saw:

> From this freshness of view there proceeded one result, the searching, unembarrassed, yet sympathetic and, as we may say, cordial criticism of England in "Our Old Home."But it also gave rise to the second noble quality, that exquisite apprehension of the real meaning of things European, both institutions and popular manners and the varied products of art. At times, Hawthorne seems to have been born for the one end of adding this final grace of definition which he so deftly attaches to the monuments of that older civilization.[23]

In *Doctor Grimshawe's Secret* Redclyffe was interested in an old, mossgrown building for the very reason Englishmen were disinterested—"because it had stood there such a weary while."[24] In *The English Notebooks* Hawthorne attempts to explain the attraction of Salisbury Cathedral:

> ...this mighty spire, and these multitudinous gray pinnacles and towers, ascend towards Heaven with a kind of natural beauty, not as if man had contrived them; they might be fancied to have grown up, just as the spires of a tuft of grass do, at the same time that they have a law or propriety and regularity among themselves.[25]

Lichfield Cathedral inspired him to write that a "Gothic cathedral is surely the most wonderful work which mortal man has yet achieved."[26] "Nevertheless," Hawthorne says in *Our Old Home*, "while an American willingly accepts growth and change as the law of his own national and private existence, he has a singular tenderness for the stone-encrusted institutions of the mother country.... I hated to see so much as a twig of ivy wrenched away from an old wall in England."[27] It is evident that Hawthorne's attraction to the institutions of England was, as Randall Stewart has said, "natural and instictive."[28]

All that has been said about the attraction England had for Hawthorne is brought into sharp relief when one considers his often critical attitude toward certain things he saw in England during 1853-57. The ambiguity which arises is somewhat perplexing, but a study of the magnetism England exerted on Hawthorne would have little value without remembering that a magnet both attracts *and* repels. An attempt to arrive at some conclusion as to why Hawthorne became so critical of English life, while it never lost its initial attraction, should be helpful in shedding some light on the seeming ambiguities.

One of the reasons Hawthorne became critical of England is suggested in the legend of the bloody footstep, which is interwoven into both *Doctor Grimshawe's Secret* and *The Ancestral Footstep.* Hawthorne intended the legend of the bloody footstep to symbolize "the baneful influence of the past as represented by family traditions and by old houses"[29] and the futility of recapturing past grandeur and to point out that the duty of the present was to throw off the yoke of the past. Perhaps Hawthorne's repudiation of the past was a result of his being "out of humour" with the way of life around him; if so, Redclyffe speaks for him in plain terms:

"I am not fit to be here,—I, so strongly susceptible of a newer, more stirring life than these men lead; I, who feel that, whatever the thought and cultivation of England may be, my own countrymen have gone forward a long, long march beyond them, not intellectually, but in a way that gives them a further start. If I come back hither, with the purpose to make myself an Englishman...then for me America has been discovered in vain, and the great spirit that has been breathed into us is in vain; and I am false to it all!"[30]

Some such renewal of patriotism on his own part resulted in Hawthorne's numerous assertions in *Our Old Home, The English Notebooks, Doctor Grimshawe's Secret,* and *The Ancestral Footstep* that America was superior to England in almost everything from nature to travelling conditions, from people to economic and social conditions. But, as Stewart asserts, "scores of petulant remarks can be set down to the irritation of the moment and need not be taken too seriously."[31]

It is evident, however, that Hawthorne felt "at home" in England only when he was with his family in his own house or withdrawn into the recesses of his mind while touring the countryside or inspecting an old tower, cathedral, graveyard, and the like. He had lived too long with the vigor of change and newness in America to be completely satisfied with musty old England. Redclyffe expresses this feeling clearly:

"All this sort of thing is beautiful; the family institution was beautiful in its day," ejaculated he aloud, to himself, not to his companion; "but it is a thing of the past. It is dying out in England; and as for ourselves, we never had it. Something better will come up; but as for this, it is past."[32]

Similarly, in *The English Notebooks* Hawthorne remarks:

> The truth is, there is a spirit lacking in England, which *we* do not lack, and for the want of which she will have to resign a foremost position among the nations, even if there were not enough other circumstances to compel her to do so.[33]

If one also remembers Hawthorne's suspicion that Englishmen were always condescending and his knowledge of the satire English tourists had written about his country, one can better understand (perhaps) his occasional patriotic flag-waving. As his alertness to "national disharmonies" developed, he convinced himself, according to Newton Arvin, that all Englishmen had a "settled, if somewhat abstract, grudge" against all Americans.[34] He found the Englishmen unattractive at a distance, but an Englishman appealing as an individual, as he says in *Our Old Home:* "Their magnetism is of a kind that repels strongly while you keep beyond a certain limit, but attracts as forcibly if you get within the magic line."[35]

At least two scholars, Leslie Stephen and Austin Warren, believe that part of the reason for Hawthorne's caustic criticisms of the English was "his fear of loving them too well."[36] Warren also agrees that "retaliation" was a prime motive.[37] Even though it may sound like a gross contradiction to state that Hawthorne "had a fear of loving" too much—the more so when recalling some of his criticisms—evidence supports the contention. In *The English Notebooks*, Hawthorne in an enthusiastic mood says:

> Yet I shall always be glad of this tour, and shall wonder the more at England, which comprehends so much, such a rich variety, within its little bounds. If England were all the world, it still would have been worth while for the Creator to have made it; and mankind would have had no cause to find fault with their abode...[38]

But, then, as if to keep from being too enthusiastic, he adds: "—except that there is not room enough for so many as might be happy here."[39]

The poverty rampant in England and many obnoxious characteristics of Englishmen in general were the principal agents which, working together, placed a damper on Hawthorne's "singular tenderness" for England's institutions and on the chance of his being altogether happy there. The opposition of Hawthorne's sentiments became increasingly painful the longer he stayed in England; and England's "beauty and magnificence" became irreconcilable with the actualities of the present. So great was the poverty impressed upon his mind that Hawthorne devoted a chapter to the subject "English Poverty" in *Our Old Home* and mentioned it frequently in his other writings which grew out of his English experiences. What bothered him as much as the misery of the sufferers was their complacency and acceptance. Because their ancestors had suffered, these people believed their condition to be thus settled. This analysis Hawthorne gives in *Our Old Home's* chapter on English poverty:

> Let me add, that, forlorn, ragged, careworn, hopeless, dirty, haggard, hungry, as they were, the most pitiful thing of all was to see the sort of patience with which they accepted their lot, as if they had been born into the world for that and nothing else. Even the little children had this characteristic in as perfect development as their grandmothers.[40]

Throughout England, even as he was enjoying the scenery and sights, he saw all around him a severe poverty the like of which was not known to him in America. An example of this unique English poverty is noted in *The English Notebooks:*

> I often see women or girls in the streets picking up fresh horse-dung with their hands, and putting it into a cloth—some accumulating large parcels of it.[41]

This destitution was irreconcilable with Hawthorne's nature. New England Puritanism ran too thick in his blood to allow him to watch peacefully without speaking out against such misery among human beings. No matter how much he loved his idea of England, he could never become so cynical, so single-minded, so narrow that he would forsake conviction.

As I have mentioned, many obnoxious characteristics of Englishmen in general also helped fan Hawthorne's discontent. The objectionable qualities he found annoying are found scattered throughout his "English" works and to discuss each one is not within the scope of this paper. However, as a matter of interest and as an illustration of the extent of his annoyance, a few characteristics which are discussed in *The English Notebooks* are noteworthy: roughness, ridiculousness, surliness, class-consciousness, lack of polish, independence, unamusement, intolerance, homeliness, and common-placeness.[42] In *Our Old Home* Hawthorne puts these characteristics into the classification of the "acrid quality in the moral atmosphere of England."[43] These "acrid" qualities forced Hawthorne to be critical of English life—not out of hate but out of love. Hawthorne always strongly defended the fairness and accuracy of his statements concerning England, and he was amused to see the "innocent wonder" with which the English regarded them. But amused or not, he was still annoyed—unhappy—about the whole general atmosphere of poverty and conceit in England and in Englishmen. This, too, added to the feelings of discontent building up within Hawthorne.

Still another possible cause for Hawthorne's cold comfort was homesickness for America. George E. Woodberry, an early biographer, states that "he was, too, always in a certain sense homesick...he was a man out of place, and had lost the natural harmonies between the outer and inner life."[44] Hawthorne had "lost the natural harmonies between the outer and inner life," but he was not homesick in the "certain sense," to use Woodberry's term, of the word. When he left England, he did not rush home—he went to Italy. To be more accurate, one could say he was tired of England and this tiredness fostered thoughts of home; but he was not *sick* for home. Even after his return to America, he yearned for Our Old Home.

In a study of this kind, dealing as it has with the attraction England had for Hawthorne and the reasons for his discontent in England, concrete conclusions are not possible. Hawthorne himself could never fully explain the situation. As has been pointed out, both the attraction and the discontent are often shrouded in inconsistencies and ambiguities. What attracted Hawthorne in the main was of an *abstract* nature—a feeling for "Our Old Home," a search for hereditary ties not actually known, a fascination for past glories and ancient oldness, a love for a group with no particular concern for its individuals. What caused his discontent was *both concrete and abstract*—mean characteristics of Englishmen, poverty, an inability to begin life anew amid different people, a fear of loving the country too well. Perhaps Hawthorne suggested the only solution he had when he proposes in *Our Old Home* that America annex England and exchange the people! Impossible or not, it was the only solution, and it is important because it shows Hawthorne's general view concerning England: place the Americans with their vitality and freshness among the leavings of their heritage in England and the result, Hawthorne seems to conclude, would be paradise. This was not feasible, however, and Hawthorne, unable to shed his American coat, was therefore burdened with agonizing "twists and turns of his imagination when forced to cope with the challenge." Nevertheless, as Hawthorne said of William Brown, Esq. in a speech in Liverpool on 15 April 1857, "Sir, it is good for both countries that there should be such men—men connected by inseparable ties with one country and the other, not the less firm to their native land, but able to serve her all the better, because they claim the next place in their heart for affection to another and a kindred land."[45]

England was for Hawthorne an abstract ideal which could not always withstand the realistic perusal of a "reasonably hard-hearted"[46] American, for it was *as an official representative of America* that

Hawthorne saw himself: "It impressed me with an odd idea of having somehow lost the property of my own person, when I occasionally heard one of them [Consulate visitors] speaking of me as 'my Consul'!" As a symbol himself, he saw the Liverpool Consulate as an emblem of America, "a little patch of our nationality imbedded into the soil and institutions of England" which "should fairly represent the American taste..." With such a view it is not surprising that England became "the gateway between the Old World and the New," a dream-vision-cumallegory world which Hawthorne inevitably imagizes as a garden of Eden, which Redclyffe sees as "the freshness of Paradise."[47] If the meeting-house in Old Salem was the "purgatory" of his childhood, then England was the proving ground of the *representative* American called Nathaniel Hawthorne. As with all things ideal, England did not always measure up to the dreams of his imagination, but it was a choice place for him to come to terms with his own identity. For Hawthorne, England was a half-real, half-ideal Vision of Mirzah: "it gratified me," says Hawthorne, "to observe what trouble and pains the English gardeners are fain to throw away in producing a few sour plums and abortive pears and apples,—as, for example, in this very garden, where a row of unhappy trees were spread out perfectly flat against a brick wall, looking as if impaled alive, or crucified, with a cruel and unattainable purpose of compelling them to produce rich fruit by torture."[48] Invariably things, objects, places, ruins—and as we have seen, England itself—are seen metaphorically and synecdochically. Hawthorne in England never loses his historical and geographical sense of place, as a cursory reading of his discussions of "English" domestic scenery, "English" ale, "English" summer days, "English" beef, "English" verdure, "English" pastimes, even "English" Englishmen, etc. suggests.[49] It was to such a symbolic place that Nathaniel Hawthorne, an Adamic American almost *ab ovo*, was instinctively pulled; and his experiences in that "Paradise" largely account for that older, wiser, less poetic man who said, "For my part, I never ate an English fruit, raised in the open air, that could compare with a Yankee turnip."[50]

The University of Alabama

---

[1]*Discovery of Europe,* ed. with a new Introduction and Comments by Philip Rahv (Garden City, N.Y.: Anchor Books, Doubleday, 1960), p. viii.

[2]Nathaniel Hawthorne, *The English Notebooks,* ed. Randall Steward (New York: The Modern Language Association of America, 1941), p. xxxviii.

[3]Nathaniel Hawthorne, *Doctor Grimshawe's Secret,* ed. Julian Hawthorne (Boston: Houghton, Mifflin and Co., 1900), Old Manse Edition, Vol. XV, p. 308.

[4]*Doctor Grimshawe's Secret,* p. 311.

[5]Nathaniel Hawthorne, *Our Old Home* (Boston: Houghton, Mifflin and Co., 1900), Old Manse Edition, Vol. XI, p. 19.

[6]Edward Mather, *Nathaniel Hawthorne, A Modest Man* (New York: Thomas Y. Crowell Co., 1940), p. 251.

[7]Edward Hutchins Davidson, *Hawthorne's Last Phase* (New Haven: Yale University Press, 1949), p.21.

[8]*Doctor Grimshawe's Secret,* p. 202.

[9]*Our Old Home,* p. 85.

[10]*Doctor Grimshawe's Secret,* p. 160.

[11]Newton Arvin, *Hawthorne* (Boston: Little, Brown and Co., 1929), p. 231.

[12]Nathaniel Hawthorne, *The Ancestral Footstep* as published as an appendix in the Old Manse Edition, Vol. XIV, of *The Dolliver Romance and Kindred Tales* (Boston: Houghton, Mifflin and Co., 1904), p. 342.

[13]*English Notebooks,* p. 213.

[14]*Nathaniel Hawthorne: Representative Selections,* ed. Austin Warren (New York: The American Book Co., 1934), p. lvii.

[15]Randall Stewart, *Nathaniel Hawthorne, A Biography* (New Haven: Yale University Press, 1948), p. 180.

[16]Davidson, p. 14.

[17]*English Notebooks,* p. 218.

[18]*English Notebooks,* p. 218.

[19]*Doctor Grimshawe's Secret,* p. 320.

[20]*Our Old Home,* p. 457.

[21]*English Notebooks,* p. xxii.

[22]*Doctor Grimshawe's Secret,* p. 229. Hawthorne himself uses the word "Paradise" in reference to England in *Our Old Home,* p. 227.

[23]George Parsons Lathrop, *A Study of Hawthorne* (Boston: J. R. Osgood, 1876), p. 250.

[24]*Doctor Grimshawe's Secret,* p. 242.

[25]*English Notebooks,* p. 356.

[26]*Our Old Home,* p. 180.

[27]*Our Old Home,* pp. 80-81.

[28]*English Notebooks,* p. xxxv.

[29]Davidson, p. 28.

[30]*Doctor Grimshawe's Secret,* p. 331.

[31]*English Notebooks,* p. xxvii.

[32]*Doctor Grimshawe's Secret,* p. 257.

[33]*English Notebooks,* p. 108.

[34]Arvin, p. 239.

[35]*Our Old Home,* p. 264.

[36]Warren (ed.), p. lvii.

[37]Warren (ed.), p.lix.

[38]*English Notebooks,* p. 182.

[39]*English Notebooks,* p. 182.

[40]*Our Old Home,* p. 420.

[41]*English Notebooks,* p. 105.

[42]*English Notebooks,* pp. 12, 30, 44, 50, 78, 97, 108, 119, 192.

[43]*Our Old Home,* p. xix.

[44]George E. Woodberry, *Nathaniel Hawthorne* (Boston: Houghton, Mifflin and Co., 1902), p. 254.

[45]Nathaniel Hawthorne, "Hawthorne's Speech to the Friends of the William Brown Library, 15 April 1857," *The Nathaniel Hawthorne Journal 1972,* ed. C. E. Frazer Clark, Jr. (Washington, D.C.: NCR Microcard Editions, 1973), p. 209.

Also consult the splendid essay entitled "Our Old Home," which is chapter IV of Lawrence Sargent Hall's *Hawthorne: Critic of Society* (Gloucester, Mass.: Peter Smith, 1966), pp. 68-100.

[46]*Our Old Home*, p. 8.

[47]See *Our Old Home*, pp. 6, 3, 7, and *Doctor Grimshawe's Secret*, p. 229.

[48]*Our Old Home*, pp. 225-26. Compare *English Notebooks*, pp. 7-8.

[49]See, for example, *Our Old Home*, pp. 222-234, a commentary on English life selected at random.

[50]*Our Old Home*, p. 226. Such feelings are, of course, identical with Redclyffe's "Yankee feelings." In *Doctor Grimshawe's Secret* we learn that the "new American was stronger in him than the hereditary Englishman" (p. 246).

Hawthorne in the English Press

GEORGE MONTEIRO

In the *Nathaniel Hawthorne Journal 1972*, C. E. Frazer Clark, Jr. pointed to three major "Unexplored Areas of Hawthorne Bibliography." One of the three is the matter of Hawthorne's publication in England. "We know almost nothing about Hawthorne's appearance in the English press," he wrote, "and we know woefully little about Hawthorne's appearances in English periodicals—in spite of the fact that Hawthorne was regularly serialized" (p. 51).

The seven items listed here—two printings, four notices and reviews along with an essay on the occasion of Hawthorne's death—contribute modestly to our knowledge in this area. Their source is *The Ladies' Companion, and Monthly Magazine,* a periodical published in London for just over two decades (1849-1870). The volumes from 1849 through 1866, both first and second series, have been examined. It is of course possible that the unexamined final four volumes in the series also contain Hawthorne material.

Printings

"Feathertop: A Moralized Legend," 2, second series (July and Aug., 1852), 25-29, 83-86. (Reprinted, apparently, from the *International Magazine,* 5 [Feb. and Mar., 1852], 182-86, 333-37.)

"Pilgrimage to Old Boston," 21, second series (Mar., 1862), 148-57. (To Hawthorne's observation that "hillocks of waste and effete mineral always disfigure the neighbourhood of ironmongering towns, and, even after a considerable antiquity, are hardly made decent with a little grass," the editor adds a note: "The process is a slow one; but at Dudley potatoes are cultivated on what were cinder-heaps; and at Coalbrook Dale we have seen these artificial eminences crowned with firs.")

Notices and Reviews

[*Twice-Told Tales* (Bohn's cheap series), 1, second series (Jan. 1, 1852), 51.]

Fanny. Americans may well be proud of Longfellow.

Mrs. Smith. Ay, and of Hawthorne—

Fanny. The author of "The Scarlet Letter," and of the House with the "Seven Gables?"

Mrs. Smith. Yes; two works that, different as they are, alike stand out as among the most remarkable works of fiction of this or any other age. For sustained power, for elaborate finish, for that truth to nature, which, just lifted out of the real into the ideal, is *more true than* any matter of fact, and for high tone and purpose, I know no story that surpasses them, and right few that are worthy to be placed on the same shelf. There is a new edition of "Hawthorne's Twice-Told Tales." You may remember we read these stories some time ago, and agreed that they were full of the promise which the author's maturity has so nobly fulfilled.

Fanny. And yet, if I remember rightly, they were published many, many years before they attracted much attention.

Mrs. Smith. Yes, and this new edition is accompanied by a mournfully pathetic preface, in which, though in no spirit of complaining, the author speaks of himself as for ten or twelve years the "obscurest man of letters in America." When one thinks of what he *has* done, and what he might have done under circumstances of generous encouragement, we feel how deeply the world has been punished for its neglect. There is something very touching in the following words, which could never have been penned but by one who had felt the "chill" and the "numbness"—

"Throughout the time above-specified, he had no incitement to literary effort in a reasonable prospect of reputation or profit; nothing but the pleasure itself of composition—an enjoyment not at all amiss in its way, and perhaps essential to the merit of the work in hand, but which in the long run will hardly keep the chill out of a writer's heart, or the numbness out of his fingers."

[*The Blithedale Romance* (Boston: Ticknor, Reed, and Fields; London: Chapman and Hall), 2, second series (Sept., 1852), 161-62]

Mrs. Smith. We were talking the other day
of American writers : here is a new work by
their great romancist, Hawthorne.*

Fanny. The author of " The Scarlet Letter"
and " The House of the Seven Gables"—is it
comparable with either of those works ?

Mrs. Smith. It is so different that I cannot
bring it into comparison with them. Some
readers will doubtless consider it an inferior
production, but I should not like to declare that
it is so. The story, it is true, has not the grand
tragic outline of " The Scarlet Letter," nor the
minute picture painting that is to be found in
" The Seven Gables ;" but for subtle touches
of wisdom, that come up as it were like trea-
sures from the deep well of truth, fine poetical
fancies, and striking delineations of character,
the " Blithedale Romance" seems to me unri-
valled, except by the predecessors which owe
their origin to the same hand.

Fanny. What is it about ? Hawthorne is so
original in the construction of his stories, that
one asks this question with more eagerness than
is felt towards ordinary writers.

Mrs. Smith. The idea is a very happy one.
A party of acquaintances resort to a certain
place, entitled " Blithedale," with the view of
leading a perfectly—as they consider it—natural
life. Social distinctions are for the time to be
swept away. High-spirited and accomplished
women are to dress in cotton gowns, cook, clean,
and milk the cows—while gentlemen of a philosophic turn of mind lend the feeble thews of
their city-weakened frames to the services of the
plough and the harvest-field. How all this ends
may be readily defined.

Fanny. In a return, I suppose, to the tram-
mels as well as the comforts of civilised social
life.

Mrs. Smith. Exactly so, but not without a
fiery play of human passions meanwhile, and
some tragic results. The character of Zenobia
is very powerfully drawn. She is the type of a
woman of high intellect, refined taste, and generous impulses, yet deficient in the binding
chain of strong principle. Then we have the

gentle tender maiden, Priscilla, reminding us all
through of a lily drenched by the storm—yet
possessing such exquisite sensibility that she is
placed by it almost on the confines of the spiritual world.

Fanny. Hawthorne dearly loves to weave into
his life-like histories a thread of the supernatural. Witness his vivid impersonation of the
Witch lady in " The Scarlet Letter."

Mrs. Smith. And he does this very delicately,
and yet effectively, in the character of Priscilla.
Then we have the self-concentrated philanthro-
pist, and the Minor Poet " beginning life with
strenuous aspirations, which die out with his

youthful error"—the latter being indeed the personage who narrates the story.

Fanny. I can imagine how gloriously Hawthorne must treat such a subject, and shall
hardly rest till I have procured the book.

Mrs. Smith. You will not be disappointed, I
am sure.

[Excerpt from J. A.'s review of Oliver Wendell Holmes' *Elsie Venner*,
18, second series (Dec., 1860), 329-32]

Those who are compelled, by their insular
prejudices, to throw aside the book unread, will
lose—a very rare thing in these days of realistic
fiction—an excellent romance. The era of
English romance has gone by. We have no
more "Udolphos" and "Frankensteins." The
writer of "Zanoni" has taken to painting
middle-class life. "Wuthering Heights" was
the last English book of note which has any
pretensions to be classed as a romance. To
America, as it seems, we are to look for this
kind of writing. Not many months ago
Hawthorne gave us "Transformation"; now
Holmes gives us "Elsie Venner."

These two books are strangely alike, not only
in the physiological fancies which form the os-
tensible groundwork of the stories, but also in
the moral hypotheses which are put forth,
vaguely and doubtfully, under cover of the
aforesaid fancies. Hawthorne's Donatello par-
takes of the animal together with the human
nature. Ages ago some fair progenitrix of the
Monte Beni house had smitten with love the
shaggy bosom of an antique Faun; and thus,
from time to time, the characteristics of the
Faun—the link between the human and the
brute creation—reappear in the race. We see
in Donatello the best side of the animal nature,
the unreasoning innocence and happiness,
the playful grace and sportive beauty, the elas-
ticity of form, the delight in mere sensual vitality. He has, too, a closer sympathy than
men have with nature, brute and inanimate.
He can summon to him the beasts in a language which they alone understand; the grapes
which his feet tread in the wine-press yield up a
sweeter juice; Dryads and Naiads, and all such
gracious legendary creatures, press towards
him as he walks the earth.

Elsie Venner, too, is compounded of the animal and human natures: but, whereas the animal nature of Donatello is *inherited*, like any
other peculiarity of race—the animal nature of
Elsie is *engrafted* by abnormal means. The
Faun-element in Donatello dates from remote
antiquity; the Lamia-element in Elsie from a

time just preceding her birth. The animal nature in Donatello is general, comprehending a
sympathy with all the brute creation and—
beyond that—with all inanimate creation. The
animal nature in Elsie is special: her instincts
are ophidian only. While in Donatello we see
the best side of animal nature, in Elsie we see
the worst. Again: the transformation which
at length comes to both, affects each oppositely.
The inherited animal nature of Donatello passes
away, and leaves his human nature matured:
the engrafted animal nature of Elsie, in passing
away from her, takes with it her human life.

There is no one, I think, who will place
Holmes's idea of the Lamia on an equality with
Hawthorne's idea of the Faun. For many reasons Hawthorne's creation must rank higher.
We feel no incongruity in Donatello: the whole
story harmonizes with this central figure, and
we feel that it is native to the scenes wherein
the drama is acted. The legendary Faun takes
his place naturally enough in those glowing
Italian landscapes. In other ways, too, Hawthorne connects, by subtle ties, this figure with
the scene. He makes Donatello, as it were, a
living reflex of the Fawn of Praxiteles—one of
the chief glories of that land of *Art*—just as he
likens Miriam to the picture of Beatrice Cenci,
and her mysterious tormentor to Guido's
Dragon. Moreover, he never insists upon the
half-animal nature of Donatello as an absolute
fact: he never dreams of hinting a scientific
explanation of it, or of canvassing with his
reader whether such a marvel be possible or no.

The treatment of Elsie Venner is utterly different. There are neither classic nor artistic
associations in the New England country-town
to harmonize with the strange idea of the
woman-serpent. Elsie is placed in the midst of
the most common-place people—parsons, and
doctors, and school-girls, and low Yankees
with abominable dialects. Her ophidian nature
is treated throughout as a scientific enigma.
Mr. Holmes is a Doctor of Medicine, and he
handles his subject as none but a Doctor of
Medicine could. The book is a treatise on
"inherited organisms;" the one abnormal "engrafted organism" establishing exceptionally
the ordinary laws.

Both authors have chosen in common the
best possible groundwork for their romances,
namely, that nebulous border-land where science and poetry meet. Holmes hangs to the
scientific side, Hawthorne to the poetical.

The vague moral hypotheses, which we spoke
of above as underlying the physiological fancies
in the two stories, are respectively these that
follow. Hawthorne tremblingly puts the question, "Whether Sin may not be an element of
human education—a baptism into a higher and
purer state?" Holmes more boldly states his
thesis, that "Crime is not Sin"! We do not

mean to meddle with these hypotheses. Thus
briefly stated, they will doubtless shock many
people who were not in the least shocked by
reading of the transformation of Donatello, and
of the poisoned moral nature of Elsie Venner.
Few people, I think, will be inclined to take
either hypothesis as a satisfactory solution of
that vexed question, the Origin of Evil.

Although in comparing this book with the
production of a higher genius we have seemed
to disparage it, yet "Elsie Venner" is well
conceived and excellently worked out. The
idea of the Faun would appear no very promising idea if "Transformation" were unwritten; nor could any other man but Hawthorne
have touched upon it without rendering it ab-
surd. The idea of the woman-serpent, on the
contrary, has in it manifestly the elements
most favourable to romance. The woman's
heart struggling with the poisonous instincts
of the serpent; the woman's beauty alternating
with the serpent's loathsomeness; the helpless
ophidian fascination mingling with the tender
love-charms of a woman's eyes—here we have
elements of tragic romance, than which none
could be better. Then we have inevitably the
awakening of human love in the heart of the
Lamia; the passion and the pathos, the dumb
anguish, the dull pain, the fury of animal desire, the intuitive reticence of feminine love, the
flashes of knowledge, the blind ignorance, the
utter chaos. And, as all-conquering love rises
supreme out of this chaos, we have the dying
away of the serpent-nature, the birth of the full
human nature, in more than mortal agonies of
death and birth—the glorious triumph and the
abject humility, the high hope and the deep
despair.

For another reason the notion of the woman-
serpent is less foreign to us than that of the
Faun. The latter belongs exclusively to a faith
that is dead; it is essentially heathen. But of
the serpent and the serpent-nature, Christians
are taught a mystical belief from their earliest
childhood. The ancient stories of the Python-
class and of the Lamiæ-class are verified and
substantiated in our minds by the Christian
doctrine of the temptation of Eve.

[*Our Old Home* (London: Smith, Elder, and Co.), 24, second series
(Nov., 1863), 276-277. By C. A. W.]

-Under
this title the author has republished those charming descriptive papers, which have appeared in
the pages of the "Atlantic Magazine," and elsewhere, from time to time; papers which record
the writer's impression of the country rather

than of the inhabitants, and paint views with
only here and there a figure in them, but when
these do occur they are not usually pretty.
Englishwomen will have occasion to draw freely
on their recollections of the "Scarlet Letter,"
"The House with the Seven Gables," and
"Mosses from an Old Manse," to forgive Mr.
Hawthorne his personal impressions of them collectively. Though, on the other hand, the harder
sex are not much more leniently dealt with, so
far as their physiognomy and persons are concerned. Here is what Mr. Hawthorne says of the
beauty of English wives and daughters :

> The comely, rather than pretty, English girls,
> with their deep, healthy bloom, which an American
> taste is apt to deem fitter for a milk-maid than a
> lady.

Again :

> I have heard a good deal of the tenacity with
> which English ladies retain their personal beauty to
> a late period of life; but (not to suggest that an
> American eye needs use and cultivation before it can
> quite appreciate the charm of English beauty at any
> age) it strikes me that an English lady of fifty is
> apt to become a creature less refined and delicate,

as far as her physique goes, than anything that we
western people class under the name of woman.
She has an awful ponderosity of frame, not pulpy,
like the looser development of our few fat women,
but massive with solid beef and streaky tallow ; so
that (though struggling manfully against the idea)
you inevitably think of her as made up of steaks
and sirloins. When she walks, her advance is ele-
phantine. When she sits down, it is on a great
round space of her Maker's footstool, where she
looks as if nothing could ever move her. She im-
poses awe and respect by the muchness of her personality, to such a degree that you probably credit
her with far greater moral and intellectual force than
she can fairly claim. Her visage is usually grim
and stern, seldom positively forbidding, yet calmly
terrible, not merely by its breadth and weight of
feature, but because it seems to express so much
well-founded self-reliance, such acquaintance with
the world, its toils, troubles, and dangers, and such
sturdy capacity for trampling down a foe. Without
anything positively salient, or actively offensive, or,
indeed, unjustly formidable to her neighbours, she
has the effect of a seventy-four gun-ship in time of
peace; for, while you assure yourself that there is
no real danger, you cannot help thinking how tremendous would be her onset, if pugnaciously inclined, and how futile the effort to inflict any coun-
ter injury. She certainly looks tenfold—nay, a
hundredfold—better able to take care of herself
than our slender-framed and haggard womenkind ;
but I have not found reason to suppose that the
English dowager of fifty has actually greater courage,
fortitude, and strength of character than our women
of similar age, or even a tougher physical endurance
than they. Morally, she is strong, I suspect, only
in society, and in the common routine of social
affairs, and would be found powerless and timid in
any exceptional strait that might call for energy
outside of the conventionalities amid which she has

grown up. You can meet this figure in the street,
and live, and even smile at the recollection. But
conceive of her in a ball-room, with her bare,
brawny arms that she invariably displays there, and
all the other corresponding development, such as
is beautiful in the maiden blossom, but a spectacle
to howl at in such an overblown cabbage-rose as
this.

And again:

To be frank however, at the first glance and to
my American eye they looked all homely alike, and
the chivalry that I suggest is more than I could have
been capable of at any period of my life. They
seemed to be country lasses, of sturdy and wholesome aspect, with coarse-grained, cabbage-rosy
cheeks, and, I am willing to suppose, a stout texture
of moral principle, such as would· bear a good deal
of rough usage without suffering much detriment.
But how unlike the trim little damsels of my native
land! I desire above all things to be courteous;
but, since the plain truth must be told, the soil and
climate of England produce feminine beauty as
rarely as they do delicate fruit, and, though admirable specimens of both are to be met with, they
are the hot-house ameliorations of refined society,
and apt, moreover, to relapse into the coarseness of
the original stock. The men are man-like; but the
women are not beautiful, though the female Bull be
well adapted to the male.

We are not inapt at repeating, in reference to
our friends and acquaintances, Burns' well-known
lines:

" Oh, would some power the gifty gie us,
    To see ourselves as others see us!" &c., &c.

And here we have the petition answered in full.
The author's impressions are certainly not flattering to our national portraiture. Mr. Bull is just
as coarsely limned in our artist's pages—for
Nathaniel Hawthorne is an artist in very truth—
and we bovine-like Englishmen and women
have been amongst the first to feel it. Here is
the pendent to the former picture:—

It being the first considerable assemblage of Englishmen that I had seen, my honest impression about
them was, that they were a heavy and homely set of
people, with a remarkable roughness of aspect and
behaviour; not repulsive, but beneath which it
requires more familiarity with the national character
than I then possessed always to detect the good
breeding of a gentleman. Being generally middle-
aged, or still further advanced, they were by no
means graceful in figure; for the comeliness of the
youthful Englishman rapidly diminishes with years,
his body appearing to grow longer, his legs to abbre-
viate themselves, and his stomach to assume the
dignified prominence which justly belongs to that
metropolis of his system. His face (what with the
acridity of the atmosphere, ale at lunch, wine at
dinner, and a well-digested abundance of succulent
food) gets red and mottled, and develops at least one
additional chin, with a promise of more; so that,
finally, a stranger recognizes his animal part at the

most superficial glance, but must take time and a
little pains to discover the intellectual. Comparing
him with an American, I really thought that our
natural paleness and lean habit of flesh gave us
greatly the advantage in an æsthetic point of view.
It seemed to me, moreover, that the English tailor
had not done so much as he might and ought for
these heavy figures, but had gone on wilfully ex-
aggerating their uncouthness by the roominess of
their garments; he had evidently no idea of accuracy
of fit, and smartness was entirely out of his line.
But, to be quite open with the reader, I afterwards
learned to think that this aforesaid tailor has a
deeper art than his brethren among ourselves,
knowing how to dress his customers with such individual propriety that they look as if they were
born in their clothes, the fit being to the character
rather than the form. If you make an Englishman
smart (unless he be a very exceptional one, of whom
I have seen a few), you make. him a monster; his
best aspect is that of a ponderous respectability.

Even while we copy this description, we half
forgive the writer, for the sake of the grains of
truth mixed up with the following, and the not
ungenial appreciation of us after all; when a
little natural indigestion on the score of our
politics has passed away, and the traveller's
green glasses are laid aside.

The English character, as I conceive it, is by no
means a very lofty one; they seem to have a great
deal of earth and grimy dust clinging about them,
as was probably the case with the stalwart and quar-
relsome people who sprouted up out of the soil,
after Cadmus had sown the Dragon's teeth. And
yet, though the individual Englishman is sometimes
preternaturally disagreeable, an observer standing
aloof has a sense of natural kindness towards them
in the lump. . . . . These Englishmen are certainly
a franker and simpler people than ourselves, from
peer to peasant; but if we can take it as compensa-
tory on our part (which I leave to be considered),
that they owe those noble and manly qualities to a
coarser grain in their nature, and that, with a finer
one in ours, we shall ultimately acquire a marble
polish of which they are unsusceptible, I believe
that this may be the truth. . . . . We, in our dry
atmosphere, are getting too nervous, haggard,
dyspeptic, extenuated, unsubstantial, theoretic,
and need to be made grosser. John Bull, on the
other hand, has grown bulbous, long-bodied, short-
legged, heavy-witted, and, in a word, too intensely
English.
The book, notwithstanding its unpleasantness,
is a charming one, full of lovely pictures and a
natural admiration of "Our Old Home."

Essay

[Charles Kendal, "Nathaniel Hawthorne," 27, second series (Jan.,
1865), 29-33.]

The present year has been to us a prolific one
in occasions of sorrow. Some of the noblest
and most highly-gifted in art and literature have,
within the eleven months that are past, written
their last line and plied the pencil for the last
time. In our land, Thackeray, Leech, and Landor have departed. On the continent the death-
roll includes the names of Uhland and Meyer-
beer: whilst across the Atlantic came, in the
spring of the year, the tidings of the death of
Nathaniel Hawthorne. Scarcely noticed among
the telegrams that supplied us with news of the
progress of the fiercest and most unjust civil
war that was ever waged, the simple announcement had, nevertheless, a deeper, though inex-
pressibly mournful, interest to not a few in
England, than all the turmoil of battle that was
compressed into the electric summary.

On the 19th of May, at his house in Plymouth, New Hampshire, with all the lovely
sights and sounds of that sweet spring-time
which he so dearly loved, the spirit of America's
greatest prose-writer faded almost imperceptibly
into eternity. Little known to the great European public, and indeed more especially en-
deared to the scholar and the dreamer than to the
general reader by his genial humour and refined
taste, he had never striven to become popular,
and therefore the announcement of his compara-
tively early death created but little excitement,
save among the reverent circle of which we have
before spoken. So retiring and modest, indeed,
were his habits, that to many of his countrymen, in that land where the privacy of a public
man is almost invariably sacrificed to the dis-
courteous curiosity of his admirers, Hawthorne
was known but by his books, and a very few
of the most refined and most intellectual men of
the day, such as Longfellow and Wendell
Holmes, were admitted to the rare delight of his
friendship; but to these few he was well known,
and with their appreciation he was content.

Kindly and gentle as a little child was the
nature of him who has left us. Somewhat too
much absorbed in his own abundant, delicate
fancyings, and seeking habitually, in commune
with his own beautiful and finer nature, a refuge
from the rough contact and jarring turmoil of
the busy world, he yet did not neglect his more
obvious duties. An ever kind and attentive
relative and friend, his name will be held in reverence, no less for these humble qualities than
for his undying productions. His countrymen
have reason to be peculiarly proud of him, for
in him America has produced the most exquisite
prose-poet and the most originally fanciful romancist of the age.

In no country of the Old or New World can
we instance any author whose name is worthy to
be placed beside that of Hawthorne on that peculiar path which was first irradiated by the

morning blush of his fancy. Many have attempted to follow him ; but they are, in almost
every case, nearly forgotten ; whilst the exquisite
dream-scenery, which Hawthorne reveals to us,
illumined by his own subtle phantasy, tinged
with his heart-searching pathos, or fitfully soft-
ened into cool shadow by the opal-hued mist-
veil of his half-mystic but all-refined humour,
still stands in ever fresh beauty, to charm all
true lovers of art. And we may safely prophesy
that it will be many ages before its subtle influence will fail, alternately to gladden and sad-
den the hearts of future readers. But though spe-
cially marked out as a possession of the "May-
flower" land by the peculiar sombre visitings of
Puritan sadness that every now and then obscure us with a deep shadow, and the glimmer-
ing sun-motes of his dreamy fancy, he is even
more generally loved and appreciated in England
than in his native country. This may, we think,
be partially attributed to the under-current of
pathetic melancholy that runs through his
gayest and most sparkling effusions, and the
ever-present, subdued tone of longing aspiration
that seems to mark his beautiful nature, as inwardly mourning over and shrinking from the
hard, stern realities of an essentially selfish and
unchivalrous age. It is like the stream of dusky
water, unreached by the rays of the sun, which
is sometimes to be seen, in spring, flowing along
the bed of a brook, whose upper surface radiates
a thousand iridescent colours, in joyous answer
to the kisses of the sun, whose ripples sparkle
along in careless merriment, when a sudden
change comes over it ; a sombre flush seems, by
some appreciable magic, to sweep over the pris-
matic play of the current ; the under-stream for
the nonce gets the upper hand : though the
happy glitter is still visible, it is clouded by
some half-sombre, half-translucent change, which
sends a not ungrateful thrill of indefinable sadness to the heart. Though this may rob a mind,
acutely alive to natural influences, of some
of the buoyant rapture consequent on the
delicious advent of spring, yet it has an
effect on a sensitive intellect, that more than
repays the momentary glooming of the landscape.

It is this, and a thousand other natural phenomena of the same kind, that suggest to the
poetic temperament more sublime and delicate
conceptions by far than the most smiling aspect
of summer, or the most gorgeously tinted landscape of autumn.

We Englishmen, belonging to the most material period of the most material country in the
world,* are, perhaps, in our heart of hearts, a
more romantic people than any that inhabit the
known globe. Not in our acts do we show it,
for they are, almost invariably, whether in public or private life, dictated by the most rigid con-

siderations of realistic expediency; but we still,
even the most conventional of us, love to
cherish, in some dark corner of our souls, an
inward hankering, scarcely even self-confessed,
toward the most Utopian and fanciful of ideals,
and almost always, though openly disclaiming it,
feel a secret, indefinable sympathy with the mind
of such a man as Nathaniel Hawthorne. His
child-like simplicity, his freshness of thought,
untainted by worldliness, and his half-sad, half-
hopeful longings, strike upon us as a much-
needed and delightful relief from the grim posi-
tivism of conventional life.

As on a sultry day we plunge into the cool
greenness of a beautiful wood, whose masses of
foliage absorb the sunlight, and, whilst neu-
tralizing its glare, assume thereby a luminous
beauty and a half-translucent depth of shadow
that is infinitely more soothing and attractive
than the brilliant splendour of the sun-gilded
plain, Hawthorne's commingled fancy and
pathos present to us an ever-welcome retreat
where we may rub-off, for a little, the dust of

---

* Some may object to this that the Americans
themselves best answer this description; but we
think that any impartial person who has followed
the shifting fortunes and consequences of the present Civil War can scarcely hold such an opinion.

---

toil, and freshen our weary minds with the dewy
flowers of his undying spring.

Again, to those of us to whom the more
delicate emanations of his brain would have no
special attraction, there would still remain the
more *real* part of his genius. The works of
one who has shown himself to be so wondrous
a depicter of varied character, so profound a
student of the human soul, could never fail to
be recognized at their full value by a great
majority of English readers. Many, perhaps,
might not feel any responsive chord struck
within them by the ethereal loveliness of the
variations which he knew so well how to con-
struct upon the melodies that live to a poet in
every natural sight and sound, who might not
be able to comprehend his subtle imagery and
the fairy flowers of his phantasy, would not fail
to acknowledge the hand of the great master in
the striking figures that stand out, in such profusion, from his canvas. The versatility of his
genius is as striking an attribute of the man as
its beauty. No thinker can ignore the creative
mind that could give us, at one time, the heart-
searing agony of "The Scarlet Letter," at
another "The Tender Beauty," shaded here
and there with gloom, of "The House of the
Seven Gables;" at one time, the half-playful,
half-earnest mysticism of "The Blithedale
Romance," and at another the sombre
horrors of some of his legends. His latest

romance, by many considered his greatest work,
"Transformation," opens up to us a field of
fiction, which no writer, before Hawthorne, has
worked in so entirely original and felicitous a
manner. The way in which he indicates the
subtle change in the mind of "Donatello,"
the weird transition from an utterly sensuous
life to the development of a higher though
pain-purchased intelligence, produced by the
entrance upon the stage of his existence of
a new and sinful agency through whose
constraining influence his happy, careless,
sunny joyance merges into the reserved
and somewhat gloomy gravity of a being conscious of the awful truths of immortality and
the heavy responsibilities of an undying soul,
is unsurpassable. There is scarcely a character
in the whole range of fiction which can compare
with it. The whole book, besides, is a mine of
beauty. In contrast with the increasing gloom
that shadows over the two principal characters,
stands out, in grateful relief, the exquisite figure
of Hilda, as lovely in its delicate beauty and its
cold and stainless purity as "The Sea-born
Venus" of another gifted American, Mr.
Fraiken. The minor personages of the story
are all sketched in with consummate art, and
the completed picture is set in a flower-fringed
frame of most delightful fancies and imagery, in
which the old classical, mythical fictions are
interwoven with modern romance in an exquisitely delicate and beautiful manner.

In his study of character, Hawthorn did not
think it beneath him to notice the least details,
the humblest links of domestic circumstance,
when by so doing he could more fully and
artistically exhibit the growth of an embryo
intelligence. Indeed, he sometimes probes the
wounds that have been left by great trials or
great sins so far and so minutely, in his search
after the hidden germ of psychical development,
that he has often been *accused* of a morbid
craving for the sensational laying open of revolting details, for word-dissection, to an extent
almost painful.

His "Scarlet Letter" is generally chosen as
the weak point on this ground; but it seems
scarcely possible to an intelligent reader that
any one, who does not make his own faults, can
study that most wonderful picture without observing how—though the subject is painful and
almost revolting, and the details of the sufferings
of Hester and the young minister would be un-
bearable if depicted by a mediocre writer—the
light genius of the author has enabled him to
make beautiful these deformities with the veiling
embellishment of his poetic thought, and to
etherealize the grosser interests and struggles of
mortals into some diviner essence, the secret of
which is known only to himself.

Old Roger Chillingworth, certainly, is a demon of unrelenting malignity in his thirst for vengeance, and his deliberate hourly, nay, momentary, re-awakening of the most cruel tortures in the young minister's breast; but much horror is removed from the sketch by the manner in which it is treated, and by the remembrance of how deeply the once kindly and gentle scholar had been wronged. Indeed, his Mephistophelian impersonation seems almost grateful to us, as a necessary and *apropos* foil to the weird and dazzling brightness of little Pearl's elfin figure. This latter character, again, with her strange, half-uncanny, all bright and beautiful ways and actions, illuminates the sombre ground of the drama with a fitful and capricious light, giving no relief to the gloom, but, like a fleeting meteor in a cloud-obscured sky, causing the shadow to seem doubly dark beside the brilliant ray. Very touching and beautiful, in its simple pathos, is the death-scene of the young minister, when he conquers the cowardly silence in which he has veiled so long his association in criminality with Hester, and lays open the blackness of his sin before that congregation, who have learned to look upon him as something almost more than mortal. A wonderful effect, too, have the weird suggestions of the future witch-mania and the temptation of the minister by the hag, that chequer the black canvas of the story with their lurid flashes of furnace flame. But we should require far more space and time than we can possibly at present occupy, if we attempted to point out a tithe of these inimitable beauties. They have been already, and will, doubtless, often again be discoursed of, by pens much more capable.

We have now before us a tiny book, of some forty pages, that contains the last ideas which the mighty magician conceived and recorded. But the short first chapter of an unfinished story, to be called the "Dolliver Romance," bears so exquisitely the impress of Hawthorne's master-hand, that we read it with even more than the old eagerness, and when we arrive at the break which can never be remedied, the void which can now never be bridged over, find fresh cause to lament the loss of the writer. It is the opening sketch of the declining age of an old New England apothecary, upon whose trembling limbs life has scarcely any hold, and for whom earth has no retaining link except the beloved presence of his little grandchild "Pansie." With one foot in the grave, and the blood in his veins frozen by the wintry breath of age, he has nothing in common with the new generation, and lives in a state of continual abstraction, from which only a child's voice can recall him. This latter, a little tottering creature of 3 years, a faint indication of a beautiful figure, is the revivifying influence of the old man's life, his

perpetual revisiting of spring, the one only thing
that remains to him here below to prevent his
weary soul from passing away.

This preliminary outline is drawn with exquisite tenderness and delicacy of hand, and we
can perceive in it the promise of a more perfect
and beautiful work than any he had as yet given
to the world.   All Hawthorne's charming peculiarities are perceptible in it. His quaint conceits
and half-humours, half-pathetic turns of thought,
are as thickly strewn over these few pages as
in many of his productions, and perhaps they
are touched off with a more loving and delicate
care.   Some of the ideas are full of so tenderly
lovely and mournful a fancy, that one cannot
but think that approaching death must have
given to his inward vision some clearer insight
into sights and secrets beyond mortal ken.
One passage, in which he describes the way in
which the old man, on whom the greeting and
business of the outside world fall with jarring
and painful strangeness, is soothed and com-
forted by the innocent companionship of his
tiny granddaughter, is of such unequalled
beauty that we cannot resist the temptation of
quoting it.

" Walking the streets seldom and reluctantly, he
felt a dreary impulse to elude the people's observation, as if with a sense that he had gone irrevocably
out of fashion, and broken his connecting links
with the network of human life; or else it was that
nightmare-feeling which we sometimes have in
dreams, when we seem to find ourselves wandering
through a crowded avenue, with the noonday sun
upon us, in some wild extravagance of dress or
nudity. He was conscious of estrangement from
his townspeople, but did not always know how or
wherefore, nor why he should be thus groping
through the twilight mist in solitude. If they
spoke loudly to him, with cheery voices, the greeting translated itself faintly and mournfully to his
ears; if they shook him by the hand, it was as if a
thick insensible glove absorbed the kindly pressure
and the warmth. When little Pansie was the companion of his walk, her childish gaiety and freedom
did not avail to bring him into closer relationship
with men, but seemed to follow him to that region
of indefinable remoteness, *that dismal Fairyland
of aged fancy*, into which old Grandsire Dolliver
had so strangely crept away. Yet there were moments, as many persons had noticed, when the
great-grandpapa would suddenly take stronger hues
of life. It was as if his faded figure had been
coloured over anew, or at least, as he and Pansie
moved along the street, as if a sunbeam had fallen
across him, instead of the grey gloom of an instant
before. His chilled sensibilities had probably been
touched and quickened by the warm contiguity of
his little companion through the medium of her
hand, as it stirred within his own, or some inflection
of her voice that set his memory ringing and chim-
ing with forgotten sounds. While that music lasted,
the old man was alive and happy. And there were
seasons, it might be, even happier than these, when

Pansie had been kissed and put to bed, and Grandsire Dolliver sat by his fireside, gazing in among
the massive coals and above their glow into those
cavernous abysses with which all men communicate.
Hence come angels or fiends into our twilight
musings, according as we may have peopled them in
bygone years. Over our friend's face, in the rosy
flicker of the fire-gleam, stole an expression of repose and perfect trust that made him as beautiful to
look at, in his high-backed chair, as the child Pansie
on her pillow ; and sometimes the spirits that were
watching him beheld a calm surprise draw slowly
over his features, and brighten into joy, though not
so vividly as to break his evening quietude. *The
gate of heaven had been kindly left ajar, that this
forlorn old creature might catch a glimpse within.*
All the night afterwards, he would be semi-conscious
of an intangible bliss diffused through the fitful
lapses of an old man's slumber, and would awake
at early dawn with a faint thrilling of the heart-
strings, as if there had been music just now wandering over them."

And so abruptly finishes this last emanation of
Hawthorne's poet-soul. Its very beauty strikes
a painful chord within us, when we note the
certain indications in these last few lines his
hand traced, how surely his genius was advancing towards the greatest heights of inspiration, how he would have exalted and delighted
the world with the ripened fruit of his maturer
age, and think that the soul which gave vent to
his poetic yearnings has fled, that we may never
more look for another magical outpouring of
artistic treasure from the hand that now lies cold
in death.

Truly the present age is a fatal one to genius.
Those who own a higher intellect and a nobler
mission than the general mass of mankind, who
are destined to give us some vague inkling of
celestial beauty, seem unwilling now to linger
amongst us, and seek in their early prime a
nobler refuge than is to be found upon earth,
and where their poetic dreams will meet with a
surer realization.

In former ages our great classic authors, in
poetry and prose, lived mostly to a good old age,
and were permitted to expand into imperishable
works, for our benefit, the clearer and nobler
thoughts of their autumn age; but now very
few great lights in literature and art remain to
us beyond their earliest manhood.

It seems not long ago that Shelley, Keats, and
Mendelssohn passed away; but the other day
that Hood, Mrs. Browning, and Macaulay received their last summons! (How they crowd
upon us as we recall them!) And now another
of the Immortals has taken wing, and departed
to that unknown place "where only," in the
words of the most beautiful epitaph in the
language, " his own harmony can be excelled."

Nathaniel Hawthorne has been taken away ;
but it may be some consolation to those who

weep for him, to know that his death was as
easy as ever was vouchsafed to mortal, and
that the gentle current of his life passed away
into the unseachable ocean of eternity, in the
painless insensibility of a swoon.

Brown University

The Reluctant Yankee in Hawthorne's Abortive Gothic Romances

RONALD T. CURRAN

The three drafts of Hawthorne's proposed romance situated in England[1] are characterized by a satiric and chauvinistic purpose that informs the story of an American in search of his lost patrimony. All three manuscripts, "The Ancestral Footstep" and "Doctor Grimshawe's Secret" (I and II), represent successive drafts of the same attempted tale. Hawthorne planned to make sport with the idiosyncrasies of both nations while finally endorsing America and democracy. The protagonist would ultimately proclaim his Yankee heritage and refute any claim to a British title or estate. Whatever embellishments Hawthorne added, his focus upon a real or bogus heir in search of his origins remained central in each manuscript. The success or failure of the hero's identity quest would discredit British aristocracy, since the establishment of the American's roots would discover a scandal in an inheritance encompassing 200 years. This exposé would then publicize a history of wrongdoing rivaling that of the Pyncheons.

Though Hawthorne never completed the romance, his attempts reveal that his theme would have been similar to that of *The House of the Seven Gables*. Family sins would haunt and corrupt successive generations of aristocrats. Renewal of the family and reversal of this repetition of wrongdoing was promised in a democratic marriage and hybridization of the pure line. Hawthorne's incomplete romance again proposes such a renewal, but at the national level. Unfortunately, his Gothic embellishments eventually absorbed and overshadowed his original purposes. When Hawthorne finally broke off writing, he was totally enmeshed in the jumbled details of a stock Gothic romance. Unable to write with the same control and originality evident in his successful romances,[2] Hawthorne in the last phase fell back upon unmodified and standard aspects of Gothic fiction. His unfinished drafts reveal the degree of his dependence upon the standard class myth,[3] motifs, characters, and devices of the Gothicists. These manuscripts testify to the significant though essentially secondary role which Gothic materials generally played in his fiction.

Hawthorne's characteristically ambivalent endorsement of democracy recurs in these unfinished drafts. It is embodied in his use of the Gothic class myth. Biographical evidence and comments in the *English Notebooks* confirm Hawthorne's identification with the hero in his romance of England. Middleton, Etherege, Ned (later Edward Redcliffe)[4] all fulfill the role of the aristocrat in search of his birthright. Edward H. Davidson notes that Hawthorne "began to toy with the idea that he was the last surviving male heir of a family long absent from the old home. In himself, he became the living visible symbol of a link between England and America." Quoting from the *English Notebooks*, Davidson finds that Hawthorne (then Consul to Liverpool) mused: "My ancestor left England in 1635. I return in 1853. I sometimes feel as if I myself had been absent these two hundred and eighteen years—leaving England emerging from the feudal system, and finding it on the verge of Republicanism."[5] Davidson also adds that in "The Ancestral Footstep" so many "narrative and descriptive elements of the romance parallel Hawthorne's own experiences in and record of England that it is suggestive to compare certain passages of the fragmentary novel with their counterparts in the English journal."[6] In these drafts we find Hawthorne concerning himself with the two social and governmental orders—feudalism and democracy. His romance of England portrays the same central conflict as "The Legends of the Province House" and *The House of the Seven Gables*. And in these posthumous works Hawthorne identifies himself with each of his protagonists who attempt to solve the secret of their ancestry in order to define their own roots and destiny.

Among his early romances, *The House of the Seven Gables* reveals the most clearly Hawthorne's concern with class and family in America. In that novel he employs with variations the Gothic class myth which reinstates a momentarily disinherited aristocrat to his lost patrimony. Superficially his novel seems to refute any notions of aristocracy and social status. But his Yankee radical, Holgrave, joins the Establishment, grows conservative, abandons his liberal beliefs, and settles on Judge Pyncheon's opulent estate. Working with the same myth in "The Ancestral Footstep" and the Grimshawe manuscripts, Hawthorne extends the problem of class identification with a quest motif that involves a search for the European roots of an American family. In both instances his biographical and notebook commentary reveal his personal involvement in the conflicts that naturally arose in any sensitive

American. Aware of the disperity between the sharp outlines of European identity and the blurred ones of the evolving American character, Hawthorne often depicted his characters' attraction for something more concrete.

Significantly, Hawthorne returns in the last phase to the same conflicts between aristocracy and democracy; pride in European ancestry, class, and wealth. Attempting to set forth the plot of "The Ancestral Footstep," he writes that "In the traditions that [Middleton] brought over, there was a key to some family secrets that were still unsolved, and that controlled the descent of estates and titles. His influence upon these matters involves [him] in divers strange and perilous adventures; and at last it turns out that he himself is the rightful heir to the titles and estate, that had passed into another name within the last half-century" (p. 445). With minor modifications we have a description of the plot of either Walpole's *Castle of Otranto* or Clara Reeve's *Old English Baron*. Both works reinstate their heroes—Theodore and Edmund respectively—in the family castle. On the other hand in *The House of the Seven Gables*, Hawthorne aborted his American democratic version of that Gothic class myth. Rather than reaffirming Holgrave's peasant identity, he upholds the concept of status in converting his Maule to a Whig conservative. The man whose classless ancestors claimed the land from a New World wilderness with bareknuckled pioneering spirit joins the rank and file. In this first posthumous draft of his romance, Hawthorne again attempts to endorse democracy. His inability to complete the narrative attests in part to his failure to do so.

Nonetheless, Hawthorne's addition of an international dimension to "The Ancestral Footstep" is significant. Seen in the light of Middleton's (his American protagonist) vision of England, Hawthorne's selection of a British setting takes on meaning: "he sought his ancient home as if he had found his way into Paradise and were endeavoring to trace out the sight [site] of Eve's bridal bower, the birthplace of the human race and its glorious possibilities of happiness and high performance" (p. 437). Great Britain becomes the setting for the revised class myth that promises a new social order. Therefore, the symbolic New England landscape in *The House of the Seven Gables* gains a rival for its part in the genesis myth of a new social order that Hawthorne entertwines with the Gothic class myth. For, essentially, he repeats the component parts and symbolic value of both myths in England. Were Middleton fully drawn and led to make the unpatriotic choice, the republican promise of progressive America would yield to a conservative reverence for the past. And the new Adam and Eve would speak with upper-class British accents.

The false heir's role in "The Ancestral Footstep," however, commits Hawthorne to American republicanism. The bogus aristocrat's negative isolation deflates British notions of birthright and class: "Eldredge's [the Italian claimant to the estate] own position as a foreigner in the midst of English home life, insulated and dreary, shall represent to Middleton, in some degree, what his own would be, were he to accept the estate. But Middleton shall not come to the decision to resign it, without having to repress a deep yearning for that sense of long, long rest in an age-consecrated home, which he had felt so deeply to be the happy lot of Englishmen. But this ought to be rejected, as not belonging to his country, nor to the age, nor any longer possible" (pp. 517-18).

Hawthorne's avowed moral, moreover, preserves the same chauvinistic message that Governor Hancock delivered on the Province House steps in "Old Esther Dudley." "The Moral, if any moral were to be gathered from these petty and wretched circumstances, was, 'Let the past alone: do not seek to renew it; press on to higher and better things,...and be assured that the right way can never be that which leads you back to the identical shapes that you long ago left behind. Onward, onward, onward!' " (XI, 488-89). Middleton, Hawthorne indicates, will echo Holgrave's same distaste for the weight of the dead hand of the past on the present. The proposed plot of the romance strongly resembles that of *The House of the Seven Gables.* However, Middleton"...resigns all the claims which he might now assert, and retires, arm in arm with Alice...The estate takes a passage into the female line, and the old name becomes extinct, nor does Middleton seek to conclude it by resuming it in place of the one long ago assumed by his ancestor. Thus he and his wife become the Adam and Eve of a new epoch, and the fitting missionaries of a new social faith, of which there must be continual hints through the book" (p. 490). Hawthorne designs Middleton's marriage to Alice to fulfill the promise that he rescinded in his ending to *The House of the Seven Gables.* Unlike Holgrave, Middleton maintains his liberal American posture. He has no taste for stone fences and venerable ancestral mansions. Middleton breaks with the old aristocratic order, whereas Holgrave returns to it.

Essentially, Hawthorne reveals himself a committed nationalist in his statements of purpose in "The Ancestral Footstep." He plans to follow the same pattern as Walpole and Reeve with his American aristocrat, only to win him estate and birthright so that he may relinquish them once and for all. "I should think ill of an American," Hawthorne asserts, "who for any causes of ambition,—any hope of wealth or rank,—or even for the sake of any of those old, delightful ideas of the past, the associations of ancestry, the loveliness of an age-long home,—the old poetry and romance that haunt these ancient villages and estates of England,—would give up the chance of acting upon the unmoulded future of America" (p. 505).

Hawthorne's teasing list of delightful things to be rejected recalls his words in the preface to *The Marble Faun,* and it reveals an appeal which tradition continually had to the author himself. Perhaps both his aims and his failing powers account for these unfinished drafts of this proposed romance. That Hawthorne should find it difficult to endorse his own country and system of government in the midst of the Civil War does not stretch credibility. The war depressed and disillusioned him, since it threatened the institutions that lay at the foundation of American life. Coincidentally, at one point, Hawthorne kills Middleton in a slip of the pen that Freudians would find not without significance. Eldredge, the Italian aristocrat and claimant to the ancestral estate, momentarily emerges as victor in the death struggle that Hawthorne eschewed from his narrative a few pages later (p. 453).

Nor is it without significance that Middleton makes *two* attempts to unlock the secret of his birthright. When he initially approaches the Lilliputian replica of his family's palace, Middleton finds no documents in the old cabinet, an architectural model of his family's fabled residence: "Yet here it was in miniature, all that he had dreamed of; a palace of four feet high! (p. 461). Pressing one of the mosaics to discover the tiny castle's Gothic apartment, Middleton observes only a "pinch of dust" (p. 462). Recasting his symbolic episode at a later phase, Hawthorne relates that "Middleton looked eagerly in, and saw that it contained documents, with antique seals of wax appended..." But closing the receptacle, Middleton decides that "The case was one demanding consideration, and he put a strong curb upon his impatient curiosity, conscious that, at all events, his first impulsive feeling was that he ought not to examine these papers without the presence of his host or some other authorized witness" (p. 511).

"The Ancestral Footstep" ends indecisively. Middleton is appointed ambassador, and his second visit to the ancestral home never materializes though Hawthorne predicts disastrous consequences when the heir asserts his claim. Hawthorne's indecisiveness about this central scene is as symbolic as the action and setting themselves. His proposal for a chauvinistic romance yields by 19 May 1858 to work on *The Marble Faun* and quite different problems.[7]

By 1861, however, Hawthorne's preliminary studies for "Doctor Grimshawe's Secret" reveal that he had not altogether abandoned his plans for a romance about England. Ideas for a double-edged satire of both English and American manners embellish his initial plot in "The Ancestral Footstep," and passages in the Grimshawe drafts reflect the same attempt.[8] In both "The Ancestral Footstep" and "Doctor Grimshawe's Secret," the essential plan and conflicts remain the same. Study "A" reveals the similarity of the latter to "The Ancestral Footstep" as well as to Gothic fiction:

The English and American ideas to be brought strikingly into contrast
and contact. The American comes back to England, somewhat with the
sense of a wronged person; for there shall have been a tradition of his ancestors having been driven away with wrong and contumely. He returns
to find them in a state of apparently greater prosperity than ever, but yet
on the verge of a crisis, which he perhaps discovers through his researches into old records and estimates by his legal knowledge. There shall,
on the other hand, be a tradition in the English family of a vanished heir,
who, if he were alive, would take all the land and estates; and this on
comparison shall coincide with the American tradition. . . Feeling himself
the heir, the American shall consider himself entitled to dispose as he
pleases of the estate and honors and so shall, in exercise of his judgment,
let the title and estate pass away. . .(p. 21)

Study "B" supplements Hawthorne's Gothic plans, emphasizing the
conflict between feudalism and republicanism. In this second plan
Hawthorne proposes that "around this American of to-day will be
made to diffuse itself a romantic, if not preternatural interest; and the
feelings of the Democrat and Aristocrat will be brought out in all the
stronger contrast. . .The great gist of the story ought to be the natural
hatred of men—and the particular hatred of Americans—to an
Aristocracy; at the same time doing a good deal of justice to the
aristocratic system by respecting its grand, beautiful, and noble characteristics" (p. 22). Hawthorne's expansion of these proposals, however,
makes only a passing attempt to satirize the contrasting political and
social systems. Such satire comprises mainly isolated commentary
which is secondary to the main action of solving the identity riddle.
The latter takes precedence over all else. Atmosphere and supporting
characters derive their functions and meaning in connection with the
protagonist's quest for his familial, social, and national identity.
Hawthorne's underlying chauvinism never develops; the hero never
gains the position of being able to repudiate his British titles and estate.
Indeed, at points in his narrative, Hawthorne develops Etherege as a
representative American in search of more solid national roots than
America—a country as yet without a clear-cut identity—could supply.
Cross-purposes seem involved when Etherege can defend his country
and national heritage in one breath and disclaim it in the next. In an
exchange with the warden of the alms house, Etherege allows that "All
this sort of thing building a home for one's posterity is beautiful; the
family institution was beautiful in its day,. . .but it is a thing of the past.
It is dying out in England; and as for ourselves, we never had it.
Something better will come up; but as for this it is past" (I, 97). Shortly
thereafter, Etherege tells Hammond that as an American he would
have no interest in investigating his parentage with a view to
recovering an hereditary title: "The title. . .ought not to be a very
strong consideration with an American. One of us would be ashamed, I

verily believe, to assume any distinction except such as may be supposed to indicate personal, not hereditary merit" (I, 116).

At a later phase of the first draft of "Doctor Grimshawe's Secret,"
however, Etherege tells Hammond quite another story. Refusing to take
the pensioner's advice and leave England, Etherege repeats aghast:

> Gone hence!...I tell you—what I have hardly hitherto told to
> myself—that all my dreams, all my wishes hitherto, have looked for-
> ward to precisely the juncture that seems now to be approaching. My
> dreaming childhood dreamt of this. If you know anything of me, you
> know how I sprang out of mystery, akin to none, a thing concocted out of
> the elements, without visible agency—how, all through my boyhood, I
> was alone; how I grew up without a root, yet continually longing for
> one—longing to be connected to somebody—and never feeling myself so.
> Yet there was ever a looking forward to this time at which I now find
> myself. If my next step were death, yet while the path seemed to lead
> onward to a certainty of establishing me in connection with my race, I
> would yet take it. I have tried to keep down this yearning to stifle it, an-
> nihilate it, with making a position for myself, with being my own past;
> but I cannot overcome this natural horror of being a creature floating in
> the air, attached to nothing; ever this feeling that there is no reality in
> the life and fortunes, good or bad, of being so unconnected. There is not
> even a grave, not a heap of dry bones, not a pinch of dust, with which I
> can claim connection, unless I find it here.' (I, 145)

Hawthorne's design in thus depicting Etherege seems linked with
the same Gothic class myth that he accepted in a modified form in *The
House of the Seven Gables*. Like Holgrave, Etherege is depicted as the archetypal Yankee radical, and that similarity continues as Hawthorne
puts the same conservatism into the latter's statements concerning birthright, ancestry, and an artisocratic identity that must lead eventually
to undemocratic notions of class. In other words the democratic order—envisioned by both Holgrave and Etherege, by Colonel Joliffe,
Captain Lincoln, Alice Vane, and Governor Hancock in the Province
House legends—never materializes. Instead, the protagonists in whom
this political philosophy is embodied often become its antagonists and
are converted to the system they initially oppose.

Earlier in the first draft, Hawthorne had begun to prepare the reader
for Etherege's conversion. After Etherege had freed himself of Yankee
legislative cares in America, Hawthorne tells us that he seized the opportunity for a visit to England. And being there "he began to feel the
deep yearning which the sensitive American—his mind full of English
thoughts, his imagination of English poetry, his heart of English character and feeling—cannot fail to be influenced by, the yearning of the
blood within his veins for that from which it had been estranged..." (I,
70).

Clearly, Hawthorne intends that Etherege's feelings are to be viewed as those of all Americans. And the new social philosophy he hinted at broadly in "The Ancestral Footstep" reappears in a later stage of development in the first draft of "Doctor Grimshawe's Secret." Voicing this theory of renewal, the pensioner says that history and observation proved, that all people...needed to be transplanted, or somehow renewed, every few generations; so that, according to this ancient philosopher's theory, it would be good for the whole people of England, now, if it could at once be transplanted to England [America]...and equally good, on the other hand, for the whole American people to be transplanted back to the original island" (I, 101). Etherege later receives the same advice from Lord Brathwaite who includes his own countrymen in the renewal theory, saying, "Indeed, Italians might do as well [as Americans]" (I, 137).

The spokesman, however, is less important than the theory itself. For the theory suggests that Hawthorne has modified his idea to make England the new Eden and Middleton and his wife "the fitting missionaries of a new social faith" (p. 490). Rather than repudiating the titles and estate, the hero threatens to remain and take part in a renewal of England. He is not pledged to marry an American expatriate with dual, equally strong national ties and return to his native land as Hawthorne proposed at one point in "The Ancestral Footstep" (p. 517). Instead, textual evidence reveals that Hawthorne considered Etherege's being the true heir (I, 121), assuming his rightful inheritance, and renewing the English. The Yankee who once prided himself on his possibly springing from the lowest origins (I, 63) threatens to defect, change citizenship and class, and continue the process of hybridization on the other side of the water. He is a Holgrave figure turned into an expatriate as well as an aristocrat. And his partly sketched role again exposes Hawthorne's misgivings about the promise of American democracy. This time his protagonist prefers renewal outside America. While his conversion may work both ways, his avowed desires to find roots and background threaten to overshadow his commitment to democracy. He will be more influenced in all likelihood by his passionately desired past than by his role as an agent in Britain's conversion to democratic government.

Hawthorne's aims change, however, and he never develops this scheme of national renewal. Avoiding the issue altogether, he sets to exploiting the Gothic possibilities inherent in the legend of the Bloody Footstep and the unlawfully-held Brathwaite estate. Etherege becomes rather foolish, prattling out of both sides of his mouth, since Hawthorne's plan to award the estate to the pensioner (I, 189) makes Etherege's comments of little consequence. His deception had been planned very early in the first draft (I, 54-55). Deluding the hero about his aristocratic birthright, Hawthorne relieves him of any major role in the narrative. To make full use of the Gothic possibilities in his romance, Hawthorne dismisses the conflict he began with. After his choice of the pensioner, Hawthorne falls into another meditative aside to ponder the future course of his narrative: "Try back again" (I, 189), he counsels himself.

Hawthorne's puzzlement at this point appears in the form of a profusion of weird Gothic additions. Choosing the pensioner, Hammond, as the heir solves none of the questions raised by Etherege's quest for his true identity. Dropping that aspect of his romance, Hawthorne drifts into Gothic flights of fancy akin to those of Monk Lewis and Poe. He initiates a revenge motif: Doctor Grimshawe has revived a criminal presumed hanged, gained control of the man's will, and dispatched him to the family household to torment and persecute successive generations of Grimshawes for a wrong they did to him (I, 189). He decides that "The spiders [are] to be much emphasized" (I, 189). Then Hawthorne ponders the question of how the nearly hanged man is to be subjugated to the Doctor's will: "He broods over a coffer in which his beloved's ashes are enclosed? Pish. He has her converted into a ring, which pinches his finger, giving him exquisite torment" (I, 190). Making his picture of Doctor Grimshawe more Gothic, Hawthorne speculates: "He might have embalmed a member of the family in some new way; so that he shall appear lifelike—to what good end? The Devil knows; I don't" (I, 190). Developing the role of the inadequately hanged man whom Doctor Grimshawe revived, the author draws a typical Gothic villain: "The man whom the doctor leaves behind must act the part of a house-hold demon to successive heirs...He fosters all wickedness in the young, and facilitates it in the old" (I, 191).

Not wishing to resolve the problems that would arise from Etherege's heirship, Hawthorne ponders what significance remains. Zealously attempting to discover the past, Etherege, as Hawthorne finally depicts him, succeeds only in destroying his illusion. The moral perhaps intended seems to be that researches in the past unearth painful realities. The golden ringlets of the persecuted maiden are a fool's-gold reminder of the wrongdoings of former generations. Discovery only releases such secrets to plague the living and to preserve the influence of former injustice in a pattern of retribution. In a sense Etherege opens the coffer not only to discover golden locks but also to enrich the Gothic possibilities of the plot. This turnabout from the narrative of national confrontation and renewal reflects his desire to write a standard Gothic romance complete with Italian villain, persecuted maidens, mysterious apartments, and haunted castles. His change from an initially benign portrait of a kindhearted Doctor Grimshawe raising orphaned children to that of a vengeful alchemist tends in the same Gothic direction. Emphasis in the second draft falls on the alchemist "wholly unradiant of hope, misanthropic, savagely morbid" (II, 264), who looks at Ned as though he'd "eat him up" (II, 242), rather than upon Etherege as a disinherited aristocrat in search of his patrimony. Hints of this Gothic intention appear throughout the meditative asides in the first draft, but their full potentiality is not sensed until Hawthorne has abandoned the hero, the quest for familial and national identity, and the resolution of the protagonist's resulting conflict of national interest. When he does so, the full Gothic potential of "Doctor Grimshawe's Secret" is released.

Nonetheless, even while Hawthorne adds Gothic embellishments to his second draft, he cannot resist recurring to his original plan. Though he has announced Doctor Grimshawe's purpose of fostering a bogus heir, Hawthorne underscores Ned's aristocratic background. In a sense Hawthorne himself recognizes the thematic consequences of discrediting Etherege. Ned dwells, we are told, in his "castle in the air" and "that visionary hall, in England" (II, 261). Later Hawthorne confides: "It is very remarkable that Ned had so much good in him as we find there; in the first place, born as he seemed to be of a vagrant stock, a seedling sown by the breezes, and falling among the rocks or sands...That unknown mother, that had no opportunity to nurse her boy, must have had gentle and noblest qualities to endow him with; a noble father, too, a long sustained descent, one would have thought. Was this an alms house child?" (II, 264). We learn that when Ned wakes up in the alms house, he finds himself equally at home as when he lived with Doctor Grimshawe in America. The family crest which ornaments nearly every item in the alms house "was just as familiar to his recollection as that of the cat which he had fondled in his childhood" (II, 227). Subsequently, he becomes intolerably irritated that the two dreams (of England and America) during his delirium "should have knotted and entangled themselves in his mind" (II, 278). Bird sounds in the English countryside impress him as familiar: "'The lark! The lark!' exclaimed the traveller, recognizing the note (though never heard before) as if his childhood had known it...'How familiar these rustic sounds!' he exclaimed. 'Surely I was born here!' " (II, 274).

In the later half of his second draft, Hawthorne changes Ned's name to Edward Redclyffe, and it seems more than mere coincidence that Sir Edward Redclyffe is the name of the benefactor of the almshouse, one of the past heirs of the family estate nearby, and of the same family whose crest decorates the almshouse and seems so familiar to Hawthorne's American who quests after his identity (II, 286). Such evidence takes on added significance when we recall Etherege's initial reaction to England: "'Oh home, my home, my forefather's home! I have come back to thee! The wanderer has come back!'" (I, 146). Hawthorne's ambivalent stand on the question of heirship cannot be dismissed. But his attraction for the conflict that would arise if Etherege were found to be the true heir seems as evident in the above statements by his hero as by his inability to meet and resolve that conflict.

In the second draft, however, at nearly the same point as in the first, Hawthorne abandons the manuscript. It ends with a conversation between the warden and Edward who contrast aspects of America and England. And they do not resolve the problem of which nation is superior to the other. In a sense they embody the debate which Hawthorne could not conclude for himself during this period. Unable to mine the cultural and psychological implications of Gothic myths, symbols, motifs, and devices, he permits them to crowd his unfinished romance with satiric materials that give it the aspect of a typical Gothic romance.

Aware of his similarity to well-known Gothic writers, Hawthorne describes the ancestral home of the Brathwaites as not having "much of the stateliness of Mrs. Radcliffe's castles with their suites of rooms opening into one another" (I, 154). Fearing his kinship with a more contemporary Gothicist, Hawthorne cautioned himself: "The story must not be founded at all on remorse or secret guilt—all that Poe wore out" (I, 105). And during his composition of "Doctor Grimshawe's Secret," he read aloud to his family from nearly all eight volumes of Sir Walter Scott's historical Gothic romances.[9]

To a degree Hawthorne's plans reflect a pattern that emerges in the meditative passages. The more he attempts to enrich his narrative with stock Gothic additions, the further confused he becomes. Instead of contrasting two systems of government, Hawthorne wishes to focus his romance upon Doctor Grimshawe's revenge plot and that scientist's qualities as a slightly-mad alchemist (II, 207). He portrays Lord Brathwaite as an archetypal Italian villain with the heartless logic of Machiavelli and the cruelty of the medieval Church. Hawthorne plans extensive Melmoth-like wanderings for the pensioner (I, 119ff.), and he considers exploiting the Gothic motif of the hero's reaction to solitary confinement (I, 168). In short, Hawthorne's more characteristic and original designs are redrawn with a Gothic ostentation that diverts and eventually dominates the narrative. All such additions serve mainly to obscure his original purpose and to entangle the novel in a confusion of subplots that retard its progress and lead to its eventual abortion. In these final works the Gothic tradition subverts rather than informs Hawthorne's creative process.

In "Septimius Felton" Hawthorne writes in the same Gothic mode as he did in the preceding posthumous works.[10] Doctor Jabez Portsoaken carries on the arachnid research of Doctor Grimshawe. And like the American bachelor-scientist, Doctor Portsoaken lives in rooms full of an "abundance of spiders, who had spun their webs about the walls and ceiling in the wildest apparent confusion" (p. 365). Reworking the legend of the bloody footstep from "Doctor Grimshawe's Secret" into "Septimius Felton," Hawthorne expands his treatment adding even more Gothic clutter.

Nonetheless, even in this posthumous manuscript, Hawthorne reintroduces the theme of inheritance characteristic of "The Ancestral Footstep" and "Doctor Grimshawe's Secret." Doctor Portsoaken tells Septimius that his family name is one "formerly of much eminence and repute" in England (p. 373) and that the ancestral estate "lies open to any well-sustained, perhaps to any plausible, claimant" (p. 376). However, Septimius' only interest in the claim-supporting documents that he uncovers in the family chest is the information they provide which helps him to decipher the formula for the elixir of life. However faithful Hawthorne remains to his central theme of immortality, he still concludes his Gothic romance with playful but significant ambiguity. He hints broadly that his protagonist foresook his quest for the elixir only to claim aristocratic privilege in England. "Rumors there have been...that there had appeared an American claimant, who had made out his right to the great estate of Smithell's Hall, and had dwelt there, and left posterity, and that in the subsequent generation an ancient baronial title had been revived in favor of the son and heir of the American" (p. 430).

Though his ending is clearly equivocal, Hawthorne finally succeeds in restoring the British patrimony of one of his American heroes. Whereas Middleton, Etherege, and Ned (later Edward Redcliffe) fall short of returning to the traditional structure of the Old World, Septimius—Hawthorne intimates with ambiguity and regret—may have effected a complete reintegration of his ancestral line in England.

It would be unjustified to claim too intimate a connection among all the posthumous works. They are after all separate and each has a somewhat unique identity. But their interconnection in theme and style urges us to attach a significant degree of importance to Septimius's reaffirmation of British birthright and class. The development of that theme in the posthumous works provides an extended view of Hawthorne's own subjective struggle with the different social orders which America and England developed. Whether the New World had progressed beyond and improved upon the old was subject to question in his mind. The evolution of Hawthorne's persistent theme of national identity shows in various degrees his disillusionment rather than his acceptance of one order or another. The rumors which describe Septimius Felton as having reclaimed his British patrimony and continued his family line there merely outline the negative extreme of Hawthorne's skepticism and conservatism at that time.

Working with these drafts we should bear in mind Hawthorne's advice to himself as he composed them: "The life is not yet breathed into this plot, after all my galvanic efforts. Not a spark of passion as yet. How shall it be attained[?]" (I, 149). Nor should the critic be unaware of Hawthorne's earlier warning: "I have not yet struck the true key-note of this Romance, and until I do, and unless I do, I shall write nothing but tediousness and nonsense...The tragic and the gentler pathetic need not be excluded by the tone and treatment. If I could write one central scene in this vein, all the rest of the Romance would readily arrange itself around that nucleus" ("The Ancestral Footstep" p. 491).

In this last phase Hawthorne piles one Gothic borrowing upon another without the details having any relation to a coherent view of the meaning of life. As a result he loses artistic, symbolic, allegorical, and aesthetic as well as moral consistency. Why Hawthorne's control became so feeble we can only guess. In one sense old age brought his consistent skepticism into full flower. For the most part Hawthorne's fictional canon chronicles a history of disillusionment. Moments of optimism are few, fleeting, and unsustained in comparison to the darker periods. Hawthorne's comment on the aspect of a proposed story of Doctor Grimshawe's spider-like entrapment of all the other characters reflects the magnitude of his pessimism at this time. "It [the story] must relate to property; because nothing else survives in this world. Love grows cold and dies; hatred is pacified by anni[hi]lation" (I, 164). Old age, the maturation of a chronic pessimism, and the loss of faith in the growth of love, partly explains Hawthorne's fragmented attempts at romances in this last phase.

Perhaps Septimius Felton's feelings of the unreality of life during a war which unseated his own faith in the dignity and progress of mankind may also reflect Hawthorne's state of mind at a similar period in American history. Describing Septimius's confusion at that moment, Hawthorne relates that "In short, it was a moment as I suppose all men feel (at least I can answer for one), when the real scene and picture of life swims, jars, shakes, seems about to be broken up and dispersed, like the picture in a smooth pond, when we disturb its tranquil mirror by throwing in a stone; and though the scene soon settles itself, and looks as real as before, a haunting doubt keeps close at hand, as long as we live asking, 'Is it stable? Am I sure of it? Am I certainly not dreaming? See; it trembles again, ready to dissolve' " (p. 336). These posthumous works reflect that same unstable and fragmented state of mind.

Hawthorne's sense of instability at this moment seems in part the outgrowth of his own identity crisis, acute during this period of civil conflict, but sustained throughout his life in one degree or another. The psychic strain of war was critical in Hawthorne's case. As his comments in these posthumous drafts admit, his faith in the stability of the American identity was weak. Sensing a form of national schizophrenia inherent in a war between brothers, Hawthorne indeed felt that "the real scene and picture of life" seemed "ready to dissolve." Hawthorne was—or felt himself to be—culturally an orphan, and his prefaces, especially to *The Marble Faun,* often publicized his sense of aesthetic insecurity. He felt the need for deeper roots than American citizenship in the nineteenth century had yet permitted to grow. Hawthorne viewed England and the security of fixed identity and tradition that it represented for him as a refuge from the unsettling dynamism of a culturally-thin nineteenth-century America on the brink of the Civil War. His fear as well as his irony, moreover, is fully engaged in the composition of Clifford's tirade on progress during his train ride with Hepzibah in *The House of the Seven Gables* and in his pointed satire of such reformers as Holgrave and Hollingsworth.

Hawthorne's manipulation of his protagonists in these posthumous manuscripts reveals a man seeking an illusive stability which he associates with union, or perhaps more accurately, *reunion,* with his assumed parent state—England. Is it any wonder, then, that Hawthorne's protagonists in this final phase of his literary career and at this critical juncture in American history go through the motions of a homecoming, are imbued with virtually a Jungian sense of "home feeling" with the English past, assume roles in a British tale of social genesis, and desire to reintegrate their ancestral line by finding its English roots? Hawthorne's characteristic ambiguity striates this issue of insecurity in national identity. In his fiction he represented himself by turns as both Yankee chauvinist in the Province House legends, for example, and nostalgic immigrant in spirit as he did sporadically in the posthumous romances. But this sense of confused and often divided allegiance between America and England, present and past, pervades his fiction and promotes his identity diffusion.

In the face of this personal and national challenge, Hawthorne allowed his conservatism to strengthen and his pessimism to deepen. His inability to maintain a coherent view of life in this latter period is revealed in his dependence upon Gothicism in the posthumous drafts. While these last works reveal starkly his artistic debts to the Gothic tradition, they also—and perhaps more importantly—tell the tale of an artist whose skepticism, conservatism, and weak sense of national identity eventually led to the fragmentation of his view of life. His disillusionment of spirit, in other words, is imaged forth in the disintegration of his talent. Unable to control and to integrate his materials by means of a coherent view of life, Hawthorne lapses into uncontrolled Gothicism which reveals his own disillusionment as well as the degree to which he depended upon the Gothic tradition in his fiction.

Hawthorne, unlike Whitman, could neither envision nor fashion any "stalwart and well-shaped heir." Ambivalence informed his portrait of the Yankee revolutionary precisely because he could not commit himself to Jacksonian democracy. Middleton, Etherege, Edward Redcliffe, and even Holgrave furnish proof that Hawthorne was skeptical of the identity and the values shaped in a basically hybrid egalitarian state. Without tradition and the social, political, and psychic continuity that Hawthorne felt it made possible, America began to seem to him less and less substantial. As his defenses and artistic control slipped away in these later years, Hawthorne began more emphatically to reflect his identity crisis in his fiction. As he grew less able to assure himself who and what he was, he ceased to be able to integrate the basically aristocratic tradition of the Gothic romance with the more democratic concerns he often advanced in his fiction.

University of Pittsburgh

---

[1]Edward H. Davidson, *Hawthorne's Last Phase* (New Haven: Yale University Press, 1949), p. vii. Davidson records also that "The Ancestral Footstep" was written between April and May of 1868 and published in 1882-83, while "Doctor Grimshawe's Secret" was composed during the years 1860-61 and published in 1882. Furthermore, Davidson adds that "Only by ignoring his most solemn injunctions against publishing any of his literary effects did the heirs reveal these romances Hawthorne never intended the world to see" (p. vii). Textual references to "The Ancestral Footstep" are from the Riverside Edition: those to "Doctor Grimshawe's Secret" are from *Hawthorne's "Doctor Grimshawe's Secret"*, Edward H. Davidson, ed. (Cambridge, Massachusetts, 1954). Professor Davidson includes two drafts (I and II) and seven (A, B, B1, C, D, E, & F) "Preliminary Studies" related to "Doctor Grimshawe's Secret" in his edition. The former will be referred to in the text by roman numeral and the latter by alphabetical signification along with the page number. [I want to express my appreciation to the Faculty of Arts and Sciences at the University of Pittsburgh whose research grant enabled me to prepare this article for publication.]

[2]Edward M. Clay, "The 'Dominating' Symbol in Hawthorne's Last Phase," *American Literature*, XXXIX (January 1968), 506-516, views Hawthorne's posthumous romances as symptomatic of his loss of artistic control. Mr. Clay focuses upon Hawthorne's inability to fuse his symbols with the ideas he intended to develop. Rather than being organically suggested by the meanings intended, the symbols are selected on the basis of their appeal to the author. Then Hawthorne attempts artificially to force them to fit the narrative he has in mind. The result is mechanical, contrived, unintegrated, and ultimately incomplete.

[3]By "class myth" I mean the narrative which reinforces and justifies the position of aristocracy in feudal society. Walpole's *The Castle of Otranto* and Reeve's *The Old English Baron* would be good examples. The hero is a disenfranchised aristocrat unaware of his birthright and seemingly a pauper who eventually learns his true identity and recaptures his family's estate from bogus heirs. The peasants in both narratives recognize that the "pauper" in their midst is too clever to be one of their number and must instead be a prince. In

the republican sense the term, "myth," is used to describe a narrative dealing with a culture hero—in this instance the Yankee, the establishment of the present order—democracy, and the delineation of culture traits—ambition, drive, ingenuity, versatility, adaptability, aggressiveness, and vitality.

[4]Hawthorne changes the name of his hero in all three drafts, often modifying his spelling from page to page.

[5]*Hawthorne's Last Phase,* p. 16.

[6]*Ibid.,* p. 23.

[7]*Ibid.,* p. 1.

[8]In the second draft of "Doctor Grimshawe's Secret" Hawthorne emphasizes the American setting for his narrative and the satire on the contrasting systems almost disappears.

[9]*Hawthorne's Last Phase,* p. 7.

[10]In *Hawthorne's Last Phase,* p. vii, Davidson indicates that "Septimius Felton" was written between 1861-63 and published in 1871-72.

RIDING BESIDE THE COLORADO
(Thinking of the Concord)

ERNEST KROLL

Those lovers of the woodlot muse,
Hawthorne and Thoreau,
What would they have said
Of this impetuous river's
Cutting its own abyss
Across a high plateau
To reach the sea without a fall,
When their own brimming stream,
If it moved ahead at all,
Moved in its bed as in a dream,
Without the slightest emphasis?

The river right for a sail
With the one, elect companion
Would sooner take the fall
Than cut itself a canyon.

Nature and Hawthorne's Religious Isolationists

DAVID B. KESTERSON

Commenting on the predominant theme of isolation in Hawthorne's fiction, Paul Elmer More has said that Hawthorne, more than any other author, presents this "one truth of the penalty of solitude laid upon the human soul...."[1] Indeed, More feels, Hawthorne's "works seem to fall together like the movements of a great symphony built upon one imposing theme."[2] Alexander Cowie has also pointed out that most of Hawthorne's themes—the violation of the soul, overindulgence in scientific experimentation, the evils of mesmerism, the search for the elixir—are "in conjunction with Hawthorne's obsession for isolation."[3] What More and Cowie have singled out thematically is manifested in Hawthorne's characterization by numerous isolated characters who run the gamut of various kinds of withdrawal, including isolation resulting from selfish pursuit or an all-absorbing quest, from pride, from harboring of secret guilt, and from simply neglecting roles and responsibilities in society. One of the most predominant groups of isolationists in Hawthorne's fiction, however, is composed of those guilty of religious excess—a fanaticism or enthusiasm that alienates its adherents from society.

Hawthorne often used nature in his fiction—as setting or background for human action and emotion, as descriptive imagery, and as symbolism—to set forth theme and enhance character depiction.[4] All aspects and conditions of floral, faunal, and mineral nature plus sun, moon, and stars, cloudy and clear skies, and elements of weather are brought to bear on theme, character, and situation. As he does with his other types of isolationists, Hawthorne employs nature imagery and symbolism with the religious monomaniacs to indicate that these

196

people have erred. Hawthorne believed that man, to establish and enjoy a normal relationship with his world, must live in harmony with his fellow beings and with nature. If man does not respect the bond of love crucial to coexistence and accept the view that all men are united in a brotherhood of imperfection, and if he does not adopt nature as an inspirational and stabilizing force in his life, he lives a sub-human existence—so self centered as to be at odds with other people and with external nature. Hawthorne's religious enthusiasts, conscious only of their spiritual goals, violate the bond with man and nature essential to living a normal life.

In one of his earliest, if not the earliest, extant tales, "Alice Doane's Appeal,"[5] Hawthorne deals with the isolation of inhumane Puritan zealots who believed in witchcraft and violated social bonds by unjustly executing fellow human beings. The subject of witchcraft appears in both the frame and narrative of the story. The frame consists of the narrator's description of a stroll to Gallows Hill he once took with two young women. When they reach the place of execution, he tells them the story of "Alice Doane's Appeal," a tale of seventeenth-century Salem murder and witchcraft. The aspects of nature found on the hill reflect the wrong doings of the witchcraft executions. Gallows Hill is green but not with grass—woodwax, a "vile and ineradicable weed," has taken over and choked out the grass (XII, 279).[6] The roots of this weed "make the soil their own, and permit nothing else to vegetate among them; so that a physical curse may be said to have blasted the spot, where guilt and frenzy consummated the most execrable scene that our history blushes to record" (XII, 280). Also along the ridge of the hill are ugly, decayed stumps of trees and, protruding from the woodwax, the "rocky substance" of the hill (XII, 281). The decadent, wild setting recalls the moral wrong of the past and, for those involved in witchcraft, alienation from all things humane and salutary.

The pleasant June afternoon in the frame of "Alice Doane" contrasts with the unpleasant winter scene and the coldness and desolation of the story proper. The girls in the frame, their mirth "brightening the gloom into a sunny shower of feeling..." (XII, 281), are foils to the guilt-ridden, abnormal characters in the tale. The destructive, cancerous woodwax is a symbol of the malignant evil of the wizard in the story who tampers with human hearts and uses black magic to shape events to please him. The narrator points out to the girls, concerning the wizard's nearby grave, that "the wood-wax had sprouted originally from his unhallowed bones" (XII, 292). The wizard's hut, incidentally, is ungraced by nature; it stands desolate beneath a range of rocks away from the town. Because of his ruthless devotion to the magic arts, the wizard is separated both from human society and the attractions and comforts of nature.

Religious fanaticism and intolerance which preclude basic understanding and appreciation of human love are dominant forces in "The Gentle Boy." Little Ilbrahim, whose Quaker father has been executed by the Puritans, becomes a victim both of Puritan bigotry and of Quaker fanaticism (in the person of his mother, who is as much a fanatic as the Puritans). He and the Pearsons, the Puritan couple who take him into their home after Tobias Pearson finds him alone and weeping on Gallows Hill, are the only ones in the community not guilty of harsh intolerance.

Despite the villagers' disapprobation of Tobias's lodging a Quaker lad, nature favors the family. Pearson's cottage is nestled in a nook of the wood-covered hill, "whither it seemed to have crept for protection" (I, 92). There, sharing the love of the couple, Ilbrahim enjoys his happiest moments; he becomes a "sunbeam, brightening moody countenances and chasing away gloom" (I, 108). The family are not isolated in nature, for they continue to meet human responsibilities and demands. They simply feel more comfortable living close to beneficent nature, away from the harsh Puritan community.

In contrast to Pearson's love-warmed spot in nature, the outside world—representing the Puritan community—is barren and hostile. The very path to the meeting house winds through "leafless woods" (I, 96), suggesting the barrenness of stern Puritan life. And Ilbrahim's world of love collapses when the village children, all offspring of Puritan bigots, beat him (even though he has given care and love to one of the boys who had once been wounded). The inhuman act crushes Ilbrahim's spirit: the "dance of sunshine" which formerly played over his countenance is destroyed by the cloud over his existence..." (I, 113). The only happiness the delicate youth regains is that which he feels immediately before his death when his mother returns from her wanderings and comes to his bedside in the Pearson home. His words, "mourn not, dearest Mother. I am happy now" (I, 125), express his only comforting thoughts in the world of inhuman persecution. An innocent life aware of human love has been harshly extinguished. The cold, tumultuous Puritan world, symbolized by the fierce wintry blasts blowing against the Pearson cottage on the night of Ilbrahim's death, has again crushed a human soul by its prejudice and dearth of human love.

The story "Endicott and the Red Cross" also deals with the harshness of extreme Puritanism and isolation from humanity. There is no association of nature imagery or symbolism, however, with the protagonist, Endicott, who is as guilty of intolerance as other religious fanatics. Rather, Hawthorne here uses nature to play up the truer religion and more balanced outlook on humanity envinced by Roger Williams and thus demonstrates Endicott's failings by implied comparison. As Williams arrives in Endicott's community from Boston one day, he stops to drink from a fountain near the meeting house—one of the many significant fountains and springs in Hawthorne's fiction. The scene illustrates the man's normal relationship with God and the world: "He laid aside his staff, and stooped to drink at a bubbling fountain which gushed into the sunshine about a score of yards from the corner of the meeting-house. But, ere the good man drank, he turned his face heavenward in thankfulness..." (I, 489). The purity and cleanliness of the fountain gushing into the sun represent Williams' religion, purer and more inspiring than Endicott's fiery, irrational devotion. The fact that the *first* action we see of Williams' is his drinking the bubbling, sun-lit water emphasizes his wholesome relationship with his world.

There are those religious isolationists in Hawthorne's fiction who, because of their own sense of self-righteousness or obsession with man's sinful nature, refuse to accept life the way it is and thus withdraw from humanity. Such are Young Goodman Brown and Mr. Hooper of "The Minister's Black Veil." Roy Male has said that in Hawthorne's fiction which deals with moral growth, "...man solves the riddle of the Sphinx by moving from action through passion to perception, a cycle that leads up to his death. He may attempt to avoid this tragic rhythm, but if he does so he is consumed, like Ethan Brand, too soon."[7] Both Goodman Brown and Parson Hooper face the initiation into life and maturity which Hawthorne recognized as a crucial human experience. But neither can meet the challenge presented by the duality of life, and thus neither matures and both are "consumed." As Melvin Askew says, Mr. Hooper escapes human responsibility by "temporizing" and Brown by "straight-forward rejection."[8] With both characters Hawthorne associates abundant nature imagery and symbols to emphasize their misdirection and subsequent isolation from man and nature. Both men are fittingly characterized by dark, dismal elements of nature, symbolizing their preoccupation with the presence of evil in humanity.

"Young Goodman Brown" is the story of a youth who undergoes an ideal-shattering revelation of the basic imperfection of man and is unable to accept the reality of such a world. After the night of his fearful experience or dream of attending the witchcraft meeting and losing his faith, he becomes "a stern, a sad, a darkly meditative, a distrustful, if not a desperate man..." (II, 106). He cannot sing hymns in church, for he hears instead an "anthem of sin"; he receives nothing from the minister's sermons but sits in expectation of the roof falling down on "the gray blasphemer and his hearers"; and he shuns his pretty wife,

Faith, and scowls at her and the family when they kneel to pray. It is no wonder that when he dies, "no hopeful verse" is carved on his tombstone: "his dying hour was gloom" (II, 106).

The story contains two sets of nature images which point up Brown's dilemma.[9] The first group, composed of gloomy, unsalutary natural objects, emphasize both the evil side of life and also the wrongness of a life spent in continual recognition of and meditation on evil. The road which Brown follows into the forest is dreary and "darkened by all the gloomiest trees of the forest, which barely stood aside to let the narrow path creep through, and closed immediately behind" (as if to admonish Brown not to take such a dark, difficult path—II, 90). The black staff of the man (or devil) with whom he has the rendezvous in the forest resembles "a great black snake, so curiously wrought that it might almost be seen to twist and wriggle itself like a living serpent" (II, 91). As Brown and his companion walk deeper into the forest, the man plucks a maple branch to serve as his walking stick, and the leaves of the branch become "strangely withered and dried up as with a week's sunshine" (II, 95). Nature demonstrates what sort of poisonous company Brown is keeping. When Brown suddenly feels that his faith has deserted him and he must given himself up to the devil, the entire forest is filled with "frightful sounds—the creaking of the trees, the howling of wild beasts, and the yell of Indians; while sometimes the wind...gave a broad roar around the traveller, as if all Nature were laughing him to scorn" (II, 99). At the witch meeting, four of the gloomy pines surrounding a crude rock (resembling either an "altar or a pulpit" are ablaze, as is the mass of foliage on the summit of the rock; and the eerie red fire in the dark trees and undergrowth presents a grotesque contrast (II, 100, 102). When the climax of the meeting has passed and Brown finds himself weak and trembling in solitude, he staggers against the rock, finding it "chill and damp"; and a low hanging twig, that had been ablaze a moment earlier, sprinkles his cheek "with the coldest dew" (II, 105).

The strange objects and events in the forest signify in part the malign spirit behind Puritan witchcraft. But more important to the central meaning of the story, the objects and events of the woods correspond to the nature of life and to Brown's situation. The forest as symbol contains two meanings. First, its eerie, unsalutary characteristics represent the evil side of life that must be recognized and accepted—no matter how unpleasant it is—by all men if they are to reach maturity of character. Evil is an inescapable part of the duality of life. Brown cannot accept the ambiguity of good and evil in life; life must be all good or all evil to him. Shocked in his naive interpretation of men's characters, he sees them as hypocrites who pretend to be good, while concealing basically evil natures. Secondly, some particular aspects of the forest represent Brown's distorted life itself. The darkness of the forest and the coldness of the rock and dew signify the gloomy, cold life Brown will lead in the future since he recognizes only the existence of evil in the world. The unnatural phenomenon of the fire which leaves its fuel cold and clammy is juxtaposed to Brown's unnatural decision to spend the remainder of his life obsessed with man's sinful nature. One circumstance is just as abnormal as the other. Brown's mind becomes gloomy and poisonous, as unhealthy as the bewitched forest itself.

The second group of nature images in the story suggest the normal world, a world in which the existence of sin is recognized but is relegated to a position inferior to the more positive aspects of life such as human love. Contrasting with the dark "heathen wilderness" through which Brown wanders that fateful night is the blue sky studded with stars above the gloom of the forest (II, 97-98). The sky is at once symbol both of heaven (which Brown doubts is really above him anymore) and also—resplendent as it is—the beautiful, wholesome aspects of life (aspects which Brown needs to recognize in order to raise himself above his state of disillusionment). But even as Brown gazes momentarily upward, "a cloud, though no wind was stirring, hurried across the zenith and hid the brightening stars" (II, 98). Brown has become too preoccupied with the existence of evil to concentrate on the optimistic side of life.

The cloud in the above passage introduces a set of sunshine-cloud images which are integral to the meaning of the story. When Brown first hears the voices of his townspeople singing in the forest, he recognizes the tones "heard daily in the *sunshine* at Salem village, but never until now from a *cloud* of night" (II, 98—italics mine).[10] And when he returns to Salem the next morning, the first sight which meets his dazed eyes is Goody Cloyse, his old Christian teacher, standing "in the early *sunshine* at her own lattice, catechizing a little girl who had brought her a pint of morning's milk" (II, 105—italics mine). The scene is significant. Old Goody Cloyse is one of the pious Puritans whom Brown saw in the bewitched forest, and to him she now represents utter hypocrisy. But actually she is no more hypocritical than anyone else who realizes that life, regardless of the presence of sin, must be lived with the illusion of goodness prevailing. Brown is the one with the wrong emphasis on life. The fact that the sun, symbol of divine approval of normal human actions, smiles down on Goody is symbolic of her rightness and Brown's error. A new day, both literal and figurative, has begun; and Brown has the choice, having been given insight into the duality of life, to mature and to develop more perception and conviction than before. But he cannot face hypocrisy and forgive foibles in those whom he has respected and upheld as flawless. As Roy Male says, Brown fails to attain "a perspective broad enough and deep enough to see the dark night as an essential part of human experience, but a part that may prelude a new and richer dawn."[11] Goodman Brown isolates himself from the world of sinners; and the appellation "Goodman"—basically a title similar to "Mister"—is here used ironically to suggest the opposite of *good man*, for Brown commits the worst sin of all in severing himself from all humanity.

The theme of "The Minister's Black Veil" is similar to that of "Goodman Brown." The Reverend Mr.Hooper, like young Brown, realizes the prevalence of sin in the world and dons his black veil as a sign to all men that either literally or figuratively they should follow suit in showing that they too are sinners. Like Brown, Mr. Hooper, because of his realization of sin, shuns love and human sympathy. The only human contacts he maintains are those which pertain to his duties as a pastor. He is like Arthur Dimmesdale in remaining faithful to his clerical responsibilities.

Nature imagery in the story once again appears as a contrast between cheery and salutary versus dark and gloomy nature. The opening scene of the story shows a crowd of people arriving on Sunday morning at Milford Meeting House. Outstanding in the crowd are pretty maidens whom "the Sabbath sunshine made...prettier than on weekdays" (I, 52). But when morose, beveiled Mr. Hooper arrives at the church, the contrast between his darkness and the cheery brightness of the sun-lit maidens is remarkable. And this sun-cloud imagery runs throughout the story. We find out later that from beneath his black veil "there rolled a cloud into the sunshine, an ambiguity of sin or sorrow, which enveloped the poor minister, so that love or sympathy could never reach him" (I, 65). Elizabeth, his fiancee, feeling the deprivation of love, begs him to "let the sun shine from behind the cloud" (I, 61). Mr. Hooper's veil, a dark cloud masking his person, "had separated him from cheerful brotherhood and woman's love, and kept him in that saddest of all prisons, his own heart; and still it lay upon his face [when he was on his death bed], as if to deepen the gloom of his darksome chamber, and shade him from the sunshine of eternity" (I, 67). He is so concerned with sin and guilt in the world that he cannot even contemplate the usually comfortable thought of a heavenly escape from guilt. His last thoughts and words are pessimistic as he sees nothing but a black veil on the faces of those present at his beside. Like Goodman Brown, Mr. Hooper cannot enjoy life as it is. The sunshine on the village maidens means nothing to him except that beneath their sunny exteriors there lurks some hidden guilt in their outwardly pure hearts. He is unable to confront, accept, and adapt himself to human life which is replete with cares and wrongdoings. As a result, he is annihilated as a human being. As Melvin Askew says, "He distinguishes himself from the common heart of humanity with his black veil and waits for the world to come round to him. He waits in vain."[12]

Hawthorne's handling of the theme of religious isolation with Hilda, young copiest in *The Marble Faun,* offers confusion and inconsistency. The problem is one of interpretation of his intentions for her role. Did he primarily intend her to be another of his religious isolationists and thus set out to depict her critically? Or did he consider her purity and piety admirable qualities and attempt to make of her a redeeming character for Kenyon and Miriam? Richard Fogle views Hilda as a symbol of heaven, living as she does in a tower among the doves and always dressed in white; she is "a Christian vestal virgin tending an eternal flame" and a symbol of "heaven's simplicity."[13] Hyatt Waggoner, who once scoffed at the idea of her representing heaven and pointed out that she cannot be a Christian symbol because heaven, unlike Hilda, is neither uncharitable nor self-righteous,[14] now defends the view that Hilda, to Hawthorne, is ultimately admirable in her rectitude because Hawthorne "does not require that young girls should grow in knowledge of the world."[15] If Hilda errs in being overly righteous, the error is "charming and admirable in innocent young girls" to the nineteenth century-mind.[16]

Waggoner's argument is convincing except when the nature imagery and symbolism associated with Hilda are taken into consideration. When these are examined, the view of Hilda taken by Peter D. Zivkovic seems to be the most reasonable explanation of what happened with the creation of Hilda. Zivkovic believes that Hilda is just as isolated from humanity as any of Hawthorne's villains. The difference between her and others is that "her *intellect* is isolated and evil, but *she* is good....Hawthorne wanted her to be good, but not good incarnate, which is ultimately evil. He wanted her to be only unusually good, not unbelievably good. He did not see her right. He did not recognize Hilda for what he made of her."[17] Zivkovic's conclusion, thus, is that Hawthorne became confused in what he was doing with Hilda and lost control of her. The nature symbols associated with Hilda bear out this thesis. Two of them—marble and delicate flowers—indicate that Hawthorne had in mind making Hilda another of his misguided isolationists; whereas one other symbol—the doves—paradoxically distorts this interpretation and suggests that perhaps he was partly viewing Hilda as having achieved an admirable spiritual state for earthly life. Such confusion in Hawthorne's interpretation can be accounted for by the fact that in *The Marble Faun* (1860) he was entering his last and deteriorating phase of his craftsmanship during which he was occasionally unable to present a consistent view of a character and sustain that presentation with consistent imagery and symbolism. This problem intensified, of course, in the fragments written in the few years following *The Marble Faun.*

That Hilda is directly related to the theme of isolation is undeniable because of her excessive attention to religious ideals. Even if Hawthorne also had other ideas in mind for her, he certainly could not have been unaware of her similarity to other fanatics whom he had already dealt with in his fiction. Hilda is aloof from man and interested only in her copying, her purity, and her shrine to the Virgin at the top of her tower. She boasts that, high above the streets of the city, "the air...so exhilarates my spirits, that sometimes I feel half-inclined to attempt a flight from the top of my tower, in the faith that I should float upward!" (C, IV, 54). Miriam points out her distance from the common affairs of man, telling Hilda,"...you dwell above our vanities and passions, our moral dust and mud, with the doves and the angels for your nearest neighbors" (C, IV, 53). These white doves, symbols of her spotless purity, sit on the edge of her tower or hover about her head when she looks out her window. The white robe she wears evokes "such an analogy to their snowy plumage, that the confraternity of artists called her Hilda The Dove, and recognized her aerial apartment as The Dove-Cote" (C, IV, 56).

Hilda, then, is religious, pure, and innocent. Roy Male has pointed out that her innocence "has its historic counterparts in the Virgin Mary and in the saint whose name she bears."[18] But she is alienated from man in her egocentric religious interests and in her self-righteousness. Kenyon observes that she "has no need of love!" (C, IV, 21). She is so heartless and concerned for her own purity that on the day after she has witnessed Miriam and Donatello commit the murder she refuses to touch Miriam or even claim her friendship when the latter comes to her tower for help. Miriam is forced to say, "You have no sin, nor any conception of what it is; and therefore you are so terribly severe! As an angel, you are not amiss; but, as a human creature, and a woman among earthly men and women, you need a sin to soften you!" (C, IV, 209).

The nature images and symbols associated with Hilda are marble, flowers, and the doves. At least two—the marble and flowers—suggest her coldness and her ethereal nature respectively, revealing her abnormality in a world of people. Male has pointed out Hawthorne's frequent association of Hilda with marble (e. g., the marble model of her hand sculptured by Kenyon) and comments on the "icy rigidity" apparent in these symbols.[19] The flower image is introduced when an old German artist in the novel, seeing that Hilda is too delicate to withstand the trials of life in Rome, advises her to return to New England: "The air...is not wholesome for a little foreign flower like you, my child, a delicate wood-anemone from the western forest-land!" (C, IV, 334-35). The metaphor emphasizes Hilda's incorporeity and shows her unfitness to take a solid place in the complex social world.

Like the delicate flower in the forest, she flourishes best when in her protective spiritual environment.

The third emblem—the doves—is the one that presents the paradox in understanding the role of Hilda. If the birds suggest a desirable heavenly or spiritual purity, then we are immediately puzzled by the conflicting aspects in Hilda of (1) her spiritual idealism, and (2) her cold aloofness from man. If the doves do not suggest ideal purity, then we have to interpret the symbol ironically, as suggesting an undesirable purity, alien to the world of men: doves—symbols usually associated with heavenly purity or peacefulness—would thus have to be considered inappropriate symbols for the human state because of their representing only spiritual essence. But if Hawthorne meant the dove symbol to be taken ironically, he is unconvincing. In too many other places he equates doves with softness and admirable purity, even referring to his own wife, Sophia, as his "Dove."[20] Because of the confusion of symbolic meaning, it seems evident that Hawthorne's concept of the character of Hilda became confused and lapsed out of control. Primarily he must have intended to imply a desirable purity when he related Hilda and the doves. But in so doing, he deviated from the pattern he had already designed for her from the first of the novel: that of the obsessed religious devotee who has failed to acknowledge herself as being a part of mankind.

Richard Digby, pious seclusionist in "The Man of Adamant," is the epitome of religious bigotry in Hawthorne's fiction. The "gloomiest and most intolerant of a stern brotherhood" (III, 564), Digby withdraws from man—thinking his ways are the only road to salvation—and holes up in a gloomy cave analogous to a sepulchre. When he refuses companionship and ignores heavenly commands, his heart stops beating, and the calcifying drippings of the cave gradually turn him into stone.

Nature imagery in the story is copious, pointing up how unfortunate was Digby's decision to flee the normal human world. On the day that he leaves to build a private tabernacle in the gloomy forest, he looks back in scorn at the village—expecting to see fire and brimstone rush in at once and destroy the place now that he, the only righteous one, is safely away—but is disappointed to see the village showered only with peaceful sunshine, symbolizing nature's approval of the human community. He continues his trek into the forest, and the deeper he penetrates the lonelier he becomes and the thicker the trees and undergrowth are. The forest shadow grows darker and darker as its gloom hides "the blessed sky" from Digby's view (III, 565).

On the third evening, Digby spies a cave in the side of a rocky hill and decides to make it his tabernacle. This cave, a gloomy recess practically concealed by a "dense veil of tangled foliage about it," is no place for man: "If Nature meant this remote and dismal cavern for the use of man, it could only be to bury in its gloom the victims of a pestilence, and then to block up its mouth with stones, and avoid the spot forever after" (III, 566). The only thing bright or cheerful near it is a bubbling fountain, "at which Richard Digby hardly threw away a glance" (III, 566). When he enters his cave, he notices that dripping stalactites hang from the ceiling; and "the fallen leaves and sprigs of foliage, which the wind had swept into the cave, and the little feathery shrubs, rooted near the threshold, were not wet with a natural dew, but had been embalmed by this wondrous process" (III, 566-67—a foreshadowing of Digby's own similar embalming later). But Digby, even though he has the same deposit "of calculous particles within his heart," which could "change his fleshly heart to stone," does not even perceive the analogy when he sees "the sprigs of marble foliage . . ., the similitude suggested by these once tender herbs" (III, 567).

Insistent on maintaining his abnormal ways, Digby refuses to drink from the clear spring or eat healthful food; instead he drinks the oozing cave water and eats unsavory herbs and roots. When the spirit of Mary Goffe—a convert to his preaching who has been dead several months —one day appears at the cave entrance in an effort to entice him back into the world, the total derangement of his mind is manifested. Mary, upon whom the sun shines radiantly, invites him back to "thy fellow-men; for they need thee . . . and thou hast tenfold need of them" (III, 569). But Digby refuses to listen to her plea for a return to normality. Then she tries to get him to drink the spring water, the "hallowed water," but he knocks aside the cup and orders her away (III, 571). He is totally lost in his bigotry. As Waggoner has pointed out, pure religion does not "reject the natural light of the sun or the pure water of the natural spring. . . ."[21]

When Digby tells Mary that she has nothing to do with his Bible, his prayers, or his heaven, and orders her not to tempt him again, his heart immediately ceases to beat, and Mary's form returns "from the sepulchral cave to heaven" (III, 571). Digby's body is discovered by farm children a century later, completely calcified and wearing "a most forbidding frown" (III, 572). Hawthorne offers the admonition that "Friendship, and Love, and Piety, all human and celestial sympathies, should keep aloof from that hidden cave . . .;" for there sits Digby "in the attitude of repelling the whole race of mortals,—not from heaven,—but from the horrible loneliness of his dark, cold sepulchre!" (III, 573).

In all the above writings Hawthorne uses nature to dramatize the necessary involvement of man with his world. The experiences of these religious isolationists underscore Hawthorne's insistence on the point that too much attention to religion or the spiritual purity of man can in itself separate man from his kind. The lives of Ilbrahim, John Endicott, Hilda, Richard Digby, the story of Alice Doane, and the actions of Young Goodman Brown and the Reverend Mr. Hooper all confirm the view that man must be careful not to sever his relationship with his fellow man. In seeking spiritual perfection, man ironically commits an unpardonable evil by ignoring the side of man that makes him human and demands the love and sympathy of others—his state of imperfection.

North Texas State University

[1]"The Solitude of Nathaniel Hawthorne," *Shelburne Essays*, First Series (New York and London, [1904], I, 27.

[2]Ibid.

[3]*The Rise of the American Novel* (New York: American Book Co., [1951], p. 349.

[4]See my unpublished doctoral dissertation, "Nature in the Life and Works of Nathaniel Hawthorne" (Arkansas, 1965), for a thorough treatment of Hawthorne's use of nature in his fiction.

[5]We Know this story was one of the early projected "Seven Tales of My Native Land," the subjects of which were witchcraft and the sea. Elizabeth Hawthorne said that Hawthorne read her the story in 1825. See Nelson F. Adkins, "The Early Projected Works of Nathaniel Hawthorne," *The Papers of the Bibliographical Society of America*, 39 (Second Quarter 1945), 121-22, and Elizabeth Chandler, "A Study of the Sources of the Tales and Romances Written by Nathaniel Hawthorne Before 1853," *Smith College Studies in Modern Languages*, 7 (July, 1926), 8-9.

[6]References to Hawthorne's stories by volume and page numbers are to *The Works of Nathaniel Hawthorne*, ed. George Parsons Lathrop, 13 vols. (Boston and New York: Houghton, Mifflin and Co., [1883]. All references appear in the text. References to *The Marble Faun*, also given in the text as *C* followed by Vol. *IV* and page numbers, are to *The Centenary Edition of the Works of Nathaniel Hawthorne*, ed. William Charvat, Roy Harvey Pearce, Claude M. Simpson (Columbus: Ohio State University Press, [1962-]).

[7]*Hawthorne's Tragic Vision* (Austin: University of Texas Press, [1957], p. 18.

[8]"Hawthorne, the Fall, and the Psychology of Maturity," *American Literature*, 34 (November, 1962), 336.

[9]For a similar treatment of nature imagery and symbolism in this story, see my article "Nature and Theme in 'Young Goodman Brown'," *The Dickinson Review*, 2 (Winter, 1970), 42-46.

[10]Richard Fogle, discussing the symbols of day and night, town and forest, also points out that "Day and the Town are clearly emblematic of Good, of the seemly outward appearance of human convention and society. They stand for the safety of unquestioning and unspeculative faith....Night and the Forest, symbols of doubt and wandering, are the domains of the Evil One, where the dark subterranean forces of the human spirit riot unchecked" (*Hawthorne's Fiction: The Light and the Dark*, Norman: University of Oklahoma Press, 1964, p. 26).

[11]*Hawthorne's Tragic Vision,* pp. 79-80.

[12]"Hawthorne, the Fall, and the Psychology of Maturity," p. 342.

[13]*Hawthorne's Fiction: The Light and the Dark,* pp. 197-98.

[14]In the first edition of *Hawthorne: A Critical Study* (Cambridge: The Belknap Press of Harvard University Press), p. 205. Waggoner went on to say that, as a representative of spirit in the first four-fifths of the novel, Hilda would make the supernatural world look "very unattractive and even immoral, inferior indeed in grace to the human world" (p. 205).

[15]In *Hawthorne: A Critical Study* (revised edition, 1963), p. 222.

[16]Ibid.

[17]"The Evil of the Isolated Intellect: Hilda, in *The Marble Faun,*" *Personalist,* 43 (Spring, 1962), p. 204.

[18]*Hawthorne's Tragic Vision,* p. 162.

[19]Ibid., p. 172.

[20]See both Hawthorne's love letters to Sophia and the *American Notebooks* for numerous such references.

[21]*Hawthorne: A Critical Study* (1963), p. 110.

"An Exceedingly Pleasant Mention": *The Scarlet Letter* and *Holden's Dollar Magazine*

RICHARD TUERK

In the June, 1850, number of *Holden's Dollar Magazine* appears a review essay entitled "The Scarlet Letter: A Romance,"[1] which bibliographies of Hawthorne as well as studies of his contemporaneous reputation, including Bertha Faust's *Hawthorne's Contemporaneous Reputation*, the Centenary introduction to *The Scarlet Letter*, and Kenneth Walter Cameron's *Hawthorne Among his Contemporaries*, overlook. Yet in his volume Cameron includes material that probably alludes to it. He reproduces a "List of Books, Etc., by and Relating to Nathaniel Hawthorne, Prepared as an Exhibition to Commemorate the Centenary of his Birth, by Victor Hugo Paltsits, Assistant Librarian, Lenox Branch" from the July, 1904, issue of the *Bulletin of the New York Public Library*, in which Paltsits paraphrases a letter written from Lenox, April 27, 1851, to E. A. Duyckinck, the noted editor,[2] who, incidently, along with his brother G. L. Duyckinck, edited the *Dollar Magazine* in 1851. In the letter itself, still housed in the Duyckinck Collection of the Manuscript Division of the New York Public Library, Hawthorne writes: "Please to thank Mr [sic] Mathews, on my behalf,for a copy of the Dollar Magazine, containing an exceedingly pleasant mention of my late book—much in a little space. It especially gratifies me that he calls my page 'changeful'; but perhaps this is merely an evidence of my yearning most for such praises as I deserve least."[3] Although this statement comes at the end of a discussion of *The House of the Seven Gables*, published in 1851, it cannot refer to a review of that book, for the *Dollar Magazine* contains none. In fact, after volume 8 (July-December, 1851) the *Dollar Magazine* merged with the *North American Miscellany*, assuming the name of the latter. Hawthorne probably refers to a "mention" of *The Scarlet Letter*, which book he discusses briefly in his letter when, in a now famous passage, he writes about *The House of the Seven Gables:* "It appears to me that you like the book better than the Scarlet Letter; and I certainly think it a more natural and healthy product of my mind, and felt less reluctant in publishing it."

The Mr. Mathews referred to in the letter is undoubtedly Cornelius Mathews (1817-1889), an author and editor as well as friend and business associate of Duyckinck with whom he co-edited *Arcturus.* Mathews contributed to the *Dollar Magazine,* writing "A Strange Walk Down Broadway"[4] and possibly writing for the section of the magazine entitled "Holden's Review," in which most of the book reviews appeared. However, if Hawthorne's words about "an exceedingly pleasant mention" refer to "The Scarlet Letter: A Romance," then they do not refer to a review written by Mathews.

Hawthorne's connection with the *Dollar Magazine* is not confined to this one review essay. In May, 1851, less than one year after the review and shortly before the demise of the magazine, it published "Ethan Brand."[5] In addition, Hawthorne may be referring to any one of three reviews of his books in the *Dollar Magazine.* None of them specifically call Hawthorne's page "changeful." In fact, only "The Scarlet Letter: A Romance" uses the term; and it does so in a context implying that one of Hawthorne's strengths is that his characters are not "changeful."[6] Thus, either this word in the letter refers to something else Mathews wrote, making it in no way helpful in determining to which review Hawthorne refers, or Hawthorne misread the passage.

The earliest of these *Dollar Magazine* reviews seems least likely to be the one involved. Appearing anonymously in "Holden's Review" for May, 1850, it treats *The Scarlet Letter*[7] and may have been written by C.F. Briggs, who is described in volume 5 as the now retiring literary editor of the *Dollar Magazine.*[8] The review says that the book is "a pure romance, and, as a work of art, is as nearly perfect as the story of Cupid and Psyche, or any of the great masterpieces that have delighted the world by their purity. And by purity we mean absence of faults." Nonetheless, the reviewer insists that Hawthorne should have omitted "The Custom House" chapter, which, he writes, "does not prepare the mind for the romance and is therefore an encumbrance" and "leaves the reader in doubt whether the facts stated in relation to the finding of the Scarlet Letter in the Upper Chamber of the Custom House be fact or fiction." Then, for one and one half of the two and one quarter pages of the review, the reviewer quotes from "The Custom House," immediately after which he writes:

> We had intended to give an extended notice of this new work by Mr. Hawthorne, but a gentleman whose thoughts will be more acceptable to our readers than our own remarks, having sent us an able review of it for

our next number, we shall do no more than to express our opinion that the Scarlet Letter is the finest production of its highly gifted author, and among the finest and most original works of fiction which our literature can boast.

The "able review" is, of course, "The Scarlet Letter: A Romance." It seems unlikely that this brief notice is the "exceedingly pleasant mention" about which Hawthorne writes to Duyckinck, in spite of its brevity, for two reasons: to a large extent it is not complimentary, in spite of its glowing beginning and ending; and it is incomplete in itself, instead pointing to the more complete, forthcoming review.

The second best possibility for the "exceedingly pleasant mention" also appears in "Holden's Review," this time in volume 7, probably for March, 1851.[9] It is exceedingly short, so it too fits the requirement of brevity; it takes up very "little space." Also, its publication date is much closer to the date of the letter than that of either of the other two possibilities, perhaps too close. It even may have been written by Cornelius Mathews himself, since he seems to have been connected with the *Dollar Magazine* at this time. It is, however, so brief and concerned with such a minor work that it seems unlikely to be the review in question. It is also debatable just how "much" this review does contain "in a little space." The entire review follows:

> *True Stories from History and Biography. By Nathaniel*
> *Hawthorne. Boston: Ticknor, Reed, and Fields.*

> Whoever has read "The Scarlet Letter" and "Mosses from an Old Manse" will feel that Nathaniel Hawthorne can write in a most attractive style in whatever department of literature he may enter, and can even accomplish that most difficult feat of writing for *children*. As Hawthorne truly observes "To make a lively and entertaining narrative for children, with such unmalleable material as is presented by the sombre, stern, and rigid characteristics of the Puritans and their descendants, is quite as difficult an attempt, as to manufacture delicate playthings out of the granite rocks on which New England is founded," but he has succeeded.

The review is "pleasant," and it certainly is "in a little space." Indeed, the phrase "my late book" in the letter to Duyckinck may refer to *True Stories from History and Biography;* but I doubt it.

Probably the letter refers to the anonymous essay entitled "The Scarlet Letter: A Romance," which is indeed "exceedingly pleasant" and which, although it is fairly long, does accomplish "much in" relatively "little space." Add to this evidence the use of the word "changeful" in the review, a piece of evidence that may or may not be relevant, and it seems more than likely that the letter refers to this particular item.

Its author can be identified on the basis of what seems to be irrefutable evidence. In the issue of the *Dollar Magazine* for August, 1850, under the heading "How Others Describe Holden's Dollar Magazine," appears the following item from the *New York Tribune:* "HOLDEN'S MAGAZINE for June is a pleasant and most readable No. of one of the most readable of magazines. It is always welcome with its gayeties and gravities, and has something adopted to every varying mood. An admirable review of Hawthorne's Scarlet Letter by Rev. Henry Giles is a piece of criticism such as is rarely met with."[10] The Reverend Henry Giles (1809-1882) had a colorful career. Born in Wexford, Ireland, and brought up as a Roman Catholic, he became a Unitarian and then a Unitarian minister. In 1840, he moved to the United States, where he soon gained a reputation as a brilliant lecturer and conversationalist.[11] He wrote many essays and a number of books, including several on literary topics. His titles include *Lectures and Essays*[12] and *Human Life in Shakespeare*[13] as well as *Illustrations of Genius in some of its Relations to Culture and Society*,[14] to which we shall return later. In *Hawthorne and his Publisher* Caroline Ticknor quotes "a contemporaneous critic" about Ticknor and Fields' Old Corner Bookstore that "Here Henry Giles scintillated with such brilliant epigrams, and outlined his thoughts so incisively that his misshaped form was forgotten."[15] In *Fields of the Atlantic Monthly: Letters to an Editor* James C. Austin prints a letter, written in London, May 20, 1860, to Hawthorne, in which Fields writes: "Giles wrote that article in the Boston Courier, Whipple tells me in his last letter." Austin comments: "The Henry Giles article in the Courier was a review of *The Marble Faun* which Hawthorne had liked,"[16] indicating that Giles' interest in Hawthorne's works and Hawthorne's interest in Giles' works did not end with *The Scarlet Letter.*

In *Illustrations of Genius* Giles included a chapter entitled "The Scarlet Letter. A Romance, By Nathaniel Hawthorne."[17] This chapter, which is indeed included in Hawthorne bibliographies although not in collections of criticism, is a slightly revised version of the essay in the *Dollar Magazine.* Giles, however, does not mention that the chapter appeared anywhere else. In fact, he seems to take pains to hide this fact, even changing the first sentence of paragraph 20 (on page 342) so that the words "our article" become "our essay." The table that follows is a collation between the text in *Holden's Dollar Magazine* and that in *Illustrations of Genius.* In making it, I have ignored end-line hyphenation of words.

Page. col. line (Holden's text)	Holden's text	Genius text
337.1.5	on,	[on
337.1.7	In "The Twice-Told Tales,"	[In the Twice-told Tales
337.1.8	in "The Mosses from an Old Manse,"	[in the Mosses from an Old Manse
337.1.10	literalness,	[literalness
337.1.11	it, fancies,	[it fancies
	Bunyan's,	[Bunyan's
337.1.12	Radcliffe.	[Radcliffe?
337.1.17	mind,	[mind;
337.1.20	author,	[author
337.1.22	Introduction	[introduction
337.1.28	again,	[again
337.1.29	tale,	[tale
337.1.32	castle,	[castle
337.1.33	indeed,—to	[indeed, to
337.1.35	Custom House.	[custom house.
337.1.37	which	[which,
337.1.38-39	Custom House:	[custom house,
337.1.40	them.—	[them.
337.1.44	transcribe:	[transcribe:—
337.1.50	the Oldest Inhabitant	[the oldest inhabitant
337.1.51	settled,	[settled
337.1.52	epoch,	[epoch
337.1.53	the Collector	[the collector
337.2.6	heart-quake.	[heartquake.
337.2.14	captains,	[captains
337.2.16	sea,	[sea
337.2.18	nook;	[nook,
337.2.20	Presidential	[presidential
337.2.28	Custom House,	[custom house
337.2.40	service;	[service,
337.2.45	practices,	[practices
337.2.46	Custom House	[custom-house
337.2.48	Custom House	[custom house
337.2.49	Paradise.	[paradise.
337.2.51	Whigs.	[whigs.
337.2.51-52	brotherhood,	[brotherhood
337.2.52	Surveyor	[surveyor
337.2.53	Democrat	[democrat
337.2.57	post,	[post

338.1.1-2	Whig Collector,	[whig collector
338.1.5	life,	[life
338.1.7	Custom House	[custom-house
338.1.9	duty,	[duty
	politician,	[politician
338.1.12	discern,	[discern
338.1.13	pained,	[pained
338.1.14	me,	[me
338.1.21	speaking-trumpet,	[speaking trumpet
338.1.27	men,	[men
338.1.28	politics,	[politics
338.1.29	Uncle.	[uncle.
338.1.30	it	[it,
338.1.35	wharves,	[wharves
338.1.36	Custom House	[custom-house
338.1.40	forenoon,	[forenoon
338.1.42	sea-stories,	[sea stories
	jokes,	[jokes
338.1.43	pass-words	[passwords
338.1.47	hearts,	[hearts
338.1.49	behalf,	[behalf
338.1.53	vessels!	[vessels.
338.1.54	matters,	[matters;
338.1.56	fingers!	[fingers.
338.1.58	wagon-load	[wagon load
	merchandize	[merchandise
338.1.59	noonday, perhaps,	[noonday perhaps
338.1.63	double-lock,	[double lock
338.1-2.63-1	sealing-wax,	[sealing wax
338.2.4	caution,	[caution
338.2.5	happened;	[happened—
338.2.6	zeal,	[zeal
338.2.7	remedy!"	[remedy."
338.2.8	the "Old Inspector"	[the Old Inspector
338.2.8-9	perfect:	[perfect;
338.2.11	presumption,	[presumption;
338.2.12	it,	[it
338.2.14	Custom House	[custom-house
338.2.15-16	the "Old Inspector;"	[the Old Inspector;
338.2.16-17	the "Inspector" provoke,	[the Inspector provoke
338.2.17	Cabinets	[cabinets
338.2.24	faculties,	[faculties
338.2.26	incidents,	[incidents;
338.2.29	goose,	[goose

338.2.32	tough,	[tough
338.2.35	hand-saw."	[handsaw."
338.2.46	Hawthorne,	[Hawthorne
338.2.47	concern.—	[concern.
338.2.49	result;	[result,
338.2.51-52	Custom House no loser:	[custom house no loser;
338.2.52	Custom House,	[custom house
338.2.53	Custom House	[custom house
338.2.55	Custom House,	[custom house
338.2.60	strange	[strange,
338.2.61	characters,—in	[characters—in
339.1.6	Indian; when	[Indian. When
339.1.10-11	occurred,	[occurred
339.1.18	cloth,	[cloth
339.1.19	letter—A.	[letter A.
339.1.22	Scarlet Letter	[scarlet letter
339.1.25	but	[but,
339.1.27	pillory,	[pillory
	life.—	[life.
339.1.28	firmly	[firmly,
339.1.32	shrinks,—she	[shrinks. She
339.1.35	Europe: and	[Europe; and,
339.1.40	sinner—but	[sinner; but
339.1.41	woman,	[woman
339.1.44	degradation,	[degradation
339.1.45	transgression,	[transgression
339.1.46	firmness—even grandeur	[firmness, even grandeur,
339.1.51	selfishness—guilt	[selfishness, guilt
339.1.56	unblest,	[unblessed,
339.1.57	last,	[last
339.2.1	woman,	[woman
339.2.2	Hester;	[Hester,
339.2.4	colony,	[colony
339.2.6	Wilson;	[Wilson—
339.2.6-7	experience;	[experience,
339.2.7	preaching,	[preaching
339.2.8	Dimmesdale; young	[Dimmesdale—young
339.2.10	distinguished	[distinguished,
339.2.13	eloquence—uniting	[eloquence, uniting,
339.2.23	sermon;	[sermon:
339.2.24	is, a	[is—a
339.2.25	ambiguous.—	[ambiguous.
339.2.28	truly,	[truly
339.2.30	see,	[see

339.2.31	mercy,	[mercy
339.2.33-34	Scarlet Letter,	[scarlet letter
339.2.37	Eschylus	[Aeschylus
339.2.43	herself,	[herself
339.2.44	another;	[another,
339.2.45-46	deserted;	[deserted,
339.2.47-48	men,—not	[men, not
339.2.49	spirit—and	[spirit, and,
339.2.51	one,	[one
	husband—the other, his loved,	[husband, the other his loved
339.2.55-56	incidents	[incidents,
340.11	living;	[living,
	child;	[child,
340.1.12	does, besides,	[does besides
340.1.20	beauty—an	[beauty, an
	witchery—a	[witchery, a
340.1.21	unearthly—an	[unearthly, an
340.1.22	loveliness—which	[loveliness, which
340.1.23	embodied	[imbodied
340.1.24	embodied	[imbodied
340.1.27	—bears	[bears
340.1.30	forgive, looks on,	[forgive looks on
340.1.34	who	[which
340.1.35	it,	[it
340.1.37	eloquence,	[eloquence
340.1.38-39	passion—with	[passion, with
340.1.41-42	of shame	[of open shame
340.1.42	side,	[side
340.1.44	joy,	[joy
340.1.51	babble,	[babble
340.1.53	ripple!	[ripple.
340.1.56	flight,	[flight
340.1.57	confession; while	[confession,—while
340.1.59	martyrdom, he	[martyrdom,—he
340.1.60-61	temptations, grotesque— strange—fascinating— illusive—terrible.	[temptations—grotesque, strange, fascinating, illusive, terrible.
340.2.2	so,	[so
340.2.6	sermon,	[sermon
340.2.10	pillory,	[pillory
340.2.12	church,	[church;
340.2.16	scaffold,	[scaffold

340.2.17	astonished	[astonished,
340.2.18	England!'	[England,'
340.2.22-23	woe—'ye,	[woe,—'ye
340.2.23	me!—ye,	[me, ye
340.2.24	holy!—behold	[holy, behold
340.2.25	last!—at last!—I	[last—at last—I
340.2.33	it!	[it.
	been,—wherever,.	[been—wherever,
340.2.35	repose,—it	[repose—it
340.2.38	you,	[you
340.2.39	shuddered!'	[shuddered.'
340.2.40	seemed,	[seemed
	point,	[point
340.2.42-43	weakness,—and,	[weakness—and,
340.2.43-44	heart,—that	[heart—that
340.2.49	fierceness;	[fierceness,
340.2.56	world!—and	[world—and
340.2.58	death-hour,	[death hour,
340.2.62	breast,	[breast;
341.1.2	heart!"	[heart!' "
341.1.7	in-looking	[inlooking
341.1.16	but by association—	[but in idea—
341.1.17	and	[and,
341.1.20	age;	[age,
341.1.21	distinctive,	[distinctive
341.1.24	laws. Yet,	[laws; yet
341.1.25	Real,	[real
341.1.26	Ideal;	[ideal;
	Ideal is the Real,	[ideal is the real,
341.1.27-28	Actual, local, temporary	[actual local, temporary,
	and changeful—in	and changeful; in
341.1.29	Real	[real
341.1.31	themselves,	[themselves;
341.1.33	Art,	[art,
341.1.40	being,	[being
341.1.40-41	conquer, and to bend	[conquer, to bend
341.1.41	aspire, and to become	[aspire, to become
341.1.46	sorrow;	[sorrow—
	source,	[source
341.1.48	fellows:	[fellows;
341.1.50	good,	[good;
341.1.52	spirit,	[spirit;
341.1.55	malignant,	[malignant;
341.1.57	it,	[it;

341.1.58	reproach,	[reproach
341.1.60	it,	[it
341.2.7	repenting;	[repenting—
341.2.12	and	[and,
341.2.24	it,	[it
341.2.28	life,	[life
341.2.30	for, then,	[for then
341.2.33	seems,	[seems;
341.2.34	rightly,	[rightly;
341.2.35	power,	[power:
341.2.37	fallen,	[fallen;
341.2.38	bad	[bad,
341.2.42	him	[him,
341.2.43	beggar	[beggar,
341.2.44	moment,	[moment
341.2.45	gain,	[gain
	through.—	[through.
341.2.50	courage,	[courage;
341.2.52	demanded,	[demanded
341.2.61	it,	[it
342.1.3-4	confession,	[confession
342.1.11	embody	[imbody
342.1.13	contrarieties,	[contrarieties
342.1.16	substance,	[substance
342.1.17	life:	[life;
342.1.24	this,	[this
341.1.26	effect,	[effect;
342.1.35	him:	[him;
	see,	[see
342.1.41-42	student,	[student
342.1.42	injury,	[injury
342.1.43	persecutor:	[persecutor,
342.1.44	villain—a	[villain, a
342.1.50	"Pearl!"	[Pearl!
342.1.51	sweet,	[sweet
342.1.52	lustre,	[lustre
342.1.59	genius,	[genius
342.1.63	"Pearl"	[Pearl
342.2.1	strongest affections,	[strongest, affections
342.2.3	possess	[possess,
342.2.4	wood-like,	[woodlike,
342.2.7	plot,	[plot
342.2.8	article	[essay
342.2.12	only by	[only one by

342.2.16	be, no doubt, on it;	[be on [it,
342.2.17	none, we are sure, will be as to the genius	[none as to its genius
342.2.19	doubtful, others,	[doubtful [others
342.2.20	well-defined;	[well defined;
342.2.21	no work	[any work
342.2.25	passion, but must,	[passion, must
342.2.26	instruct	[instruct,
342.2.29	compact	[compact,
342.2.34	Genius	[Genius,
342.2.35	freedom,	[freedom
342.2.45	his	[*his*
342.2.46	nature, and	[nature; and,
342.2.48	creation,	[creation
342.2.48-49	suggestiveness,	[suggestiveness
342.2.51	"Truth."	["truth."
342.2.54	life,	[life
342.2.60	relations:	[relations;
343.1.1	Now	[Now,
343.1.5	utmost,	[utmost;
343.1.8	weaken	[weaken,
343.1.20	that	[*that*
343.1.23	life	[*life*
343.1.25	self-respect.—	[self-respect.
343.1.34	divinely	[divinely,
343.1.37	away,	[away
343.1.40	he accuse,	[He [accuse
343.1.59	and	[and,
343.2.6	tempted human:	[tempted, [human;
343.2.7	but	[but,
343.2.12	humanity	[humanity,
343.2.18	untrue,	[untrue
343.2.21-22	nobleness,	[nobleness
343.2.25	phenomenal; and that	[phenomenal, and that,
343.2.29-30	force, because	[force; because,
343.2.41	for	[for,
343.2.44	TRUTH.	[TRUTH,
343.2.48	him,	[him
343.2.52	prophet,	[prophet
343.2.53	But,	[But

	change,	[change
343.2.59	trial	[trial,
	virtue.—	[virtue.
344.1.8	sinner,	[sinner
344.1.9	But,	[But
344.1.14	turbulent,	[turbulent;
344.1.16	society,	[society;
344.1.17	ambition, remain	[ambition—remain
344.1.27	THOUGHT	[THOUGHT
344.2.2	evil it is,	[evil as it is
344.2.6	affectionate	[affectionate,
344.2.10	until,	[until
344.2.10-11	revelation,	[revelation
344.2.12-13	"Chillingworth"	[Chillingworth
344.2.19	it	[it,
344.2.23	this,	[this
344.2.24	needful,	[needful

As can be easily seen, most of the changes are minor, involving punctuation, especially insertions and deletions of commas, dashes, and hyphens; rarely do any of these changes affect the meaning of the sentences (but see 341.1.27-28). Other frequent changes involve substitution of lower case for upper case letters. Thus, "Custom House" becomes "custom house" or, when used as an adjective, "custom-house"; "Democrat" becomes "democrat"; and "Whig Collector" becomes "whig collector," wherever these phrases appear in the chapter. Sometimes the chapter drops quotation marks used in the article and makes corresponding changes in capitalization (see for examples 337.1.7, 337.1.8, 338.2.8, 338.2.15-16, and 338.2.16-17). Most of the changes in wording are also minor, sometimes involving clarification (see 340.1.34, 340.1.41-42, 341.1.16, 342.2.12, 342.2.17, 342.2.21 and 342.2.25, and 342.2.2), and sometimes involving elimination of wordiness (see 341.1.40-41, 342.2.16, and 342.2.17).

In addition to being important because of these biographical and bibliographical considerations, the review is important in its own right, for even though it is clearly a child of the nineteenth century, it is in some ways surprisingly modern. The reviewer's recognition that the book is a tightly unified whole and that the characters must be judged in the context of that whole anticipates many of the tenets of new criticism. Yet especially interesting is his insistence that the romance treats relationships of man to man in society. At the same time that he recognizes the psychological depths of Hawthorne's portrayals of individual characters, the reviewer points out that of paramount importance are their interactions and that this tale of woe is profoundly

·social in its implications. Thus, this anonymous nineteenth-century essay anticipates modern studies of *The Scarlet Letter,* such as Quentin Anderson's in *The Imperial Self,* [18] by pointing out how unjust the community's ostracism of Hester is, since all the members of any community are themselves sinners. For the anonymous reviewer writes, "We have all of us, potentially, the elements of every sin. That sin does not come into consciousness or commission may be a negation of trial and not a triumph of virtue," and he asks: "what right have we to claim kindred with the saint and exclude the sinner?" a question that seems central not just to *The Scarlet Letter* but to the bulk of Hawthorne's works. In these words the reviewer seems to put his finger on some of the central issues of the romance. Because the review itself as well as the chapter are in no modern collections of Hawthorne criticism and are not readily available in their original form and because the review is especially difficult to obtain, the entire review follows.

East Texas State University

THE SCARLET LETTER:

A ROMANCE. BY NATHANIEL HAWTHORNE.

No writer has this country produced, that is more distinctive than Nathaniel Hawthorne. Familiar to us all is that quaintness of manner, which, at first simple as an old wife's talk, gradually beguiles us on, until we are lost amidst the wildest scenes and the most ideal interests. In "The Twice-told Tales," and in "The Mosses from an Old Manse," who has not felt the peculiar charm of that homely New England literalness, which conceals beneath it, fancies, often as bold as Bunyan's, and as exciting as those of Radcliffe. The present story develops all the peculiarities of the author's genius, but of his genius put forth with a strength beyond any former effort. It has the unmistakeable stamp on it of the writer's mind, yet there is a sort of power in it which we did not expect, though it does not surprise us. It is the most decisive production of the author, and one of the remarkable stories of the age.

The Introduction is an opening that will detain the reader on the threshold of the feast. This part of the volume gives a new illustration to the old truism, that with genius no topic is exhausted. We had no idea that the machinery of neglected documents could ever be used again, without causing the reader to yawn at the beginning of a tale, and deterring him from going further. But, then, we always connected such documents with the library of an old castle, or the concealments of an old church: it was new to us, indeed,—to find that the materials of a romance could be secreted in a Custom House. Not less new to us, and as delightful as new, the poetry and pathos with which as with a halo and mist of fancy and emotion, he encircles that old Custom House: enlivened with gleamings of humor, that fitfully and mildly irradiate them.— Thus we might characterize the whole of the preparatory matter. The following passage, in allusion to his official relations and companions, we venture to transcribe:

"I doubt greatly—or rather, I do not doubt at all—whether any public functionary of the United States, either in the civil or military line, has ever had such a patriarchal body of veterans under his orders as myself. The whereabouts of the Oldest Inhabitant was at once settled, when I looked at them. For upwards of twenty years before this epoch, the independent position of the Collector had kept the Salem Custom House out of the whirlpool of political vicissitude, which makes the tenure of office generally so fragile. A soldier,—New England's most distinguished soldier,—he stood firmly on the pedestal of his gallant services; and, himself secure in the wise liberality of the successive administrations through which he had held office, he had been the safety of his subordinates in many an hour of danger and heart-quake. General Miller was radically conservative; a man over whose kindly nature habit had no slight influence; attaching himself strongly to familiar faces, and with difficulty moved to change, even when change might have brought unquestionable improvement. Thus, on taking charge of my department, I found few but aged men. They were ancient sea captains, for the most part, who, after being tost on every sea, and standing up sturdily against life's tempestuous blast, had finally drifted into this quiet nook; where, with little to disturb them, except the periodical terrors of a Presidential election, they one and all acquired a new lease of existence. Though by no means less liable than their fellow-men to age and infirmity, they had evidently some talisman or other that kept death at bay. Two or three of their number, as I was assured, being gouty and rheumatic, or perhaps bedridden, never dreamed of making their appearance at the Custom House, during a large part of the year; but, after a torpid winter, would creep out into the warm sunshine of May or June, go lazily about what they termed duty, and, at their own leisure and convenience, betake themselves to bed again. I must plead guilty to the charge of abbreviating the official breath of more than one of these venerable servants of the republic.— They were allowed, on my representation, to rest from their arduous labors, and soon afterwards—as if their sole principle of life had been zeal for their country's service; as I verily believe it was—withdrew to a better world. It is a pious consolation to me, that, through my interference, a sufficient space was allowed them for repentance of the evil and corrupt practices, into which, as a matter of course, every Custom House officer must be supposed to fall. Neither the front nor the back entrance of the Custom House opens on the road to Paradise.

"The greater part of my officers were Whigs. It was well for their venerable brotherhood, that the new Surveyor was not a politician, and, though a faithful Democrat in principle, neither received nor held his office with any reference to political services. Had it been otherwise,—had an active politician been put into his influential post, to assume the easy task of making head against a Whig Collector, whose infirmities withheld him from the personal administration of his office,— hardly a man of the old corps would have drawn the breath of official life, within a month after the exterminating angel had come up the Custom House steps. According to the received code in such matters, it would have been nothing short of duty, in a politician, to bring every one of those white heads under the axe of the guillotine. It was plain enough to discern, that the old fellows dreaded some such discourtesy at my hands. It pained, and at the same time amused me, to behold the terrors that attended my advent; to see a furrowed cheek, weather-beaten by half a century of storm, turn ashy pale at the glance of so harmless an individual as myself; to detect, as one or another addressed me, the tremor of a voice, which, in long-past days, had been wont to bellow through a speaking-trumpet, hoarsely enough to frighten Boreas himself to silence. They knew, these excellent old persons, that, by all established rule,—and, as regarded some of them, weighed by their own lack of efficiency for business,—they ought to have given place to younger men, more orthodox in politics, and altogether fitter than themselves to serve our common Uncle. I knew it too, but could never quite find in my heart to act upon the knowledge. Much and deservedly to my own discredit, therefore, and considerably to the detriment of my official conscience, they continued, during my incumbency, to creep about the wharves, and loiter up and down the Custom House steps. They spent a good deal of time, also, asleep in their accustomed corners, with their chairs tilted back against the wall; awaking, however, once or twice in a forenoon, to bore one another with the several thousandth repetition of old sea-stories, and mouldy jokes, that had grown to be pass-words and countersigns among them.

"The discovery was soon made, I imagine, that the new Surveyor had no great harm in him. So. with lightsome hearts. and the happy consciousness of being usefully employed,— in their own behalf, at least, if not for our beloved country,—these good old gentlemen went through the various formalities of office. Sagaciously, under their spectacles, did they peep into the holds of vessels! Mighty was their fuss about little matters, and marvellous, sometimes, the obtuseness that allowed greater ones to slip between their fingers! Whenever such a mischance occurred,—when a wagon-load of valuable merchandize had been smuggled ashore, at noonday, perhaps, and directly beneath their unsuspicious noses,— nothing could exceed the vigilance and alacrity with which they proceeded to lock, and double-lock, and secure with tape and sealing-wax, all the avenues of the delinquent vessel. Instead of a reprimand for their previous negligence, the case seemed rather to require an eulogium on their praiseworthy caution, after the mischief had happened; a grateful recognition of the promptitude of their zeal, the moment that there was no longer any remedy!"

The sketch of the "Old Inspector" is perfect: but we cannot extract it. To attempt to give an idea of it in other than the author's words would be presumption, and to curtail it, would be to do it violence. No picture that we remember in Addison or Goldsmith excels it. Hawthorne was a Custom House officer that he might draw the "Old Inspector;" and glad, hearty laughter will the "Inspector" provoke, when Cabinets and their changes will be the lumber of old Time. The old Inspector lived, it seems, a life, in which the cares of office never spoiled his appetite, in which no sickly fancies or laborious thoughts disturbed digestion. Happy, however, though he was according to the measure of his faculties, and the activity of his functions, his course of life was not entirely untroubled. It had its painful incidents, but they were not many. "The chief tragic event of the old man's life, our historian tells us, was his mishap with a certain goose, which lived and died some twenty or forty years ago; a goose of most promising figure, but which at table proved so inveterately tough, that the carving knife would make no impression on its carcass, and it could only be divided with an axe and a hand-saw." In happy contrast to this is the sketch of General Miller, serious, appreciating, happily conceived, and written with an impressive and kindly eloquence.

The slight personal revealings which he gives of himself are not the least in the attractions of this introduction. We doubt not that all who sympathize with literature, and with its place in American culture and American fame, have feelings and opinions connected with the dismissal of Mr. Hawthorne, with which party tendencies have no concern.— Whatever may be our thought concerning the matter, we cannot regret the result; since humanity is the gainer and the Custom House no loser: for though humanity might lose a poet in the Custom House, there is not much danger that the Custom House will lose many officers in poetry. Yet, as our author found the hint of his story in the Custom House, we are thankful to those who put him in: as he could not use it while he remained there, we are benefitted by those who turned him out.

It is a deep. dark, strange and solemn story; deep, dark, strange and solemn in its scene, narrative, characters,—in the meanings which it conceals and in the moral which it implies. Though most distinctly told, there is yet a mystic and a mythic obscurity around it. It is well placed in an age of witchcraft—in an age when religious feeling allied itself with ferocious superstitions, and when the moral sense was a kind of internal savageism, ere the land was cleared of the Indian; when the settlements in New England were yet girded by dismal forests, and the minds of New England were ruled over by dismal doctrines, the events of this story are supposed to have occurred, and its personages to have lived. A crowd is gathered round a prison door. Faces are anxious and expectant. The door opens, and out from the jail there comes a woman in the bloom of youth and beauty. An infant, some three months old, clings alarmed to her neck. On her breast she wears, shaped from scarlet cloth, and elegantly embroidered, the letter—A. This woman is Hester Prynne, an immigrant in the colony of about two years. Sne is to stand in the pillory, and this Scarlet Letter is the initial of her sin and of her shame. She might have been punished with death according to the severe laws of the colony; but as many mitigating circumstances plead in her behalf, she is to be exposed on the pillory, and to wear this letter for life.—Not impudently, yet firmly she ascends; she stands upon the scaffold; she listens respectfully to the admonition of the clergy; she bears bravely the gaze of the crowd, and only once she shrinks,—she sees, as she looks into that crowd, the pallid face of an elderly and deformed man. He is her husband: he had staid behind in Europe: and thus exposed, she saw him in a strange land for the first time. The moment passed. There was yet another soul present, bound to the spirit of the woman by a stronger and a darker interest.

The woman here exposed is a sinner—but she has sinned after the manner of woman, and even in sin appears a whole woman, in weakness and in strength. The meanness and degradation, which man displays in his transgression, is often in strange contrast with the firmness—even grandeur which woman sometimes shows in hers. The deeper crimes of man come from his passions and his appetites; the most grievous sins of woman are frequently from her heart. Thus, while guilt in man is selfishness—guilt in woman may be sacrifice. While it bears down man to cowardly degradation, it may display in woman some of her most heroic qualities. Even, as in this instance, with a love sincere, though unhappy and unblest, she can still be faithful to the last, and strong as a martyr. She will bear all tortures and all shames, and no power can wring out the secret which she has locked within her heart. In the faith which will endure disgrace, and endure it in a solitary silence, woman has ever proved her superiority to man. This attribute in the moral being of

woman, our author finely brings out in the whole character of Hester; but especially in her conduct on the pillory.

Among other magnates of the colony, two clergymen are present. One is the grave and elderly Mr. Wilson; a man of much experience; quiet in his preaching, and sober in his godliness. The other is Mr. Dimmesdale; young, handsome, and a man of genius; a man distinguished in general repute, for a piety to which good men grown hoary in the service of God did homage; a man of matchless eloquence—uniting, as it seemed, a seraph's zeal to a prophet's speech. This is the man that is called on to exhort Hester to make confession as to who is the partner of her sin. The venerable Mr. Wilson has exhausted all his skill and failed. Regarding the persuasiveness of his younger colleague as not to be resisted, he urges the evidently unwilling priest to use this persuasiveness on the unyielding culprit. The youthful priest does pour out an impressive sermon; a sad sermon it is, a sermon sounding with the melancholy of despair. Sincere, it is yet ambiguous.—Hester's ear might take it, and not falsely, as an exhortation to speak out; but her woman's heart would feel it truly, as an appeal to hold her peace. Hester does hold her peace. We can here easily see, that her exhorter is at her mercy, and that he is the companion of her guilt. She steps down from the stage of her exposure, to wear upon her bosom the Scarlet Letter, until it shall burn into her flesh and blood, through heart and soul, and scorch all her moral and her living womanhood. But, since the muse of Eschylus made men stand aghast by pictures of awe and sorrow, was ever a more tragic group than we have here presented to the imagination? Here is the unconscious infant that shall never know a father; here is the exposed mother, whose sin has all the pain of open shame for herself, and the burden of concealment for another; without any remorse for the man she has deserted; without any support from the man she has loved. And here are these two men, —not revealed to each other or to the people, yet confronted spirit to spirit—and by a sort of occult instinct, present mind to mind—the one, an unloved husband—the other, his loved, but wretched rival. What group more desolate was ever brought together?

This tragic power in the opening deepens in the progress of the story; and passions, incidents and persons are fraught with it to the end. We feel it in the oath of Hester to her husband, in that sad interview when she swears not to discover her relation to him: we feel it in the anguish with which she beholds the malign influence that the wily and revengeful man exercises on the priest, in whom he knows he has found his rival, in whom he secures his victim: we feel it in that force of sorrow which, after years have fled, leads her to break up this companionship, and in the desperate efforts which she makes to arouse in her lover the courage and resolve of manhood. There is a Grecian sublimity in the manner in which she meets and goes through her destiny. Year after year she lives solitary, yet not selfish; unsocial, but not inhuman; strong, but not ungentle. She works for her living; nurtures her child; and does, besides, aught she can of neighborly charity. She still wears the letter, but few attach the original significance to it: nay, so conciliating is patience, so powerful is the might of uncomplaining endurance, that this letter, from a symbol of infamy, comes at last to stand for loving and honorable meanings. The child grows apace, and is a thing of dreamful beauty—an infant witchery—a mixture of the human and the unearthly—an incarnate loveliness—which we know not how to name, whether to call it an embodied angel from the skies, or an embodied fairy from the woods. The outcast woman wears her scarlet letter on her garment; the tortured priest—bears his, burning in his breast. The fire that is never quenched consumes him; the worm that never dies devours him; and the enemy that cannot forgive, looks on, and glories in his sufferings. They have done their work. They have worn out his life. The scarlet letter has done its work. Hester, reckless of a society who had so bruised her, would now quit it, and take the priest along with her. There is, in this portion of this deep prose tragedy, great eloquence, and a most profound searching into human passion—with dashes of poetic sunshine, the brighter for the gloom. The interview between Hester and Dimmesdale, after so many years of shame on her side, and so many of secret remorse on his, in the silent and secluded forest, is a scene of sorrow and joy, and of inward human struggle, upon which we pondered in long reflection and with thoughtful admiration. It is a pregnant page out of the volume of humanity. Then, in contrast with these situations and persons so agitated with sad memories and excited passions, is the child at the brook, questioning its babble, and giving the meaning of its own sweet fancies to the music of its ripple! But life must no more wrestle with remorse. The time has come for confession, and confession ends in death. While the minister temporarily meditates flight, and has not yet resolved upon confession: while his brain reels between desire and conviction, between earthly escape and spiritual martyrdom, he is visited by a series of temptations, grotesque — strange—fascinating—illusive—terrible. Extraordinary as these are, every man has that in his experience which will convince

him of their reality. This is a great piece of psychological painting; and so, too, with a dramatic grandeur in addition, is the close of the minister's life. The people and the fathers of the people are assembled. It is election day. The preacher has pronounced a sermon, which the council and the multitude throb under as a voice from heaven. The priest is on the pinnacle of fame for sanctity and genius. Hester Prynne stands near the pillory, on which seven years before she was exposed. Throngs have left the church, they are coming towards this scaffold. The preacher, pale and tottering, is among them. Here the minister stops: with Hester and her child he ascends the scaffold, in the presence of the bewildered, the astonished assembly.

"'People of New England!' cried he, with a voice that rose over them, high, solemn and majestic,—yet had always a tremor through it, and sometimes a shriek, struggling up out of a fathomless depth of remorse and woe,—'ye, that have loved me!—ye, that have deemed me holy!—behold me here, the one sinner of the world! At last!—at last!—I stand upon the spot where, seven years since, I should have stood; here, with this woman, whose arm, more than the little strength wherewith I have crept hitherward, sustains me, at this dreadful moment, from grovelling down upon my face! Lo, the scarlet letter which Hester wears! Ye have all shuddered at it! Wherever her walk hath been,—wherever, so miserably burdened, she may have hoped to find repose,—it hath cast a lurid gleam of awe and horrible repugnance round about her. But there stood one in the midst of you, at whose brand of sin and infamy ye have not shuddered!'

"It seemed, at this point, as if the minister must leave the remainder of his secret undisclosed. But he fought back the bodily weakness,—and, still more, the faintness of heart,—that was striving for the mastery with him. He threw off all assistance, and stepped passionately forward a pace before the woman and the child.

"'It was on him!' he continued, with a kind of fierceness; so determined was he to speak out the whole. 'God's eye beheld it! The angels were for ever pointing at it! The Devil knew it well, and fretted it continually with the touch of his burning finger! But he hid it cunningly from men, and walked among you with the mien of a spirit, mournful because so pure in a sinful world!—and sad, because he missed his heavenly kindred! Now, at the death-hour, he stands up before you! He bids you look again at Hester's scarlet letter! He tells you, that, with all its mysterious horror, it is but the shadow of what he bears on his own breast, and that even this,

his own red stigma, is no more than the type of what has seared his inmost heart!"

Then, in a last and wild "farewell," he expires.

The leading characters are conceived, contrasted and evolved, not with artistic skill only, but with an in-looking soul that has gone far down to the deep places of the human affections and to the mysteries of the human will. The several individualities are admirably sustained. It would be no fair method of criticism to judge them as we would persons of like condition now; for, though they belong to what we esteem the order of common life, their era is so remote from ours—not indeed by years, but by association—as to render them mythical; and besides the dimness of tradition, there is the mystery about them of peculiar and solemn destinies. Their age is to ours in this country a sort of heroic age; and they are beings created to be distinctive, even in their age. They are in the highest sense poetic beings, and to be estimated by poetic laws. Yet, by such laws we do not take them from the Real, by regarding them as of the Ideal; for the Ideal is the Real, but separated from all that renders the Actual, local, temporary and changeful—in fact, consists of those elements of the Real which are permanent and universal. These beings are consistent with themselves, and this is all that the rule by which they are to be estimated requires. In the world of Art, in the world of Imagination, they are complete and vital unities; and this is their proper world. Hester is ever the strong soul, still only with the strength of a soul that has sinned. Superior in her nature, she lives only in the force of nature, and ascends not into that sphere of spiritual being, in which to yield is to conquer, and to bend is to aspire, and to become lowly is to become exalted. She is not a Christian, but a stoic. The outward cannot conquer her; but neither does she conquer the outward. She has not learned the divinity of Christian sorrow; the godliness of its source, and the beauty of its manifestation. She is greater than her fellows: not, however, by heavenly, but human energy. She is too noble for revenge. She does them good, but it is not meekly done. She does them good, because good is the action of a grand spirit, and hers was a grand spirit. Though not evangelically benevolent, she could not be malevolent, vengeful, or malignant, for that were to be base. She earns good opinion without caring for it, and when she has worn out reproach, she despises reconciliation. In taking her sin, and the odium, and the penalty of it, on her own isolated, absolute individuality, we have an impressive example of mental and moral prowess. In bearing all the scorching and scathing shame of it on her own un-sheltered bosom, without appeal, apology, excuse, or equivocation, we almost forget the crime in the courage, and lose sight of the sinner in the heroine. She is not of those paltry creatures who will first have such enjoyment as sin affords and then expect to be petted for repenting; creatures who seem willing to put off their manhood, if they can evade retributive censure in the simulated incapacity of idiots or infants. But Hester was not of such. She would not charge her deed upon circumstance or others; and odious as that scarlet letter was, she could not put it off, if, in doing so, she must put off with it the moral majesty of her individual personality.

Dimmesdale, too, whether considered as a psychological conception, or as an artistic creation, or as a moral agent, is a character in which we find evidence of a genius that seems to have elements in common with the apparently irreconcilable minds of Coleridge and of Crabbe. In one sense, it is a character not uncommon; but the author, in opening to us the inward workings of it, and the spirit of these workings, evinces a searching and sagacious intellect, acting in company with an imagination that is as keen in its questionings of actual life, as it is original in its forms of ideal life. Dimmesdale is not a hypocrite; for, then, it would be easy to paint him. He has committed sin, and conceals it. Still he is not false: he knows that he is not what he seems, yet he does not deceive. He has genius which he would use rightly, and yet he has not rectitude. He has power, he would not apply his power to evil ends; but still he is not a good man. He has fallen, yet he is not a hardened, nor by habit a bad man. He loves fame, reputation, glory, influence; but he would give the universe for the one minute's courage which would blast them all, strip him to the soul, and place him a spiritual bankrupt and beggar before the hooting multitude. That moment, it costs him years of agony to gain, and his life to go through.— There is deep moral import for us in this character. It is one to tax profound attention, and it merits the profoundest. It will not do to call such a man a hypocrite. It will not even do to say that he wanted courage, for a man who had courage equal to the sacrifice which his trial demanded, would not be a man who could be exposed to such a trial. Our remarks on character are often extremely inconsistent, and often we prove ourselves to be fools in our criticism of folly. There are instances when, by giving way to sudden passion, a man brings upon himself a measureless woe. Now, frequently, this is not so much the result of the deed itself as of the concealment of it, and of the complications which belong to the concealment. Why, we ask, was not a frank and free confession made?

Let us just think below the surface, and we shall discover that the coolness and the strength which would be equal to the confession, would never be subject to the passion. There are actions which are morally contradictory, as there are terms which are logically cntradictory; and the latter do not more necessarily exclude each other than do the former. Dimmesdale is one of those mixed characters, which, as they are the hardest to judge in life, are also the hardest to embody in literature. He is an example of those spiritual contrarieties, which we should find in essence in the heart of every man that walks, could we see into it. In him, as poetry requires, they are intensified: in substance, they are of the stuff of common life: it is only in degree that they are ideal and romantic. His being is a secret strife between passion and principle; between the power of conviction and feebleness of will; between desire and devotion; between the consciousness of being wrong and the longing to be right. With all this, there is an interior centre of moral imposition. Vanity abides in that centre. He lives in excitement and for effect, and the illusion which deceives the world is not greater than that which deceives himself.

Chillingworth is not a character that it is very pleasant to contemplate. He is, however, a character to excite thought and to afford instruction. His character, like the others, is depicted with a singular originality. But, he is disagreeable. Still, we find a moral use in him: and we do not see, that, consistently with the plot or spirit of the story, he could well be other than he is. Yet, however real or natural the fact may be, it is painful to behold, as we do in Chillingworth, worthy qualities changed into wicked ones; to behold an honest, intelligent, earnest, and reflective student, transformed by any injury, to a mean, insidious, vindictive persecutor: a simulating and smiling villain—a deliberate and fiendish assassin, who turns his mind into spiritual passion by which to consume and to kill his victim.

But, then, in what a wonder of contrast to this hateful and contemptible character is that of the enchanting little "Pearl!" A true jewel she is, glistening and gleaming with sweet, yet unsettled and uncertain lustre, amidst all the darker fragments of the story; a playful sprite, and yet sorrowful; a cherub that seems to have lost its pathway out of heaven and found itself on earth, smiling with the sweetness of higher spheres, yet sombre also with the melancholy of this lower world. Nothing, perhaps, has more tested genius, than to give the ideal of childhood. We have now before our minds the Mignone of Goèthe, the Fenella of Scott, the Little Nell of Dickens; but we think that "Pearl" takes hold of our last, almost strongest affections, by a wildness, a delicacy, an enchantment, which none of them possess—which they certainly do not possess as she does, in union with a weird, wood-like, sylvan witchery.

We have been thus full in our outline of the plot, and in our analysis of the characters, not that we would have our article a substitute for the story, for we suppose that all our readers are already familiar with this extraordinary volume: we have chosen our method as the only by which we could naturally and easily indicate the impressions which have been left upon our mind by a tale so original and peculiar. Differences of opinion there will be, no doubt, on the tendencies of it; but none, we are sure, will be as to the genius in it. Some might consider the moral influence doubtful, in a few instances; in others, the purpose does not seem clear or well-defined; but in substance, and on the whole, no work which reveals, as this does, the deep places of our nature, which so lays bare the subtle concealments of conscience, and which so brings out the tragic results of passion, but must, in its very sadness, solemnize, instruct and purify us.

We have not indulged in quotation; for in a story so thorough in its unity, so compact and so condensed, we found but few passages that we could, without injury, displace.

Our closing remarks must now be made. They must not be many, although there is no want of suggestiveness in our text. Genius working by its freedom, in a work of art, has no formal moral for its end. The moral should be in the spirit of purity and power with which it acts. When a spirit of purity and power is in the man, no badness or baseness can be in the artist. You may draw fifty or five thousand moral influences from his work; you may make fifty or five thousand moral uses of his work; your influences and your uses may be right; but not one of them may have been in his contemplation. He works within boundless nature, and in conformity with nature, power goes out from him through his creation, with an infinity of suggestiveness, and in an infinity of ways. The author does in the present instance faintly indicate a moral in the single word—" Truth." But the real moral of his story covers the entire of life; any word which expressed a danger or duty of life, would be but a part of the moral; the whole of it would require many words, significant of many dangers and many duties. But, as the author has chosen his word, we have no right to change it. We will only dwell on it in a few very general relations: as, for example, in the relation of society to the individual; in relation of the individual to society; and in relation of the individual to himself.

Now in the relation of society to the individual, the treatment by the community of Hester was void of truth; it was false; it was bad. Rude society has always the error of pushing ignominy to the utmost, and we may doubt if any society is yet so instructed as to be entirely right and true in this matter. We would not destroy, nay, we would not weaken the moral supervision of society; we would not strip from it the solemn right to rebuke and punish. The retributive action of society on the individual is a part of nature; it is an extension of the instinct of self-preservation into the wider though vaguer instinct of social preservation. Nor is this action without its individual moral use. Society becomes a mirror to conscience; and in that mirror a man often, for the first time, beholds the true moral image of himself. Let society punish, even to death, if that must be; let society expose, if exposure is necessary: but there is a bound which society has no claim to cross; there is a life which no criminal can forfeit— the life of his inward being, the very vitality of his soul, the last recess of self-respect.— To intrude on this is worse than murder; for it is an attempt to kill that which is the life of life, the last retreat of hope, the last shelter in which consciousness can fold itself and bear existence even for an hour. Every man has this while he remains a man: let him wholly lose it, and in the same instant he flings off life. Jesus Christ, who knew all that is in man, knew how deeply, how divinely this is in him, and he revered it. He would not even *look* at the woman brought to him for judgment, but turned away, as if he would write upon the ground: and thus, while savage sanctimoniousness would brand with a scarlet stain, he whom no one could accuse, would not wound by a glance. Even the secret and silent punishment of God spares this thing in man; for, until remorse blackens to despair, it is that by which man ever finds in some part of his soul a drop of comfort. When society tries to corrupt this drop, or squeeze it out, then does society provoke man in his soul to hate it, to resist it as a tyrant, towards whom resistance is virtue.

Society may go beyond its just jurisdiction, but the individual reacts against the barbarism of society. When exposure has done all, it has done its worst; when nothing is concealed, there is no more to fear; and there can be but slight excitement to shame where there is no motive for gratitude. But when it is the individual that is false with society, he is feeble with himself. The sense of unfitness will perplex him; and while any moral sensibility is alive, the sense of untruth will torment him. If a scarlet letter is to be worn, it is greatly better that it should be stitched upon the garment, ay, even branded on the forehead, than that it should burn ever in the heart. Every man is pledged to society in the way of general honesty; but some men are pledged additionally by the special relations of consecrated office. A judge may be tempted and he is but human; so may a priest; but until all sacred associations are taken from magistracy and priesthood, sin in judge or priest will ever appear darker than in other men. The argument will not hold which urges that duty is one; that it is the same in all men; that it belongs to humanity and not to office. The mere acceptance or assumption of an office is an open vow, a deliberate engagement; and in the degree of the trust given in the office are the expectations formed of the man. Satisfy these outwardly as a man may, while he is inwardly untrue, he cannot be at peace, except his conscience die; then that would be intellectual as well as moral death. To a man with any innate nobleness, no humiliation can be deeper, no shame more scalding, than to know that his life is not a reality, that his position is but phenomenal; and that while mistaken for a prophet, he is only an actor. To have any secret which involves such feelings is a killing thing. It complicates the spirit; it confuses motive; it deprives a man of inherent force, because in taking away his peace and his simplicity, it takes away his courage and his strength. However grand or energetic his efforts may be, they are but fitful and spasmodic; they have no continuous life; they are united to no fixed centre; below the most rapturous applause there are the stunning whisperings of fear, and in the brightest noon of fame the inward eye will shape to itself the accusing spectre of remorse. The distinction of what is natural in morality from what is conventional gives no relief; for in all the permanent relations of society, the natural and the conventional merge into the law of TRUTH, and that is immutable and eternal. A man with any spiritual life in him only fears society because he has first condemned himself; and no censure from without can fatally disturb him, if it has not interpretation from within. "*Thou art the man*," says the lowly seer to the mighty king; it was the voice in the heart of the king which gave import to the voice of the prophet, and gave it terror.

But, though society can make no change, nor even conscience in aught that is dark, yet the best has need to watch and to be humble. We have all of us, potentially, the elements of every sin. That sin does not come into consciousness or commission may be a negation of trial and not a triumph of virtue.— Why should we not apply the great idea of our human identity, our human oneness, to guilt as well as to goodness? To feel that the situation of the direst criminal was possible to any of us, seems to us truly as needful to justice as to mercy—a sure bond of genuine charity. And what right have we to claim kindred with the saint and exclude the sinner? We are of common nature with them both; we are brothers in humanity; and we sanctify that humanity not less by pity towards the sinner, than we do by aspiration towards the saint. But, there is a class of sins of which society takes no cognizance, and of which a man is not quick to suspect himself. They are quiet sins, but they may become very deadly. They are sins of the spirit. They are not turbulent, but they cause often tempests of distress. Sins of the carnal passions become soon odious to society, but sins of the spirit—envy, vanity, bigotry, ambition, remain unrebuked, or are insensible to rebuke. The sins of the outward passions begin in the senses, and are in their last stage and worst when they reach the soul. The sins of the inward passions begin in the soul, and are direct and immediate evil in the source of life. But their agency does not stop within the soul; it goes far abroad; and, if allied with intellectual energy, it becomes as much more fearful for evil in the world as THOUGHT is greater than appetite. We would speak here, however, only on the evil it is, in the individual himself. One such sin may work the most direful ruin in him; it may corrupt him in the essence of his soul; eat out of it every tolerant, every affectionate disposition; it may so deceive his faculties, so pervert his sentiments, that he minds not the inward wickedness that is in him, or the perdition to which he has come, until, in some late and revolting revelation, he finds himself incurably miserable in hating and being hated. In the "Chillingworth" of this story we have this moral fact impressed on us. A man of thought, and not originally of unkindly temper, he allows a fatal provocation to overmaster him; he lets in the spirit of vengeance to his breast; helps its growth by brooding meditation; strengthens it by exercise and habit, until victory brings him to despair; until all the man within him dies and nothing but the fiend is living. "From envy, hatred, malice, and all uncharitableness, good Lord deliver us!" Than this, there is no more needful, and no more solemn petition within the compass of human supplication.

---

[1]"The Scarlet Letter: A Romance. By Nathaniel Hawthorne," *Holden's Dollar Magazine*, 5 (June, 1850), 337-344.

[2]Kenneth Walter Cameron, *Hawthorne Among His Contemporaries. A Harvest of Estimates, Insights, and Anecdotes from the Victorian Literary World and an Index* (Hartford: Transcendental Books, 1968), pp. 512-513. The paraphrase appears on pp. 320-321 of the *Bulletin of the New York Public Library* (July, 1904).

[3]Autograph letter, signed.

[4]*Dollar Magazine*, 8 (1851), 43-44.

[5]Nina E. Browne, *A Bibliography of Nathaniel Hawthorne* (Boston: Houghton, Mifflin, 1905), p. 71, erroneously lists the May, 1851, number of the *Dollar Magazine* as the first place of publication. Hugh Cathcart, *Bibliography of the Works of Nathaniel Hawthorne* (Cleveland: The Rowfant Club, 1905), p. 40, correctly conjunctures that "Ethan Brand" "probably" appeared first in the *Boston Literary Museum*, entitled "The Unpardonable Sin." Neither bibliography lists the reviews of Hawthorne's works that are in the *Dollar Magazine*.

[6]See 341.1.28.

[7]*Dollar Magazine*, 5 (1850), 312-314.

[8]*Dollar Magazine*, 5 (1850), 442.

[9]*Dollar Magazine*, 7 (1851), 136. The volumes I used do not distinguish between numbers in volume 7.

[10]*Dollar Magazine*, 6 (1850), [447].

[11]"Henry Giles," *Appleton's Cyclopaedia of American Biography*, ed. James Grant Wilson and John Fiske (New York: D. Appleton, 1888).

[12]*Lectures and Essays*, 2 vols. (Boston: Ticknor, Reed, and Fields, 1850).

[13]*Human Life in Shakespeare* (Boston: Lee and Shepherd, 1868).

[14]*Illustrations of Genius in some of its Relations to Culture and Society* (Boston: Ticknor and Fields, 1854).

[15]*Hawthorne and His Publisher* (1913; rpt. Port Washington, N.Y.: Kennikat Press, 1969), p.24.

[16]*Fields of the Atlantic Monthly:Letters to an Editor, 1861-1870* (San Marino, Ca.: The Huntington Library, 1953), p. 212.

[17]*Illustrations of Genius,* pp. 66-90.

[18]*The Imperial Self: An Essay in American Literary and Cultural History* (New York: Alfred A. Knopf, 1971), pp. 59-87.

The Mischianza Ball and Hawthorne's "Howe's Masquerade"

FUMIO ANO

Hawthorne makes it clear that as historical background for "Howe's Masquerade" (1838)[1], the first of the four "Legends of the Province House," he used the siege of Boston and probably Sir William Howe's departure from the city during the American Revolution.[2] It has been pointed out, too, that he drew also on a play called "The Blockade of Boston," in which there is a caricature of George Washington similar to that in the tale.[3] Howe's masquerade of the tale is one of the entertainments at the Province House, the "mansion of the old royal governors of Massachusetts," held "during the latter part of the siege of Boston," and probably just before the British evacuated the city on March 17, 1776.

For the magnificence of Howe's masquerade ball and the fantastic elements in the tale, Hawthorne seems to have had an additional source, the extravagant ball arranged by Major John André for Howe on May 18, 1778, to celebrate his departure from Philadelphia. This ball, at the time called *Mischianza*, meaning a medley of festivities, "is said to have exceeded in magnificence of exhibition even those of Louis XIV,"[4] and historians have referred to it as an unusual affair. Ira D. Gruber, for example, regards it as difficult to explain why Sir William Howe would have allowed his officers to stage a magnificent pageant to celebrate his departure, considering his failure to end the rebellion and the frustrations he had experienced in dealing with the ministry.[5]

It is most likely that Hawthorne read at least one report of the Mischianza Ball: "Particulars of the Mischianza in America," a copy of a long letter from an officer at Philadelphia to his correspondent in London. This letter appeared in the August, 1778, issue, volume XLVIII, of the *Gentleman's Magazine*. Hawthorne drew this volume from the

231

Salem Athenaeum on July 6, 1830.[6] The letter, which is said to have been written by Major André,[7] depicts full particulars of the Mischianza, the "most splendid entertainment...ever given by an army to their General."[8]

The Mischianza, offering a variety of entertainment, was given to General William Howe by twenty-two of his field officers on May 18, 1778. The entertainment began with a grand regatta which consisted of three divisions of galleys dressed out in a variety of colors and streamers; Sir William and his brother, Lord Howe, and Sir Henry Clinton were in the Hussar galley in the center. In front of the whole were three flat boats with a band of music in each, and the transport ships, crowded with spectators, appeared in a long line and provided the most picturesque scene. "God save the King" was played and as soon as the general's barge was seen to push for the shore, a salute of guns was fired from two ships, the *Roebuck* and the *Vigilant.* The company, as they disembarked, arranged themselves in a procession and advanced through an avenue which led to a square lawn, where the White Knights and the Black Knights engaged in a tilt and tournament, according to the customs and ordinances of ancient chivalry, in the presence of their chosen ladies in Turkish costumes. After that they passed under the first triumphal arch, erected in the Tuscan order in honor of Lord Howe, and then, under the second arch, dedicated to General Howe, into a garden, from where they ascended a flight of steps, covered with carpets which led into a spacious hall. In this hall and the adjoining rooms were prepared tea, lemonade, and other beverages.

The following paragraphs from the letter in the *Gentleman's Magazine* describe the ball itself:

> From these apartments we were conducted up to a ball-room, decorated in a light elegant stile of painting. The ground was a pale blue, pannelled with a small gold bead, and in the interior filled with dropping festoons of flowers in their natural colours. Below the surbase the ground was of rose-pink, with drapery festooned in blue. These decorations were heightened by 85 mirrours, decked with rose-pink silk ribbands, and artificial flowers; and in the intermediate spaces were 34 branches with wax-lights, ornamented in a similar manner.
>
> On the same floor were four drawing-rooms, with side-boards of refreshments, decorated and lighted in the same stile and taste as the ball-room. The ball was opened by the Knights and their Ladies; and the dances continued till ten o'clock, when the windows were thrown open, and a magnificent bouquet of rockets began the fire-works. These were planned by Capt. Montresor, the chief engineer, and consisted of twenty different exhibitions, displayed under his direction with the happiest success, and in the highest stile of beauty. Towards the conclusion, the interior part of the triumphal arch was illuminated amidst an uninterrupted flight of rockets and bursting of baloons. The military trophies

on each side assumed a variety of transparent colours. The shell and flaming heart on the wings sent forth Chinese fountains, succeeded by fire-pots. Fame appeared at top, spangled with stars, and from her trumpet blowing the following device in letters of light, *Tes Lauriers sont immortels.*—A *sauteur* of Rockets, bursting from the pediment, concluded the *feu d'artifice.*

At twelve supper was announced, and large folding doors, hitherto artfully concealed, being suddenly thrown open, discovered a magnificent saloon of 210 feet by 40, and 22 in height, with three alcoves on each side, which served for side-boards. The cieling was the segment of a circle, and the sides were painted of a light straw-colour, with vine-leaves and festoon-flowers, some in a bright, some in a darkish green. Fifty-six large pier-glasses, ornamented with green silk artificial flowers and ribbands; 100 branches with three lights in each, trimmed in the same manner as the mirrors; 18 lustres each, with 24 lights, suspended from the cieling, and ornamented as the branches; 300 wax-tapers, disposed along the supper tables; 430 covers; 1200 dishes; 24 black slaves, in oriental dresses, with silver collars and bracelets, ranged in two lines, and bending to the ground as the General and Admiral approached the saloon: all these, forming together the most brilliant assemblage of gay objects, and appearing at once as we entered by an easy descent, exhibited a *coup d'oeil* beyond description magnificent.

Towards the end of supper, the Herald of the Blended Rose, in his habit of ceremony, attended by his trumpets, entered the saloon, and proclaimed the King's health, the Queen, and Royal Family, the Army and Navy, with their respective Commanders, the Knights and their Ladies, the Ladies in general: each of these toasts was followed by a flourish of music. After supper we returned to the ball-room, and continued to dance till four o'clock.[9]

Although the particulars of the Mischianza Ball do not appear in Hawthorne's description of Howe's masquerade, these two affairs are similar in that both are pompous and fantastic beyond description. It is possible to think that Hawthorne was impressed by "all the pomp and splendor of the *Mischianza*" which have been noted by many historians—a regatta on the Delaware, a medieval tournament on land, triumphal arches, dressed-up knights, ladies in Turkish costumes, fireworks, a surprise supper, and a gorgeous ball—and that the ball was enough to suggest to him the pomp and fantasticality of Howe's masquerade in his tale, which he called the "most gay and gorgeous affair that had occurred in the annals of the government."

Howe's masquerade of his tale is given "to hide the distress and danger of the period, and the desperate aspect of the siege, under an ostentation of festivity," just before Howe's departure from the Province House at Boston; the Mischianza was held on the eve of his departure from Philadelphia and ultimately from America, as a result of his failure to end the rebellion. Both are held under somewhat similar conditions, but obviously, in this respect, Hawthorne kept in mind Howe's departure from Boston on March 17, 1776, because the

English had a very hard time of it at Boston,[10] while they could spend fairly good time in Philadelphia. It may be supposed, therefore, that Hawthorne transferred the Mischianza to the period of the siege of Boston in order, first of all, to create a tenser, more dramatic situation. It should be noted also that the Revolutionary period in American history was not *hoarly antique* to Hawthorne and his contemporary readers and that he, as a romance writer, had to "attempt to throw the spell of hoar antiquity over localities with which the living world, and the day that is passing over us, have aught to do," though he thought it "desperately hard work" to do so. In transferring the time and place of the Mischianza to the period of the siege of Boston, Hawthorne could, after all, create a proper setting for his tale: a "neutral territory." He could, with the best energy of his imagination, "throw a tinge of romance and historic grandeur over the realities of the scene."

Tohoku University
Sendai, Japan

---

[1] The text of "Howe's Masquerade" used for this article is the "Old Manse Edition," ed. Rose Hawthorne Lathrop and Horace E. Scudder (Boston: Houghton, Mifflin and Company, 1900), II, 1-25.

[2] An entry in *The American Notebooks* relates to the material of this story: "A phantom of the old royal governors, or some such shadowy pageant, on the night of the evacuation of Boston by the British." *The American Notebooks*, ed. Claude M. Simpson (Ohio State University Press, 1972), p. 186. The story was published in May, 1838; the notebook entry appears under the year 1840, but it is not unlikely that Sophia Hawthorne, in editing the notebooks, shifted this note from an earlier date.

[3] See *Twice-Told Tales*, ed. J. Hubert Scott (Boston: Houghton, Mifflin and Company, 1907), pp. 569-570: "On a January evening of 1776, when Gage had been recalled and Howe had held the command for three months, a farce, *The Blockade of Boston*, was presented at Faneuil Hall. Howe was one of the audience amused by the appearance on the stage of a caricatured Washington bearing a rusty sword and attended by a grotesque squire."

[4] Benson J. Lossing, *Seventeen Hundred and Seventy-Six, or the War of Independence* (New York: Edward Walker, 1847), p. 259.

[5] *The Howe Brothers and the American Revolution* (New York: Atheneum, 1972), p. 298.

[6] *Gentleman's Magazine*, XLVIII (Aug., 1778), 353-357. The same letter appeared in the *Annual Register for 1778* (London, 1800), pp. 264-270. According to Kesselring's list, Hawthorne drew the 1758, 1834, and 1836 issues of the *Annual Register* from the Salem Athenaeum, but the 1778 issue is not included in his list. Marion L. Kesselring, *Hawthorne's Reading: 1828-1850* (New York: New York Public Library, 1949), pp. 28, 43, and 51.

[7] See Gruber, *The Howe Brothers*, p. 299n. and Lossing, *Seventeen Hundred and Seventy-Six*, p. 259n.

[8] *Gentleman's Magazine*, XLVIII, 356.

[9]Ibid., 356.

[10]See, for example, William Edward Hartpole Lecky, *The American Revolution: 1763-1783* (New York: D. Appleton and Company, 1907), p. 234: "The blockade of Boston became more severe; sickness disabled many of the British soldiers; swarms of privateers made it very difficult to obtain provisions; and at last, on the night of March 4, 1776, the Americans obtained possession of Dorchester heights, which commanded the harbour. The town was now no longer tenable. On March 17, Howe, with the remainder of his army, consisting of about 7,600 men, sailed for Halifax, and Washington marched in triumph into the capital of Massachusetts."

Thomas Shepard and Crèvecoeur: Two Uses of the Image of the Bosom Serpent before Hawthorne

THOMAS WERGE

In his "Bosom Serpents before Hawthorne: The Origins of a Symbol," Sargent Bush, Jr. demonstrates that a tradition concerning the bosom serpent existed long before 1843, the year in which Hawthorne's "Egotism; or, the Bosom Serpent," appeared.[1] The tradition, he contends, "Hydra-like in its many branches," is comprised of four main sources on which Hawthorne might well have drawn for his conception of the symbolic serpent: Spenser's *The Faerie Queene*, contemporary newspaper stories of current medical cases, earlier medical accounts, and theological writings of the seventeenth and eighteenth centuries. Bush concludes that Hawthorne must have been at least partially aware of each element in the tradition.

> However much, or little, of it Hawthorne knew, we cannot say with certainty; we will, however, rightly continue to associate bosom serpents chiefly with his name, for his was the mind which transformed these several approaches to a common idea into a lasting literary symbol for the insidious and corrupting effect of sin on the soul of man.[2]

Two authors Bush does not include in his analysis—Crèvecoeur, in *Letters from an American Farmer*, and Thomas Shepard, in *The Sincere Convert*—also make use of this same image of the serpent. Each usage reinforces Bush's general argument, and Shepard's invocation of the bosom serpent further emphasizes the significance of the image in the Puritan tradition.[3]

Crèvecoeur's account is of a copperhead snake biting a man rather than dwelling inside his heart or stomach. But his description of the victim's physical symptoms, and of the responses of those he confronts, bears a clear relationship to Hawthorne's narrative of Roderick Elliston:

> his eyes were filled with madness and rage, he cast them on all present with the most vindictive looks: he thrust out his tongue as the snakes do; he hissed through his teeth with inconceivable strength, and became an object of terror to all by-standers. To the lividness of a corpse he united the desperate force of a maniac; they hardly were able to fasten him, so as to guard themselves from his attacks.[4]

Bush does not single out any one of Hawthorne's four possible sources as the most plausible origin of his symbol. Since Hawthorne would seem to have been aware of all of them, he argues, it is unnecessary to emphasize one source to the exclusion of another. Yet Bush acknowledges the presence of the bosom serpent as a symbol in the religious writings of the seventeenth and eighteenth centuries, and notes that it "occasionally" is found in the works of the American Puritans.[5] He refers to the sermons of Thomas Hooker, in which the bosom serpent is used as an image for man's sinful heart and guilty conscience, to demonstrate his contention. Despite his awareness that Hawthorne may have encountered the image in other theological works as well as in Hooker's, however, Bush warns that "not all American Puritan preachers had imaginations fertile enough to produce such poignantly symbolic metaphors as [those] from Hooker's writings, so that efforts to find similar passages in the writings of other Puritans are by no means guaranteed to be successful."[6]

Thomas Shepard, whose stature as a theologian and as a powerful, imaginative preacher in Puritan New England equalled that of Hooker, also describes the unregenerate heart as a poisonous creature.[7] It is as full of sin, he states, "as a Toad is of poyson."[8] Its sinfulness is continual and pervasive:

> Actual sins of the life fly out like sparks, and vanish, but this brand is always glowing within: the toad spits poyson sometimes, but it retains and keeps a poysonful nature alwayes. Hence the Apostle calls it, *"Sin that dwels in me,"* that is, which always lies and remains in me (pp. 56-57).

Any goodness in this foul nest is "but as a drop of Rosewater in a bowl of poyson; where fallen, it is all corrupted" (p. 53).

As the source of the poison of man's sinfulness, then, the depraved heart "contains, breeds, brings forth, suckles all the litter" of actual sins (pp. 56-57). And while "thou feelest not all these [sins] stirring in thee at one time," insists Shepard, "they are in thee like a nest of Snakes in an old hedge. Although they break not out in thy life[,] they lie lurking in thy heart" (p. 54).

If Crèvecoeur's description anticipates Hawthorne's delineation of Roderick Elliston's physical characteristics, it is far more limited in its meaning than either Shepard's or Hawthorne's use of the bosom serpent. Shepard, like Hawthorne, and like the Puritan tradition, sees the physical symbol as emblematic of a moral state. Serpent and heart, image and soul, are related organically. The bosom serpent is an important image in the Puritan tradition. It remains significant for Hawthorne not for narrowly literary reasons, but for the way in which it embodies and reveals an intensely real and constant dimension of man's moral experience.

University of Notre Dame

---

[1]"Bosom Serpents before Hawthorne: The Origins of a Symbol," *American Literature,* XLIII (May 1971), 181-199.

[2]"Bosom Serpents before Hawthorne," p. 199.

[3]There is no explicit evidence that Hawthorne read Crèvecoeur or Shepard, nor is there evidence that he read Thomas Hooker, whose writings Bush uses to support his contentions. See Marion Louise Kesselring, "Hawthorne's Reading, 1828-1850," *Bulletin of the New York Public Library,* LIII (Feb., Mar., Apr., 1949), 55-71, 121-138, 173-194. It is clear, of course, that Hawthorne's reading was not limited to the works or time span Kesselring documents. In light of Hawthorne's wide and deep reading, especially in literature and in religious writings, it would be foolish to allow a lack of positivist evidence to detract from the strong possibility that he had read these authors.

[4]*Letters from an American Farmer* (New York: E. P. Dutton, 1957), p. 170. Crèvecoeur's victim, unlike Hawthorne's, who is redeemed by the love and faith of the Beatrice-like Rosina, dies from the effects of the poison: "In the space of two hours death relieved the poor wretch from his struggles, and the spectators from their apprehensions" (p. 170).

[5]Although Bush's observation that "the full notion of a snake's residing in the human heart does not derive from the Bible" ("Bosom Serpents before Hawthorne," p. 197) is technically accurate, the close relationship in the Bible between man's heart and tongue, his will and speech, lends a special importance to those Biblical passages in which the tongue is seen as a poisonous serpent or creature. The tongue is identified with, and expresses, the proud and sinful heart. See, for example, the serpent's speech in Genesis, Psalm 58.4 and James 3.7-8: "the whole nature of beastes...hathe bene tamed of the nature of man. But the tongue can no man tame. It is an unrulie evil, full of deadelie poyson" (Geneva Bible). One of the lines Bush cites in Hooker—"The sting of the serpent is in their hearts, and the poison of asps is under their lips" ("Bosom Serpents before Hawthorne," p. 198)—echoes the Psalms: "Thei have sharpened their tongues like a serpent: adders poyson is under their lippes" (Ps. 140.3, Geneva Bible). Shepard, in *The Sincere Convert* (London, 1648), reflects a similar Biblical language in stating that *"the tongue is a world of mischief"* because it is bound to the sinful heart:*"For out of the abundance of the*

heart the tongue speaketh" (p. 53). Roderick Elliston's hissing utterances must be seen as part of this aspect of the Biblical tradition.

[6]"Bosom Serpents before Hawthorne," p. 198. Bush's tone here is curiously ambivalent. There can be no quarrel, finally, with the obvious recognition that not "all" such divines are as imaginative as Hooker. Not all Russian novelists are as imaginative as Dostoyevsky—which is hardly reason for dismissing them. If Bush is willing to grant the Puritan use of the image of the bosom serpent, he is clearly condescending toward the American Puritan literary tradition apart from Hooker and Edward Taylor. He apparently does not share the assumption that Perry Miller, Kenneth Murdock, and many contemporary scholars have effectively dispelled the older conventional wisdom concerning the Puritans' supposed lack of literary imagination and ability.

[7]Moses Coit Tyler indicates Shepard's prominence: "Of all the great preachers who came to New England in our first age, there were three who, according to the universal opinion of their contemporaries, towered above all others,—Thomas Hooker, Thomas Shepard, John Cotton. These three could be compared with one another; but with them could be compared no one else" *(A History of American Literature 1607-1765* [New York: Crowell-Collier, 1962], p. 183).

[8]*The Sincere Convert* (London, 1648), p. 52. All quotations are taken from this edition. The consistent popularity of *The Sincere Convert* is evidenced by its having gone through some twenty-one editions between 1641 and 1812. A three-volume edition of Shepard's *Works* was published in 1853.

Paulding's "The Dumb Girl,"
A Source of *The Scarlet Letter*

LOUIS OWENS

In 1830, twenty years before Nathaniel Hawthorne wrote *The Scarlet Letter*, James K. Paulding published *The Chronicles of the City of Gotham*. Among the tales published in this collection was "The Dumb Girl," a story which may have been a significant and largely overlooked source of *The Scarlet Letter*. Perhaps an examination of "The Dumb Girl" will serve to place Paulding in a long-deserved position of respect in the lists of Hawthorne's sources and influences.

Similarities between Paulding's tale and the story of Hester Prynne were first suggested in 1926 by Amos L. Herold in his critical biography of Paulding. In this book, Herold touched briefly upon the subject of "The Dumb Girl," and observed that "Special interest attaches to "The Dumb Girl" (1830), because it resembles and may have influenced *The Scarlet Letter* (1850)."[1] Herold failed to convince Luther S. Mansfield, who in 1948, in *The Literary History of the United States*, declared such comparisons between the two works "extravagant."[2] Though the subject appeared again in 1956, when Ralph M. Aderman, editor of a volume of Paulding's letters, cited Herold's discovery and agreed that "the correspondences are so close as to preclude the possibility of coincidence,"[3] it appears that no critic has as yet pursued a comparison of the two works beyond Herold's original two paragraphs on the subject.

An examination of "The Dumb Girl" makes apparent several impressive similarities and parallels between it and *The Scarlet Letter*, resemblances which indicate that perhaps Hawthorne owed much more to the influence of James K. Paulding than has been previously noted. The plot of "The Dumb Girl" is relatively simple: Walter, a young squire, returns to Tarrytown from six years of adventurous life at sea, and instantly becomes the romantic hero of the small village. He is attracted to Phoebe, a young woman who is "dumb," and succeeds in a short while in deceiving and seducing her. Phoebe vanishes from the community and is believed by all, including her seducer, to be dead; suspicion of murder falls upon Walter. Though Walter's guilt cannot be proven, he suffers for seven years from both the torments of his conscience and the condemnation of the village before being partially absolved of guilt by the knowledge that Phoebe is alive. He continues to suffer remorse for his seduction of Phoebe, however, for the rest of his life.This plot is summarized and accurately recorded, as Herold points out, in Hawthorne's *American Notebooks* for September 7, 1835, in which he noted: "A young man to win the love of a girl, without any serious intentions, and to find that in that love, which might have been the greatest blessing of his life, he had conjured up a spirit of mischief, which pursued him throughout his whole career—and this without any revengeful purposes on the part of the deserted girl."[4]

The heroine of the tale is Phoebe Angevine, a young woman of great beauty, set apart from other girls of the village by a combination of her physical affliction, an idiot brother who is her constant companion, poverty, and the envy the others feel toward her natural beauty. Phoebe bears a striking resemblance to Hester Prynne: Phoebe's "hair was amazingly long, luxuriant and silky, of a dark brown colour to match her eyes;"[5] Hester has "dark and abundant hair, so glossy that it threw off the sunshine with a gleam...and deep black eyes."[6] Phoebe "displayed the character and impress of most intense passion, or sensibility, or both"; Hester displays such passion and sensibility throughout her novel. Phoebe has an instinct for beautiful dress, of which Paulding wrote "Everybody wondered how she always kept herself so neat—for she was neatness itself. It was partly innate delicacy, and partly personal vanity" (p. 169). Hester has an "oriental" love of the voluptuous; her dress "was of a splendor in accordance with the taste of the age, but greatly beyond what was allowed by the sumptuary regulations of the colony" (p. 42). Hester, too, acts partly from personal vanity.

Hester vows at the beginning of *The Scarlet Letter*, "I will not speak!" (p. 53), committing herself to a lifetime of silence; Phoebe cannot speak, and her affliction seals her passion within her as deeply as Hester's vow. Paulding wrote, "Phoebe became gradually absorbed in the all-devouring passion. She could not relieve her heart and express her feelings in speech, and thus they preyed upon her almost to suffocation" (p. 180). Hawthorne appeared to view Hester's silence as an affliction similar to Phoebe's "dumbness," when he wrote that Hester was "as much alone as if she inhabited another sphere, or communicated with the common nature by other organs and senses than the rest of human kind" (p. 63).

When Phoebe's seduction becomes public knowledge, she is judged and condemned by the town gossips in a chorus of ten characters with such names as Mrs. Ratsbane, Mrs. Fadladdle and Mrs. Cackle. Hawthorne, with a much firmer style, created only five matrons to judge Hester outside the jail, a smaller and more effective chorus than Paulding's. Hawthorne added to his censurers a sympathetic soul in the person of the young wife, who says "O, peace, neighbors, peace!...Do not let her hear you! Not a stitch in that embroidered letter, but she has felt it in her heart" (p. 43). Paulding added to his harsh chorus "Mrs. Daisey," who like the young wife answers the condemnations with sympathy for the condemned: "Well, after all, let us hope for the best" (p. 180).

Phoebe's seduction occurs in a woodland scene, where "A high rock gloomed over the bank of the river, as it whirled violently round a sharp angle, deep and turbid," in "a little greensward, shadowed by lofty sycamores, and shut in on all sides" (p. 187). Hester's forest meeting with Dimmesdale occurs in "a little dell...with a leaf-strewn bank rising gently on either side, and a brook flowing through the midst," a brook which formed "eddies and black depths at some points" (p. 134). Paulding calls his scene "a scene made for love," which "might easily be desecrated to a more malignant passion." It is there, he says, in "the wicked twilight of the quiet woods," where "the purest heart sometimes swells with the boiling eddies of a youthful fancy" (p. 179). It is a setting which might come from either "The Dumb Girl" or *The Scarlet Letter.*

In the villagers' stern condemnation of Phoebe's fall, and later in their ostracism of Walter, Paulding illustrated what is perhaps a central moral of his tale, a moral which might effectively be applied to one aspect of *The Scarlet Letter.* Paulding admonishes: "Vice thrives apace where it carries with it no other penalty than that denounced by the law. It is the inquest, the censure, the terrible verdict of the society in which we live and move and have our very being, that constitutes the severest punishment" (p. 181). In this passage Paulding suggested one of the main currents which would later run through Hawthorne's romance; in Hester's seven years of cruel punishment one can find an illustration of the truth of Paulding's insight.

The eloquence and accomplishments of Phoebe's seducer make him the most admired man in the village, "the lion of the day, the wonder of the men, and the admiration of the ladies, old and young" (p. 172). Like Dimmesdale, Walter is a fresh arrival in the village; Walter has come from the sea, and Dimmesdale has "come from one of the great English universities, bringing all the learning of the age into our wild forest-land" (p. 51). Walter has captured the admiration of the villagers by his eloquent and enthusiastic stories; Dimmesdale has won over the people of Boston by his "eloquence and religious fervor." One seducer tells stories and the other preaches sermons. Each seducer feels he cannot be united publicly with his lover because such an action would damage or destroy his position in society, for Hester is married, and Phoebe is dumb and poor.

"The Dumb Girl" contains an avenue of experience which is but suggested as possibility by Hawthorne in *The Scarlet Letter:* Phoebe flees the scene of her disgrace. She removes to a place where she is unknown, and begins a new life, realizing the possibility which (Hawthorne makes this explicit) was always available to Hester. Though believed to have drowned, Phoebe had been swept downstream by the river, and pulling herself from the water, had "crossed the mountain which bordered the river, and became an outcast and a wanderer." She establishes a new life among new people, where she is "treated with kindness, as one on whom the hand of Providence had inflicted the sorest evils; and she made herself useful by her habits of industry. At this time news did not travel as fast as now; for there were few readers, and fewer newspapers to trumpet forth murders and accidents of flood and field" (p. 196). Like Hester, Phoebe is a value to her community with her "habits of industry," and like Hester, she refuses to give up the child of sin: "When her child was born, they wished to take it away, and place it at nurse in a poor-house; but she would not consent. She nursed it and brought it up, without being a burden to any living soul" (p. 197). That Hester is free to make Phoebe's decision to start a new life is obvious when Hawthorne says:

> It may seem marvellous, that, with the world before her,—kept by no restrictive clause of her condemnation within the limits of the Puritan settlement, so remote and so obscure,—free to return to her birthplace, or to any other European land, and there hide her character and identity under a new exterior, as completely as if emerging into another state of being,—and having also the passes of the dark, inscrutable forest open to her, where the wildness of her nature might assimilate itself with a people whose customs and life were alien from the law that had condemned her,—it may seem marvellous, that this woman should still call that place her home, where, and where only, she must needs be the type of shame (p. 60).

Phoebe had actually taken the option of going into the "passes of the dark, inscrutable forest" to a different people.

If Phoebe defies a fate like Hester's and opts for a new life, Walter does not. Paulding was most concerned with Walter's crime, not Phoebe's moral weakness. Dimmesdale sinned against the Puritan God, and in so doing, sinned against the Puritan community; but Walter sinned against the human soul when he betrayed Phoebe, and thus sinned against all humanity. It is Walter, rather than Phoebe, who must face the censure and "terrible verdict" of society. Walter's suffering may serve as a prototype for the later torments of both Hester and Dimmesdale; he suffers both the "severest punishment" of social ostracism, and the terrible ravages of conscience which would destroy Dimmesdale. Walter becomes a man apart, like the bearer of the scarlet letter: "He stood, a marked man, feared and hated by all; in the midst of society he was alone, and he sought to be alone." He avoids facing people because "he feared they might behold the refelction of his crime in that mirror of his soul" (p. 191). Like Dimmesdale, he wonders that people cannot see his guilt. Walter begins to suffer much as Dimmesdale later would:

> The days of Walter were days of bitterness, his nights were nights of horror. It seemed as if guilt had unmanned him entirely...He became the slave of conscience and superstition combined, and never knew a night of tranquil and unbroken rest. Awake, he lay perspiring in vague indefinite horrors; and sleeping, he rolled from side to side, muttering unintelligible words, and moans that seemed to rend his very vitals (p. 192).

He is haunted by his guilt, the "impression uppermost in his mind was his crime. The figure of Phoebe was ever present to his waking hours;—what wonder, then, if it haunted his dreams" (p. 192). Like the Puritan minister, Walter has dream-visions of his lover appearing before him. In *The Scarlet Letter* Hawthorne wrote: "And now, through the chamber which these spectral thoughts had made so ghastly, glided Hester Prynne, leading along little Pearl, in her scarlet garb, and pointing her forefinger, first at the scarlet letter on her bosom, and then at the clergyman's own breast" (p. 106). Paulding wrote of Walter's dreams, "that night the figure of Phoebe appeared to him as usual, pointing to a leaf in the pocket-book he had given her," and of the scene of Phoebe's return, "Phoebe pointed to their child; then placed her hand on her heart" (p. 193).

The guilt preys on Walter's physical and mental health: "By degrees, as his mind and body became gradually weakened by being thus constantly assailed, a firm conviction fastened itself on his imagination, that this besetting phantasy was a malignant fiend, empowered by a just Providence to assume the shape of his victim, to punish him for his crime" (p. 193). The great difference between the torment of Walter and that of Dimmesdale is that Hawthorne chose to personify the ravages of conscience in the form of a "malignant fiend" named Chillingworth, who "has become a fiend for especial torment" (p. 124). Perhaps it was here, in "The Dumb Girl," that Chillingworth was born.

Like Dimmesdale, "Walter Avery had paid the full penalty of his crime, in the misery of seven long years" (p. 197). At the end of the seven years, Phoebe sends her son to Walter, uniting father and child for the first time, and making Walter realize he is not guilty of Phoebe's death; he is partially absolved. Walter's surprise at finding Phoebe to be still alive is similar to the forest meeting between Hester and Dimmesdale, when Dimmesdale cries "Hester! Hester Prynne!...is it thou? Art thou in life?", and she answers "Even so!...In such life as has been mine these seven years past!" (p. 136). And the child's question of Walter, "What is a father?", will be later echoed with variations in precocious Pearl's insistant queries of Hester.

Walter does not find complete absolution until the climax scene of the story, in which Phoebe returns to him as he is dying, and they are united at last. He begs her forgiveness and calls for a minister of God so that they can be married. Walter's rejection of a physician and demand for a doctor of divinity resembles Dimmesdale's refusal to confess to Chillingworth, an "earthly physician," in which he says "Not to thee! But if it be the soul's disease, then do I commit myself to the one Physician of the soul!" (p. 100). When Walter has been forgiven by Phoebe, he clasps hands with her and with the child, and united with both before the eyes of God, he cries "May God forgive me!" and dies—two weeks later (p. 199).

It is obvious that the climax scenes of "The Dumb Girl" and *The Scarlet Letter* are structurally very similar: both serve to unite the lovers before the eyes of God (minister or Puritan people); both bring together the illigitimate child with its parents; both allow the chief sinner to repent and die; and both leave a wife or lover and child to continue living within the society. Like Hester, Phoebe chooses to live out her life in the village in which her disgrace occured; like Hester she becomes highly respected and a favorite ear for the confesssions of the villagers. Both women are perfect audiences, for one cannot speak and the other will not. The old gossips who first condemned Phoebe decide in the end that "she was one of the most agreeable creatures in the world" (p. 199).

It would seem justifiable, in light of the considerable correspondences between the two works, to consider Paulding's tale of major importance in any study of the creation of Hawthorne's classic. The tale of thirty pages cannot compare as a work of art, of course, with *The Scarlet Letter*. Paulding was by no means the consummate craftsman that Hawthorne was; he created his tales quickly and spent little or no time in revision of them. His stories are often without any internal unity and consequently fail to achieve a whole effect. "The Dumb Girl" is perhaps Paulding's best story, demonstrating the author's admirable talent for writing clear, concise prose, and containing psychological insight often as penetrating as that of Hawthorne. The story does not work effectively, as does *The Scarlet Letter*, in terms of culminating action; there are serious impediments to the movement of the tale, such as the union of father and child before the ultimate union of the lovers, which drain away the power of the final climax scene. Paulding was unable to restrain his satirical inclination, and thus damaged the story in the final lines by telling us that to be a good listener, "in this talking republic of ours, is better than having the eloquence of a Patrick Henry, a Randolph, or a Clay" (p. 199). Though Hawthorne had a similar fondness for satire, as exemplified by the "work of vast ability in the somniferous school of literature" (p. 101), which put Dimmesdale to sleep, he kept his satire well governed.

Paulding's investigation into the psychology of his time, the phenomenon of guilt and penance (or crime and punishment), and the function of society as a tool for social punishment, all predate and prefigure Hawthorne's major work. Even the famous "Custom-House" sketch is paralleled by Paulding's "Memoir of the Unknown Author," in which he insists that he is merely the editor of the tales, having purchased the manuscripts in a public auction of the estate of a deceased man who perhaps purchased them years before from the original author, the name of which author it is impossible to discover. Though this "Memoir" was not published in *The Chronicles of the City of Gotham*, it was included by Paulding's son, William I. Paulding, in his 1867 edition of *Tales of A Good Woman* along with "The Dumb Girl," a combination he states was his father's original intention. This essay introduces the tales in a similar way to that in which "The Custom-House" introduces the story of Hester Prynne. When Hawthorne said "It will be seen, likewise, that this Custom-House sketch has a certain propriety, of a kind always recognized in literature, as explaining how a large portion of the following pages came into my possession, and as offering proofs of the authenticity of a narrative therein contained" (p. 7), he was referring to a tradition which went back to Paulding's "Memoir," and beyond to Defoe.

Hawthorne emphasized the role of "Mr. Surveyor Pue," insisting that "it should be borne carefully in mind, that the main facts of that story are authorized and authenticated by the document of Mr. Surveyor Pue...I have allowed myself, as to such points, nearly or altogether as much license as if the facts had been entirely of my own invention. What I contend for is the authenticity of the outline" (p. 29). Herold, in his critical biography, suggests that Paulding might well be Hawthorne's "Surveyor Pue." The fact that Paulding served the government for forty years, he contends, makes him a convenient model for Hawthorne's source, in whose day "a man's office was a life-lease."[7] Perhaps when Hawthorne said "it was my chief trouble, therefore, that I was likely to grow gray and decrepit in the Surveyorship, and become much such another animal as the old Inspector" (p. 34), he was expressing not only the obvious fear, but also the fear of

becoming, like Paulding, another minor writer of tales soon to be
'forgotten.

Fred Lewis Pattee, in his *Development of the American Short Story*, calls
Hawthorne "an anomaly in the midcentury, seemingly without for-
bears, and, for a time at least, seemingly without followers."[8] He
suggests, however, that the essay form of Hawthorne's early tales can
be traced to the influence of Washington Irving. It would seem from a
reading of "The Dumb Girl," that Hawthorne had a forebear in
Paulding, whose favorite literary form was that of the essay. Pattee ad-
mits that Irving "was interested primarily in picturesque externals, in
the genially human," while "Hawthorne, on the contrary, would
search below the surfaces of life and find morals and motives and
spiritual interpretations."[9] Clearly, given such an interpretation of
styles, Hawthorne is much closer to the author of "The Dumb Girl"
than to Irving. It seems probable that Paulding should have been a
major influence on Hawthorne's early work when we realize that between 1824 and 1834 Paulding published at least fifty tales. It was
during this time that Hawthorne was writing the stories which would
be published in 1837 as the first series of *Twice-Told Tales.* Between 1825
and 1837 Hawthorne wrote approximately fifty tales; it is natural that a
writer concentrating on the short story form as Hawthorne was, would
read and study the most popular works in that form in his day. We
know that Hawthorne was a thorough reader of current periodicals,
and that between 1826 and 1832 Paulding published thirteen tales in
the *Atlantic Souvenir,* the most prestigeous literary magazine of the
period.[10] We also know that a manuscript catalogue of the library of the
Athenaeum Society for 1829 lists works by Paulding,[11] and that
Hawthorne withdrew from the Athenaeum on July 7, 1828, specimens
of Paulding's verse.[12] During the years from 1824 to 1832, Paulding's
most productive period, Irving published no tales, and both Hawthorne
and Poe were just beginning to write seriously. Paulding so dominated
the short narrative form during this time that Herold felt justified in
referring to the decade as "the Paulding decade of the short story."[13]
Pattee calls Paulding one of the two writers of greatest import to
readers of the decade, the other being Miss Catharine Sedgewick.

Hawthorne's familiarity with the writings of Paulding is firmly
established in a letter, dated May 31, 1840, which Hawthorne sent to
Paulding while the latter served as Secretary of the Navy. In the letter,
Hawthorne appeals for a discharge for a young seaman named James
Cook, and says: "It is with reluctance, Sir, that I have taken this liberty,
as being unknown to you personally, nor perhaps by reputation; and
yet, apart from your official character, I cannot but feel it one of my
birth-rights to address Mr. Paulding; who has made himself the admired and familiar friend of every reader in the land."[14]

In the first half of the nineteenth century, Paulding wrote 70 tales, Hawthorne wrote 110, Willis 60, and Poe 70.[15] In Pattee's list of the "Leading Stories of the Twenties," Paulding's titles far outnumber those by any other author, with twenty-two stories listed, including the two collections entitled *Tales of A Good Woman* (1829), and *The Chronicles of the City of Gotham.* The name which begins to appear most frequently with Paulding's after the end of the decade is Hawthorne's, beginning with his "Sights From a Steeple" in 1831.[16] Both Paulding and Hawthorne contributed to the *Token* for 1836, with Paulding's "The Magic Spinning Wheel," and Hawthorne's "The Wedding Knell," "The Minister's Black Veil," and "The May-Pole of Merry Mount" appearing in that publication.[17] Another indication of Hawthorne's awareness of Paulding's work is the fact, pointed out by Arlin Turner, that Hawthorne drew upon Paulding's *A Life of Washington* for material published in *The American Magazine of Useful and Entertaining Knowledge* in 1836.[18]

In the *Pioneer*, for February 1843, Hawthorne published an early version of "The Hall of Fantasy," in which he attempted to characterize many of his contemporary writers. In this sketch Hawthorne commented on no less than thirty of his fellow writers, including such figures as Emerson, Bryant and Cooper, along with John Neal, Poe, Catharine Sedgwick and Nathaniel Willis.[19] Strikingly absent in the list of names is that of James K. Paulding, the most prolific writer of the period, and one whom Hawthorne had professed admiration for just three years before. This omission could only have been a deliberate decision by Hawthorne to ignore Paulding, a decision which has been largely affirmed by critics for more than a century in their general exclusion of Paulding from a place of prominence in the history of American literature. Remembered today chiefly as a letter-writer and collaborator with Washington Irving, it is perhaps time that Paulding be looked to as an influencer of at least one great American writer.

University of California, Santa Barbara

---

[1]Amos L. Herold, *James K. Paulding: Versatile American* (1926; rpt. New York: AMS Press, 1966), p. 82.

[2]Luther S. Mansfield, "Diversity and Innovation in the Middle States," *Literary History of the United States*, ed. Robert E. Spiller et al., 3rd ed., rev. (New York: Macmillan, 1963), p. 275.

[3]Ralph M. Aderman, "The Case of James Cook, A Study in Political Influence in 1840," *Essex Institute Historical Collection*, 92 (1956), 64.

[4]Herold, p. 82.

[5]James K. Paulding, "The Dumb Girl," *Tales of A Good Woman*, ed. William I. Paulding (New York: Charles Scribner, 1867), p. 169. Subsequent quotations from "The Dumb Girl" are from this edition.

[6]Nathaniel Hawthorne, *The Scarlet Letter*, Norton Critical Editions (New York: W. W. Norton, 1962), p. 42. Subsequent quotations from *The Scarlet Letter* are from this edition.

[7]Herold, p. 83.

[8]Fred Lewis Pattee, *The Development of the American Short Story* (New York: Harper & Brothers, 1923), p. 98.

[9]Pattee, p. 100.

[10]Herold, p. 72.

[11]Randall Stewart, *Nathaniel Hawthorne: A Biography* (New Haven: Yale University Press, 1948), p. 19.

[12]Aderman, "The Case of James Cook," p. 64.

[13]Herold, p. 66.

[14]Aderman, p. 63.

[15]Herold, p. 72.

[16]Pattee, p. 50.

[17]Aderman, p. 64.

[18]Arlin Turner, *Hawthorne as Editor, Selections From His Writings in the American Magazine of Useful and Entertaining Knowledge,* (Louisiana: Louisiana State U. Press, 1941), p. 263.

The Coverdale Translation:
Blithedale and the Bible

JOAN MAGRETTA

To say that an author has a specific place in literary history is to
define not only a context in which individual texts are most fully
realized but also the dominant "mental set"[1] which that author shares
with others. Hawthorne's work clearly belongs in a Christian tradition
whose essential texts are Spenser's *Faerie Queen*, Milton's *Paradise Lost*,
Bunyan's *Pilgrim's Progress* and ultimately, the Bible itself.[2] Given that
most students of Hawthorne would readily assent to this lineage, it is
curious that no attention has been paid to the Biblical elements in *The
Blithedale Romance*.

Miles Coverdale was the translator of the so-called Coverdale Bible
of 1535, the first complete version of the Bible printed in English.
Blithedale critics have noted this, but have failed to explore any but the
most superficial implications arising from Hawthorne's choice of this
name for his narrator. Roy Male's commentary, as brief as it is, seems
to be the most extensive to date. He remarks that Coverdale, like his
prototype, ought to be a translator, "but one of the book's recurrent
ironies is that during the empty religious experience" of Blithedale,
"...no translation—moral or artistic—occurs."[3] That the work exists
in its peculiar form should immediately refute the charge that artistic
translation has not been accomplished. *The Blithedale Romance* is
Coverdale's "testament" in the double sense of that word: it is both an
account of events he has witnessed and his legacy to posterity, left in
the hope it may guide future generations.

The Old Testament begins at the beginning, Genesis accounting for
the creation as God's fundamental designation of the most basic of
natural oppositions, day and night, light and dark. Coverdale's freely

imaginative reconstruction of Old Moodie's origins, the chapter entitled "Fauntleroy," is his version of the creation of the fictional world which informs the romance, and Hawthorne, like God, is here concerned with the source of radical oppositions, light and dark.

Stylistically this interpolated tale is set off from the rest of the narrative, the description of Zenobia's birth as, "And there was born to him a child,"[4] sounding an unmistakably Biblical tone. Hawthorne's technique is such that, if we perceive the parallels to Genesis which infuse the chapter, we are not drawn *away from* Coverdale's version and *to* Genesis, but rather we see that this, *like* Genesis, is an explanation of the origin of things, and that this account has the same kind of function and validity within *The Blithedale Romance* as Genesis has within its context of Holy Scriptures.

The genesis imagined in "Fauntleroy" is wholly consistent with Hawthorne's moral and aesthetic sensibilities. The apparently antithetical qualities of light and dark are comprehended within a single individual, the two halves of one man represented by the mirror images, Fauntleroy and Old Moodie. The daughter of pride and the daughter of shame, experience and innocence, body and spirit, are inextricable sisters, sharing one father, receiving life from a common source.

Repeated allusions to Eden and Paradise identify the Blithedale experiment as an attempt to return to a prelapsarian state of existence. But there can be no ignoring the fact that man is fallen and, in fact, the practical foundation of the community is "the curse of Adam's posterity," (p. 206) the toil of agriculture. The parallel between Blithedale and the Happy Valley of Johnson's *Rasselas* has been noted, but Hawthorne's irony extends to a more fundamental source. As a result of original sin, man was expelled from the blithe dale of Eden and condemned to make his way in the vale of tears. (It is interesting to note that "The valley of the shadow of death" is a verbal creation of the Coverdale Bible of 1535.) In the end, Zenobia's suicide fulfills this tragic irony of the fallen world, but from the very first night at Blithedale the shadow of death is overhead, ominous and portentous:

> From the bank of the distant river, which was shimmering in the moonlight, came the black shadow of the only cloud in heaven, driven swiftly by the wind, and passing over the meadow and hillock—vanishing amid tufts of leafless trees, but reappearing on the hither side—until it swept across our door-step.
> How cold an Arcadia was this! (p. 38)

Among Hawthorne's debts to the Bible for literary forms or devices is his use of parable. The story of Fauntleroy, as it is contained in the brief interpolated tale, is the parable of a man deceived by appearances and blinded to spiritual realities. Fauntleroy's crime, which is purposely never specified, looms over the whole narrative as a primal transgression. The resemblance of Old Moodie to the Scandanavian god, Odin, suggests the parallel that both suffered the mutilation of one eye as the price of learning the oracular secrets of the lower world. The *mythos* of Fauntleroy-Moodie is comprised of a pattern of blindness, crime, escape, and withdrawal, and seen in this light is paradigmatic for the separate *mythoi* of Hollingsworth, Zenobia and Coverdale.

The New Testament parables of Christ are a specialized form of the genre, defined by their subject matter, the relation of faith to life. Zenobia's legend, "The Silvery Veil," is cast in this mold. This interpolated tale is so blatantly a moral and a message that readers have been misled by its apparent over-simplicity. The rewards of faith and the wages of skepticism are so openly expressed, and the link between Theodore and Coverdale made so obviously, that the legend has been interpreted as a rather clear moral statement, a self-contained unit which functions entirely within the limits of the romance. There is, however, more involved in this parable than a simple lesson of faith.

If Theodore will kiss the Veiled Lady sight unseen, she promises that "'from that instant, Theodore, thou shalt be mine, and I thine, with never more a veil between us! And all the felicity of earth and of the future world shall be mine and thine together.' " (p. 113) The language of this passage points, once again, to the Bible. The full implications of the Lady's promise are perhaps best illuminated by this well-known passage from the Epistle of St. Paul to the Corinthians:

> For we know in part, and we prophesy in part.
> But when that which is perfect is come, then that which is in part shall be done away.
> When I was a child, I spake as a child, I understood as a child, I thought as a child: but when I became a man, I put away childish things.
> For now we see through a glass darkly; but then face to face: now I know in part; but then I shall know even as also I am known. (1 Corinthians 13.9-12)

Hollingsworth, Zenobia, Coverdale and Moodie look at the world through the medium of self, and thus all see through a glass darkly. Imprisonment within the ego prevents any true communion, the meeting of men face to face. Priscilla, the child of the story, is the only one who can hold out the promise of removing forever the veils which isolate men.

Priscilla, the wearer of the literal veil, has paradoxically escaped the horrors of the metaphoric veil. She is not ego-bound, ego imprisoned. Whereas the Self-ishness of the other characters is a source of blindness, Priscilla's Self-lessness gives her great visionary gifts. She is a true clairvoyant, or "clear-seeing" person, representing the truth of Christ's statement in the Sermon on the Mount that the pure in heart see God. This ability to see is a source of life enabling Priscilla to survive whereas her three companions are destroyed, their fate demonstrating that "where there is no vision, the people perish." (Proverbs 29.18)

A second paradox lies in the fact that Priscilla's bondage to Westervelt, the most literal "possession" of the narrative, leaves her the most free character in the story. She is physically enslaved but spiritually free, the others being physically free but psychological or spiritual prisoners. This is related to the New Testament theme presented in the statement, "Ye shall know the truth and the truth shall make you free." (John 8.32) With her ability to see clearly to the heart of matters, Priscilla possesses spiritual truth.[5]

She may not be a very appealing character when "put exactly side by side with nature," (p. 2) but Hawthorne goes to the trouble of indicating, in the Preface, that this is not to be done. Priscilla is not "real" even in the limited sense that Hollingsworth, Zenobia and Coverdale are, but more to the point, she is "functional." This is clearly seen in the chapter of her rescue by Hollingsworth, where she is not essentially the girl, Priscilla, but a figure like the Lady of *Comus* whose chastity has magical powers. Repeatedly referred to as an object of sacrifice, Priscilla is associated with the lamb of the New Testament who is restored to life on the Day of Judgment. It is only at the close of the romance, when the stories of her three companions have been played out and her function has been fulfilled, that Priscilla shows signs of having developed into a "real" woman.

Too many critics have been guilty of the error of Sweet Fern in Hawthorne's *Wonder Book*, that is, inquiring so minutely into factual detail and literal probability that they are insensitive to the imaginative possibilities of a figure like Priscilla. Her veil, as container which protects, imprisons and alters vision is the work's central metaphoric expression of the Self. The physical qualities of the veil are in themselves quite apt to convey Hawthorne's sense of what the Self is, but to discover his attitude toward the Self we must turn to the associative qualities of the veil as religious symbol.

The white veil worn by vestal virgins, novitiates, and brides is a traditional symbol of purity, mystery and consecration. The most significant veil of the Bible, however, is the one which God commanded to be placed around the ark of the temple, the ark which served as a medium for oracles and which signified divine nearness. In the book of Exodus, God indicated that the veil was to separate the sanctuary, or holy place, from the most holy, or holy of holies.

Here lies the crux of Hawthorne's vision, that the Self is ultimately a profound mystery in the religious sense of the word, and it deserves the most awesome respect and reverence.[6] In his creation of Priscilla, Hawthorne is at pains to indicate the sacred nature of the enigma of her identity. Those characters in the story who attempt to tamper with the "weakly Maiden" do not fare very well. Their fate might well serve as a warning to the readers of *Blithedale.*

As interpolated tales set apart from the narrative, it is not difficult to see the parabolic quality of "The Silvery Veil" and "Fauntleroy." There is still another parable of consequence to be considered, the third interpolated tale of the text—the story of Blithedale itself. This story can only be approached as an inserted tale in a specific and limited sense, but the perspective thus gained is useful.

As Coverdale is the narrator of the story, his attitude toward the materials with which he works is as important as the materials themselves. To Coverdale, the socialist experiment has been a lesson, a parable, an experience from which a moral can and must be extracted. After leaving the farm he muses:

> True; if you look at it in one way, it had been only a summer in the country. But considered in a profounder relation, it was part of another age, a different state of society, a segment of an existence peculiar in its aims and methods, a leaf of some mysterious volume interpolated into the current history which Time was writing off. (p. 146)

The lesson of Blithedale, in essence, is consonant with the central themes of the work as a whole. The community is an experiment in brotherhood whose goal is to replace Pride (Self-ishness) with Familiar Love (Self-lessness). Cooperation and communion are to supplant competition and isolation.

The experiment fails, the quest for a better life which it represents is unsuccessful. Although the original vision is treated with respect throughout, Blithedale as the One True System is shown to be ridiculous, just as Hollingsworth's originally benevolent project becomes odious when revered as the One True Scheme. When Coverdale concludes that they had struck on what "ought to be a truth," (p. 246) he is closer to the mark.

Just as he pronounces the final "flesh is grass" epitaph over Zenobia's grave, it is Coverdale who issues the last words over the corpse of Blithedale, extracting the moral of the parable:

> The experiment, so far as its original projectors were concerned, proved long ago a failure, first lapsing into Fourierism, and dying, as it well deserved, for this infidelity to its own higher spirit. (p. 246)

From socialism to Fourierism, from selflessness to the selfish principle,[7] from benevolence to egotism, the lapse of Blithedale and the lapse of Hollingsworth are one and the same, the sad pattern of infidelity and betrayal. In the confusion of chaos both Hollingsworth and Blithedale went astray and chose the path leading to ruin. The central quest of this Coverdale testament, related explicitly to Bunyan's warning that "from the very gate of Heaven, there is a by-way to the pit," (p. 243) leads finally to this injunction from the Gospel of Matthew:

> Enter ye in at the strait gate: for wide is the gate, and broad is the way, that leadeth to destruction, and many there be which go in thereat:
> Because straight is the gate, and narrow is the way, which leadeth unto life, and few there be that find it. (Matthew 7.13-14)

Very few indeed find life in *The Blithedale Romance*. And the attempt to find new truths by which to live is shown to be futile, at least for Hawthorne's would-be communitarians. As Zenobia says when formulating the final moral for the proposed ballad of Blithedale, "'There are no new truths, much as we have prided ourselves on finding some.' " (p. 224) That there are no new truths under the sun is the wisdom of Ecclesiastes. That the seasons come and go, that human endeavor is all vanity, that the generations pass but the earth abides forever—this is finally the wisdom which Coverdale has accumulated, albeit too late for his own salvation. This is ultimately what he has come to see and the vantage point from which his testament is issued.

The University of Michigan

---

[1]For a full discussion of the importance of "mental set" in the creation and perception of works of art see E. H. Gombrich, *Art and Illusion* (New York: Bollingen Foundation, 1960).

[2]Hawthorne's relationship to this tradition is established convincingly by F.O. Matthiessen, *American Renaissance* (New York: Oxford University Press, 1941).

[3]Roy R. Male, *Hawthorne's Tragic Vision* (Austin: University of Texas Press, 1957), p. 154.

[4]Nathaniel Hawthorne, *The Blithedale Romance* (Columbus: Ohio State University Press, 1964), p. 182. The text used is Volume III of the Centenary Edition. Subsequent references to this edition will appear in the text.

[5]Secondary sources may be helpful in the re-creation of a concept as illusive as "mental set." In John T. Codman's *Brook Farm: Historic and Personal Memoirs* (Boston: Arena Publishing Company, 1894), the author, a participant in the Brook Farm experiment, describes the attitude of the communitarians in the following terms: "They all believed in the motto, 'The *truth* shall make you *free*.' " (p. 38).

⁶In a journal entry dated October 18, 1841, Hawthorne beseeched his bride-to-be not to dabble in mesmerism. The following passage may be found in *The Heart of Hawthorne's Journals,* edited by Newton Arvin (Boston: Houghton Mifflin Company, 1929), pp. 84-85:

> I am unwilling that a power should be exercised on thee of which we know neither the origin nor the consequence...Supposing that this power arises from the transfusion of one spirit into another, it seems to me that the sacredness of an individual is violated by it; there would be an intrusion into thy holy of holies.

⁷Whatever one's interpretation of Fourierism, it is defined in *The Blithedale Romance* as depending for its operation on the "selfish principle." See Chapter VII, "The Convalescent."

Poe and the
Second Edition of Hawthorne's
Twice-Told Tales

D. M. McKEITHAN

It has not been clearly established, so far as I know, whether the fiction of Poe or Hawthorne was much influenced by the work of the other. Resemblances have been noted between Poe's *The Oval Portrait,* which appeared[1] in *Graham's Magazine* for April, 1842, and Hawthorne's *The Prophetic Pictures,* which had appeared in the Boston *Token* for 1837 and in the first edition of *Twice-Told Tales* (1837). Both stories deal with dedicated artists who could make this portrait paintings very lifelike. Hawthorne's artist could paint "not merely a man's features, but his mind and heart. He catches the secret sentiments and passions and throws them upon the canvas." Hawthorne's story and the source which he cites[2] indicate that his purpose was to depict an artist so understanding of human character and so skillful in painting that he could detect insanity in a subject earlier than most people and suggest it to perceptive observers of his work.

In Poe's story there is no insanity in subject or portrait, though the artist's obsession with his art and his blindness to his wife's decline make him a sort of madman. Poe's artist—studious, moody, passionate, and wild, more concerned about his art than his wife—combines some of the traits of Hawthorne's artist (who cared only for his art although he had no wife) and Walter, the husband of Elinor (his increasing moodiness, for instance). In Poe's story the young wife is "full of glee," whereas Hawthorne's Elinor is sad and frightened at times by a look she has observed on Walter's face. Poe's artist is not a prophet and his pictures are not prophetic. There are striking differences between the stories as well as similarities. I see no evidence of plagiarism. If there is indebtedness, it is tenuous and difficult to demonstrate; it is nothing more tangible than inspiration. Perhaps Killis Campbell had this in mind when he called Poe's story "moral" and "Hawthornesque" and added that "in 'The Oval Portrait' Poe seems to have affected for once the manner of Hawthorne."[3] Inspiration to write the story—if that is what Poe derived from Hawthorne—is a far greater indebtedness than a few details of plot or characterization.

Hawthorne's *The Birthmark*, which appeared in Lowell's magazine, the *Pioneer* (March, 1843), resembles *The Oval Portrait* in that each tells the story of a wife who permitted herself to be sacrificed to please her husband in his professional work. In Poe's story the wife sits as model "for many weeks in the dark high turret-chamber" while her artist husband paints her portrait. The life and color are drained from her to go into the portrait, but when it has become quite lifelike, she is dead. In Hawthorne's story the wife permitted her husband, a scientist, to use her in a scientific experiment. He removed a birthmark from her cheek, but she died. In Hawthorne's story the wife was reluctant at first to become the subject of her husband's experiment just as in Poe's story the wife was reluctant to become her husband's model. In each story the wife consented to do what her husband desired out of her deep devotion to him. Arthur Hobson Quinn notes the similarity between these stories and reaches this conclusion:"The similarity of theme to Hawthorne's 'The Birthmark'...is apparent, but Hawthorne's treatment is so different that there can be no question of plagiarism."[4] Since *The Oval Portrait* appeared in the same issue of *Graham's Magazine* as Poe's preliminary notice of the second edition of *Twice-Told Tales*, Hawthorne had probably read it. It is impossible to determine with certainty whether he used an idea or two from it, either consciously or unconsciously, but his treatment is original and Quinn is correct in saying that there is no plagiarism here. Moreover, Hawthorne had the theme of his story in mind several years before *The Oval Portrait* appeared. (See *The American Notebooks*, Centenary Edition, pages 165, 184.)

Seymour L. Gross, in his article "Poe's Revision of 'The Oval Portrait,' "[5] suggests the possibility that Poe may have revised *The Oval Portrait* as it had appeared in *Graham's Magazine* for publication in the *Broadway Journal* of April 26, 1845, after he had read *The Birthmark* and under its influence. There can be little doubt that Poe had read *The Birthmark*, which had appeared in the *Pioneer* for March, 1843. He was in correspondence with Lowell, the editor of the *Pioneer*, in February and March, 1843, and was receiving and reading the *Pioneer*, to which both Poe and Hawthorne were contributors.[6] If indebtedness exists, however, it is nothing resembling plagiarism and Professor Gross is correct in not suggesting any.

Students of Poe and Hawthorne have often expressed regret that Poe marred his otherwise fine review of the second edition of *Twice-Told Tales* in *Graham's Magazine* for May, 1842, by suggesting that

Hawthorne might have plagiarized the climax of *Howe's Masquerade* from *William Wilson*, and they have pointed out that *Howe's Masquerade* had been published in the *Democratic Review* for May, 1838, a year before Poe's *William Wilson* appeared in *The Gift* for 1840 (*The Gift* for 1840 came out in May, 1839, and the story was reprinted in *Burton's Gentleman's Magazine* for October, 1839). Poe wrote:

> In "Howe's Masquerade" we observe something which resembles a plagiarism—but which *may* be a very flattering coincidence of thought. We quote the passage in question.
>
> > *"With a dark flush of wrath* upon his brow they saw the general *draw his sword* and *advance to meet* the figure *in the cloak* before the latter had stepped one pace upon the floor.
> > *'Villain, unmuffle yourself,'* cried he, 'you pass no farther!'
> > "The figure, without blenching a hair's breadth from the sword which was pointed at his breast, made a solemn pause, and *lowered the cape of the cloak* from his face, yet not sufficiently for the spectators to catch a glimpse of it. But Sir William Howe had evidently seen enough. The sternness of his countenance gave place to a look of wild amazement, if not horror, while he recoiled several steps from the figure, *and let fall his sword* upon the floor." See vol. 2, page 20.

The idea here is, that the figure in the cloak is the phantom or reduplication of Sir William Howe; but in an article called "William Wilson," one of the "Tales of the Grotesque and Arabesque," we have not only the same idea, but the same idea similarly presented in several respects. We quote two paragraphs, which our readers may compare with what has been already given. We have italicized, above, the immediate particulars of resemblance.

> "The brief moment in which I averted my eyes had been sufficient to produce, apparently, a material change in the arrangement at the upper or farther end of the room. A large mirror, it appeared to me, now stood where none had been perceptible before: and as I stepped up to it in extremity of terror, mine own image, but with features all pale and dabbled in blood, *advanced* with a feeble and tottering gait to meet me.
> "Thus it appeared I say, but was not. It was Wilson, who then stood before me in the agonies of dissolution. Not a line in all the marked and singular lineaments of that face which was not even identically mine own. *His mask and cloak lay where he had thrown them, upon the floor."*—vol. 2, p. 57.

Here it will be observed that, not only are the two general conceptions identical, but there are various *points* of similarity. In each case the figure seen is the wraith or duplication of the beholder. In each case the scene is a masquerade. In each case the figure is cloaked. In each, there is a quarrel—that is to say, angry words pass between the parties.[7] In each the beholder is enraged. In each the cloak and sword fall upon the floor.[8]

The "villain, unmuffle yourself," of Mr. H. is precisely paralleled by a
passage at page 56 of "William Wilson."[9]

Despite any resemblances between the two episodes, "there can be no
question of plagiarism" here since Hawthorne's story was published
first and since Poe did not know it and thought his own had been
published first.

George Edward Woodberry stated that the idea developed in *William
Wilson*, "the conception of a double dogging one's steps and thwarting
one's evil designs," is a very old one and found in many places in
literature.[10] Killis Campbell,[11] Horace E. Thorner,[12] and others thought
that the most likely immediate source of Poe was Washington Irving's
"An Unwritten Drama of Lord Byron," published in the *Knickerbocker*,
VI, 2 (August, 1835), 142-144, and in *The Gift* for 1836, pages 166 through
171. Thorner, among others, believed that Poe had read Irving's article
because *The Gift* for 1836 also reprinted Poe's *Manuscript Found in a Bot-
tle*, pages 67 through 87. Irving said that he had learned the story from
Medwin, who had heard it from Byron, and that Shelley had told
Byron about a dream he had had of seeing his own ghost after having
read a play by Calderon.

The story which Byron had planned to tell in a dramatic poem is
summarized in detail by Irving. Its hero, Alfonso, a wild and passionate
young Spanish nobleman, is harassed by an unknown "masked and
muffled" person who follows him everywhere, becoming his
"shadow—his second self," "thwarting his schemes, and marring all
his intrigues of love and of ambition": "a voice, like the voice of his
own soul, whispers in his ear," checking him in his evil designs.
Alfonso's resentment turns into a rage when he suspects the mysterious
stranger of having supplanted him in the affections of his mistress, and
Alfonso attacks him with fury. "They fight; his rival scarcely defends
himself; at the first thrust he receives the sword of Alfonso in his
bosom. . . . The mask and mantle of the unknown drop off, and Alfonso
discovers his own image—the spectre of himself. . . ."Irving states:
"The spectre is an allegorical being, the personification of conscience,
or of the passions," and adds: "The foregoing sketch of the plot may
hereafter suggest a rich theme to a poet or dramatist of the Byron
school."[13]

Of the Calderon play which Shelley had been reading, Woodberry
wrote: "The reference is plainly to *El Purgatorio de San Patricio*, a
favorite of Shelley's (from which he took a passage of *The Cenci*), in
which Un Hombre Embozado is a character."[14] Poe sent a copy of *Burton's* for October, 1839, containing *William Wilson* to Washington Irving, and in a letter to Poe dated November 6, 1839, Irving praised
William Wilson but said nothing about its source.[15] Such an original

elaboration of an old idea was considered entirely proper by Byron (who was planning to do it), by Irving (who tried to do it), and by Poe (who did it).

Since Poe did not know that *Howe's Masquerade* was published earlier than *William Wilson*, neither story owes anything to the other. Doubtless Poe found all the suggestions he needed for *William Wilson* in Irving's "An Unwritten Drama of Lord Byron"—Woodberry[16] and Quinn[17] thought it unlikely that Poe had read the Calderon drama. If Hawthorne also read Irving's article, his only possible indebtedness to it is in his concluding episode, in which Sir William Howe approaches with drawn sword the muffled figure representing himself and drops the sword in amazement or horror when the figure reveals his face. It should be pointed out, however, that this concluding episode is merely the logical climax of Hawthorne's plot, which is otherwise entirely different from Irving's story, and Hawthorne would very likely have written it in the same way whether or not he had read Irving's story. In other words, there is not in *Howe's Masquerade* enough evidence to justify our saying positively that Hawthorne had read "An Unwritten Drama of Lord Byron." If he had been conscious of adapting an episode from Irving, it is probable that he would have indicated the source as he did in such stories as *The Minister's Black Veil*, *Wakefield*, and *The Prophetic Pictures*.

In a letter from Philadelphia dated June 21, 1841, Poe invited Washington Irving to write for *Graham's Magazine*.[18] He said he hoped to secure contributions from "the most distinguished pens (of America)" or "at least, to procure the aid of some five or six of the most distinguished." He named those whom he had in mind: "We shall endeavor to engage the permanent services of yourself, Mr. Cooper, Mr. Paulding, Mr. Kennedy, Mr. Longfellow, Mr. Bryant, Mr. Halleck, Mr. Willis, and, perhaps, one or two others." From this letter it seems logical to conclude that as late as June 21, 1841, Poe had not read enough of Hawthorne's work to realize that Hawthorne was one of the best writers in America.

In 1847 Poe wrote: "It was never the fashion (until lately) to speak of him [Hawthorne] in any summary of our best authors."[19] In a letter of February 4, 1843, congratulating Lowell on his magazine the *Pioneer*, Poe mentions Hawthorne as a writer whom he would like to have as a permanent contributor if he were editing a magazine of his own.[20] In another letter to Lowell on March 27, 1843, Poe says he hopes to bring out the first number of a new magazine to be called the *Stylus* on July 1 and requests Lowell to procure for the magazine a short article from Hawthorne.[21] Sometime between June 21, 1841, and February 4, 1843, Poe became convinced that Hawthorne was a great writer. I think it was early in 1842. Poe says in his review of the second edition of *Twice-Told Tales:*

> Of Mr. Hawthorne's Tales we would say, emphatically, that they belong to the highest region of Art—an Art subservient to genius of a very lofty order. We had supposed, with good reason for so supposing, that he had been thrust into his present position by one of the impudent *cliques* which beset our literature, and whose pretensions it is our full purpose to expose at the earliest opportunity; but we have been most agreeably mistaken. We know of few compositions which the critic can more honestly commend than these "Twice-Told Tales." As Americans, we feel proud of the book.[22]

I take this to be Poe's confession that before he began reading the second edition of *Twice-Told Tales* he had never read enough of Hawthorne to form an opinion of his worth. We can imagine how amazed Poe was to discover that such an artist and genius as Hawthorne was at work in America. It is my conjecture that the immediate effect upon Poe was the inspiration to write *The Oval Portrait* and *The Masque of the Red Death*.[23] Another effect on Poe might have been the clarification of his ideas of the short story as an art form. It was in his review of this book that he first explained his theory of the short story. His study of the short stories of Hawthorne might very well have helped him formulate his theory even though it was based on his own practice in writing the short story. Doubtless Poe derived more inspiration from the second edition of *Twice-Told Tales* than from any other American book he ever reviewed.

Although Hawthorne's *Howe's Masquerade* had appeared in the *Democratic Review* for May, 1838, it is obvious that Poe had not seen it until he started reading the second edition of *Twice-Told Tales*. His main review of the two volumes appeared in *Graham's Magazine* for May, 1842, which also contained *The Masque of the Red Death*. An impressive number of possible sources of Poe's story have been suggested by various scholars,[24] and nothing that I write here is intended to cast the slightest doubt on the validity of any of these suggestions. It was noted by W. D. Armes over sixty years ago, for instance, that the story might be indebted to William Harrison Ainsworth's *Old Saint Paul's*, in which a London grocer provisions his house with food and keeps his family indoors during a part of the Great Plague.[25] Killis Campbell thought that Poe might have read a letter from N. P. Willis in the New York *Mirror* for June 2, 1832: in Europe Willis had attended a masked ball at which there were a cholera waltz, a cholera galopade, and a masked figure impersonating the cholera.[26]

Cortell Holsapple wrote:

> It seems, then, that certain of the ideas which appear in *The Masque,*

published in 1842, had been in his mind years earlier; they may possibly have been suggested by his reading as early as 1832. Late in 1841 or early in 1842, stimulated by necessity, Poe's memory and imagination combined to generate and produce *The Masque*. And, even if the sources listed should be supplemented by additional research, the originality of Poe's work in this tale is not to be denied.[27]

Possibly the stimulation that came to Poe early in 1842 (like a catalyst accelerating a chemical reaction) was his reading Hawthorne's *Lady Eleanore's Mantle* and *Howe's Masquerade* in the second edition of *Twice-Told Tales*.

Seventy years ago, in discussing the tales of Poe and Hawthorne, George D. Latimer pointed out similarities and differences between *Lady Eleanore's Mantle* and *The Masque of the Red Death*.[28] Although he does not suggest that Poe's story is indebted to Hawthorne's, he noted that in each story the pestilence made its appearance at a ball and there is some stress on the color of blood. He was also interested in differences—Hawthorne's moral purpose and Poe's single effect of horror with his artistic, impressive, but "terrible picture of Death Triumphant."

There are, indeed, similarities between *Lady Eleanore's Mantle*[29] and *The Masque of the Red Death*. At Governor Shute's ball in honor of Lady Eleanore the guests were "the principal gentry of the colony." They wore no masks but rivaled in splendor Prince Prospero and his thousand courtiers: "the ladies shone in rich silks and satins,...the gentlemen glittered in gold embroidery, laid unsparingly upon the purple, or scarlet, or sky-blue velvet." Lady Eleanore's mantle, the handiwork of a woman dying of smallpox, was "gorgeous" and of "fantastic splendor." Since it was accidentally "sprinkled" with a brimming goblet of consecrated wine, it was—presumably—stained with red spots.

Lady Eleanore's illness at the ball was apparently identified by Dr. Clarke as the smallpox, which shortly thereafter swept through the colony. The "dreadful epidemic, which...was wont to slay its hundreds and thousands on both sides of the Atlantic,...was distinguished by a peculiar virulence." Hawthorne refers to the "red brand" of "that mighty conqueror—that scourge and horror of our forefathers—the Small-Pox." Hawthorne continues: "Graves were hastily dug.... The public councils were suspended.... This conqueror had a symbol of his triumphs. It was a blood-red flag, that fluttered in the tainted air, over the door of every dwelling into which the Small-Pox had entered."

In Poe's story much stress is put on the idea of red spots on the faces of the victims of the pestilence. Of the figure representing the Red Death Poe says: "His vesture was dabbled in *blood*—and his broad brow, with all the features of the face, was besprinkled with the scarlet horror." In Poe's story "no pestilence had been ever so fatal, or so hideous. Blood was its Avator and its seal—the redness and the horror of blood....The scarlet stains upon the body and especially upon the face of the victim, were the pest-ban...." Such words might have described Lady Eleanore, the victim of the smallpox, when her mad lover exclaimed: "Fie! Heap of diseased mortality, why lurkest thou in my lady's chamber?" Finally, in each story the pestilence made its appearance at a ball, and the festivities were abruptly terminated.

There are great differences between *Howe's Masquerade* and *The Masque of the Red Death* with reference to plot, style, and purpose. Hawthorne's style is leisurely, while Poe's is compressed and concise. Poe uses an unidentified foreign setting, possibly eighteenth-century Italy; Hawthorne reveals his great interest in New England history in colonial and Revolutionary times, concealing neither his anti-British feeling nor his patriotism. Poe seems mainly concerned with producing an artistic story with an effect of horror, making masterful use of color and bizarre details.

Nevertheless, there are similarities between the two stories. The setting of each is a masked ball, given for the elite, at a time of great peril, and for the same general purpose—to bolster morale. In *Howe's Masquerade* Sir William Howe, the last of the old royal governors of Massachusetts, gave a masked ball in Boston at the Province House to which were invited the officers of the British army, the loyal gentry of the province, and a few prominent patriots. The time was the latter part of the siege of Boston. Washington's army was steadily approaching and was soon to occupy the city. Sir William's purpose in giving the ball was "to hide the distress and danger of the period, and the desperate aspect of the siege, under an ostentation of festivity."

In *The Masque of the Red Death* during a great plague Prince Prospero had retired with a thousand guests from his court to one of his castellated abbeys, well provisioned with food and all means of pleasure and entertainment. The Prince gave a masked ball toward the close of the fifth or sixth month of his seclusion "while the pestilence raged most furiously abroad." The Prince's guests were able to "bid defiance to contagion. The external world could take care of itself. In the meantime it was folly to grieve, or to think." There were food, entertainment, "and security...within. Without was the 'Red Death.'"

Each was a gay affair, and the apartments were crowded. The ball in *Howe's Masquerade* "was the most gay and gorgeous affair that had occurred in the annals of the government," and "the brilliantly-lighted apartments were thronged with figures." In *The Masque of the Red Death* there were seven rooms or apartments. The deep blood colored lights streaming on the black velvet tapestries and the gigantic clock of ebony in the seventh room kept most people out. "But these other apartments were densely crowded, and in them beat feverishly the heart of life."

At each ball there was a great variety of costumes, though they were more grotesque and bizarre in Poe's story. In *Howe's Masquerade* the costumes were from history, romance, the London theatres, or comedy—knights of the Conquest, bearded statesmen and high-ruffled ladies of the court of Queen Elizabeth, a parti-colored Merry Andrew with cap and bells, a Falstaff provocative of laughter, a Don Quixote with bean pole and pot lid. In *The Masque of the Red Death* the costumes "were grotesque. There were much glare and glitter and piquancy and phantasm . . .; arabesque figures with unsuited limbs and appointments, . . . much of the beautiful, much of the wanton, much of the *bizarre*, something of the terrible."

The guests in *Howe's Masquerade*—mostly British officers and loyalists—were surprised to see in attendance the stern old figure of Colonel Joliffe, with his fair granddaughter, whose Whig principles and patriotism were well known. The loyalists affirmed that the old colonel's "black puritanical scowl threw a shadow round about him." But despite "his sombre influence their gayety continued to blaze higher." In *The Masque of the Red Death* the check on the merriment was more formidable. In the seventh room, where "the effect of the firelight that streamed upon the dark hangings through the blood-tinted panes was ghastly in the extreme," there stood "a gigantic clock of ebony." The sound that came from its "brazen lungs" every time it struck the hour was "of so peculiar a note and emphasis" that the musicians and dancers stopped, "there was a brief disconcert of the whole gay company," and "the giddiest grew pale." Then light laughter was resumed and continued until the momentary fear and paralysis returned next time the clock struck the hour. "But, in spite of these things, it was a gay and magnificent revel."

Toward midnight unexpected events disrupted the two masked balls. In *Howe's Masquerade* the gayety was suddenly checked half an hour after the clock of the Old South had struck eleven times. A band outside the door began playing a funeral march. Inside, down the stairway came a procession of allegorical figures representing the governors of the province, from the old Puritan governors of the original democracy of Massachusetts down to the last of the royal governors. Colonel Joliffe and his granddaughter served as chorus to interpret for Sir William. The young lady explained that "the ghosts of these ancient governors had been summoned to form the funeral procession of royal authority in New England."

When the figure representing Gage—Sir William's immediate predecessor—passed down the staircase and out the door, tense excitement reached a higher pitch, for everyone knew that the next figure would represent Sir William himself. Miss Joliffe taunted Sir

William and added: "Perhaps he will not suffer the next to pass unchallenged." He assured her that he would not: "The next that takes his
leave shall receive due courtesy." The excitement increased as a figure
appeared, seeming to mould itself amid the gloom, "so dusky was the
area whence it emerged."

The tall figure moved down the stairway "with a stately and martial
tread," his military cloak "drawn up around the face," so that the
features "were completely hidden." His clothing, gait, and bearing
resembled Sir William's. "With a dark flush of wrath upon his brow,"
Sir William drew "his sword and advance[d] to meet the figure."
" 'Villain, unmuffle yourself!' cried he. 'You pass no farther!' " Though
the sword "was pointed at his breast," the figure did not blench "a
hair's breadth," but after "a solemn pause...lowered the cape of the
cloak from about the face." Sir William's stern look changed to one of
"wild amazement, if not horror." He recoiled a few steps and "let fall
his sword upon the floor." The martial figure again concealed his face
and left the Province House.

As the band outside moved away, "its dismal strains were mingled
with the knell of midnight from the steeple of the Old South, and with
the roar of artillery, which announced that the beleaguering army of
Washington had intrenched itself upon a nearer height than before."
As the cannon boomed, Colonel Joliffe told Sir William that "the em-
pire of Britain in this ancient province is at its last gasp to-
night...and methinks the shadows of the old governors are fit mourn-
ers at its funeral!" The masquerade was "the last festival that a British
ruler ever held in the old province of Massachusetts Bay."

The Masque of the Red Death leads to a bloodcurdling climax. As the
ebony clock began striking twelve strokes for midnight, the music
ceased, the dancers stood still, and many became aware of the presence
of a masked figure that none had noticed before. All were filled with
horror, for "the figure in question" was shrouded "in the habiliments of
the grave," its mask exactly resembled a corpse, and the whole countenance was besprinkled with blood. At sight of the figure, the Prince
was convulsed with a shudder of distaste or terror, and "his brow red-
dened with rage." He ordered his courtiers to seize and unmask the
figure, but all were paralyzed with fear, and the figure passed close to
the Prince with "solemn and measured step" and moved through five
of the rooms and into the sixth before any effort was made to stop him.
Finally, the Prince himself, "maddening with rage and the shame of
his own momentary cowardice," dashed in pursuit. With drawn dagger
held high, he had nearly caught up with the figure when the latter
"turned suddenly round and confronted his pursuer. There was a sharp
cry—and the dagger dropped gleaming upon the sable carpet, upon
which instantly afterwards, fell prostrate in death the Prince Pros-

pero." Other revelers seized the blasphemer and found "the grave-cerements and corpse-like mask...untenanted by any tangible form." The Red Death had invaded the stronghold. The ebony clock ran down, "the flames of the tripods expires," the revelers dropped one by one. "And Darkness and Decay and the Red Death held illimitable dominion over all."

I have not intended to suggest that *Howe's Masquerade* is *the* source of *The Masque of the Red Death*: many plausible sources and influences have been cited, including *William Wilson* and Irving's account of Byron's unwritten drama. It is possible, however, that Poe had not written *The Oval Portrait* or *The Masque of the Red Death* when he read *The Prophetic Pictures*, *Howe's Masquerade*, and *Lady Eleanore's Mantle* in the second edition of *Twice-Told Tales*. His reading of Hawthorne might have been the catalyst that set in motion his creative energies. The stimulation or inspiration might have enabled him to compose the two stories so quickly that he was able to publish *The Oval Portrait* along with his preliminary notice of *Twice-Told Tales* and *The Masque of the Red Death* in the same issue as his main review. The two stories together cover only seven and a half pages in the Modern Library edition. It seems to me that their compact style and brevity support this theory concerning their composition under the impetus of inspiration. The tremendous impact on Poe of his reading of *Twice-Told Tales* is further indicated by the possibility that it clarified his thinking and enabled him to define his theory of the short story. The fact that he had never explained his theory of the short story until he had read *Twice-Told Tales* and the further fact that he chose to explain it in his review of Hawthorne's work do at least suggest a casual relationship.

Moreover, I am not suggesting that Poe was guilty of plagiarizing from Hawthorne to any extent whatsoever. What we have here, I think, is not plagiarism, but one of the finest examples of the correct use of books. According to Emerson, "They are for nothing but to inspire."

Much has been made of the fact that in his review of *Twice-Told Tales* and *Mosses from an Old Manse* in *Godey's Lady's Book* for November, 1847, Poe said that Hawthorne had no originality, that he was "infinitely too fond of allegory," and that he should cast off the influence of the Transcendentalists. Equal stress should be put on the fact that Poe was still of the opinion that Hawthorne was the best writer in America.

He has the purest style, the finest taste, the most available scholarship, the most delicate humor, the most touching pathos, the most radiant imagination, the most consummate ingenuity; and with these varied good qualities he has done *well* as a mystic.[30]

Poe began this review by quoting and reaffirming a statement he had made about Hawthorne in the preface of his sketches of the New York Literati. In spite of Hawthorne's shortcomings, Poe said, "he evinces extraordinary genius, having no rival either in America or elsewhere."[31]

University of Texas

[1]Under the early title of *Life in Death.*

[2]An episode in William Dunlap's *History of the Rise and Progress of the Arts of Design in the United States.*

[3]Killis Campbell (editor), *Poe's Short Stories* (New York, Harcourt, Brace and Company, 1927), pp. xvii and xxii.

[4]Arthur Hobson Quinn, *Edgar Allan Poe: A Critical Biography* (New York, Appleton-Century-Crofts, 1941), p. 331.

[5]Seymour L. Gross, "Poe's Revision of 'The Oval Portrait,' " *Modern Language Notes,* LXXIV (January, 1959), 16-20.

[6]Quinn, *op. cit.,* pp. 365-366, 382-384.

[7]In *Howe's Masquerade* no words are spoken by the masked figure.

[8]In *Howe's Masquerade* no cloak falls upon the floor. In *William Wilson* no sword falls upon the floor.

[9]*Graham's Magazine,* XX (May, 1842), 299-300. In *William Wilson* the masked figure is called "scoundrel! imposter! accursed villain!" and later he throws his mask and cloak upon the floor, but he is not ordered to unmask or unmuffle himself.

[10]George E. Woodberry, *The Life of Edgar Allan Poe* (Boston and New York, Houghton Mifflin Company, 1909), I, 232 and 232 n.

[11]Killis Campbell, *op. cit.,* p. xxii.

[12]Horace E. Thorner, "Hawthorne, Poe, and a Literary Ghost," the *New England Quarterly,* VII (March, 1934), 146-154.

[13]Washington Irving, "An Unwritten Drama of Lord Byron," *The Gift: A Christmas and New Year's Present for 1836* (edited by Miss Leslie, Philadelphia, E. L. Carey & A. Hart), pp. 166-171.

[14]Woodberry, *op. cit.,* I, 232 n.

[15]*Ibid.,* pp. 216-217.

[16]*Ibid.,* p. 232 n.

[17]Quinn, *op. cit.,* p. 286 n.

[18]New York *Times,* January 12, 1930, Section 2, pp. 1 and 4.

[19]In his review of *Twice-Told Tales* and *Mosses from an Old Manse* in *Godey's Lady's Book* for November, 1847, reprinted in *The Complete Works of Edgar Allan Poe* (ed. James A. Harrison, New York, 1902), XIII, 142.

[20]Quinn, *op. cit.,* pp. 365-366.

[21]*Ibid.,* pp. 382-383.

[22]*Graham's Magazine,* XX (May, 1842), 299.

[23]*Ibid.,* pp. 257-259, where the title read *The Mask of the Red Death.*

[24]Some are mentioned by Gerald E. Gerber, "Additional Sources for 'The Masque of the Red Death,' " *American Literature,* 37, No. 1 (March, 1965), 52-54, and by those critics whom he cites.

[25] *Transactions and Proceedings of the American Philological Association* for 1907, p. xxxi. Cited by Killis Campbell in *The Mind of Poe and Other Studies* (New York, Russell & Russell, 1962: first published in 1933 by the Harvard University Press), p. 171 and 171 n.

[26] Killis Campbell (editor), *Poe's Short Stories*, p. xxi.

[27] Cortell King Holsapple, "*The Masque of the Red Death* and *I Promessi Sposi*," University of Texas *Studies in English*, XVIII (1938), 139.

[28] George D. Latimer, "The Tales of Poe and Hawthorne," *New England Magazine*, 30 (August, 1904), 692-703.

[29] Published in the *Democratic Review* for December, 1838.

[30] Reprinted in *The Complete Works of Edgar Allan Poe*, ed. James A. Harrison (New York, 1902), XIII, 155.

[31] *Ibid.*, p. 141. Poe's introduction to "The Literati of New York City" appeared in *Godey's Lady's Book* for May, 1846, and was reprinted in the Harrison edition, XV, 1-5.

James's *Washington Square:*
More on the Hawthorne Relation

THADDEO KITASIMBWA BABIIHA

In a recent article, "James's *Washington Square:* The Hawthorne Relation,"[1] R. E. Long discusses very well the bearing "Rappaccini's Daughter" has on *Washington Square.* I would like now to point out a specific passage in *Washington Square* which parallels another in "Rappaccini's Daughter," and two other passages in James's story which parallel a pair of passages in *The Scarlet Letter.*

Among the similarities Long discusses are those between Dr. Sloper and Dr. Rappaccini. Both doctors are guilty of intellectual pride, and have little warmth of heart. Dr. Sloper, especially, continually refers to his "fine perceptions" acquired through his profession, and his "thirty years medical practice." He likes to observe people (Catherine and Morris are his geometrical "surfaces"; he knows their "measure"), and is always interrogating them and gathering information. He is sure of his judgements too. While at dinner with Morris for the first time (chapter vii), Dr. Sloper "observed" his guest "attentively," and "asked him several questions." In the same paragraph, James tells us that Dr. Sloper (emphases in both quotations are mine):

> prided himself on being a *physiognomist;* and while the young man, chatting with easy assurance, puffed his cigar and filled his glass again, the Doctor sat with *his eyes quietly fixed* on his bright, expressive face.

In "Rappaccini's Daughter," Dr. Rappaccini first sees Giovanni while the latter is speaking with Professor Baglioni. The two had just met on the streets of Padua, and as they talked, "there came a man in black along the street." Hawthorne continues:

> As he passed, this person . . . *fixed his eyes* upon Giovanni with an intentness that seemed *to bring out whatever was within him* worthy of notice.

Nevertheless, there was a peculiar *quietness* in the look, as if taking merely a speculative, not human interest, in the young man.

In James, we read "physiognomist"; in Hawthorne, "to bring out whatever was within him." In James, again we find "his eyes quietly fixed"; in Hawthorne, "fixed his eyes" and "quietness." Even the words "young man" appear in both quotations.

Another similarity Long mentions—although in more general terms—is that between Catherine's situation and Beatrice's. I would like to point out here another affinity Catherine has with another Hawthorne heroine, namely, Hester Prynee of *The Scarlet Letter*.

In chapter xiii of *The Scarlet Letter*, one reads the following (the emphasized words in this quotation are for clearer reference to those emphasized in the second quotation from *Washington Square*):

> Years had come and gone...[Hester] *had long been a familiar object to the townspeople...a species of general regard had ultimately grown up in reference to her*...she was quick to acknowledge her sisterhood with the race of man whenever benefits were to be conferred. None was so ready as she to give of her little substance to every demand of poverty...In all seasons of calamity...the outcast of society at once found her place. She came...into the household that was darkened by trouble...the embroidered letter...was the taper of the sick chamber...Her breast...was but the softer pillow for the head that needed one. She was self-ordained a Sister of Mercy.

In chapter xxxii of *Washington Square*, one reads:

> As time went on...[Catherine] became an admirable old maid...[and] interested herself in charitable institutions, asylums, hospitals, and aid societies.

She even knits and embroiders just as Hester does.

In chapter xxiv of *The Scarlet Letter*, again one reads:

> But there was a more real life for Hester Prynne here, in New England...And, as she had no selfish ends, nor lived in any measure for her own profit or enjoyment, people brought all their sorrows and perplexities, and besought her counsel, as one who had herself gone through a mighty trouble. Women, more especially—in the continually recurring trials of wounded, wasted, wronged, misplaced, or erring and sinful passion; or with the dreary burden of a heart unyielded...came to Hester's cottage, demanding why they were so wretched and what the remedy! Hester comforted and counseled them as best she might.

And, in the same chapter xxxii of *Washington Square*, one reads that Catherine

*mingled freely in the usual gayeties of the town, and she became at last an
inevitable figure at all respectable entertainments. She was greatly liked,* and as
time went on she grew to be a sort of kindly maiden-aunt to the younger
portion of society. Young girls were apt to confide to her their love affairs. . .and young men were fond of her without knowing why.

The passages in both these cases are so similar—allowing for James's
concise style—as to almost suggest a direct source.

I have pointed out these specific passages with the hope that they
will reinforce Long's conclusion that Hawthorne's archetypes do loom
in the background of *Washington Square.*

Brown University

---

[1]Robert Emmet Long, "James's *Washington Square:* The Hawthorne Relation,"
New England Quarterly, 46, No. 4 (Dec. 1973), 573-90.

Industrial Imagery in
The House of The Seven Gables

RICHARD F. FLECK

It has been generally conceived that Nathaniel Hawthorne made little or no reference to the Insutrial Age in his works except for one chapter in *The House of The Seven Gables*. Of his tales and sketches Mark Van Doren claims, "Industrial is as absent as the other side of the moon."[1] Leo Marx approaches the problem of an "apparent lack" of industrial references in Hawthorne's work by analyzing the sublimated or "suggested" inferences in such stories as "Ethan Brand" with its dominant fire imagery.[2] With specific regard to *The House of The Seven Gables*, several critics have examined Hawthorne's use of the railroad in "The Flight of Two Owls." Henry G. Fairbanks and G. Ferris Cronkhite, for instance, discuss the railroad as subdued for the literary purpose of contrasting the past with the present.[3] However, a close reading of the entire romance uncovers a significant number of industrial images which, along with the railroad, collectively function, for the most part, as metaphors of mental states. It is curious that Hawthorne should depict mentalities so dominated by the past with contemporary industrial imagery.

Early in the book Hepzibah's first nervous encounters with the irritating shop bell are described with industrial imagery which transcends to her mental state: "But, at this instant, the shop-bell, right over her head, tinkled as if it were bewitched. The old gentlewoman's heart seemed to be attached to the same steel-spring; for it went through a series of sharp jerks, in unison with the sound."[4] Here the image of "steel-spring" works as a symbol of power snapping her from her musings into an aristocratic past to the unlady-like present circumstance of having to manage a shop. Hawthorne is bordering upon a modern technique of stream of consciousness seen in Joyce or Faulkner.

One of her early customers is a drunkard who is also described with industrial imagery: "Shortly afterwards, a man in a blue cotton-frock, much soiled, came in and bought a pipe; filling the whole shop, meanwhile, with the hot odor of strong drink, not only exhaled in the torrid atmosphere of his breath, but oozing out of his entire system, like an inflammable gas."[5] The effects of alcohol being like "an inflammable gas" illustrates Hawthorne's definite use of the contemporary scene and is not unlike a grievous mental state described in his short story "The Celestial Railroad." As the celestial railroad passes through "The Valley of the Shadow of Death," the narrator remarks, "It was gratifying, likewise, to observe how much care had been taken to dispel the everlasting gloom and supply the defect of cheerful sunshine, not a ray of which has ever penetrated among these awful shadows. For this purpose, the inflammable gas which exudes plentifully from the soil is collected by means of pipes, and thence communicated to a quadruple row of lamps along the whole extent of the passage. Thus a radiance has been created even out of the fiery and sulphurous curse that rests forever upon the valley—a radiance hurtful, however, to the eyes."[6] In both cases "inflammable gas" represents a type of specious radiance.

Inflammable gas again figures in Hawthorne's description of a despondent Hepzibah who is suddenly enlightened with flickering dreams of hidden wealth: "These were some of the fantasies which she had long dreamed about; and, aided by these, Uncle Venner's casual attempt at encouragement kindled a strange festal glory in the poor, bare, melancholy chambers of her brain, as if that inner world were suddenly lighted up with gas."[7]

Electricity also serves as a metaphor of Hepzibah's mental state, this time through her tone of voice: "Fewer words than before, but with the same mysterious music in them! Mellow, melancholy, yet not mournful, the tone seemed to gush up out of the deep well of Hepzibah's heart, all steeped in its profoundest emotion. There was a tremor in it, too, that,—as all strong feeling is electric—partly communicated itself to Phoebe."[8] Clifford, her moody brother returned from thirty years imprisonment, is depicted with similar electric terminology: "But if she [Hepzibah] were a long while absent, he became pettish and nervously restless, pacing the room to-and-fro, with the uncertainty that characterized all his movements; or else would sit broodingly in his great chair, resting his head on his hands, and evincing life only by an electric sparkle of ill-humor, whenever Hepzibah endeavored to arrouse him."[9] Electricity in both cases functions as a metaphor of emotion or mood.

The railroad's "obstreperous howl" affects Clifford even before "The Flight of Two Owls" in the chapter "The Arched Window." As he viewed the railroad from his window, he is stunned by its "terrible energy."[10] Five chapters later, after he and Hepzibah take flight from their decaying house to board a train, it is the railroad in Clifford's mind that becomes a metaphor of newness and futurity. Clifford observes, "It had just occured to me, on the contrary, that this admirable invention of the railroad—with the vast and inevitable improvements to be looked for, both as to speed and convenience—is destined to do away with those stale ideas of home and fireside, and substitute something better."[11] Shortly after this comment he exclaims, "they spiritualize travel!"[12] While he is still in his short-lived mood which is as quick flowing as the train ride itself, Clifford philosophically links electricity to thought: "Is it a fact—or have I dreamt it—that, by means of electricity, the world of matter has become a great nerve, vibrating thousands of miles in a breathless point of time? Rather, the round globe is a vast head, a brain, instinct with intelligence! Or, shall we say, it is itself a thought, nothing but thought, and no longer the substance which deemed it?"[13] Here Hawthorne has Clifford create metaphors out of his encounter with the Industrial Age to reflect his short-lived but significant exuberance. It is ironic that Clifford and Hepzibah settle on the country estate of Judge Pyncheon after much discussion of the need for mobility, but they obviously cannot escape the all-encompassing Industrial Age any more than Henry Thoreau could at Walden Pond.

The House of The Seven Gables has significant industrial images which function as metaphors of the mind. Hawthorne is comparable to Thoreau and Whitman in his poetic use of contemporary industrial America.

University of Wyoming

---

[1]Mark Van Doren, Nathaniel Hawthorne (New York: William Sloane Associates, 1949), p. 95.

[2]Leo Marx, "The Machine in the Garden," *New England Quarterly*, XXIX (March, 1956), 27-42.

[3]Henry G. Fairbanks, "Hawthorne and the Machine Age," *American Literature*, XXVIII (May, 1956), 155-163 and G. Ferris Cronkhite, "The Transcendental Railroad," *New England Quarterly*, XXIV (September, 1951), 306-328.

[4]Nathaniel Hawthorne, *The House of The Seven Gables*, ed. Harry Levin (Columbus, Ohio: Charles E. Merrill Publishing Company, 1965), p. 49. Hereafter referred to as *The House.*

[5]*The House*, p. 53.

[6]Nathaniel Hawthorne, "The Celestial Railroad," *Mosses from an Old Manse* (Boston: Houghton, Mifflin and Company, 1882), p. 220.

[7]*The House*, p. 65.

[8]*The House*, p. 96.

[9] *The House*, p. 138.
[10] *The House*, p. 161.
[11] *The House*, p. 259.
[12] *The House*, p. 260.
[13] *The House*, p. 264.

A Mexican Flower
in Rappaccini's Garden:
Madame Calderon de la Barca's
Life in Mexico Revisited

RICHARD CLARK STERNE

Madame Calderon de la B (in Life in Mexico) speaks of persons who have been inoculated with the venom of rattlesnakes, by pricking them in various places with the tooth. These persons are thus secured forever against the bite of any venomous reptile. They have the power of calling snakes, and feel great pleasure in playing with and handling them. Their own bite becomes poisonous to people not inoculated in the same manner. Thus a part of the serpent's nature appears to be transfused into them.[1]

Randall Stewart remarks that this passage in Hawthorne's *American Notebooks* "suggests an analogy to 'Rappaccini's Daughter'...in which Beatrice, imbued with the poison of flowers, becomes poisonous to others."[2] Led by Stewart's observation to Madame Calderon's *Life in Mexico* (first published in 1843), I found there what seems to be a source of Hawthorne's conception of the resplendent shrub in "Rappaccini's Daughter" (first published in December, 1844[3]), and of the "purple print," in the form of four fingers and a thumb, which appears on Giovanni's hand.

In "Letter the Thirteenth" of *Life in Mexico*, Madame Calderon tells of her visit to

the Mineria, the Botanic Garden, the Museum, etc., all which [sic] leave a certain disagreeable impression on the mind, since, without having the dignity of ruins, they are fine buildings neglected.[4]

She depicts the Botanic Garden as

a small, ill-kept enclosure, where there still remain some rare plants of the immense collection made in the time of the Spanish government,

277

when great progress was made in all the natural sciences, four hundred thousand dollars having been expended in botanical expeditions alone.

She then describes "El Arbol de las Manitas" (the tree of the small hands) as "the most curious which we saw in the garden":

The flower is of a bright scarlet, in the form of a hand, with five fingers and a thumb; and it is said that there are only three of these trees in the republic. The gardener is an old Italian, who came over with the viceroys, and though now one hundred and ten years old, and nearly bent double, possesses all his faculties. The garden is pretty from the age of the trees, and luxuriance of the flowers, but melancholy as a proof of the decay of the science in Mexico.[5]

Hawthorne's Giovanni Guasconti, having moved into a "desolate and ill-furnished apartment," looks down from his window into what "he judged to be one of those botanic gardens which were of earlier date in Padua than elsewhere in Italy or in the world"; he sees, among some "gorgeously magnificent" flowers,

one shrub in particular, set in a marble vase in the midst of the pool, that bore a profusion of purple blossoms, each of which had the lustre and richness of a gem; and the whole together made a show so resplendent that it seemed enough to illuminate the garden, even had there been no sunshine.

Later, while conversing with Beatrice in the garden, Giovanni steps toward the shrub, intending to "pluck it as a memorial of this interview." Beatrice shrieks, catches his hand, and draws it back, crying, "Touch it not!...Not for thy life! It is fatal!" The next morning, after awakening "to a sense of pain," Giovanni becomes aware

of a burning and tingling agony in his hand—in his right hand—the very hand which Beatrice had grasped in her own when he was on the point of plucking one of the gemlike flowers. On the back of that hand there was now a purple print like that of four small fingers, and the likeness of a slender thumb upon his wrist.

Hawthorne has evidently transposed the "form of a hand" from the flower described by Madame Calderon, to Giovanni's flesh. In effecting the transposition, he emphasizes the intimacy of the relationship between Beatrice and the shrub which she calls her "sister"; the "four small fingers, and...slender thumb" are marks made by Beatrice's hand, while their purple color recalls the "purple blossoms" of the shrubs.

It may be noted that Hawthorne has no need, in a story already Gothic enough, of the extra finger on the flower described by Madame

Calderon. As for the apparent discrepancy between the "bright scarlet" color of the flower in the Mexican Botanic Garden and the rich "purple" of the blossom imagined by Hawthorne, Alfred J. Kloeckner has pointed out that both Milton, in Paradise Lost, and Hawthorne in this tale, clearly use "purple" to signify "crimson."[6]

The very atmosphere of decay evoked by Madame Calderon in her account of "the Mineria, the Botanic Garden, the Museum," seems to have been transported by Hawthorne to a Paduan "botanic garden." It is even possible that Madame Calderon's "old Italian" gardener, who, "though now one hundred and ten years old, and nearly bent double possesses all his faculties," was rejuvenated—if that is the word—as Dr. Rappaccini. In any case, it appears that among the scenes and images from life and literature which Hawthorne metamorphosed in "Rappaccini's Daughter," was a flower in the form of a hand, on "El Arbol de las Manitas."

Simmons College

---

[1]Randall Stewart, ed., *The American Notebooks by Nathaniel Hawthorne* New Haven, 1932), p. 98.

[2]*Notebooks*, p. 297.

[3]*The United States Magazine and Democratic Review*, LXXVIII (December, 1844), 545-560.

[4]Mme. Calderon de la Barca, *Life in Mexico During a Residence of Two Years in That Country* (New York, 1931), p. 125.

[5]*Life*, p. 126.

[6]"The Flower and the Fountain: Hawthorne's Chief Symbols in 'Rappaccini's Daughter' ", *American Literature*, XXXVIII (Nov., 1966), 329.

Hawthorne in Portuguese (3)

GEORGE MONTIERO

To my earlier checklists of Hawthorne in Portuguese translation (*NJH 1971* and *NHJ 1972*) can be added seven items. They are drawn from John E. Englekirk's *A Literatura Norteamericana no Brasil* (Mexico, 1950), pp. 75, 101-102. Enumeration corresponds to the system employed in the earlier checklists.

I. Novel

B. *The House of the Seven Gables*
    4. *A casa dos sete oitoes.* Trans. Sodre Viana. Colecao Fogos Cruzados. Livraria Jose Olympio Editora. Rio de Janeiro. N.d.

C. *The Blithedale Romance*
    2. *O romance do Vale Feliz.* Trans. Sodre Viana. Livraria Jose Olympio Editora. Rio de Janeiro. N.d.

D. *The Marble Faun*
    3. *O fauno de marmore.* Trans. Sodre Viana. Livraria Jose Olympio Editora. Rio de Janeiro. N.d.

II. Tales and Sketches

B. *David Swan*
    3. *David Swan.* Trans. J. da Cunha Borges. Collected in *Os mais belos contos norteamericanos.* Editora Vecchi. Rio de Janeiro. 1945.

E. *Dr. Heidegger's Experiment*
    3. *A experiencia do dr. Heidegger.* Trans. W[ilson] L[ousada]. *Correio da manha* [Rio de Janeiro] (September 30, 1945).

H. *The Ambitious Guest*
    2. *O hospede ambicioso.* Trans. W[ilson] L[ousada]. *Correio da manha* [Rio de Janeiro] (February 24, 1946).

M. *The Wedding Knell*
    1. *O dobre nupcial.* Trans. W[ilson] L[ousada]. *Correio da manha* [Rio de Janeiro] (February 10, 1946).

Brown University

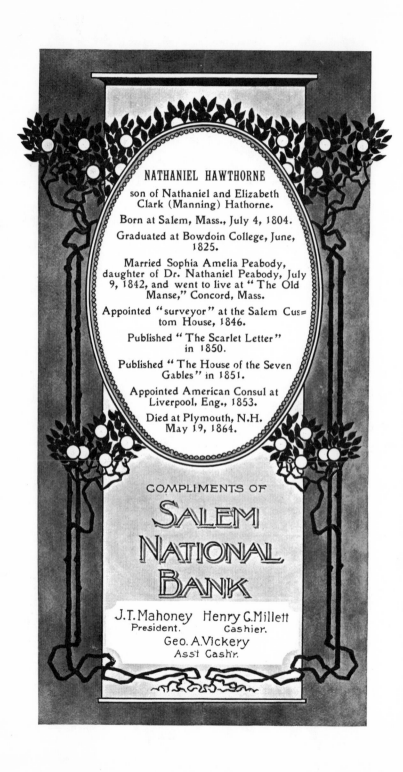

NATHANIEL HAWTHORNE

son of Nathaniel and Elizabeth
Clark (Manning) Hathorne.

Born at Salem, Mass., July 4, 1804.

Graduated at Bowdoin College, June,
1825.

Married Sophia Amelia Peabody,
daughter of Dr. Nathaniel Peabody, July
9, 1842, and went to live at "The Old
Manse," Concord, Mass.

Appointed "surveyor" at the Salem Cus=
tom House, 1846.

Published "The Scarlet Letter"
in 1850.

Published "The House of the Seven
Gables" in 1851.

Appointed American Consul at
Liverpool, Eng., 1853.

Died at Plymouth, N.H.
May 19, 1864.

COMPLIMENTS OF

SALEM

NATIONAL

BANK

J.T. Mahoney   Henry C.Millett
President.   Cashier.

Geo. A.Vickery
Ass't Cash'r.